Praise for *Just Enough Software Architecture: A Risk-Driven Approach*

If you're going to read only one book on software architecture, start with this one. *Just Enough Software Architecture* covers the essential concepts of software architecture that everyone — programmers, developers, testers, architects, and managers — needs to know, and it provides pragmatic advice that can be put into practice within hours of reading.

—Michael Keeling, professional software engineer

This book reflects the author's rare mix of deep knowledge of software architecture concepts and extensive industry experience as a developer. If you're an architect, you will want the developers in your organization to read this book. If you're a developer, do read it. The book is about architecture in real (not ideal) software projects. It describes a context that you'll recognize and then it shows you how to improve your design practice in that context.

—Paulo Merson, practicing software architect and
Visiting Scientist at the Software Engineering Institute

Fairbanks' focus on "just enough" architecture should appeal to any developers trying to work out how to make the architecting process tractable. This focus is made accessible through detailed examples and advice that illustrate how an understanding of risk can be used to manage architecture development and scope. At the same time, Fairbanks provides detail on the more academic aspects of software architecture, which should help developers who are interested in understanding the broader theory and practice to apply these concepts to their projects.

—Dr. Bradley Schmerl, Senior Systems Scientist, School of
Computer Science, Carnegie Mellon University

The Risk-Driven Model approach described in George Fairbanks' *Just Enough Software Architecture* has been applied to the eXtensible Information Modeler (XIM) project here at the NASA Johnson Space Center (JSC) with much success. It is a must for all members of the project, from project management to individual developers. In fact, it is a must for every developer's tool belt. The Code Model section and the anti-patterns alone are worth the cost of the book!

—Christopher Dean, Chief Architect, XIM,
Engineering Science Contract Group – NASA Johnson Space Center

Just Enough Software Architecture

A Risk-Driven Approach

George Fairbanks

Published by Marshall & Brainerd
2445 7th Street
Boulder, CO 80304
(303) 834-7760

Library of Congress Control Number: 2010910450

ISBN 978-0-9846181-0-1

First printing, August 2010

Foreword

In the 1990s software architecture emerged as an explicit subfield of software engineering when it became widely recognized that getting the architecture right was a key enabler for creating a software-based system that met its requirements. What followed was a dizzying array of proposals for notations, tools, techniques, and processes to support architectural design and to integrate it into existing software development practices.

And yet, despite the existence of this body of material, principled attention to software architecture has in many cases not found its way into common practice. Part of the reason for this has been something of a polarization of opinions about the role that architecture should play. On one side is a school of thought that advocates architecture-focused design, in which architecture plays a pivotal and essential role throughout the software development process. People in this camp have tended to focus on detailed and complete architectural designs, well-defined architecture milestones, and explicit standards for architecture documentation. On the other side is a school of thought that deemphasizes architecture, arguing that it will emerge naturally as a by-product of good design, or that it is not needed at all since the architecture is obvious for that class of system. People in this camp have tended to focus on minimizing architectural design as an activity separate from implementation, and on reducing or eliminating architectural documentation.

Clearly, neither of these camps has it right for all systems. Indeed, the central question that must be asked is "How much explicit architectural design should one carry out for a given system?"

In this book, George Fairbanks proposes an answer: "Just Enough Architecture." One's first reaction to this might be "Well, duh!" because who would want too much or too little. But of course there is more to it than that, and it is precisely the detailing of principles for figuring out what "just enough" means that is the thrust of this book. As such, it provides a refreshing and non-dogmatic way to approach software architecture — one with enormous practical value.

Fairbanks argues that the core criterion for determining how much architecture is enough is risk reduction. Where there is little risk in a design, little architecture is needed. But when hard system design issues arise, architecture is a tool with tremendous potential. In this way the book adopts a true engineering perspective on architecture, in the sense that it directly promotes the consideration of the costs and benefits in selecting a technique. Specifically, focusing on risk reduction aligns engineering benefits with costs by ensuring that architectural design is used in situations where it is likely to have the most payoff.

Naturally, there are a lot of secondary questions to answer. Which risks are best addressed with software architecture? How do you apply architectural design principles to resolve a design problem? What do you write down about your architectural commitments so that others know what they are? How can you help ensure that architectural commitments are respected by downstream implementers?

This book answers all of these questions, and many more — making it a uniquely practical and approachable contribution to the field of software architecture. For anyone who must create innovative software systems, for anyone who is faced with tough decisions about design tradeoffs, for anyone who must find an appropriate balance between agility and discipline — in short, for almost any software engineer — this is essential reading.

David Garlan
Professor, School of Computer Science
Director of Professional Software Engineering Programs
Carnegie Mellon University
May 2010

Preface

This is the book I wish I'd had when I started developing software. At the time, there were books on languages and books on object-oriented programming, but few books on design. Knowing the features of the C++ language does not mean you can design a good object-oriented system, nor does knowing the Unified Modeling Language (UML) imply you can design a good system architecture.

This book is different from other books about software architecture. Here is what sets it apart:

It teaches risk-driven architecting. There is no need for meticulous designs when risks are small, nor any excuse for sloppy designs when risks threaten your success. Many high-profile agile software proponents suggest that some up-front design can be helpful, and this book describes a way to do just enough architecture. It avoids the "one size fits all" process tar pit with advice on how to tune your architecture and design efforts based on the risks you face. The rigor of most techniques can be adjusted, from quick-and-dirty to meticulous.

It democratizes architecture. You may have software architects at your organization — indeed, you may be one of them. Every architect I have met wishes that all developers understood architecture. They complain that developers do not understand why constraints exist and how seemingly small changes can affect a system's properties. This book seeks to make architecture relevant to all software developers, not just architects.

It cultivates declarative knowledge. There is a difference between being able to hit a tennis ball and knowing why you are able to hit it, what psychologists refer to as *procedural knowledge* versus *declarative knowledge*. If you are already an expert at designing and building systems then you will have employed many of the techniques found here, but this book will make you more aware of what you have been doing and provide names for the concepts. That declarative knowledge will improve your ability to mentor other developers.

It emphasizes the engineering. People who design and build software systems have to do many things, including dealing with schedules, resource commitments, and stakeholder needs. Many books on software architecture already cover software development processes and organizational structures. This book, in contrast, focuses on the technical parts of software development and deals with what developers do to ensure a system works — the *engineering*. It shows you how to build models and analyze architectures so that you can make principled design tradeoffs. It describes the techniques software designers use to reason about medium- to large-sized problems and points out where you can learn specialized techniques in more detail. Consequently, throughout this book, software engineers are referred to as *developers*, not differentiating architects from programmers.

It provides practical advice. This book offers a practical treatment of architecture. Software architecture is a kind of software design, but design decisions influence the architecture and vice versa. What the best developers do is drill down into obstacles in detail, understand them, then pop back up to relate the nature of those obstacles to the architecture as a whole. The approach in this book embraces this drill-down/pop-up behavior by describing models that have various levels of abstraction, from architecture to data structure design.

About me

My career has been a quest to learn how to build software systems. That quest has led me to interleave academics with industrial software development. I have the complete collector's set of computer science degrees: a BS, an MS, and a PhD (the PhD is from Carnegie Mellon University, in software engineering). For my thesis, I worked on software frameworks because they are a problem that many developers face. I developed a new kind of specification, called a design fragment, to describe how to use frameworks, and I built an Eclipse-based tool that can validate their correct usage. I was enormously fortunate to be advised by David Garlan and Bill Scherlis, and to have Jonathan Aldrich and Ralph Johnson on my committee.

I appreciate academic rigor, but my roots are in industry. I have been a software developer on projects including the Nortel DMS-100 central office telephone switch, statistical analysis for a driving simulator, an IT application at Time Warner Telecommunications, plug-ins for the Eclipse IDE, and every last stitch of code for my own web startup company. I tinker with Linux boxes as an amateur system administrator and have a closet lit by blinking lights and warmed by power supplies. I have supported agile techniques since their early days — in 1996 I successfully encouraged my department to switch from a six-month to a two-week development cycle, and in 1998 I started doing test-first development.

Who is this book for?

The primary audience for this book is practicing software developers. Readers should already know basic software development ideas — things like object-oriented software development, the UML, use cases, and design patterns. Some experience with how real software development proceeds will be exceedingly helpful, because many of this book's basic arguments are predicated on common experiences. If you have seen developers build too much documentation or do too little thinking before coding, you will know how software development can go wrong and therefore be looking for remedies like those offered in this book. This book is also suitable as a textbook in an advanced undergraduate or graduate level course.

Here is what to expect depending on what kind of reader you are:

Greenhorn developers or students. If you already have learned the basic mechanics of software development, such as programming languages and data structure design, and, ideally, have taken a general software engineering class, this book will introduce you to specific models of software that will help you form a *conceptual model* of software architecture. This model will help you make sense of the chaos of large systems without drawing a lot of diagrams and documentation. It may give you your first taste of ideas such as *quality attributes* and *architectural styles*. You will learn how to take your understanding of small programs and ramp it up to full industrial scale and quality. It can accelerate your progress toward becoming an effective, experienced developer.

Experienced developers. If you are good at developing systems then you will invariably be asked to mentor others. However, you may find that you have a somewhat idiosyncratic perspective on architecture, perhaps using unique diagram notations or terminology. This book will help you improve your ability to mentor others, understand why you are able to succeed where others struggle, and teach you about standard models, notations, and names.

Software architects. The role of software architect can be a difficult one when others in your organization do not understand what you do and why you do it. Not only will this book teach you techniques for building systems, it will also give you ways to explain what you are doing and how you are doing it. Perhaps you will even hand this book to co-workers so that you can better work as teammates.

Academics. This book makes several contributions to the field of software architecture. It introduces the *risk-driven model* of software architecture, which is a way of deciding how much architecture and design work to do on a project. It describes three approaches to architecture: *architecture-indifferent design*, *architecture-focused design*, and *architecture hoisting*. It integrates two perspectives on software architecture: the functional perspective and the quality-attribute perspective, yielding a single conceptual model. And it introduces the idea of an *architecturally-evident coding style* that makes your architecture evident from reading the source code.

Acknowledgments

This book would not have been possible without the generous assistance of many people. Several worked closely with me on one or more chapters and deserve special recognition for their help: Kevin Bierhoff, Alan Birchenough, David Garlan, Greg Hartman, Ian Maung, Paulo Merson, Bradley Schmerl, and Morgan Stanfield.

Others suffered through bad early drafts, caught huge numbers of problems, and provided needed guidance: Len Bass, Grady Booch, Christopher Dean, Michael Donohue, Daniel Dvorak, Anthony Earl, Hans Gyllstrom, Tim Halloran, Ralph Hoop, Michael Keeling, Ken LaToza, Thomas LaToza, Louis Marbel, Andy Myers, Carl Paradis, Paul Rayner, Patrick Riley, Aamod Sane, Nicholas Sherman, Olaf Zimmermann, and Guido Zgraggen. Thank you.

I would be remiss if I did not acknowledge all the people who have mentored me over the years, starting with my parents who provided more support than I can describe. My professional mentors have included Desmond D'Souza and the gang from Icon Computing; my thesis advisors, David Garlan and Bill Scherlis; and the faculty and students at Carnegie Mellon.

The wonderful cover illustration was conceived and drawn by my friend Lisa Haney (http://LisaHaney.com). Alan Apt has been a source of guidance and support through the book writing process.

The preparation of this book was done primarily with open source tools, including the Linux operating system, the LyX document processor, the Memoir LaTeX style, the LaTeX document preparation system, and the Inkscape drawing editor. Most diagrams were created using Microsoft Visio and Pavel Hruby's Visio UML template.

Contents

Chapter 1

Introduction

Decade after decade, software systems have seen orders-of-magnitude increases in their size and complexity. This is remarkable — and more than a little scary for those of us who build software. In contrast, imagine how hard basketball would be if it scaled up the same way, with 5 people on the floor one decade, then 50, then 500. Because of this growth, today's software systems are arguably the largest and most complex things ever built.

Software developers are always battling the ever-stronger foes of complexity and scale, but even though their opponent grows in strength, developers have staved off defeat and even reveled in victory. How have they done this?

One answer is that the increases in software size and complexity have been matched by advances in software engineering. Assembly language programming gave way to higher-level languages and structured programming. Procedures have, in many domains, given way to objects. And software reuse, which used to mean just subroutines, is now also done with extensive libraries and frameworks.

It is no coincidence that the battle between developers and software complexity always seems to be at a stalemate. Since developers cannot grow bigger brains, they have instead improved their weapons. An improved weapon gives developers two options: to more easily conquer yesterday's problems, or to combat tomorrow's. We are no smarter than developers of the previous generation, but our improved weapons allow us to build software of greater size and complexity.

Software developers wield some tangible weapons, such as Integrated Development Environments (IDEs) and programming languages, but intangible weapons arguably make a bigger impact. Returning to our basketball metaphor, consider a coach and a rookie (a novice sports player) watching the same game. The coach sees more than the rookie — not because the coach's eyes are more acute, but because he has an intangible weapon. He has built up a set of mental abstractions that allow him to convert his perceptions of raw phenomena, such as a ball being passed, into a condensed and integrated understanding of what is happening, such as the success of an offensive strategy. The coach watches the same game that the rookie does, but he understands it better. Alan Kay has observed that your "point of view is worth 80 IQ points" (Kay, 1989).

Software is similar in that there are lots of low-level details. If developers have built up a set of mental abstractions (i.e., a conceptual model), they can convert those details into a condensed understanding: where before they saw just code, perhaps they now see a thread-safe locking policy or an event-driven system.

1.1   Partitioning, knowledge, and abstractions

To be successful at combating the scale and complexity of software in the next decade, developers will need improved weapons. Those weapons can be categorized, perhaps with a bit of shoehorning, into three categories: partitioning, knowledge, and abstraction. Developers *partition* a problem so that its parts are smaller and more tractable, they apply *knowledge* of similar problems, and they use *abstractions* to help them reason. Partitioning, knowledge, and abstraction are effective because they enable our fixed-sized minds to comprehend an ever-growing problem.

- **Partitioning**. Partitioning is effective as a strategy to combat complexity and scale when two conditions are true: first, the divided parts must be sufficiently small that a person can now solve them; second, it must be possible to reason about how the parts assemble[1] into a whole. Parts that are encapsulated are easier to reason about, because you need to track fewer details when composing the parts into a solution. You can forget, at least temporarily, about the details inside the other parts. This allows the developer to more easily reason about how the parts will interact with each other.

- **Knowledge**. Software developers use knowledge of prior problems to help them solve current ones. This knowledge can be implicit know-how or explicitly written down. It can be specific, as in which components work well with others, or general, as in techniques for optimizing a database table layout. It comes in many forms, including books, lectures, pattern descriptions, source code, design documents, or sketches on a whiteboard.

---

[1]Mary Shaw has remarked that when dividing and conquering, the dividing is the easy part.

- **Abstraction**. Abstraction can effectively combat complexity and scale because it shrinks problems, and smaller problems are easier to reason about. If you are driving from New York to Los Angeles, you can simplify the navigation problem by considering only highways. By hiding details (excluding the option of driving across fields or parking lots), you have shrunken the number of options to consider, making the problem easier to reason about.

You should not expect any *silver bullets*, as Fred Brooks called them, that will suddenly eliminate the difficulties of software development (Brooks, 1995). Instead, you should look for weapons that help you partition systems better, provide knowledge, and enable abstraction to reveal the essence of the problem.

Software architecture is one such weapon and it can help you address the complexity and scale of software systems. It helps you *partition* software, it provides *knowledge* that helps you design better software, and it provides *abstractions* that help you reason about software. It is a tool in the hands of a skilled developer. It helps software developers to routinely build systems that previously required virtuosos (Shaw and Garlan, 1996), but it does not eliminate the need for skilled software developers. Instead of removing the need for ingenuity, it allows developers to apply their ingenuity to build bigger and more complex systems.

1.2 Three examples of software architecture

That is what software architecture *does* for you, but what *is* it? Roughly speaking, architecture is the macroscopic design of a software system. Chapter 2 of this book discusses a more careful definition, but perhaps it is best to understand software architecture using some concrete examples first.

It can be hard to "see the forest for the trees," which in this case means finding the architecture amidst the design details. But by comparing multiple similar systems with different architectures you should be able to notice what is different and therefore identify their architectures. What follows is a description of three systems with the same functionality, yet different architectures, based on the experiences at Rackspace.

Rackspace is a real company that manages hosted email servers. Customers call up for help when they experience problems. To help a customer, Rackspace must search the log files that record what has happened during the customer's email processing. Because the volume of emails they handle kept increasing, Rackspace built three generations of systems to handle the customer queries (Hoff, 2008b; Hood, 2008).

Version 1: Local log files. The first version of the program was simple. There were already dozens of email servers generating log files. Rackspace wrote a script that would use ssh to connect to each machine and execute a grep query on the mail log file. Engineers could control the search results by adjusting the grep query.

This version initially worked well, but over time the number of searches increased and the overhead of running those searches on the email servers became noticeable. Also, it required an engineer, rather than a support tech, to perform the search.

Version 2: Central database. The second version addressed the drawbacks of the first one by moving the log data off of the email servers and by making it searchable by support techs. Every few minutes, each email server would send its recent log data to a central machine where it was loaded into a relational database. Support techs had access to the database data via a web-based interface.

Rackspace was now handling hundreds of email servers, so the volume of log data had increased correspondingly. Rackspace's challenge became how to get the log data into the database as quickly and efficiently as possible. The company settled on bulk record insertion into merge tables, which enabled loading of the data in two or three minutes. Only three days worth of logs were kept so that the database size would not hinder performance.

Over time, this system also encountered problems. The database server was a single machine and, because of the constant loading of data and the query volume, it was pushed to its limit with heavy CPU and disk loads. Wildcard searches were prohibited because of the extra load they put on the server. As the amount of log data grew, searches became slower. The server experienced seemingly random failures that became increasingly frequent. Any log data that was dropped was gone forever because it was not backed up. These problems led to a loss of confidence in the system.

Version 3: Indexing cluster. The third version addressed the drawbacks of the second by saving log data into a distributed file system and by parallelizing the indexing of log data. Instead of running on a single powerful machine, it used ten commodity machines. Log data from the email servers streamed into the Hadoop Distributed File System, which kept three copies of everything on different disks. In 2008, when Rackspace wrote a report on its experiences, it had over six terabytes of data spanning thirty disk drives, which represented six months of search indexes.

Indexing was performed using Hadoop, which divides the input data, indexes (or "maps") in jobs, then combines (or "reduces") the partial results into a complete index. Jobs ran every ten minutes and took about five minutes to complete, so index results were about fifteen minutes stale. Rackspace was able to index over 140 gigabytes of log data per day and had executed over 150,000 jobs since starting the system.

As in the second system, support techs had access via a web interface that was much like a web search-engine interface. Query results were provided within seconds.

When engineers thought up new questions about the data, they could write a new kind of job and have their answer within a few hours.

1.3 Reflections

The first thing to notice from looking at these three systems is that they all have roughly the same functionality (querying email logs to diagnose problems) yet they have different architectures. *Their architecture was a separate choice from their functionality.* This means that when you build a system, you can choose an architecture that best suits your needs, then build the functionality on that architectural skeleton. What else can these systems reveal about software architecture?

Quality attributes. Despite having the same functionality, the three systems differ in their modifiability, scalability, and latency. For example, in the first and second version, ad hoc queries could be created in a matter of seconds, either by changing the grep expression used for the search or by changing the SQL query. The third system requires a new program to be written and scheduled before query results can be obtained. All three support creating new queries, but they differ in how easy it is to do (modifiability).

Notice also that there was no free lunch: promoting one quality inhibited another. The third system was much more scalable than the other two, but its scalability came at the price of reduced ability to make ad hoc queries and a longer wait before results were available. The data in the first system was queryable online (and the second could perhaps be made nearly so), but the third system had to collect data then run a batch process to index the results, which means that query results were a bit stale.

If you are ever in a situation in which you can get great scalability, latency, modifiability, etc., then you should count yourself lucky, because such *quality attributes* usually trade off against each other. Maximizing one quality attribute means settling for less of the others. For example, choosing a more modifiable design may entail worse latency.

Conceptual model. Even without being a software architecture expert, you could read about these three systems and reason about their design from first principles. What advantage would come from being a software architecture expert (i.e., being a coach instead of a rookie)? Both coaches and rookies have an innate ability to reason, but the coach has a head start because of the *conceptual model* he carries in his head that helps him make sense of what he sees.

As an architecture expert, you would be primed to notice the partitioning differences in each system. You would distinguish between chunks of code (modules), runtime chunks (components), and hardware chunks (nodes, or environmental elements). You would notice and already know the names of the architectural patterns each system employs. You would know which pattern is suited for achieving which quality attributes, so you would have predicted that the client-server system would have lower latency than the map-reduce system. You would sort out and relate domain facts, design choices, and implementation details — and notice when someone else has jumbled them together. Being an expert in software architecture helps you to use your innate reasoning abilities more effectively.

Abstractions and constraints. In software, bigger things are usually built out of smaller things. You can always reason about the smaller things in a system (like individual lines of code) but usually you will find it more efficient to reason about the larger things (like clients and servers). For example, the third system in the Rackspace example scheduled jobs and stored data in a distributed file system. If you needed to solve a problem about how jobs flow through that system, then it would be most efficient to reason about the problem at that level. You could begin your reasoning process by considering the small bits, like objects and procedure calls, but that would be inefficient and likely to swamp you with details.

Furthermore, a "job" is an abstraction that obeys more constraints than an arbitrary "chunk of code" does. The developers imposed those constraints to make reasoning about the system easier. For example, if they constrain jobs to have no side effects, they can run the same job twice, in parallel, just in case one becomes bogged down. It is hard to reason about an arbitrary chunk of code specifically because you cannot tell what it *does not* do. Developers voluntarily impose constraints on the system in order to amplify their reasoning abilities.

1.4   Perspective shift

In 1968 Edsger Dijkstra wrote a now famous letter titled "GOTO Considered Harmful" advocating the use of structured programming. His argument is roughly as follows: Developers build programs containing static statements that execute to produce output. Developers, being human, have a hard time envisioning how the static statements of a program will execute at runtime. GOTO statements complicate the reasoning about runtime execution, so it is best to avoid GOTO statements and embrace structured programming.

Looking back at this debate today, it is hard to imagine disagreeing strongly, but at the time the resistance was substantial. Developers were accustomed to working within the old set of abstractions. They focused on the constraints of the new abstractions rather than the benefits and objected based on corner cases that were hard to express using structured programming. Each similar increase in abstraction is opposed by some who are familiar with the old abstractions. During my programming career, I have seen developers resist abstract data types and object-oriented programming, only to later embrace them.

New architecture abstractions rarely replace old abstractions, but instead coexist with them. Using abstractions such as components and connectors does not mean that objects, methods, and data structures disappear. Similarly, forest fire fighters switch between thinking about individual trees or entire forests depending on what part of their job they are doing at the moment.

Effectively applying software architecture ideas requires a conscious and explicit shift to embrace its abstractions, such as components and connectors, rather than only using the abstractions found in mainstream programming language (often just classes or objects). If you do not consciously choose the architecture of your systems, then it may end up being what Brian Foote and Joseph Yoder call a *big ball of mud* (Foote and Yoder, 2000), which they estimate is the most common software architecture. It is easy to understand this architecture: Imagine what a system with 10 classes would look like, then scale it up to 100, 1000, ..., without any new abstractions or partitions, and let the objects in the system communicate with each other as is expedient.

1.5 Architects architecting architectures

I have sometimes seen software developers design systems with beautiful architectures, then voice their resistance to software architecture. This resistance may stem from resistance to bureaucracy-intensive up-front design processes, to pompous architects, or to having been forced to waste time making diagrams instead of systems. Fortunately, none of these problems need to be a part of creating software architecture.

Job titles, development processes, and engineering artifacts are separable, so it is important to avoid conflating the *job title* "architect," the *process* of architecting a system, and the *engineering artifact* that is the software architecture.

- **The job role: architect.** One possible job title (or role) in an organization is that of a software architect. Some architects sit in corner offices and make pronouncements that are disconnected from the engineering reality, while other architects are intimately involved in the ongoing construction of the software. Either way, the title and the office are not intrinsic to the work of designing or building software. All software developers, not just architects, should understand their software's architecture.

- **The process: architecting.** There is no software at the beginning of a project, but by the end of the project there is a running system. In between, the team performs activities (i.e., they follow a process) to construct the system. Some teams design up-front and other teams design as they build. The process that the team follows is separable from the design that emerges. A team could follow any number of different processes and produce, for example, a 3-tier system. Or put another way, it is nearly impossible to tell what architecting process a team followed by looking only at the finished software.

- **The engineering artifact: the architecture.** If you look at an automobile, you can tell what type of car it is, perhaps an all-electric car, a hybrid car, or an internal combustion car. That characteristic of the car is distinct from the process followed to design it, and distinct from the job titles used by its designers. The car's design is an engineering artifact. Different choices about process and job titles could still result in their creating, for example, a hybrid car. Software is similar. If you look at a finished software system, you can distinguish various designs; for example: collaborating peer-to-peer nodes in a voice-over-IP network, multiple tiers in information technology (IT) systems, or parallelized map-reduce compute nodes in internet systems. Every software system has an architecture just as every car has a design. Some software is cobbled together without a regular process, yet its architecture is still visible.

This book discusses process in Chapter 2 and Chapter 3. The rest of the book treats architecture as an engineering artifact: something to be analyzed, understood, and designed so that you can build better systems.

1.6   Risk-driven software architecture

Different developers have had success with different processes. Some succeeded with agile processes that have little or no up-front work. Others succeeded with detailed up-front design work. Which should you choose? Ideally, you would have a guiding principle that would help you choose appropriately.

This book suggests using *risk* to decide how much architecture work to do. One way to understand how risk can guide you to good choices about architecture it is to consider the story of my father installing a mailbox.

My father has two degrees in mechanical engineering, but when he put up a mailbox he did it like anyone else would: he dug a hole, put in the post, and filled the hole with some cement. Just because he could calculate moments, stresses, and strains does not mean he must or should. In other situations it would be foolish for him to skip these analyses. How did he know when to use them?

Software architecture is a relatively new technology, and it includes many techniques for modeling and analyzing systems. Yet each of these techniques takes time that could otherwise be spent building the system. This book introduces the *risk-driven model* for software architecture, which guides you to do just enough architecture by selecting appropriate architecture techniques and knowing when you can stop.

Your effort should be commensurate with your risk of failure. Perhaps your system has demanding scalability requirements because you run a popular web service. It would be best to ensure that your system will handle the expected number of users[2] before you invest too much energy in its design (or the site goes live). If modifiability is less of a concern for your system (or usability, etc.), you would spend little time worrying about that risk.

Each project faces different risks, so there is no single correct way to do software architecture: you must evaluate the risks on each project. Sometimes the answer is to do no architecture work, because some projects are so highly precedented that there is almost no risk as long as you reuse a proven architecture. However, when you work in novel domains or push an existing system into uncharted territory you will want to be more careful.

The idea of consistently working to reduce engineering risks echoes Barry Boehm's *spiral model* of software development (Boehm, 1988). The spiral model is a full software development process that guides projects to work on the highest risk items first. Projects face both management and engineering risks, so managers must prioritize both management risks (like the risk of customer rejection) and engineering risks (like the risk that the system is insecure or inefficient).

Compared to the spiral model, the risk-driven model helps you answer narrower questions: How much architecture work should you do, and what kind of architecture techniques should you use? Because the risk-driven model only applies to design work, it means that it can be applied to agile processes, waterfall processes, spiral processes, etc. Regardless of process, you must design the software — the difference is when design happens and which techniques are applied.

1.7 Architecture for agile developers

Agile software development is a reaction to heavyweight development processes and it emphasizes efficiently building products that customers want (Beck et al., 2001). It is increasingly popular, with one study showing 69% of companies trying it on at least some of their projects (Ambler, 2008).

In their desire to cut out unnecessary steps in software development, some agile developers believe they should avoid software architecture techniques. This reluctance is not universal, as many important voices in agile community support some planned design work, including Martin Fowler, Robert Martin, Scott Ambler, and Granville Miller (Fowler, 2004; Martin, 2009; Ambler, 2002; Miller, 2006). Refactoring a poor architecture choice can be prohibitively expensive on large systems. This

---

[2]Recall that before the popular Facebook and MySpace social networking sites there was Friendster, but it could not handle the rush of users and became too slow to use.

book can help agile developers to use software architecture in a way that is consistent with agile principles for two primary reasons:

- **Just enough architecture.** The risk-driven model of architecture guides developers to do just enough architecture then resume coding. If you only foresee risks on your project that can be handled by refactoring then you would not do any architecture design. But if you are an agilist who is also concerned that refactoring may not be enough to get the security or scalability you need, now you have a way to mitigate those risks — even in your Nth iteration — then get back to coding.

- **Conceptual model.** Agile's primary contribution is to software development process, not design abstractions, and offers a limited number of techniques (such as refactoring and spikes) to produce good designs. The contents of this book augment agile processes by providing a conceptual model to reason about a system's architecture and design, a set of software design and modeling techniques, and expert software architecture knowledge.

This is not a book specifically about agile software architecture, but you will find that its risk-driven approach is well suited to agile projects. In particular, Section 3.11 provides a sketch of how to integrate risks into an iterative, feature-centric process.

1.8   About this book

This book focuses on software architecture as it relates to the *construction of software*, and describes the techniques used to ensure that software satisfies its engineering demands. This book is largely process agnostic because the engineering techniques themselves are largely process agnostic. You will not find advice on management activities like the political responsibilities of architects, when to hold specific kinds of meetings, or how to gather requirements from stakeholders.

This book is divided into two parts. This first part introduces software architecture and the risk-driven approach. The second part helps you build up a mental conceptual model of software architecture and describes in detail the abstractions like components and connectors. What follows is short summaries of each part.

Part I: Risk-driven software architecture

A definition of software architecture is difficult to pin down precisely, but several things about it are quite clear. Software developers, like engineers in other specialties, use abstraction and models to solve large and complex problems. Software architecture acts as the skeleton of a system, influences quality attributes, is orthogonal to functionality, and uses constraints to influence a system's properties. Architecture is most important when the solution space is small, the failure risks are high, or you face difficult quality attribute demands. You can choose from architecture-indifferent design, architecture-focused design, or even architecture hoisting.

Risks can be used to guide you regarding which design and architecture techniques you should use and regarding how much design and architecture you should do. At its core, the risk-driven model is simple: (1) identify and prioritize risks, (2) select and apply a set of techniques, and (3) evaluate risk reduction.

To reveal the risk-driven model in practice, Chapter 4 provides an example of applying the risk-driven model to a Home Media Player system. The developers on that system have the challenges of team communication, integration of COTS components, and ensuring metadata consistency.

The first part of the book concludes with advice on using models and software architecture, including: use models to solve problems, add constraints judiciously, focus on risks, and distribute architecture skills throughout your team.

Part II: Architecture modeling

The second part of the book helps you build a mental conceptual model of software architecture. It starts with the canonical model structure: the domain model, the design model, and the code model. The domain model corresponds to things in the real world, the design model is the design of the software you are building, and the code model corresponds to your source code. You can build additional models that show selected details, called views, and these views can be grouped into viewtypes.

Building encapsulation boundaries is a crucial skill in software architecture. Users of a component or module can often ignore how it works internally, freeing their minds to solve other hard problems. And the builders of an encapsulated component or module have the freedom to change its implementation without perturbing its users. Builders will only have that freedom if the encapsulation is effective, so this book will teach you techniques for ensuring that it is effective.

A great number of architectural abstractions and modeling techniques have been built up over the years. This book consolidates software architecture techniques found in a variety of other sources, integrating techniques emphasizing quality attributes as well as techniques emphasizing functionality. It also discusses pragmatic ways to build effective models and debug them.

The second part of the book concludes with advice on how to use the models effectively. Any book that covered the advantages but not the pitfalls of a technology should not be trusted, so it also covers problems that you are likely to encounter. By the end of the second part, you should have built up a rich conceptual model of abstractions and relationships that will help you see software systems the way a coach sees a game.

Part I

Risk-Driven Software Architecture

Chapter 2

Software Architecture

Before understanding how you can use risk to decide how much software architecture work to do, you need to understand what software architecture is. This chapter digs into what software architecture is and why it is important. It provides a foundation so that you can understand how risk relates to software architecture.

Software architecture is about the design of your system and the impact it has on the system's qualities, qualities like performance, security, and modifiability. Rather than provide yet another definition of software architecture that is subtly different, this chapter uses a popular definition from the Carnegie Mellon Software Engineering Institute (SEI). It discusses how architecture differs from detailed design and how some of your biggest design decisions can have implications deep into the code.

Your software architecture choices are important because your architecture acts as the skeleton of your system, influences its quality attributes, and constrains the system. It is mostly orthogonal to the system's functionality, so to some extent you can mix-and-match architecture and functionality, though some combinations will work better than others.

Sometimes any architecture you choose will work out fine; other times it is not obvious that a solution is even possible. The harder the problem is, the more you will need to pay attention to your architecture choices. Your architecture choices are most important when the solution space is small, the risk of failure is high, you have difficult quality attribute requirements, or when you are working in a new domain.

This chapter discusses three levels of engagement with architecture. In architecture-indifferent design, you pay little attention to the architecture, perhaps using a highly precedented presumptive architecture, such as a 3-tier system on an information technology (IT) project. In architecture-focused design, you deliberately choose an architecture that is compatible with your system's goals. And with architecture hoisting, you design the architecture such that it can ensure a goal or property of the system.

2.1   What is software architecture?

In this book, you will learn how to use models and abstractions to reason about your software systems, specifically about their software architecture. Your design will impact how well your system succeeds, for example if it is fast, secure, or modifiable. Your design will have that impact whether you write it down in carefully labeled binders, or if you simply keep it in your head.

Architecture and detailed design. A software system's *design* consists of the decisions and intentions that are in the heads of the developers. Design can be partitioned into *software architecture* (often shortened to just *architecture*) and *detailed design*.

In practice, you will often find it difficult to differentiate architecture from detailed design. You will not be alone, since experts generally agree about the broad strokes of architecture but disagree about the fine details, such as where architecture stops and detailed design begins. Perhaps the best description of how architecture differs from detailed design comes from two leaders in the field, Mary Shaw and David Garlan (Shaw and Garlan, 1996):

> As the size and complexity of software systems increase, the design and specification of overall system structure become more significant issues than the choice of algorithms and data structures of computation. Structural issues include the organization of a system as a composition of components; global control structures; the protocols for communication, synchronization, and data access; the assignment of functionality to design elements; the composition of design elements; physical distribution; scaling and performance; dimensions of evolution; and selection among design alternatives. This is the *software architecture* level of design.

Definition. A great variety of definitions of software architecture have been proposed and there is general agreement that architecture deals with macroscopic, sweeping issues in software design. One of the most popular definitions is from the Software Engineering Institute (Clements et al., 2010):

> The software architecture of a computing system is the set of structures needed to reason about the system, which comprise software elements, relations among them, and properties of both.

This definition lists topics that are important to software architecture: elements, relations, and properties. Yet it does not simply say these structures comprise the architecture, it says that the architecture is the set of structures you need to reason about the system.

As an analogy, consider the architecture of the United States. Schoolchildren learn that the country is composed of fifty states and have lessons in which they memorize the states' locations. However, this structural information is insufficient to reason about the country. So they later learn that the size of the states is related to when they were settled, that states differ in their resources, and that the size and population of the states influenced the structure of the national legislature. With this improved understanding, they can reason about why the most and least populous states both have just two senators each, despite differing by more than 60 times in population.

The value of this analogy is that it shows that if you want to reason about the architecture of a system (the United States), you must usually go beyond a mechanical recitation of its structure. It also gives us a chance to preview a theme of this book: you can often reason about a system without having a complete model of it. The question, "Which U.S. cities can you travel to by boat?" does not require a complete model of the country.

What counts as architectural? Defining architecture as the set of structures needed to reason about a system is useful in that it focuses attention on the purpose of the architecture (reasoning), but problematic in that it blurs the line between architecture and detailed design. It is simpler and more clear to say that architecture is the macroscopic parts of the design, such as modules and how they are connected, leaving detailed design to cover everything else.

But there are plenty of examples of architectural details that are not limited to the biggest parts in a system. The original Java Beans spec required a naming pattern for exposed Bean properties because, behind the scenes, it would use reflection to convert methods like getTargetVelocity into an exposed property called TargetVelocity. The naming pattern for methods is about as low-level a decision as possible, yet it is architecturally significant for Java Beans. Similarly, an architecture may prohibit threads, require a method to complete within 100ms, require computation to be divided into jobs, or other details that are down deep in the code.

It is unsatisfactory to conclude that architecture concerns the macroscopic parts of design, except sometimes when it does not. In such a definition, who would decide what counts as architecture? Perhaps the designers of houses and skyscrapers can explain the difference between architecture and design. Like software, house designers have architectural designs and detailed designs, but while software is only about a half century old, houses have been built for millennia.

My brother builds skyscrapers and he tells me that, in his field, the architect will usually specify some low-level details, but leave others to be decided by the construction company. The architect includes details in the architecture if they contribute to an overall quality of the building, such as its watertightness, aesthetic appeal, or constructability. Otherwise a detail is considered non-architectural. On a recent job of my brother's, the architect insisted that the gap between windows be quite small because this detail was important for the architect's intention about the building's appearance.

Intentionality. To distinguish architectural details from other details, it would appear that intentionality is the key: there is a *chain of intentionality* from a few high-level intentions or decisions of the architect that reaches down to some low-level details. Most of the details are left open to any reasonable implementation, but some are constrained, via a chain back to the top-level intentions of the designer. An architectural description could be a mixture of macroscopic and microscopic details. It could even be incomplete, perhaps not describing every top-level module, but (like Java Beans) constraining the naming pattern of methods.

The idea of architectural chains of intentionality is imperfect, since it is difficult to be precise about what a "high-level intention or decision" is, and some systems have details that are architectural yet unintentional. However, the idea is helpful in that it does not divide architecture from design at an arbitrary place, or based on the whim of an architect. It also seems to match the kinds of architectural decisions made on real systems, which are a mixture of high- and low-level decisions. As with skyscrapers, if a detail is important to achieve an overall quality of the system, it is probably architectural.

2.2   Why is software architecture important?

It is important to pay attention to software architecture because of its impact on your systems. When you choose it deliberately, you reduce your risks and chance of failure.

- **Architecture acts as the skeleton of a system.** Every system has an architecture, whether its developers consciously chose it or not. There is no single right architecture, but there are more or less suitable skeletons for the job.

- **Architecture influences quality attributes.** Quality attributes are externally visible properties, such as security, usability, latency, or modifiability. Metaphorically speaking, different skeletons are better or worse at handling different burdens, so choosing the right architecture can make achieving desired qualities easier.

- **Architecture is (mostly) orthogonal to functionality.** It is possible to build the same system as a 3-tier architecture or as a peer-to-peer system. When the architecture is poorly matched to the functionality, however, developers will struggle against it.

- **Architecture constrains systems**. Architecture is the art of imposing just enough constraints so that the system has the quality attributes you want. For example, a design that ensures scalability may require some components to be stateless in order to achieve that scalability.

The following sections look at each of these ideas in turn.

Architecture as skeleton. It is useful to consider the imperfect metaphor of architecture as a skeleton. A skeleton provides the overall structure for an animal and influences what it can do. Birds are good at flying and kangaroos are good at jumping largely because of their skeletons. Most fast animals have four legs, but while the two-legged ones are slower, they might be able to use tools more easily.

You cannot say that one skeleton is better than another unless you can say that jumping is better than flying. You can, however, say whether a skeleton is well suited to its function or not, since it would take a lot of work to make a kangaroo skeleton fly.

Software is similar. A 3-tier architecture enables IT systems to localize changes and handle transactional loads. A cooperating-processes architecture is well suited to operating systems because it isolates faults. It is hard to imagine a distributed VOIP network like Skype using anything other than a peer-to-peer architecture. (Architectural styles are discussed in Chapter 14).

The skeleton metaphor is imperfect, however, because an architecture is more than the big visible parts (i.e., the bones), and the invisible parts (such as constraints) are often more important. For example, your locking policy, memory management strategy, or technique for integrating third-party components can all be part of the architecture, yet each of these is invisible in a running system or in its source code.

Architecture influences qualities. Developers must pay attention to what their software does, that is, its *functionality*. Accounting software that fails to account, or animation software that fails to animate, is not useful. Systems have additional requirements that are not related to their function, referred to as *quality attribute* requirements. Developers must pay attention to quality attribute requirements too, since accounting software that lets bad guys read secret accounts or animation software that runs too slowly is not particularly useful either. Quality attributes are discussed in depth in Chapter 7.

Beyond supporting required functionality, a system's architecture enables or inhibits qualities such as security or performance. The skeletons of a person and a horse both support the function of taking apples to market, but consider how each differs in throughput or accommodates varying tasks. It is usually possible to make any architecture choice work, but some choices make the qualities easy to achieve, while other choices make them hard.

Functional requirements that evolve over time are a challenge to any system, but evolving quality attributes can force drastic changes. A system that was designed to support a hundred users may be impossible to scale up to a hundred thousand without an architectural change. You often see successive generations or waves of an application as it outgrows its old architecture, somewhat like a crab outgrowing its shell.

Architecture is (mostly) orthogonal to functionality. There is no single best architecture, but architectures, like skeletons, are more suited to some tasks than others. A kangaroo with hollow bones might be too fragile and a bird with strong legs would fly like an ostrich. On the other hand, you can take a skeleton and force it to work in an inappropriate context. For example, while fish can breathe underwater and mammals cannot, whales manage to get the job done despite their mammal skeletons, with some difficulty.

It is important to recognize that you can mix-and-match architecture and functionality. That is, you could change a system's architecture yet keep its functionality, or reuse the same architecture on a system with different functionality. But some combinations work better than others.

Although a system's architecture is a separate choice from its functionality, a poor architecture choice can make functionality and quality attributes difficult to achieve. Here is an analogy: what your factory produces and where it is located are two distinct dimensions, and you can choose them independently. Putting a ship factory in the desert[1] is possible, but harder than putting it on the coast. With enough effort you probably could build any system using any architecture, but developers will struggle when the architecture is unsuitable.

Architecture constrains programs. All systems are constrained. Some must interoperate with older systems, some must use subcomponents from preferred vendors, and others must stay within memory or time budgets. Constraints like these are often thought of as an obstacle that makes the developer's job more difficult, but there is another way of thinking about constraints.

When designing a system, your choices constrain it to be one way and not another. Sometimes these choices are arbitrary. But some choices constrain the system with the intention of guiding it to a destination of your choosing. Constraints like these act as *guide rails* and are essential in the construction of a system, in its ability to perform its job, and in the ability to maintain it over time.

---

[1]The ancient Egyptians appear to have done this, building ships along the Nile in Koptos, disassembling them, carrying the parts a hundred miles across the desert to Saww on the Red Sea, then reassembling them.

What a system *does not do* is as important as what it does. To ensure that a system possesses certain qualities, you must constrain it so that you know what it will *not* do. For example, a secure system will not exchange data with untrusted parties, and a usable system will not start long-running computations without providing a cancel option.

You can voluntarily choose to constrain your design in order to achieve qualities such as performance or security. For example, a train is severely constrained by its tracks, and consequently lacks flexibility in its destinations. But this constraint specifically enables other qualities, such as low rolling friction leading to efficiency. Security is another benefit, as it is impractical to hijack a train. An unconstrained design can, by definition, do anything, so if you are to have any hope of analyzing it, you must constrain it. The use of constraints is a theme that runs throughout this book and we will return to it, providing detailed examples.

Engineers use constraints to ensure that the systems they design do what they intend. Appropriately applied, you can gain many benefits through constraints:

- **Embody judgment**. Constraints are a means to transfer wisdom or understanding from one developer to another. Senior engineers have a detailed and nuanced understanding of the domain they work in, and it takes time to convey this knowledge to others. Through constraints on the design, they can guide other engineers to acceptable solutions without fully transferring their knowledge.

- **Promote conceptual integrity**. Fred Brooks argues that conceptual integrity of a system is an important goal of system design, and that a single good idea consistently applied is better than several brilliant ideas scattered across a system (Brooks, 1995). Desmond D'Souza taps into the same idea when he argues that architectural constraints "reduce needless creativity" of developers, enabling them to use that creativity in places where it is needed (D'Souza and Wills, 1998).

- **Reduce complexity**. As a corollary to conceptual integrity, constraints can factor out complexity, yielding a system with evident underlying principles. In contrast, an unconstrained system can do similar things in arbitrarily different ways in different places, hindering its comprehensibility until you master its fussy details. A constraint can cut through[2] that complexity, giving you something that

---

[2]Several years ago, I was making changes to an unfamiliar codebase and was making good progress on the problem until I discovered that some setter methods were not only failing to set variables, they were performing unprincipled complex logic, including sending event notifications to other parts of the code. At that point I realized that my assumptions about the code's constraints were false, and that the task would take much longer, since a method called launchSpaceShuttle() might be doing no such thing. Understanding a codebase is easier with constraints, for example the constraints that setter methods do indeed set the variable and only have local effects.

you can count on. For example, if data can be saved only to a database, then you know where to look for it.

- **Understand runtime behavior**. Source code can be inspected directly, yet it can be difficult to predict how it behaves at runtime. You can write tricky code whose runtime behavior is nearly impossible to understand, or you can constrain it so that its runtime behavior is evident.

At some point you will have chafed at constraints placed by others on your system. Though constraints are sometimes used poorly, you cannot design without them because constraints impose organization on chaos, the engineer's mortal enemy. You must use them responsibly, like a sharp tool that can just as easily remove a finger as cut a board, rather than reject them outright. Designing a system's architecture requires reasoned choices about what is allowed and what is not. Any hesitation about imposing constraints originates not from the enlightened way that *you* would use them, but from the coarse and ignorant way that *others* use them.

2.3   When is architecture important?

Getting your software architecture right can be crucial to your project's success, but other times it can be a minor factor. When you are building the software equivalent of a doghouse, say a website to collect registrations for a family picnic, you are unlikely to spend much time thinking about your architecture. Conversely, you would hope that the developers of hospital software are paying attention to their architecture. How do you decide when architecture is important?

Architecture is likely to require more attention in systems with large scale or high complexity. Here are five specific cases with high architecture risk.

- **Small solution space.** Architecture is important when the solution space is small or it is hard to design any acceptable solution. Consider the difficulty of creating a human powered airplane compared to creating a faster car. The airplane will require that everything is just right, including low weight and high efficiency. Conversely, up to a point, making a faster car is often no harder than adding a bigger engine.

- **High failure risk.** Any time your failure risks are high, it is probably important to get your architecture right. People might die if your hospital system fails, and your company might never recover its reputation after a serious security failure.

- **Difficult quality attributes.** Architecture influences your ability to satisfy quality attributes, so while making another email system seems easy, making one with quick performance that supports millions of users is hard.

- **New domain.** You will need to pay more attention when the domain is new, or at least new to you. If you are building your tenth interactive desktop application, you will instinctively avoid poor designs, but if you are building your first then the architecture deserves your attention.

- **Product lines.** Some sets of products share a common architecture. Their product-line architecture will make some kinds of product variations easy and others hard to build.

The overarching answer is to look at how bad it would be to get the architecture wrong. When your system is small or simple, its architecture is unlikely to sink your project, so you will pay little attention to it. Amdahl's law says that speeding up one part of a system has an impact proportional to that part's contribution. Similarly, the benefit to getting the architecture right is proportional to its contribution to overall system risk.

2.4 Presumptive architectures

People used to say that nobody ever got fired for buying IBM. IBM mainframe systems dominated the market and the assumption was that choosing an IBM system was reasonable. Today, many domains have a software architecture that dominates the same way that IBM mainframes once did. These are presumptive architectures.

A *presumptive architecture* is a family of architectures that is dominant in a particular domain. Rather than justifying their choice to use it, developers in that domain may have to justify a choice that differs from the presumptive architecture. Incurious developers may not even seriously consider other architectures or may have the misapprehension that all software should conform to the presumptive architecture.

Presumptive architectures are similar to reference architectures. A *reference architecture* is a family of architectures that describes an architectural solution to a problem and it is usually written down as a specification. You can find reference architectures for high-reliability embedded systems or for using a particular vendor's technology to build web-based systems. A publisher of a reference architecture may hope that it becomes a presumptive architecture, but that may never happen. That is, a reference architecture is often an aspirational standard, while a presumptive architecture is a de facto standard.

Presumptive architectures succeed because the architecture is a good match for the common risks in the domain. For example, IT systems often face concurrent access to shared data, shifting business rules, and long-lived data. A tiered system is a good match for those problems. One tier handles the user interface, another handles the business processing logic, and another stores data to a transactional (and often relational) database.

Another example of a presumptive architecture is the use of cooperating processes in an operating system, which is a long-running system that must gracefully recover from faults occurring in its software. Operating systems differ in many ways, but almost all of them are constructed with a kernel and a set of cooperating systems processes. By running tasks in separate processes, faults in an individual task can be isolated and the task can be restarted, preserving overall system functionality.

The term presumptive architecture is introduced in this book because it would be a mistake to ignore these 800-pound gorillas and instead believe that all developers will start with first principles in their software architecture. IT developers who use the presumptive N-tier architecture will almost always do fine. In fact, their real architectural decisions may only be which COTS (Commercial Off-The-Shelf) software will be used on each tier, for example, which brand of relational database or web application server to use.

2.5   How should software architecture be used?

Software architects may be loath to admit it, but many systems can succeed even when their developers ignore software architecture. On the other hand, there have also been plenty of failures that could have been avoided by paying attention to software architecture. By reading this book, you should be prepared enough to understand which situation you are in.

Roughly speaking, developers can take one of three approaches to software architecture: They can ignore it, embrace it, or hoist it. Let's give these approaches names so that it is easier to talk about them.

- **Architecture-indifferent design**. With this approach, you pay little attention to architecture. Your system may become a big ball of mud, a distinct architecture may emerge without your conscious choice, or you may be guided by norms in your domain to a presumptive architecture.

- **Architecture-focused design**. With this approach, you deliberately choose your software architecture. You design an architecture that is suitable to achieve your goals, which include functionality and quality attributes.

- **Architecture hoisting**. This is a kind of architecture-focused design where developers design the architecture with the intent of guaranteeing a goal or property of the system. Once a goal or property has been hoisted into the architecture, developers will not need to write any additional code to achieve it.

A developer could apply the first approach, architecture-indifferent design, either through ignorance or because the system she is developing is unchallenging. By learning about software architecture, you ensure that you will not choose this option through ignorance and take on risks unwittingly.

The second and third approaches are similar and we will discuss their differences in detail below. For now, consider architecture-focused design to be choosing an architecture that is compatible with your goals, though that choice does not provide assurances, only opportunities. Architecture hoisting requires your architecture to play an active role, one that you can rely on to achieve your goals.

Perhaps a car analogy will help illuminate the differences in these approaches. When I was in college, a housemate of mine had a beautiful step-side Ford pickup truck. The only problem, however, was that its designers were architecturally indifferent to safety, in that the truck had no seatbelts. Apparently they were just hoping we did not crash (and we did not). When I graduated, I bought a Volkswagen GTI. Its designers had followed architecture-focused design and included seatbelts, but I had to remember to buckle them each time. Its architecture was compatible with safety, but did not guarantee it. Today, it is impossible to buy a car that has not hoisted safety into its architecture, because every car is required to have airbags that deploy automatically. The following sections discuss each approach in more detail.

2.6 Architecture-indifferent design

In *architecture-indifferent design*, developers are oblivious to their system's architecture and *do not* consciously choose an architecture to help them reduce risks, achieve features, or ensure qualities. The developers may simply ignore their architecture, copy the architecture from their previous project, use the presumptive architecture in their domain, or follow a corporate standard.

Notice that in discussing a developer's approach to architecture we are discussing a person, not a discernable characteristic of their software. Every system has an architecture, whether it is deliberately chosen or not. Following an architecture-indifferent approach will yield an architecture, just not one that has been chosen deliberately, and not one that the developers are consciously aware of.

Indifference to the architecture does not mean that the architecture is unsuitable, only that an opportunity to choose a suitable architecture was passed up. If the architecture is suitable, it is only by accident. If the architecture is unsuitable, the developers must struggle against it, but they may succeed if they are diligent and resourceful.

Architecture-indifferent design is most suited to low-risk projects. Stand-alone systems with few challenging requirements are relatively low risk, surprisingly common, and easy to build without focusing on architecture. Systems that follow presumptive architectures usually succeed.

Architecture-indifferent design has several drawbacks. A system with a suitable architecture can degrade over time into an unsuitable one when the team of developers lacks a shared architectural vision. For example, developers may try to speed up the system through various local and unprincipled changes. Over time, the complexity of the system will rise, perhaps beyond the ability of the developers to effectively maintain it.

The architecture-indifferent approach opens the door to complexity and, once complexity has joined the party, it can be difficult to send it home. At first, developers may experience no harm from lacking a clear vision of their system's architecture. However, if they later need to analyze a design that lacks consistency, they will find the task much more difficult. Analysis works best when a model is simple, and an architecture-indifferent approach may yield a complex system with lots of local exceptions to rules. An architecture that was not chosen deliberately may not lend itself to any particular analysis.

The drawbacks of architecture-indifferent design are partly mitigated by mature and powerful off-the-shelf connectors and components, such as service buses and relational databases. They handle difficult problems, such as concurrency or scaling, that would otherwise require architectural attention from developers. These same factors also contribute to the ability of developers to evolve a system without anticipating their architectural needs.

2.7   Architecture-focused design

When developers follow the *architecture-focused design* approach, they are aware of their system's software architecture and they have chosen it deliberately so that their system can achieve its goals. At a minimum, that means that the architecture is suitable and does not impede the goals. All software architecture books (including this one) assume that you should be following this approach.

Most problems have interesting challenges that you must overcome when designing a solution. Some of the challenges will be functional, such as how to compute bond interest, and others will relate to quality attributes, such as how to scale to thousands of users. Architecture-focused design recognizes that the architecture you choose can make these challenges easier or harder. So it makes sense to choose an architecture that helps you to overcome your challenges.

Many developers already follow architecture-focused design even if they do not realize it. For example, if your system needs to acquire locks, you may follow an ordering convention to avoid deadlocks. If your system has no garbage collection, you may have a standard for how memory is freed to prevent leaks, such as freeing memory based on module scope. If your system uses a cache, you may restrict access to ensure that the cache coherency is maintained. If your system processes orders, you may use a message queue with durability guarantees so that order messages cannot be lost. These are all design choices, arguably architectural ones, that are intended to achieve architectural qualities.

Notice that in these examples the solution was global (i.e., universally applied) rather than local. Another way to avoid memory leaks, for example, is to simply fix them once you discover the leak. Architecture-focused design seeks architectural solutions, rather than local fixes, to problems you face.

Architecture-focused design often entails reasoning about your problems using architectural abstractions (e.g., components and connectors) and architectural views (e.g., module, runtime, and allocation views). For example, it is almost tautological that components running in their own threads require thread-safe connectors, and that distributed components cannot assume references will be in the same memory space. But these observations are easily obscured if you are instead reasoning from individual lines of code.

Architecture-focused design means you must be on the lookout for requirements that will influence your architecture choices, but these requirements are rarely stated clearly. They may be hidden in a cryptic statement from a stakeholder or be common to other systems in your domain. When you recognize one of these, you should be asking yourself how your system will do that, and if it is something that your architecture will help or hinder.

Your system will always have an architecture, and when you choose architecture-focused design, you are choosing to pay attention to it. Paying attention to the architecture does not necessarily mean documenting it. In big projects, documenting the architecture can be a big help. In a startup company where all three developers live in the same garage, documenting the architecture is less important.

Architecture-focused design is compatible with any software development process. When thinking about architecture, there is a temptation to assume a waterfall process, with up-front architecture design, but the design of your architecture is just another engineering task like designing modules, objects, or data structures. Some things will be easier if you choose the architecture early, but this is also true of your choice of programming languages, interfaces, and frameworks.

2.8 Architecture hoisting

In architecture-focused design, developers deliberately choose an architecture that is compatible with what they need their system to do. Architecture hoisting is a stricter kind of architecture-focused design. When following an *architecture hoisting* approach, developers design the architecture with the intent of guaranteeing a goal or property of the system. Guarantees are difficult to come by in any kind of software design, but architecture hoisting strives to guarantee a goal or property through ar-

Approach	Description
Architecture-indifferent design	You pay little attention to architecture. Your system may become a big ball of mud, a distinct architecture may emerge without your conscious choice, or you may be guided by norms in your domain to a presumptive architecture.
Architecture-focused design	You deliberately choose your software architecture. You design an architecture that is suitable to achieve your goals, which include functionality and quality attributes.
Architecture hoisting	A kind of architecture-focused design in which developers design the architecture with the intent of guaranteeing a goal or property of the system. Once a goal or property has been hoisted into the architecture, developers should not need to write any additional code to achieve it.

Figure 2.1: A summary of the three approaches to software architecture.

chitecture choices. The idea is that once a goal or property has been hoisted into the architecture, developers should not need to write any additional code to achieve it.

For developers, the shift from architecture-indifferent design to architecture-focused design was obvious — it was evident in that they consciously choose an architecture that was compatible with their needs. The shift to architecture hoisting can be more subtle. They will notice the difference in that instead of simply choosing an architecture that lets them to do their work, they are asking the architecture to do work for them or make their work easier.

Let's look at an example to make this idea more concrete. Imagine that your performance requirements say that your system must respond to requests within 50ms. Here are some possible ways that you could approach the system's architecture, given the three design approaches:

- **Architecture-indifferent design.** If you followed architecture-indifferent design, you could copy the distributed processing architecture from your last system and discover, hopefully not too late, that its inter-machine messaging overhead eats up most of that 50ms, leaving little time to do the real processing. To succeed, you either change the architecture or write very efficient code that can complete in 10ms.

- **Architecture-focused design.** If you followed architecture-focused design, you would deliberately choose an architecture that is compatible with that requirement, such as a client-server architecture. The single remote call to the server might take 10ms, which leaves you a reasonable 40ms to do the real processing.

- **Architecture hoisting.** If you hoist the performance goal into the architecture, you would ask yourself how the architecture could ensure that a 50ms response was always achievable. Perhaps your investigation reveals that there are peak demand times that could overload your servers, so you build software to recruit additional processing, perhaps from a cloud of servers.

When developers are writing the code to process messages, they must be aware of the performance requirement. In the architecture-indifferent and architecture-focused designs, developers are entirely responsible for satisfying the requirement. In the architecture hoisting case, sloppy code could still result in failure (i.e., there are no guarantees), but the architecture is shouldering part of the burden through active recruitment of additional servers.

Notice that in the architecture-indifferent or architecture-focused designs there was no code that you could point to and say, "This is the code that ensures our 50ms response time." In contrast, with architecture hoisting you could point to the code that regulated the number of servers. When you hoist a goal or a property into the architecture, you will either find (1) code that manages it, or (2) a deliberate structural constraint (often with reasoning or calculations) that ensures it. Examples of structural constraints would be putting sensitive data behind a firewall, or communicating via an event bus that has durability and performance guarantees.

Some mainstream examples of architecture hoisting exist. An application server, such as one used for web applications, is a program that handles several runtime qualities of another program. An application server may handle running many copies of an application on a single machine (hoisting concurrency) or even spreading out the copies across multiple machines (hoisting scaling). An Enterprise Java Bean (EJB) application server hoists concurrency, scalability, and persistence, providing an architectural solution to these common problems. The Eclipse framework hoists many features, properties, and qualities, such as resource management, concurrency, and platform independence.

When properties or quality attributes are hoisted, the application must adhere to some constraints in order to work within the architecture. For example, EJB disallows applications from starting their own threads or writing to local disk. These restrictions make sense, since it would be difficult for the EJB server to handle concurrency if applications could create their own threads, and difficult for it to move applications between servers when they have data on a local disk.

Architecture hoisting usually involves tradeoffs. Automatic garbage collection can be seen as hoisting memory management, making that task easier for developers to handle, but it can make achieving performance targets more difficult. Domain-specific concurrency patterns may be more efficient than a hoisted general-purpose mechanism.

Architecture hoisting can be seen as a kind of tyranny over developers, burdening them with additional constraints and bureaucracy. Or it can be seen as liberation for developers, freeing them to focus on functionality instead of quality attributes. Hoisting is just a mechanism and can be used appropriately or not. It is effective when the system design requires quality attributes but achieving them would be a burden to developers. Often developers may be experts in a domain but not on how to ensure a quality like security or performance, so hoisting can enable experts to work within their specialty.

2.9   Architecture in large organizations

This book is *not* about which software development process to follow, how to be an architect, or how to structure the software development roles inside your organization. Consequently, it refers to software engineers as *developers*, not differentiating architects from programmers.

However, software development within large organizations brings its own challenges as a result of scale. Large companies and organizations divide themselves into divisions, departments, and teams. They introduce roles and assign responsibilities. While there are better and worse ways to organize a company, none is perfect. You should be aware that any way of dividing a company will solve some problems while creating others.

A common organization pattern in large companies is to create an *enterprise architecture* group and give it, among other responsibilities, the job of cultivating the architecture that spans applications. This organization gives rise to two job roles: *enterprise architects* and *application architects*.

Enterprise architects. Enterprise architects are developers who are responsible for many applications. Enterprise architects do not control the functionality of any one application. Instead, they design an ecosystem inside which individual applications contribute to the overall enterprise. How well the enterprise architects cultivate the ecosystem will help or hinder the enterprise in achieving its goals, usually things like integrating applications, enabling variability across regions or markets, and standardizing deployment environments. Enterprise architects are like *movie producers* in that they influence the outcome only indirectly. Since they cannot directly influence qualities in the software, i.e., they cannot write code or design individual applications, enterprise architects exert influence by applying architecture-focused design or architecture hoisting. Enterprise architects constrain the application architects by choosing architectures and constraints with the intent of achieving their desired qualities and goals.

Application architects. Application architects are developers who are responsible for a single application. It is possible for them to understand and manage thousands of objects that comprise their application. Application architects are like movie directors whose daily actions create the shape of the product. Application architects can be successful in using an architecture-indifferent approach because they design an application's functionality in addition to its architecture. They can also apply architecture-focused design for their application, or architecture hoisting.

Pros and cons. The separation of enterprise architecture from application architecture helps a company avoid the heterogeneity and resulting chaos that would happen without a deliberate effort to standardize. This benefit comes with some challenges. The first is the multiple-bosses problem. Developers, application architects, and enterprise architects rarely report to the same boss, which means their priorities may be different. Conflicts may arise, often regarding schedules, integration, architectural constraints, and platforms. The second problem is choosing suitable architectural constraints. Enterprise architects may over-constrain the architecture because they do not fully understand the needs of individual applications. Programmers may undervalue the benefit of standardizing across applications, believing their application should be exempted from onerous enterprise architecture constraints.

Since no organization structure is without flaws, the best you can hope for is to understand the tradeoffs and anticipate the problems. Knowing why enterprise architecture groups exist separately from development and knowing the kinds of trouble that can arise means that everyone can watch out for early warning signs and work to mitigate them.

Ideally, all developers would have software architecture skills, as will be discussed more in Section 5.3. Having a separate enterprise architect group is not a bad idea, but its chance of success is higher if all developers understand core architecture principles, understand that architectural constraints exist in order to achieve goals and qualities, and understand how the chosen architecture suits their project.

2.10 Conclusion

Software architecture is a kind of design that deals with the large-scale decisions and macroscopic elements (e.g., modules, components, and connections). It can be difficult to draw the line between architecture and detailed design because some of your architectural decisions will have impact deep into the code.

Your software architecture choices are important because your architecture acts as the skeleton of your system, influences its quality attributes, and constrains the system. It is mostly orthogonal to your system's functionality, so to some extent you can mix-and-match architecture and functionality. If your architecture is suitable for your desired features and quality attributes, you will have an easier time building the system. If your architecture is unsuitable, you will struggle to meet your requirements, and may have to make compromises.

Software architecture imposes constraints on the system you build, so by choosing an architecture you are limiting your options. Your instinct might be to minimize constraints, but they are essential and beneficial, enabling you to embody your judgments, promote conceptual integrity, reduce complexity, and understand the runtime behavior of your system.

Architecture is just one of the many tasks competing for your scarce attention, so it is helpful to know how much attention it deserves. When your systems are small or low-risk, architecture is less important because the chance or impact of failure is low. Conversely, making good architecture choices is important when your solution space is small, the risk of failure is high, the desired quality attributes are difficult to achieve, you are working in a new domain, or you are building a product-line architecture. Generally speaking, you should pay as much attention to architecture as it contributes risk to the overall project, since if there is little architecture risk then optimizing it only helps a little.

If you are not paying much attention to architecture, you are probably following *architecture-indifferent design*, meaning that you focus on local changes to achieve the goals of your system. You are not asking the architecture to shoulder any burdens and may use a *presumptive architecture* by default. Many projects will succeed despite their developers following an architecture-indifferent design approach, but they are taking an unnecessary risk of failure.

This book, like every other book on software architecture, suggests that architecture is important enough to understand and choose deliberately. In *architecture-focused design*, you deliberately choose an architecture that is suited to the demands of your project, perhaps an architecture that makes scalability or modifiability easier to achieve. You can follow a stricter version of architecture-focused design by *hoisting* problems into the architecture, for example, letting an application server handle concurrency problems, or a garbage collector handle memory management.

You may well find yourself in a large organization that has divided architectural responsibilities between various teams, often with a separate enterprise architecture group. Every organizational choice has pros and cons, so your best strategy is to be aware of the possible problems so you can work to overcome them. The *enterprise architects* cultivate a garden where individual applications can flourish, which means imposing architectural constraints and applying architecture-focused design.

2.11 Further reading

The term *architecture hoisting* originated with NASA/JPL Mission Data System (MDS) developers, including Daniel Dvorak, Kirk Reinholtz, Nicholas Rouquette, and Kenny

Meyer (Meyer, 2009). Their use of the term was meant to emphasize how existing space-systems code could obscure details about, for example, the spacecraft position or velocity. In their usage, architecture hoisting was making important things visible in the architecture, including essential state variables and previously emergent behavior such as scheduling. Over time, I have come to adopt the definition presented in this chapter, which is consistent with their original intent.

This chapter refers to one of computer science's famous laws, Amdahl's law (Amdahl, 1967). Other famous laws include Brooks' law, "adding manpower to a late software project makes it later" (Brooks, 1995) and Conway's law, "any organization that designs a system ... will inevitably produce a design whose structure is a copy of the organization's communication structure." (Conway, 1968).

The term *software architecture* has been defined in many ways. There are several flavors of definitions, but you should know about the two most popular ones. An example of the first flavor is the one presented in this chapter from the Software Engineering Institute (SEI), which says architecture is about the structure of the elements and their relationships (Clements et al., 2010). The second flavor is discussed by Martin Fowler and Ralph Johnson, who say "Architecture is the set of design decisions that must be made early in a project" (Fowler, 2003b). This is also known informally as the "stuff that's hard to change later" definition. Notice that this definition does not constrain what the decisions or stuff is, so it could include things like your choice of programming language. This book uses the SEI definition partly because it emphasizes the architecture-as-artifact point of view, rather than roles or process.

The distinction between the job title called architect, the process of architecting a system, and the engineering artifact called the software architecture has been highlighted for years by Bredemeyer Consulting (Bredemeyer and Malan, 2010), even appearing in their logo.

Academic results on software architecture are generally reported in conferences and workshops. Ones to watch include:

- **WICSA**: Joint Working IEEE/IFIP Conference on Software Architecture
- **ECSA**: European Conference on Software Architecture
- **QoSA**: Quality of Software Architectures
- **SHARK**: SHAring and Reusing Architectural Knowledge
- **ICSE**: International Conference on Software Engineering
- **SPLASH**: Systems, Programming, Languages, and Applications: Software for Humanity (formerly OOPSLA)

Additionally, the SEI website frequently publishes technical reports (SEI Library).

This book avoids discussing how architects must work within organizations because other books already do a good job at this, including Bass, Clements and Kazman

(2003) and Lattanze (2008). For a business management view on what software architecture provides to the bottom line, Ross, Weill and Robertson (2006) discusses a conceptual framework for how architecture strategy should be aligned with business strategy. The financial benefits of architecture are discussed in Maranzano (2005) and Boehm and Turner (2003).

Enterprise architecture is a large field unto itself, and this chapter offers just a cursory glimpse of it from the perspective of software design. Jeanne Ross, Peter Weill, and David Robertson do a good job of showing how business strategy should coordinate with software architecture (Ross, Weill and Robertson, 2006). Martin Fowler's book is a good place to look for the standard patterns of enterprise architecture (Fowler, 2002). Several conceptual models exist for enterprise architecture, often called *enterprise architecture frameworks*, including The Open Group Architecture Framework (TOGAF) (The Open Group, 2008), Department of Defense Architecture Framework (DoDAF) (Wisnosky, 2004), and the Zachman Framework (Zachman, 1987).

Chapter 3

Risk-Driven Model

As they build successful software, software developers are choosing from alternate designs, discarding those that are doomed to fail, and preferring options with low risk of failure. When risks are low, it is easy to plow ahead without much thought, but, invariably, challenging design problems emerge and developers must grapple with high-risk designs, ones they are not sure will work.

Building successful software means anticipating possible failures and avoiding designs that could fail. Henry Petroski, a leading historian of engineering, says this about engineering as a whole:

> The concept of failure is central to the design process, and it is by thinking in terms of obviating failure that successful designs are achieved. ... Although often an implicit and tacit part of the methodology of design, failure considerations and proactive failure analysis are essential for achieving success. And it is precisely when such considerations and analyses are incorrect or incomplete that design errors are introduced and actual failures occur. (Petroski, 1994)

To address failure risks, the earliest software developers invented design techniques, such as domain modeling, security analyses, and encapsulation, that helped them build successful software. Today, developers can choose from a huge number of design techniques. From this abundance, a hard question arises: *Which design and architecture techniques should developers use?*

If there were no deadlines then the answer would be easy: use all the techniques. But that is impractical because a hallmark of engineering is the *efficient* use of resources, including time. One of the risks developers face is that they waste too much time designing. So a related question arises: *How much design and architecture should developers do?*

There is much active debate about this question and several kinds of answers have been suggested:

- **No up-front design.** Developers should just write code. Design happens, but is coincident with coding, and happens at the keyboard rather than in advance.

- **Use a yardstick.** For example, developers should spend 10% of their time on architecture and design, 40% on coding, 20% on integrating, and 30% on testing.

- **Build a documentation package.** Developers should employ a comprehensive set of design and documentation techniques sufficient to produce a complete written design document.

- **Ad hoc.** Developers should react to the project needs and decide on the spot how much design to do.

The ad hoc approach is perhaps the most common, but it is also subjective and provides no enduring lessons. Avoiding design altogether is impractical when failure risks are high, but so is building a complete documentation package when risks are low. Using a yardstick can help you plan how much effort designing the architecture will take, but it does not help you choose techniques.

This chapter introduces the *risk-driven model* of architectural design. Its essential idea is that the effort you spend on designing your software architecture should be commensurate with the risks faced by your project. When my father installed a new mailbox, he did not apply every mechanical engineering analysis and design technique he knew. Instead, he dug a hole, put in a post, and filled the hole with concrete. The risk-driven model can help you decide when to apply architecture techniques and when you can skip them.

Where a software development process orchestrates every activity from requirements to deployment, the risk-driven model guides only architectural design, and can therefore be used inside any software development process.

The risk-driven model is a reaction to a world where developers are under pressure to build high quality software quickly and at reasonable cost, yet those developers have more architecture techniques than they can afford to apply. The risk-driven model helps them answer the two questions above: how much software architecture work should they do, and which techniques should they use? It is an approach that helps developers follow a middle path, one that avoids wasting time on techniques that help their projects only a little but ensures that project-threatening risks are addressed by appropriate techniques.

In this chapter, we will examine how risk reduction is central to all engineering disciplines, learn how to choose techniques to reduce risks, understand how engineering risks interact with management risks, and learn how we can balance planned design with evolutionary design. This chapter walks through the ideas that underpin the risk-driven model, but if you are the kind of person who would prefer to first see an example of it in use, you can flip ahead to Chapter 4.

3.1 What is the risk-driven model?

The *risk-driven model* guides developers to apply a minimal set of architecture techniques to reduce their most pressing risks. It suggests a relentless questioning process: "What are my risks? What are the best techniques to reduce them? Is the risk mitigated and can I start (or resume) coding?" The risk-driven model can be summarized in three steps:

1. Identify and prioritize risks

2. Select and apply a set of techniques

3. Evaluate risk reduction

You do not want to waste time on low-impact techniques, nor do you want to ignore project-threatening risks. You want to build successful systems by taking a path that spends your time most effectively. That means addressing risks by applying architecture and design techniques but only when they are motivated by risks.

Risk or feature focus. The key element of the risk-driven model is the promotion of risk to prominence. What you choose to promote has an impact. Most developers already think about risks, but they think about lots of other things too, and consequently risks can be overlooked. A recent paper described how a team that had previously done up-front architecture work switched to a purely feature-driven process. The team was so focused on delivering features that they deferred quality attribute concerns until after active development ceased and the system was in maintenance (Babar, 2009). The conclusion to draw is that teams that focus on features will pay less attention to other areas, including risks. Earlier studies have shown that even architects are less focused on risks and tradeoffs than one would expect (Clerc, Lago and van Vliet, 2007).

Logical rationale. But what if your perception of risks differs from others' perceptions? Risk identification, risk prioritization, choice of techniques, and evaluation of risk mitigation will all vary depending on who does them. Is the risk-driven model is merely improvisation?

No. Though different developers will perceive risks differently and consequently choose different techniques, the risk-driven model has the useful property that it yields arguments that can be evaluated. An example argument would take this form:

> We identified A, B, and C as risks, with B being primary. We spent time applying techniques X and Y because we believed they would help us reduce the risk of B. We evaluated the resulting design and decided that we had sufficiently mitigated the risk of B, so we proceeded on to coding.

This allows you to answer the broad question, "How much software architecture should you do?" by providing a plan (i.e., the techniques to apply) based on the relevant context (i.e., the perceived risks).

Other developers might disagree with your assessment, so they could provide a differing argument with the same form, perhaps suggesting that risk D be included. A productive, engineering-based discussion of the risks and techniques can ensue because the rationale behind your opinion has been articulated and can be evaluated.

3.2 Are you risk-driven now?

Many developers believe that they already follow a risk-driven model, or something close to it. Yet there are telltale signs that many do not. One is an inability to list the risks they confront and the corresponding techniques they are applying.

Any developer can answer the question, "Which features are you working on?" but many have trouble with the question, "What are your primary failure risks and corresponding engineering techniques?" If risks were indeed primary then they would find it an easy question to answer.

Technique choices should vary. Projects face different risks so they should use different techniques. Some projects will have tricky quality attribute requirements that need up-front planned design, while other projects are tweaks to existing systems and entail little risk of failure. Some development teams are distributed and so they document their designs for others to read, while other teams are co-located and can reduce this formality.

When developers fail to align their architecture activities with their risks, they will over-use or under-use architectural techniques, or both. Examining the overall context of software development suggests why this can occur. Most organizations guide developers to follow a process that includes some kind of documentation template or a list of design activities. These can be beneficial and effective, but they can also inadvertently steer developers astray.

Here are some examples of well-intentioned rules that guide developers to activities that may be mismatched with their project's risks.

- The team must always (or never) build full documentation for each system.
- The team must always (or never) build a class diagram, a layer diagram, etc.
- The team must spend 10% (or 0%) of the project time on architecture.

Such guidelines can be better than no guidance, but each project will face a different set of risks. It would be a great coincidence if the same set of diagrams or techniques were always the best way to mitigate a changing set of risks.

Example mismatch. Imagine a company that builds a 3-tier system. The first tier has the user interface and is exposed to the internet. Its biggest risks might be usability and security. The second and third tiers implement business rules and persistence; they are behind a firewall. The biggest risks might be throughput and scalability.

If this company followed the risk-driven model, the front-end and back-end developers would apply different architecture and design techniques to address their different risks. Instead, what often happens is that both teams follow the same company-standard process or template and produce, say, a module dependency diagram. The problem is that there is no connection between the techniques they use and the risks they face.

Standard processes or templates are not necessarily bad, but they are often used poorly. Over time, you may be able to generalize the risks on the projects at your company and devise a list of appropriate techniques. The important part is that the techniques match the risks.

The three steps to risk-driven software architecture are deceptively simple but the devil is in the details. What exactly are risks and techniques? How do you choose an appropriate set of techniques? And when do you stop architecting and start/resume building? The following sections dig into these questions in more detail.

3.3 Risks

In the context of engineering, *risk* is commonly defined as the chance of failure times the impact of that failure. Both the probability of failure and the impact are uncertain because they are difficult to measure precisely. You can sidestep the distinction between perceived risks and actual risks by bundling the concept of uncertainty into the definition of risk. The definition of risk then becomes:

$$\text{risk} = \text{perceived probability of failure} \times \text{perceived impact}$$

A result of this definition is that a risk can exist (i.e., you can perceive it) even if it does not exist. Imagine a hypothetical program that has no bugs. If you have never run the program or tested it, should you worry about it failing? That is, should you perceive a failure risk? Of course you should, but after you analyze and test the program, you gain confidence in it, and your perception of risk goes down. So by

Project management risks	Software engineering risks
"Lead developer hit by bus"	"The server may not scale to 1000 users"
"Customer needs not understood"	"Parsing of the response messages may be buggy"
"Senior VP hates our manager"	"The system is working now but if we touch anything it may fall apart"

Figure 3.1: Examples of project management and engineering risks. You should distinguish them because engineering techniques rarely solve management risks, and vice versa.

applying techniques, you can reduce the amount of uncertainty, and therefore the amount of (perceived) risk. You can also under-appreciate or fail to perceive a risk, which we will discuss shortly.

Describing risks. You can state a risk categorically, often as the lack of a needed quality attribute like modifiability or reliability. But often this is too vague to be actionable: if you do something, are you sure that it actually reduces the categorical risk?

It is better to describe risks such that you can later test to see if they have been mitigated. Instead of just listing a quality attribute like reliability, describe each risk of failure as a testable *failure scenario*, such as "During peak loads, customers experience user interface latencies greater than five seconds."

Engineering and project management risks. Projects face many different kinds of risks, so people working on a project tend to pay attention to the risks related to their specialty. For example, the sales team worries about a good sales strategy and software developers worry about a system's scalability. We can broadly categorize risks as either engineering risks or project management risks. *Engineering risks* are those risks related to the analysis, design, and implementation of the product. These engineering risks are in the domain of the engineering of the system. *Project management risks* relate to schedules, sequencing of work, delivery, team size, geography, etc. Figure 3.1 shows examples of both.

If you are a software developer, you are asked to mitigate engineering risks and you will be applying engineering techniques. The technique type must match the risk type, so only engineering techniques will mitigate engineering risks. For example, you cannot use a PERT chart (a project management technique) to reduce the chance of buffer overruns (an engineering risk), and using Java will not resolve stakeholder disagreements.

Project domain	Prototypical risks
Information Technology (IT)	Complex, poorly understood problem
	Unsure we're solving the real problem
	May choose wrong COTS software
	Integration with existing, poorly understood software
	Domain knowledge scattered across people
	Modifiability
Systems	Performance, reliability, size, security
	Concurrency
	Composition
Web	Security
	Application scalability
	Developer productivity / expressability

Figure 3.2: While each project can have a unique set of risks, it is possible to generalize by domain. Prototypical risks are ones that are common in a domain and are a reason that software development practices vary by domain. For example, developers on Systems projects tend to use the highest performance languages.

Identifying risks. Experienced developers have an easy time identifying risks, but what can be done if the developer is less experienced or working in an unfamiliar domain? The easiest place to start is with the requirements, in whatever form they take, and looking for things that seem difficult to achieve. Misunderstood or incomplete quality attribute requirements are a common risk. You can use Quality Attribute Workshops (see Section 15.6.2), a Taxonomy-Based Questionnaire (Carr et al., 1993), or something similar, to elicit risks and produce a prioritized list of failure scenarios.

Even with diligence, you will not be able to identify every risk. When I was a child, my parents taught me to look both ways before crossing the street because they identified cars as a risk. It would have been equally bad if I had been hit by a car or by a falling meteor, but they put their attention on the foreseen and high priority risk. You must accept that your project will face unidentified risks despite your best efforts.

Prototypical risks. After you have worked in a domain for a while, you will notice *prototypical risks* that are common to most projects in that domain. For example, Systems projects usually worry more about performance than IT projects do, and Web projects almost always worry about security. Prototypical risks may have been encoded as *checklists* describing historical problem areas, perhaps generated from architecture reviews. These checklists (see Section 15.6.2) are valuable knowledge for less experienced developers and a helpful reminder for experienced ones.

Knowing the prototypical risks in your domain is a big advantage, but even more important is realizing when your project differs from the norm so that you avoid blind spots. For example, software that runs a hospital might most closely resemble an IT project, with its integration concerns and complex domain types. However, a system that takes 10 minutes to reboot after a power failure is usually a minor risk for an IT project, but a major risk at a hospital.

Prioritizing risks. Not all risks are equally large, so they can be *prioritized*. Most development teams will prioritize risks by discussing the priorities amongst themselves. This can be adequate, but the team's perception of risks may not be the same as the stakeholders' perception. If your team is spending enough time on software architecture for it to be noticeable in your budget, it is best to validate that time and money are being spent in accordance with stakeholder priorities.

Risks can be categorized[1] on two dimensions: their priority to stakeholders and their perceived difficulty by developers. Be aware that some technical risks, such as platform choices, cannot be easily assessed by stakeholders.

Formal procedures exist for cataloging and prioritizing risks using risk matrices, including a US military standard MIL-STD-882D. Formal prioritization of risks is appropriate if your system, for example, handles radioactive material, but most computer systems can be less formal.

3.4 Techniques

Once you know what risks you are facing, you can apply *techniques* that you expect to reduce the risk. The term technique is quite broad, so we will focus specifically on *software engineering risk reduction techniques*, but for convenience continue to use the simple name *technique*. Figure 3.3 shows a short list of software engineering techniques and techniques from other engineering branches.

Spectrum from analyses to solutions. Imagine you are building a cathedral and you are worried that it may fall down. You could build models of various design alternatives and calculate their stresses and strains. Alternately, you could apply a known solution, such as using a flying buttress. Both work, but the former approach has an analytical character while the latter has a known-good solution character.

Techniques exist on a spectrum from pure analyses, like calculating stresses, to pure solutions, like using a flying buttress on a cathedral. Other software architecture and design books have inventoried techniques on the solution-end of the spectrum, and call these techniques *tactics* (Bass, Clements and Kazman, 2003) or *patterns*

---

[1]This is the same categorization technique used in ATAM to prioritize architecture drivers and quality attribute scenarios, as discussed in Section 12.11.

Software engineering	Other engineering
Applying design or architecture pattern	Stress calculations
Domain modeling	Breaking point test
Throughput modeling	Thermal analysis
Security analysis	Reliability testing
Prototyping	Prototyping

Figure 3.3: A few examples of engineering risk reduction techniques in software engineering and other fields. Modeling is commonplace in all engineering fields.

(Schmidt et al., 2000; Gamma et al., 1995), and include such solutions as using a process monitor, a forwarder-receiver, or a model-view-controller.

The risk-driven model focuses on techniques that are on the analysis-end of the spectrum, ones that are procedural and independent of the problem domain. These techniques include using models such as layer diagrams, component assembly models, and deployment models; applying analytic techniques for performance, security, and reliability; and leveraging architectural styles such as client-server and pipe-and-filter to achieve an emergent quality.

Techniques mitigate risks. Design is a mysterious process, where virtuosos can make leaps of reasoning between problems and solutions (Shaw and Garlan, 1996). For your process to be repeatable, however, you need to make explicit what the virtuosos are doing tacitly. In this case, you need to be able to explicitly state how to choose techniques in response to risks. Today, this knowledge is mostly informal, but we can aspire to creating a handbook that would help us make informed decisions. It would be filled with entries that look like this:

> If you have <a risk>, consider <a technique> to reduce it.

Such a handbook would improve the repeatability of designing software architectures by encoding the knowledge of virtuoso architects as mappings between risks and techniques.

Any particular technique is good at reducing some risks but not others. In a neat and orderly world, there would be a single technique to address every known risk. In practice, some risks can be mitigated by multiple techniques, while others risks require you to invent techniques on the fly.

This frame of mind, where you choose techniques based on risks, helps you to work efficiently. You do not want to waste time (or other resources) on low-impact techniques, nor do you want to ignore project-threatening risks. You want to build successful systems by taking a path that spends your time most effectively. That means only applying techniques when they are motivated by risks.

Optimal basket of techniques. To avoid wasting your time and money, you should choose techniques that best reduce your prioritized list of risks. You should seek out opportunities to kill two birds with one stone by applying a single technique to mitigate two or more risks. You might like to think of it as an *optimization problem* to choose a set of techniques that optimally mitigates your risks.

It is harder to decide which techniques should be applied than it appears at first glance. Every technique does something valuable, just not the valuable thing your project needs most. For example, there are techniques for improving the usability of your user interfaces. Imagine you successfully used such techniques on your last project, so you choose it again on your current project. You find three usability flaws in your design, and fix them. Does this mean that employing the usability technique was a good idea?

Not necessarily, because such reasoning ignores the *opportunity cost*. The fair comparison is against the other techniques you could have used. If your biggest risk is that your chosen framework is inappropriate, you should spend your time analyzing or prototyping your framework choice instead of on usability. Your time is scarce, so you should choose techniques that are maximally effective at reducing your failure risks, not just somewhat effective.

Cannot eliminate engineering risk. Perhaps you are wondering why we should try to create an optimal basket of techniques when we should go all the way and eliminate engineering risk. It is tempting, since engineers hate ignoring risks, especially those they know how to address.

The downside of trying to eliminate engineering risk is *time*. As aviation pioneers, the Wright brothers spent time on mathematical and empirical investigations into aeronautical principles and thus reduced their engineering risk. But, if they had continued these investigations until risks were eliminated, their first test flight might have been in 1953 instead of 1903.

The reason you cannot afford to eliminate engineering risk is because you must balance it with non-engineering risk, which is predominantly project management risk. Consequently, a software developer does not have the option to apply every useful technique because risk reductions must be balanced against time and cost.

3.5   Guidance on choosing techniques

So far, you have been introduced to the risk-driven model and have been advised to choose techniques based on your risks. You should be wondering how to make good choices. In the future, perhaps a developer choosing techniques will act much like a mechanical engineer who chooses materials by referencing tables of properties and making quantitative decisions. For now, such tables do not exist. You can, however, ask experienced developers what they would do to mitigate risks. That is, you would choose techniques based on their experience and your own.

However, if you are curious, you would be dissatisfied either with a table or a collection of advice from software veterans. Surely there must be principles that underlie any table or any veteran's experience, principles that explain why technique X works to mitigate risk Y.

Such principles do exist and we will now take a look at some important ones. Here is a brief preview. First, sometimes you have a problem to *find* while other times you have a problem to *prove*, and your technique choice should match that need. Second, some problems can be solved with an *analogic* model while others require an *analytic* model, so you will need to differentiate these kinds of models. Third, it may only be efficient to analyze a problem using a particular type of model. And finally, some techniques have *affinities*, like pounding is suitable for nails and twisting is suitable for screws.

Problems to find and prove. In his book *How to Solve It*, George Polya identifies two distinct kinds of math problems: problems to *find* and problems to *prove* (Polya, 2004). The problem, "Is there a number that when squared equals 4?" is a problem to find, and you can test your proposed answer easily. On the other hand, "Is the set of prime numbers infinite?" is a problem to prove. Finding things tends to be easier than proving things because for proofs you need to demonstrate something is true in all possible cases.

When searching for a technique to address a risk, you can often eliminate many possible techniques because they answer the wrong kind of Polya question. Some risks are specific, so they can be tested with straightforward test cases. It is easy to imagine writing a test case for "Can the database hold names up to 100 characters?" since it is a problem to find. Similarly, you may need to design a scalable website. This is also a problem to find because you only need to design (i.e., find) one solution, not demonstrate that your design is optimal.

Conversely, it is hard to imagine a small set of test cases providing persuasive evidence when you have a problem to prove. Consider, "Does the system always conform to the framework Application Programming Interface (API)?" Your tests could succeed, but there could be a case you have not yet seen, perhaps when a framework call unexpectedly passes a null reference. Another example of a problem to prove is deadlock: Any number of tests can run successfully without revealing a problem in a locking protocol.

Analytic and analogic models. Michael Jackson, crediting Russell Ackoff, distinguishes between *analogic models* and *analytic models* (Jackson, 1995; Jackson, 2000).

In an analogic model, each model element has an analogue in the domain of interest. A radar screen is an analogic model of some terrain, where blips on the screen correspond to airplanes — the blip and the airplane are analogues.

Analogic models support analysis only indirectly, and usually domain knowledge or human reasoning are required. A radar screen can help you answer the question, "Are these planes on a collision course?" but to do so you are using your special purpose brainpower in the same way that an outfielder can tell if he is in position to catch a fly ball (see Section 15.6.1).

An analytic (what Ackoff would call *symbolic*) model, by contrast, directly supports computational analysis. Mathematical equations are examples of analytic models, as are state machines. You could imagine an analytic model of the airplanes where each is represented by a vector. Mathematics provides an analytic capability to relate the vectors, so you could quantitatively answer questions about collision courses.

When you model software, you invariably use symbols, whether they are Unified Modeling Language (UML) elements or some other notation. You must be careful because some of those symbolic models support analytic reasoning while others support analogic reasoning, even when they use the same notation. For example, two different UML models could represent airplanes as classes, one with and one without an attribute for the airplane's vector. The UML model with the vector enables you to compute a collision course, so it is an analytic model. The UML model without the vector does not, so it is an analogic model. So simply using a defined notation, like UML, does not guarantee that your models will be analytic. *Architecture description languages* (ADLs) are more constrained than UML, with the intention of nudging your architecture models to be analytic ones.

Whether a given model is analytic or analogic depends on the question you want it to answer. Either of the UML models could be used to count airplanes, for example, and so could be considered analytic models.

When you know what risks you want to mitigate, you can appropriately choose an analytic or analogic model. For example, if you are concerned that your engineers may not understand the relationships between domain entities, you may build an analogic model in UML and confirm it with domain experts. Conversely, if you need to calculate response time distributions, then you will want an analytic model.

Viewtype matching. The effectiveness of some risk-technique pairings depends on the type of model or view used. *Viewtypes* are not fully discussed until Section 9.6. For now, it is sufficient to know about the three primary viewtypes. The *module viewtype* includes tangible artifacts such as source code and classes; the *runtime viewtype* includes runtime structures like objects; and the *allocation viewtype* includes allocation elements like server rooms and hardware. It is easiest to reason about modifiability from the module viewtype, performance from the runtime viewtype, and security from the deployment and module viewtypes.

Each view reveals selected details of a system. Reasoning about a risk works best when the view being used reveals details relevant to that risk. For example, reasoning about a runtime protocol is easier with a runtime view, perhaps a state machine, than with source code. Similarly, it is easier to reason about single points of failure using an allocation view than a module view.

Despite this, developers are adaptable and will work with the resources they have, and will mentally simulate the other viewtypes. For example, developers usually have access to the source code, so they have become quite adept at imagining the runtime behavior of the code and where it will be deployed. While a developer can make do with source code, reasoning will be easier when the risk and viewtype are matched, and the view reveals details related to the risk.

Techniques with affinities. In the physical world, tools are designed for a purpose: hammers are for pounding nails, screwdrivers are for turning screws, saws are for cutting. You may sometimes hammer a screw, or use a screwdriver as a pry bar, but the results are better when you use the tool that matches the job.

In software architecture, some techniques only go with particular risks because they were designed that way and it is difficult to use them for another purpose. For example, Rate Monotonic Analysis primarily helps with reliability risks, threat modeling primarily helps with security risks, and queuing theory primarily helps with performance risks (these techniques are discussed in Section 15.6).

3.6   When to stop

The beginning of this chapter posed two questions. So far, this chapter has explored the first: Which design and architecture techniques should you use? The answer is to identify risks and choose techniques to combat them. The techniques best suited to one project will not be the ones best suited to another project. But the mindset of aligning your architecture techniques, your experience, and the guidance you have learned will steer you to appropriate techniques.

We now turn our attention to the second question: How much design and architecture should you do? Time spent designing or analyzing is time that could have been spent building, testing, etc., so you want to get the balance right, neither doing too much design, nor ignoring risks that could swamp your project.

Effort should be commensurate with risk. The risk-driven model strives to efficiently apply techniques to reduce risks, which means not over- or under-applying techniques. To achieve efficiency, the risk-driven model uses this guiding principle:

Architecture efforts should be commensurate with the risk of failure.

If you recall the story of my father and the mailbox, he was not terribly worried about the mailbox falling over, so he did not spend much time designing the solution or applying mechanical engineering analyses. He thought about the design a little bit, perhaps considering how deep the hole should be, but most of his time was spent on implementation.

When you are unconcerned about security risks, spend no time on security design. However, when performance is a project-threatening risk, work on it until you are reasonably sure that performance will be OK.

Incomplete architecture designs. When you apply the risk-driven model, you only design the areas where you perceive failure risks. Most of the time, applying a design technique means building a model of some kind, either on paper or a whiteboard. Consequently, your architecture model will likely be detailed in some areas and sketchy, or even non-existent, in others.

For example, if you have identified some performance risks and no security risks, you would build models to address the performance risks, but those models would have no security details in them. Still, not every detail about performance would be modeled and decided. Remember that models are an intermediate product and you can stop working on them once you have become convinced that your architecture is suitable for addressing your risks.

Subjective evaluation. The risk-driven model says to prioritize your risks, apply chosen techniques, then evaluate any remaining risk, which means that you must decide if the risk has been sufficiently mitigated. But what does sufficiently mitigated mean? You have prioritized your risks, but which risks make the cut and which do not?

The risk-driven model is a framework to facilitate your decision making, but it cannot make judgment calls for you. It identifies salient ideas (prioritized risks and corresponding techniques) and guides you to ask the right questions about your design work. By using the risk-driven model, you are ahead because you have identified risks, enacted corresponding techniques, and kept your effort commensurate with your risks. But eventually you must make a subjective evaluation: will the architecture you designed enable you to overcome your failure risks?

3.7   Planned and evolutionary design

You should now be prepared, at a conceptual level at least, to go out and apply software architecture on your projects. You may still have some questions about how to proceed, however, since we have not yet discussed how the risk-driven model interacts with other kinds of guidance you already know, things like planned and evolutionary design, software processes, and specifically agile software development.

The remainder of the chapter shows how the risk-centric model is compatible with each of these and can be used to augment their advice.

We start by discussing three styles of design: planned, evolutionary, and minimal planned design. Planned and evolutionary are the two basic styles of design and minimal planned design is a combination of them.

Evolutionary design. *Evolutionary design* "means that the design of the system grows as the system is implemented" (Fowler, 2004). Historically, evolutionary design has been frowned upon because local and uncoordinated design decisions yield chaos, creating a hodgepodge system that is hard to maintain and evolve any further.

However, recent trends in software processes have re-invigorated evolutionary design by addressing most of its shortcomings. The agile practices of *refactoring*, *test-driven design*, and *continuous integration* work against the chaos. Refactoring (a behavior-preserving transformation of code) cleans up the uncoordinated local designs (Fowler, 1999), test-driven design ensures that changes to the system do not cause it to lose or break existing functionality, and continuous integration provides the entire team with the same codebase. Some argue that these practices are sufficiently powerful that planned design can be avoided entirely (Beck and Andres, 2004).

Of the three practices, refactoring is the workhorse that reduces the hodgepodge in evolutionary design. Refactoring replaces designs that solved older, local problems with designs that solve current, global problems. Refactoring, however, has limits. Current refactoring techniques provide little guidance for architecture scale transformations. For example, Amazon's sweeping change from a tiered, single-database architecture to a service-oriented architecture (Hoff, 2008a) is difficult to imagine resulting from small refactoring steps at the level of individual classes and methods. In addition, legacy code usually lacks sufficient test cases to confidently engage in refactoring, yet most systems have some legacy code.

Though some projects use evolutionary design recklessly, its advocates say that evolutionary design must be paired with supporting practices like refactoring, test-driven design, and continuous integration.

Planned design. At the opposite end of the spectrum from evolutionary design is *planned design*. The general idea behind planned design is that plans are worked out in great detail before construction begins. Analogies with bridge design and construction are often brought up, since bridge construction rarely begins before its design is complete.

Few people advocate[2] doing planned design for an entire software system, an approach sometimes called *Big Design Up Front (BDUF)*. However, complete planning

---

[2]Model Driven Engineering (MDE) is an exception since it needs a detailed model to generate code.

of just the architecture is suggested by some authors (Lattanze, 2008; Bass, Clements and Kazman, 2003), since it is often hard to know on a large or complex project that *any* system can satisfy the requirements. When you are not sure that any system can be built, it is best to find this out early.

Planned architecture design is also practical when an architecture is shared by many teams working in parallel, and therefore useful to know before the sub-teams start working. In this case, a planned architecture that defines the top-level components and connectors can be paired with *local designs*, where sub-teams design the internal models of the components and connectors. The architecture usually insists on some overall invariants and design decisions, such as setting up a concurrency policy, a standard set of connectors, allocating high-level responsibilities, or defining some localized quality attribute scenarios. Note that architectural modeling elements like components and connectors will be fully described in the second part of this book.

Even when following planned design, an architecture or design should rarely, if ever, be 100% complete before proceeding to prototyping or coding. With current design techniques, it is nearly impossible to perfect the design without feedback from running code.

Minimal planned design. In between evolutionary design and planned design is *minimal planned design*, or *Little Design Up Front* (Martin, 2009). Advocates of minimal planned design worry that they might design themselves into a corner if they did all evolutionary design, but they also worry that all planned design is difficult and likely to get things wrong. Martin Fowler puts estimated numbers on this, saying he does roughly 20% planned design and 80% evolutionary design (Venners, 2002).

Balancing planned and evolutionary design is possible. One way is to do some initial planned design to ensure that the architecture will handle the biggest risks. After this initial planned design, future changes to requirements can often be handled through local design, or with evolutionary design if the project also has refactoring, test-driven-design, and continuous integration practices working smoothly.

If you are concerned primarily with how well the architecture will support global or emergent qualities, you can do planned design to ensure these qualities and reserve any remaining design as evolutionary or local design. For example, if you have identified throughput as your biggest risk, you could engage in planned design to set up throughput budgets (e.g., message deliveries happen in 25ms 90% of the time). The remainder of the design, which ensured that individual components and connectors met those performance budgets, could be done as evolutionary or local design. The general idea is to perform *architecture-focused design* (see Section 2.7) to set up an architecture known to handle your biggest risks, allowing you more freedom in other design decisions.

Which is best? Regardless of which design style you prefer, you must design software before you write the code, whether it is ten minutes before or ten months before. Both design styles have devoted proponents and their debate relies on anecdotes rather than solid data, so for now opinions will vary. If you have high confidence in your ability to do evolutionary design, you will do less planned design.

Realize that different systems will lend themselves to different styles of design. Consider the slow changes to the Apache web server over the past decade. It is suitable for planned design because its design resembles an optimization problem for a stable set of requirements (e.g., high reliability, extensibility, and performance). On the other hand, many projects have rapidly changing requirements that favor evolutionary design.

The essential tension between planned and evolutionary design is this: A long head start on architectural design yields opportunities to ensure global properties, avoid design dead ends, and coordinate sub-teams — but it comes at the expense of possibly making mistakes that would be avoided if decisions were made later. Teams with strong refactoring, test-driven development, and continuous integration practices will be able to do more evolutionary design than other teams.

The risk-driven model is compatible with evolutionary, planned, and minimal planned design. All of these design styles agree that design should happen at some point and they all allocate time for it. In planned design, that time is up-front, so applying the risk-driven model means doing up-front design until architecture risks have subsided. In evolutionary design, it means doing architecture design during development, whenever a risk looms sufficiently large. Applying it to minimal planned design is a combination of the others.

3.8 Software development process

Few developers build systems using only a design style, say evolutionary design, and a compiler. Instead, their activities are structured using a software development process that has been designed to increase their chances of successfully delivering a good system. A good software development process does more than just minimize engineering risks, since it must also factor in other business needs and risks, such as time-to-market pressures.

When you broaden your attention from pure engineering risks to the overall project risks, you find many more risks to worry about. Will the customer accept your system? Will the market have changed by the time you deliver? Will you deliver on time? Did your requirements reflect the customer's desires? Do you have the right people, are they doing the right jobs, and are they communicating effectively? Will there be lawsuits?

Software development process. A *software development process* orchestrates a team's activities with the goal of balancing both engineering and project management risks. It is tempting, but impossible, to cleanly separate engineering process from project management process. A software development process helps you prioritize risks across both engineering and project management, and perhaps to decide that even though engineering risks still exist, other risks outweigh them.

Risk as shared vocabulary. Risks are the shared vocabulary between engineers and project managers. A manager's job is to understand tradeoffs and make decisions across the risks on a project. A manager may not be technical enough to understand why a module does not work as desired, but he will understand the risk of its failure, and the engineer can help him assess the risk's probability and severity.

The concept of a risk is positioned in the common ground between the world of engineering and the world of project management. Engineers may choose to ignore office politics and marketing meetings, and managers may choose to ignore the database schema and performance estimates, but in the idea of risks they find common ground to make decisions about the system.

Baked-in risks. If you had never seen a software development process before, you might imagine it was like a control loop in a program, where during each iteration it prioritizes the risks and plans out the next step accordingly, looping until the system is delivered. In practice, some risk mitigation steps are deliberately *baked-in* to the software development process.

At a large company worried about team coordination, the process might insist on various forms of documentation at project milestones. Agile processes bake-in worries about time-to-market and customer rejecting the product, and consequently insist that the software be built and delivered in short iterations. IT-specific processes often face risks associated with unknown and complex domains, so their processes may bake-in constructing domain models. Whenever I leave the house, I pat my pockets to ensure that I have my wallet and keys because it is enough of a risk to bake-in to my habits.

Baking risk mitigation techniques into the software development process can be a blessing. It is a blessing when the process bakes-in risks that you would prioritize anyway, so it saves you the time of every day deciding that, for example, you should stick to two-week iterations rather than slipping the schedule. It is an efficient means of conveying expertise from experienced software developers, because they can point to successful results of following a process, rather than explaining their philosophy on software development that was baked-in. In an agile method such as XP, a team following the process can succeed even if they do not understand why XP chose its particular set of techniques.

Baking risks into the software development process can be a curse when you get it wrong. Many years ago, I interviewed with a tiny startup company. The project manager, formerly with $BIGCOMPANY, asked me what I thought about process and I told him that it needed to be appropriate for the project, the domain, and the team. Above all else, I said, applying a process from a book, unaltered, was unlikely to work. Like a scene from a comedy, he swiveled in his chair and picked up a book describing $BIGCOMPANY's development process and said, "This is the process we will be following." Needless to say, I did not end up working there, but I wish I could have seen the five co-located engineers producing detailed design documents and other bureaucracy that are baked-in to processes for large, distributed teams.

If you decide to tailor your software development process to bake-in risks, some important features to consider include project complexity (big, small), team size (big, small), location (distributed, co-located), domain (IT, finance, systems, embedded, safety-critical, etc.), and kind of customer (internal, external, shrink-wrapped).

3.9 Understanding process variations

Before you can see how to apply the risk-driven model to a software development process, you will need to know about the broad categories of processes and some details about them. This section offers an overview that omits details of each process, but it provides adequate background so that you can think about how to apply the risk-driven model.

This overview fits each process into a simple two-part template: An optional up-front design part with one or more iterations that follow. Not every development process here has up-front design, but all of them have at least one iteration. The template varies on four points:

1. Is there up-front design?

2. What is the nature of the design (planned/evolutionary; redesign allowed)?

3. How is work prioritized across iterations?

4. How long is an iteration?

Figure 3.4 summarizes the processes and highlights some of their differences.

Two other important variation points that arise when talking about development process are: how detailed should your design models be, and how long you should hold on to your design models? None of the above processes commits to an answer for these, except for XP, which allows modeling but discourages keeping the models around past an iteration. Applying this simple template to software development processes yields the following descriptions:

Process	Up-front design	Nature of design	Prioritization of work	Iteration length
Waterfall	In analysis & design phases	Planned design; no redesign	Open	Open
Iterative	Optional	Planned or evolutionary; redesign allowed	Open, often feature-centric	Open, usually 1-8 weeks
Spiral	None	Planned or evolutionary	Riskiest work first	Open
UP / RUP	Optional; design activities front-loaded	Planned or evolutionary	Riskiest work first, then highest value	Usually 2-6 weeks
XP	None, but some do in iteration zero	Evolutionary design	Highest customer value first	Usually 2-6 weeks

Figure 3.4: Examples of software development processes and how they treat design issues. For comparison purposes, a waterfall process is treated as having a single long iteration.

Waterfall. The waterfall process proceeds from beginning to end as a single long block of work that delivers the entire project (Royce, 1970). It assumes planned design work that is done in its analysis and design phases. These precede the construction phase, which can be considered a single iteration. With just one iteration, work cannot be prioritized across iterations, but it may be built incrementally within the construction phase. Applying the risk-driven model would mean doing architecture work primarily during the analysis and design phases.

Iterative. An iterative development process builds the system in multiple work blocks, called iterations (Larman and Basili, 2003). With each iteration, developers are allowed to rework existing parts of the system, so it is not just built incrementally. Iterative development optionally has up-front design work but it does not impose a prioritization across the iterations, nor does it give guidance on the nature of design work. Applying the risk-driven model would mean doing architecture work within each iteration and during the optional up-front design.

Spiral. The spiral process is a kind of iterative development, so it has many iterations, yet it is often described as having no up-front design work (Boehm, 1988). Iterations are prioritized by risk, with the first iteration handling the riskiest parts of a project. The spiral model handles both management and engineering risks. For

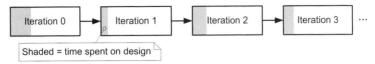

Figure 3.5: An example of how the amount of design could vary across iterations based on your perception of the risks. Based on the amount of time spent, you can infer that the most risk was perceived in iteration 0 and iteration 2.

example, it may address "personnel shortfalls" as a risk. The spiral process gives no guidance about how much architecture/design work to do, or about which architecture and design techniques to use.

[Rational] Unified Process (RUP). The Unified Process and its specialization, the Rational Unified Process, are iterative, spiral processes (Jacobson, Booch and Rumbaugh, 1999; Kruchten, 2003). They highlight the importance of addressing risks early and the use of architecture to address risks. The (R)UP advocates working on architecturally-relevant requirements first, in early iterations. It can accommodate either planned or evolutionary design.

Extreme Programming (XP). Extreme Programming is a specialization of an iterative and agile software development process, so it contains multiple iterations (Beck and Andres, 2004). It suggests avoiding up-front design work, though some projects add an *iteration zero* (Schuh, 2004), in which no customer-visible functionality is delivered. It guides developers to apply evolutionary design exclusively, though some projects modify it to incorporate a small amount of up-front design. Each iteration is prioritized by the customer's valuation of features, not risks.

3.10 The risk-driven model and software processes

It is possible to apply the risk-driven model to any of these software development processes while still keeping within the spirit of each. The waterfall process prescribes planned design in its analysis and design phases, but does not tell you what kind of architecture and design work to do, or how much of it. You can apply the risk-driven model during the analysis and design phases to answer those questions.

The iterative process does not have a designated place for design work, but it could be done at the beginning of each iteration. The amount of time spent on design would vary based on the risks. Figure 3.5 provides a notional example of how the amount of design could vary across iterations based on your perception of the risks.

The spiral process and the risk-driven model are cousins in that risk is primary in both. The difference is that the spiral process, being a full software development process, prioritizes both management and engineering risks and guides what happens across iterations. The risk-driven model only guides design work to mitigate engineering risks, and only within an iteration. Applying the risk-driven model to the spiral model or the (R)UP works the same as with an iterative process.

You will have noticed that, of the processes listed in Figure 3.4, XP (an agile process) has the most specific advice. Consequently, it is trickiest to apply the risk-driven model into the XP process (or other feature-centric agile processes), so we will look at that process in more depth.

3.11   Application to an agile processes

The following description of using the risk-driven model on an agile project highlights some core issues, such as when to design, and how to mix risks into a feature-driven development process. Since agile projects vary in their process, this description assumes one with a two-week iteration that plays a *planning game* to manage a *feature backlog*. On the engineering side, there are software architecture risks that you should fold into this process, which includes identification, prioritization, mitigation, and evaluation of those risks. The big challenges are: first, how to address initial engineering risks, and second, how to incorporate engineering risks that you later discover into the stack of work to do.

Risks. You will have identified some risks at the beginning of the project, such as the initial choices for architectural style, choice of frameworks, and choice of other COTS (Commercial Off-The-Shelf) components. Some agile projects use an iteration zero to get their development environment set up, including source code control and automated build tools. You can piggyback here to start mitigating the identified risks. Developers could have a simple whiteboard meeting to ensure everyone agrees on an architectural style, or come up with a short list of styles to investigate. If performance characteristics of COTS components are unknown but important, some quick prototyping can be done to provide approximate speed or throughput numbers.

Risk backlog. At the end of an iteration, you need to evaluate how well your activities mitigated your risks. Most of the time you will have reduced a risk sufficiently that it drops off your radar, but sometimes not. Imagine that at the end of the iteration you have learned that prototyping shows that your preferred database will run too slowly. This risk can be written up as a testable feature for the system. This is the beginning of a *risk backlog*. Whenever possible, risks should be written up as testable items.

Some risks are small enough that they can be handled as they arise during an iteration, and never show up on the backlog. But larger risks will need to be scheduled just like features are.

Note that this is not an excuse to turn a nominal iteration zero into a de facto Big Design Up-Front exercise. Instead of extending the time of iteration zero, risks are

Figure 3.6: One way to incorporate risk into an agile process is to convert the feature backlog into a *feature & risk backlog*. The product owner adds features and the software team adds technical risks. The software team must help the product owner to understand the technical risks and suitably prioritize the backlog.

pushed onto the backlog. This raises a question: how can we handle both backlogged features and risks?

Prioritizing risks and features. Many agile projects divide the world into product owners, who create a prioritized list of features called the backlog, and developers, who take features from the top of the backlog and build them.

It is tempting to put both features and risks on the same backlog, but managing the backlog becomes more complex once you introduce risks, because both features and risks must be prioritized together. Who is qualified to prioritize both?

If you give the product owner the additional responsibility to prioritize architectural risks alongside features, you can simply change the feature backlog into a feature & risk backlog, as seen in Figure 3.6. Software developers may see a feature low in the backlog asking for security. It is their job to educate the product owners that if they ever want to have a secure application, they need to address that risk early, since it will be difficult or impossible to add later. As part of the reflection at the end of each iteration, you should evaluate architectural risks and feed them into the backlog.

Summary. An agile process can handle architectural risks by doing three things. Architectural risks that you know in advance can be (at least partially) handled in a time-boxed iteration zero, where no features are planned to be delivered. Small architectural risks can be handled as they arise during iterations. And large architectural risks should be promoted to be on par with features, and inserted into a combined feature & risk backlog.

3.12   Risk and architecture refactoring

Over time, system developers understand increasingly well how a system should be designed. This is true regardless of which kind of process they follow (e.g., waterfall or iterative processes). In the beginning, they know and understand less. After some work (design, prototyping, iterations, etc.) they have better grounded opinions on suitable designs.

Once they recognize that their code does not represent the best design (e.g., by detecting *code smells*), they have two choices. One is to ignore the divergence, which yields *technical debt*. If allowed to accumulate, the system will become a big ball of mud (see Section 14.7). The other is to refactor the code, which keeps it maintainable. This second option is well described by Brian Foote and William Opdyke in their patterns on software lifecycle (Coplien and Schmidt, 1995).

Refactoring, by definition, means re-design and the scale of that redesign can vary. Sometimes a refactoring involves just a handful of objects or some localized code. But other times it involves more sweeping architectural changes and is called *architecture refactoring*. Since little published guidance exists for refactoring at large scale, architecture refactoring is generally performed ad hoc.

The example from the introduction where Rackspace implemented their query system three different ways (see Section 1.2) is best thought of as architecture refactoring. There, each refactoring of the architecture was precipitated by a pressing failure risk. Object-level refactorings take a negligible amount of time and therefore need little justification, so you should just go ahead and, for example, rename a variable to be more expressive of its intent. An architecture refactoring is expensive, so it requires a significant risk to justify it.

Two important lessons are apparent. First, *design does not exclusively happen up-front*. It is often reasonable to spend time up-front making the best choices you can, but it is optimistic to think you know enough to get all those design decisions right. You should anticipate spending time designing after your project's inception.

Second, *failure risk can guide architecture refactoring*. By the time it is implemented, nearly every system is out of date compared to the best thinking of its developers. That is, some technical debt exists. Perhaps, in hindsight, you wish you had chosen a different architecture. Risks can help you decide how bad it will be if you keep your current architecture.

3.13   Alternatives to the risk-driven model

The risk-driven model does two things: it helps you decide when you can stop doing architecture, and it guides you to appropriate architecture activities. It is not good at predicting how long you will spend designing, but it helps you recognize when you have done enough. There are several alternatives to the risk-driven model, with their own advantages and disadvantages.

No design. The option of not designing is a bit of a misnomer, especially if you believe that every system has an architecture, because the developers must have thought about it at some point. Perhaps they were thinking about the design (i.e., what they will code) immediately before they start typing, but they do think about the design. Such projects likely borrow heavily from presumptive architectures (see Section 2.4), where the developers pattern their system off of similar successful systems, explicitly or implicitly.

Documentation package. Some people suggest, or at least imply, that you should build a full documentation package that describes your architecture. If you follow this guidance, you will build a set of models and diagrams and write them down in such a way that someone else could read and understand the architecture, which can be quite desirable. If you need documentation, the Documenting Software Architectures book (Clements et al., 2010) will guide you to an effective set of models and diagrams to record.

However, few projects will need to create a full documentation package, and the "3 guys in a garage" startup probably cannot afford to write anything down.

Yardsticks. Empirical data can help you decide how much time should be spent on architecture and design. Barry Boehm has calculated the optimal amount of time to spend on the architecture for small, medium, and large projects based on a variant of his COCOMO model (Boehm and Turner, 2003). For various project sizes, he has plotted curves of architecture effort vs. total project duration. His data indicates that most projects should spend 33-37% of their total time doing architecture, with small projects spending as little as 5% and very large projects spending 40%.

A yardstick like "spend 33% of your time on architecture" can be used by project managers for planning project activities and staffing requirements, yielding a time budget to spend in design.

Yardsticks, however, are little help to developers once the architecture work has started. No reasonable developer should continue design activities for additional days after the risks have been worked out, even if the yardstick provides that budget. Nor should a reasonable developer switch to coding when a major failure risk is outstanding.

It is best to view such yardsticks as heuristics derived from experience combating risks, where projects of a certain size historically needed about that much time to mitigate their risks. That yardstick does not help you decide whether one more (or one less) day of architecture work is appropriate. Also, yardsticks only suggest broad categorical activities rather than guide you to particular techniques.

Ad hoc. When choosing how much architecture to do, most developers probably do not follow any of the alternatives above. Instead, they make a decision in the moment, based on their experience and their best understanding of the project's needs.

This may indeed be the most effective way to proceed, but it is dependent upon the skill and experience of the developer. It is not teachable, since its lessons are not explicit, nor is it particularly helpful in creating project planning estimates. It may be that, in practice, the ad hoc approach is a kind of informal risk-driven model, where developers tacitly weigh the risks and choose appropriate techniques.

3.14   Conclusion

This chapter set out to investigate two questions. First, *which design and architecture techniques should developers use?* And second, *how much design and architecture should developers do?* It reviewed existing answers, including doing no design, using yardsticks, building documentation packages, and proceeding ad hoc. It introduced the *risk-driven model* that encourages developers to: (1) prioritize the risks they face, (2) choose appropriate architecture techniques to mitigate those risks, and (3) re-evaluate remaining risks. It encourages just enough design and architecture by guiding developers to a prioritized subset of architecture activities. Design can happen up-front but it also happens during a project.

The risk-driven model is inspired by my father's work on his mailbox. He did not perform complex calculations — he just stuck the post in the hole then filled it with concrete. Low-risk projects can succeed without any planned architecture work, while many high-risk ones would fail without it.

The risk-driven model walks a middle path that avoids the extremes of complete architecture documentation packages and architecture avoidance. It follows the principle that your architecture efforts should be commensurate with the risk of failure. Avoiding failure is central to all engineering and you can use architecture techniques to mitigate the risks. The key element of the risk-driven model is the promotion of risk to prominence. Each project will have a different set of risks, so it likely needs a different set of techniques. To avoid wasting your time and money, you should choose techniques that best reduce your prioritized list of risks.

The question of how much software architecture work you should do has been a thorny one for a long time. The risk-driven model transforms that broad question into a narrow one: "Have your chosen techniques sufficiently reduced your failure risks?" Evaluation of risk mitigation is still subjective, but it is one that developers can have a focused conversation about.

Engineering techniques address engineering risks, but projects face a wide variety of risks. Software development processes must prioritize both management risks and engineering risks. You cannot reduce engineering risks to zero because there are also project management risks to consider, including time-to-market pressure. By applying the risk-driven model, you ensure that whatever time you devote to software architecture reduces your highest priority engineering risks and applies relevant techniques.

Agile software development approaches often emphasize evolutionary design over planned design. A middle path, minimal planned design, can be used to avoid the extremes. The essential tension is this: A long head start on architectural design yields opportunities to ensure global properties, avoid design dead ends, and coordinate sub-teams — but it comes at the expense of possibly making mistakes that would be avoided if decisions were made later. Agile processes focusing on features can be adapted slightly to add risk to the feature backlog, with developers educating product owners on how to prioritize the feature & risk backlog.

Some readers may be frustrated that this chapter does not prescribe a list of techniques to use and a single process to follow. These are missing because the techniques that work great on one project would be inappropriate on another. And there is not yet enough data to overcome opinions about the best process to recommend. Indeed, you may not have a choice about which process you follow, but within that process you likely have the ability to use the risk-driven model. This chapter has tried to provide relevant information about how to make your own choices so that you can do just enough architecture for your projects.

3.15   Further reading

The invention of risk as a concept likely occurred quite early, with references to it in Greek antiquity, but it took on its modern, more general, idea as late as the 17th century, where it increasingly displaced the concept of *fortunes* as what drove life's outcomes (Luhmann, 1996). A few minutes after that, project managers started using risk to drive their projects. This longstanding tradition in project management has carried over into software process design, with many authors emphasizing the role of risk in software development, including Philippe Kruchten (Kruchten, 2003), Ivar Jacobson, Grady Booch, and James Rumbaugh (Jacobson, Booch and Rumbaugh, 1999), and specifically noting the connection between architecture and risk.

Barry Boehm wrote about risk in the context of software development with his paper on the spiral model of software development (Boehm, 1988), which is an interesting read even if you already understand the model. The risk-driven model would, on first glance, appear to be quite similar to the spiral model of software development, but the spiral model applies to the entire development process, not just the design activity. A single turn through the spiral has a team analyzing, designing, developing, and testing software. The full spiral covers the project from inception to deployment. The risk-driven model, however, applies just to design, and can be incorporated into nearly any software development process. Furthermore, the spiral model guides a team to build the riskiest parts first, but does not guide them to specific design activities. Both the spiral model and the risk-driven model are in strong agreement in their promotion of risk to a position of prominence.

Barry Boehm and Richard Turner followed this up with a book on risk and agile processes (Boehm and Turner, 2003). The summary of their judgment is, "The essence of using risk to balance agility and discipline is to apply one simple question to nearly every facet of process within a project: Is it riskier for me to apply (more of) this process component or to refrain from applying it?"

Mark Denne and Jane Cleland-Huang discuss both architecture and risk in the context of software project management (Denne and Cleland-Huang, 2003). They advocate managing projects by chunking development into Minimum Marketable Features, which has the consequence of incrementally constructing your architecture.

The risk-driven model is similar to *global analysis* as described by Christine Hofmeister, Robert Nord, and Dilip Soni (Hofmeister, Nord and Soni, 2000). Global analysis consists of two steps: (1) analyzing organizational, technical, and product factors; and (2) developing strategies. Factors and strategies in global analysis map to risks and activities in the risk-driven model. Factors are broader than the technical risks in the risk-driven model, and could include, for example, headcount concerns. Both global analysis and the risk-driven model are similar in that they externalize a structured thought process of the form: I am doing X because Y might cause problems. In the published descriptions, the intention of global analysis is not to optimize the amount of effort spent on architecture, but rather to ensure that all factors have been investigated.

Two publications from the SEI can help you become more consistent and thorough in your identification and explanation of risks. Carr et al. (1993) describe a taxonomy-based method for identifying risks and Gluch (1994) introduces the condition-transition-consequence format for describing risks.

The risk-driven model advocates building limited architecture models that have detail only where you perceive risks. Similarly, authors have been advocating building minimally sufficient models for years, including Desmond D'Souza, Alan Wills, and Scott Ambler (D'Souza and Wills, 1998; Ambler, 2002). Tailoring the models built on a project to the nature of the project (greenfield, brownfield, coordination, enhancement) is discussed in Fairbanks, Bierhoff and D'Souza (2006).

The idea of cataloging techniques, or tactics, is described in the context of Attribute Driven Design in Bass, Clements and Kazman (2003). Attribute Driven Design (ADD) relies on a mapping from quality attributes to tactics (discussed in Section 11.3.4), much like global analysis. The concept in this book of mapping development techniques is similar in nature. ADD guides developers to an appropriate design (a pattern), while the risk-driven model guides developers to an activity, such as performance modeling or domain analysis. The risk-driven model can be seen as taking the promotion of risk from the spiral model and adapting the tabular mapping of ADD to map risks to techniques.

Knowing what tactics or techniques to apply would be valuable knowledge to include in a software architecture handbook, and would accelerate the learning of novice developers. Such knowledge is already in the heads of *virtuosos*, as described by Mary Shaw and David Garlan (Shaw and Garlan, 1996). The better our field encodes this knowledge, the more compact it becomes and the faster the next generation of developers absorbs it and sees farther.

Though tactics and techniques were described in this chapter as tables, they could be expressed as a pattern language, as originally described by Christopher Alexander for the domain of buildings (Alexander, 1979; Alexander, 1977), and later adapted to software in the Design Patterns book (Gamma et al., 1995) by Erich Gamma and others.

Martin Fowler's essay, "Is Design Dead?" (Fowler, 2004) provides a very readable introduction to evolutionary design and the agile practices that are required to make it work.

Merging risk-based software development and agile processes is an open research area. Jaana Nyfjord's thesis (Nyfjord, 2008) proposes the creation of a Risk Management Forum to prioritize risk across products and projects in an organization. Since the goal here is to handle architecture risks that are only a subset of all project risks, a smaller change to the process may work.

This book uses risk to help you decide which techniques to use and how many of them to apply, assuming the requirements are not negotiable. Another way to use it is to help determine the scope of the projects, assuming the requirements can be changed. Such a quantitative technique is described in Feather and Hicks (2006), with the result being a bag of requirements that gives you the most benefit for the risk that you take on.

With many developers seeking lighter weight processes, agile development is popular. Ambler (2009) provides an overview of how architecture can be woven into agile processes, and Fowler (2004) discusses how evolutionary design can complement planned design. Boehm and Turner (2003) discuss the tension between moving fast and getting it right. A thorough treatment of a practical process for software architecture is found in (Eeles and Cripps, 2009).

Chapter 4

Example: Home Media Player

This book advocates a risk-driven approach to software architecture, where developers identify engineering risks and choose a set of architecture and design techniques to mitigate them. This sounds simple and obvious, because what kind of developer would choose techniques unrelated to the risks? But most developers are not following a risk-driven approach. This chapter aims to show how risk can drive design work rather than merely being yet another thing that developers think about.

Here is an exaggerated way of highlighting what is different about the risk-driven approach. Developers who follow a risk-driven approach may feel that there is a record in their heads repeating endlessly: "What are my risks? What are the best techniques to reduce them? Is the risk mitigated and can I start (or resume) coding?" Avoiding failure by reducing risks is the primary driver of a developer's actions. Like every recursive algorithm, it has a termination condition, so developers break out of the design cycle and start coding as soon as possible.

Chapter 3 described the risk-driven model of software architecture. This chapter shows examples of applying the risk-driven model so that you can get a feel for how it works. This chapter has other goals too, including showing how to minimize your architecture modeling so that it can fit into an agile or spiral development process, how to apply software architecture techniques, and when to stop designing and start prototyping or coding. The example that runs through the chapter is for a home theater media player, described as follows.

> The Home Media Player is a computer that plays media (like music, videos, and pictures) on a television and stereo. It is a normal computer like a laptop with a single audio and video output that is hooked up to a television

and optionally to a stereo. This Home Media Player is able to play media in multiple formats from its local hard disk or streamed from the internet. It can simultaneously play music and display a slideshow of pictures, or show a video and browse information about that video. Third parties can build extensions to enable the system to play steaming media or collect metadata (e.g., song lyrics or actor biographies) from internet sites.

The example is motivated by a code-level inspection of a real system. This system is interesting as an example because in some ways it is similar to a prototypical Systems problem with performance and reliability concerns, and in other ways it is like an IT problem with concerns about handling the complex metadata for music and videos. Consequently you can see different types of risks and techniques in a single example.

This chapter is organized chronologically. It assumes that we are members of a team that has built a prototype Home Media Player and, as the chapter progresses, we are asked to address three issues that arise:

1. **Team communication:** Since the system has been successful, new developers at a remote location have been added to the growing project. We worry that the new developers may fail to understand the design and architecture, and will be ineffective contributors or even accidentally break the architecture.

2. **Integration of COTS components:** The prototype system only ran on a single platform. We are asked to integrate third-party COTS (Commercial Off-The-Shelf) components into the system with the intent of enabling the system to run on different platforms. We worry that the new components will not integrate successfully.

3. **Metadata consistency:** There are many ways to represent music and video metadata. We worry that the internal metadata representation will be incompatible with ones found on the internet, meaning that third parties would fail to build extensions.

Since the focus of this chapter is on showing an example of a risk-driven approach, it does not cover many aspects of software development. This chapter treats the requirements as perfectly understood, so it does not cover how we learn about the requirements or how they are expressed. It does not distinguish different roles inside the development team. It is process agnostic. And it assumes that the team and the project sponsors are in perfect agreement about the quality attribute priorities. These and other ideas are omitted not because they are unimportant, but so that we can focus on the design.

This chapter applies architectural concepts and uses architecture models that are described in the second part of this book, but this should not present much difficulty since you have probably seen similar things before and they are explained as the chapter progresses.

4.1 Team communication

We are part of a team that has built a successful prototype of the Home Media Player system, and while we are not literally building it in a garage, it has been built in startup fashion, with the developers co-located and working long hours together. All of the developers have participated in the design decisions and know the architecture and detailed design, but it is only in our heads. We have been told that because of our success, the company is planning to launch the product later this year. They have decided to add additional developers to the project. The new developers will not be co-located with our team, nor do they know anything about the domain or system.

We are worried that during the rapid push to turn this prototype into a launch-ready product, the new developers will inadvertently write code that goes against the design. This is sometimes called *architectural erosion* or *architectural drift* (Perry and Wolf, 1992). Even if we catch errors they introduce, we remember Fred Brooks' advice about adding developers to projects (Brooks, 1995), so we worry about how quickly we can make the new developers into productive members of the team who can make independent contributions and help us meet the launch deadline.

We decide to address the risk by communicating the design to the new developers. In doing so, we keep in mind the three primary models — the domain, the design, and the code models — and also the three primary architectural viewtypes — the module, runtime, and allocation views. As we apply techniques to address the risk, we consider how well the new developers will understand these aspects of the system. We start with the least expensive techniques and select more expensive ones until we think the risk has subsided.

4.1.1 Reading source code

Our prototype system is not yet very big, so it is tempting to simply ask the new developers to read the source code. This can work pretty well and does not cost our current team any time or effort since the code already exists, while additional diagrams or documents will require effort to create. We are tempted by mantras like "Use the source, Luke," and "The code is the truth," which advocate learning systems by reading source code.

Our code is organized into directories in the filesystem, as seen in Figure 4.1, which yields clues to someone examining it. They can see that we are using external libraries and that the code is organized into some rough chunks, including the application, GUI, and media player, but it is unclear if these rough chunks are modules, and the directory structure cannot express module dependencies.

Figure 4.1: The directory structure for Home Media Player source code. The organization of directories yields clues, but it would be a mistake to assume that each directory corresponds to a module of source code.

There are limits to using the code as the only communication. Our particular system is a prototype with the concerns about code quality that go along with that, plus we are aware of the inherent model-code gap (discussed in Section 10.1). That means that design intent will always be lost between the design and the code, even if the design only ever existed in our heads. As a team, we debated design decisions, discovered tradeoffs, and deliberately imposed design constraints, yet none of these is expressed in the code.

Beyond that, asking all the new developers to go read code for many days is likely an inefficient use of time. Even with the preparation time, it is probably more efficient for someone to communicate with them directly or write some design documents than to have so many people scouring the code.

The source code does an OK job of communicating the module viewtype and a good job of communicating the code model, but it does a poor job of communicating the other viewtypes (runtime and allocation) and the other primary models (domain and design). Perhaps we can skip the allocation viewtype since it is pretty clear: there is just one machine we deploy onto. We decide to keep looking for more ways to reduce the communication risk. Our decision as to whether or not the risk is mitigated is not objective, but it has the advantage that the goal is clear (risk reduction by communicating the design) and some metrics are available (coverage of the viewtypes and primary models).

4.1.2 Module model

Having decided to communicate our design to the new developers, we start by building a view that is easy to build: the module model. We would have chosen a variant such as a layer diagram, but our system is not built using a layered architecture style. In contrast to the directories on disk we saw earlier, a module model clearly iden-

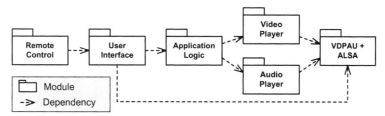

Figure 4.2: The module structure for Home Media Player system. Notice that these modules do not line up with the directories shown in Figure 4.1 and the module dependencies could not have been inferred either.

tifies the modules and the dependencies between them. It may include additional constraints, such as there should be no dependencies on vendor-specific API's, or no dependency cycles. If we had been more careful, our modules would have more closely aligned with our directory structure (see Section 10.3 for why this is a good idea).

Figure 4.2 shows the modules and dependencies for our system. The new developers who read the model can infer major functional areas from the module names, and the dependencies between modules allow them to infer how some standard scenarios might work. For example, a play command comes in from the Remote Control module to the User Interface, which tells the Application Logic to play the currently selected song, which tells the Audio Player to load the song file and decode it using an appropriate codec, which streams it to the ALSA API for playback. Figuring out this scenario involves quite a bit of guessing, but we have chosen our module names well so perhaps they will guess correctly.

We realize that there are domain terms (like codecs) and technical details (like VDPAU and ALSA API's) implicit in our module model that we would expect new developers to learn. Luckily, we are not working in a proprietary domain, so we can point the new developers to existing reference material. We collect a set of links to web pages that describe the Audio/Video domain and related technologies.

Re-evaluating our risk, we see that the code model and the module viewtype have been clarified for new developers and that perhaps the domain is now sufficiently clear. However, the runtime viewtype is still unclear — new developers would have to make guesses based on the modules or mentally animate the source code. Also, they are in the dark on many design issues, notably how our Home Media Player differs from other media players. We decide to discuss the quality attribute priorities, tradeoffs, scenarios, and architecture drivers. These should provide background on design issues, including why we made the design choices we did.

4.1.3   Quality attributes and design decisions

Our team was not given much guidance on prioritizing quality attributes, but we had seen how other media players worked and failed to satisfy. We identified several relevant quality attributes, and prioritized them this way:

> UI responsiveness (latency) > Audio/Video playback smoothness (consistent, on-time frame playback) > reliability > modifiability > playback efficiency (framerate) > portability

Our thinking was that most media players do their basic job, playing back audio and video, but many fail to provide a satisfactory solution because their user interfaces are sluggish. We also found that media players differed in their ability to provide smooth and reliable playback, and that this was important in our perception of a good system. Since we envisioned this system as being bundled with hardware, portability was not a major concern.

We identified two tradeoffs that forced us to make decisions.

- **Tradeoff**: Portability and smooth playback. Portability usually entails adding an extra software layer that provides a uniform interface to different hardware or software platforms. Unfortunately, this new layer increases latency and sometimes hurts the audio fidelity. Since we prioritized playback smoothness, we coded directly to the platform-specific API's, knowing that this will make portability more difficult.

- **Tradeoff**: Playback efficiency and modifiability. Often there are tweaks that can improve video playback, especially framerates, that are dependent on the video source or codec. But since most video playback was happening sufficiently well on the hardware we had chosen, we decided to build a system that allowed easy plug-ability of new codecs and video sources.

While we had never written down a quality attribute scenario, we often talked about two scenarios and used them as architecture drivers in our design and testing. We considered these to be drivers since they dealt with our two highest priority quality attributes and were technically challenging to achieve:

- **Architecture Driver**: When a user gives a command, such as pressing pause on the remote control, the system should comply with the command within 50ms. When the 50ms command deadline cannot be met, such as when starting playback of a video stream from the internet, the system should provide feedback such as a progress bar showing the expected wait time.

- **Architecture Driver**: Our reference H.264/MPEG-4 AVC video from local disk should play smoothly on our reference hardware.

We made several other design decisions that are consistent with our prioritization of quality attributes. We included these in the descriptions for the new developers since our team did spend considerable time discussing alternatives and because it would be hard to infer them from reading the source code.

- **Design Decision**: To promote reliability, each top-level component will run in its own process to isolate faults, like services in an operating system.

- **Design Decision**: The Media Rendering/Playback component communicates using shared memory with the Media Buffer component to minimize latency, considering the high rate of data movement.

- **Design Decision**: To help ensure smoothness of playback, disk and internet data sources are buffered in RAM since their streams are potentially unreliable.

- **Design Decision**: All media metadata is stored in the Metadata Repository, even if it is redundant with metadata embedded in the source file (e.g., ID3 tags).

- **Design Decision**: Only the Media Player Core component is allowed to write to the Metadata Repository.

At this point the only thing that we are categorically missing is a description of the runtime behavior of the system, including components, connectors, and scenarios. We have been hinting at runtime elements, for example mentioning communication paths, names of components (Metadata Repository, Rendering/Playback, Media Buffer) and connectors (shared memory, message passing, database writing). We decide to clearly describe these to the new developers.

4.1.4 Runtime models

The most valuable and least effort way to describe the runtime components and connectors is to simply list them and their responsibilities, as shown in Figure 4.3. Assigning responsibilities explains what each one does and reduces the chance of *architectural drift* because the new developers are less likely to expediently force-fit new behavior someplace it should not go. Note that the table is a view of the system design, even though it is an easy-to-create list. Not every view must be graphical.

The table will not answer every question regarding how things work, but the new developers now know the kinds of components and connectors that exist at runtime. They can make informed guesses about how everything fits together. We can go one step further and make that explicit by drawing a component assembly diagram. Figure 4.4 shows a steady-state configuration of component and connector instances in our Home Media Player system. If the system had interesting startup or shutdown

Component or Connector	Responsibilities
Media Rendering / Playback	Plays media files to the audio and video outputs. Renders elements of the user interface such as menus.
Media Player Core	Essential logic of the media player application, including the user interface and logic to coordinate activities.
Command Input	Collects raw user gestures (e.g., button presses, mouse movement) issued from remote controls, keyboards, etc., and translates them into a common vocabulary of events.
Media Buffer	Caches media files to memory to reduce jitter in data stream. Makes data available in shared memory.
Metadata Repository	A database containing metadata on all media files, for example, song names and movie directors.
Media Files	Media files stored on the normal filesystem. Could be local storage, or mounted remote drives.
Messaging Connector	An asynchronous connector enabling bi-directional message passing.
Shared Memory Connector	A synchronous connector implemented with shared memory to minimize latency, and locking to prevent corruption. Both components using this connector must be deployed on the same machine.
Pipe Connector	An asynchronous connector that delivers messages in-order, and only in one direction.
DB Connector	A synchronous connector that uses SQL to extract data from a database.
Internet Connector	A synchronous connector that uses internet protocols such as HTTP to retrieve data from the internet.
Filesystem Connector	A synchronous connector to read data from a filesystem. Uses memory mapped I/O for greater performance.

Figure 4.3: A listing of component and connector responsibilities.

configurations we might draw component assemblies for those too, but our system does not, so we will stick with this one diagram.

Note that the User, Television, and Stereo are not software components. This diagram bends the rules a bit to include them as components on this diagram, where a strict component assembly diagram would omit them. The benefit is that including

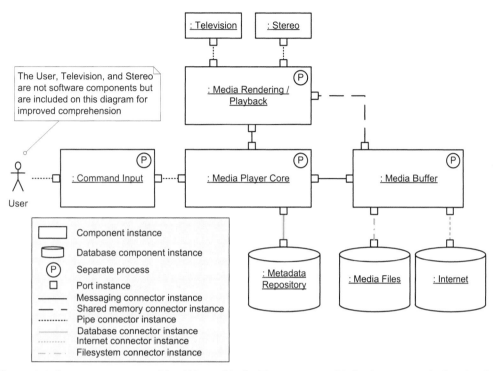

Figure 4.4: A component assembly of Home Media Player system. Notice how many design details are revealed through the legend.

them makes clear which component generates the audio and video streams and which component receives commands from the user, which otherwise might require cross-referencing to the table of responsibilities, or might just confuse the reader. Also note that a connector between two components means that they communicate at runtime. That is different than a dependency in the earlier module diagram, which means only that changes to one module could impact the other. In this system, there is just one instance of each component type, but you could imagine having a keyboard and remote control as two instances of Command Input components.

This component assembly view is effective partly because it focuses attention on issues that are important. We could have annotated the connectors to indicate if the datatypes were Big Endian or Little Endian, but that would have been a distraction since that is not one of our risks. Instead, the model contains details on issues we are concerned about getting right. By showing one kind of detail instead of another, we telegraph our concerns to the new developers.

As with the module view, we could let the new developers guess how the components behave, but this time we decide to provide a functionality scenario, one that

Name: Pause a playing video
Initial state: A video is playing.
Participants: User, Command Input, Media Player Core, Media Rendering / Playback
Steps:
1. The User presses the pause button on the remote control.
2. The Command Input component receives the button press and interprets it as the pause button. It sends a PAUSE BUTTON PRESSED message to the Media Player Core component over the event bus.
3. The Media Player Core, knowing the current state of playback is PLAYING, interprets the message as a desire to pause playback of the currently playing video. It sends a PAUSE VIDEO PLAYBACK message to the Media Rendering / Playback component.
4. The Media Rendering / Playback component freezes the current video frame and suspends audio playback. It ceases pulling data from the Media Buffer. It sends a message to the Media Player Core indicating that the video is paused.
5. The Media Player Core updates its current state of playback to PAUSED.

Figure 4.5: A functionality scenario that describes how the components collaborate to interpret commands and play video. It applies to the component assembly in Figure 4.4.

shows a representative trace of behavior through many of the components. Figure 4.5 shows how a command from the user flows through the components. While a single scenario like this does not show all behavior, it is quick to produce and easy to understand. We could also create a list of actions our system supports to complement the specific scenario, but since the new developers can play with the running prototype we have little worry about them misunderstanding that.

4.1.5   Reflection

It is difficult to ensure that a team of developers understands a design and avoids architectural drift. We were confronted with the problem of communicating our project design to new developers who were not co-located with us. One option was to simply let them figure out the system from reading the code, something that was possible given the size of this prototype. However, we were aware of the model-code gap so we knew that considerable design intent is not present in the code, so it seemed less risky and more efficient for our team to put together some documentation about the system.

As we created the documentation, we were aware of providing coverage of the three primary models — the domain, the design, and the code models — and also the three primary architectural viewtypes — the module, runtime, and allocation views. We started with the easiest documentation to produce and gradually added in more expensive parts. After each one, we asked ourselves if the risk had substantially reduced and we calibrated that evaluation based on our coverage of the viewtypes and models. When possible, we built representative and textual models rather than fully general and graphical ones. We decided to create a graphical model of our modules and component assembly since they were relatively easy to produce and conveyed more information than our textual models. We stopped when we had covered the primary models and viewtypes, trusting that the new developers would be able to use what we provided as a skeleton of understanding and would hang detailed knowledge from it.

4.2 Integration of COTS components

Now that we have a working prototype on a single platform and a newly expanded team that understands the system, we are asked to make the Home Media Player work across multiple platforms. This entails using a new component called Cross Platform AV that works on every major platform. We are also asked to use a new video rendering component called NextGenVideo, which is provided by partner company. These are often referred to as COTS (Commercial Off-The-Shelf) components, even if they are open source components or a non-commercial group. The good news is that the NextGenVideo component is higher performance than our current video component and it plays back more kinds of video files. The bad news is that it has a reputation for crashing when the source video file is imperfect.

Based on what we have been asked to do, we create a list of failure risks. Some of our risks involve quality attributes while others involve functionality.

1. **Integration.** Can we fit these new components into our architecture? Will we face architecture mismatch problems (see Section 15.7)? We know little about NextGenVideo and Cross Platform AV and are not even sure the two new components are compatible.

2. **Reliability.** Given that the NextGenVideo component has a reputation for crashing, we will need to insulate the whole Home Media Player system from what happens to NextGenVideo. While we wish it did not crash and perhaps could fix it if we had the source code, we have to live with it and work around its warts.

3. **On-Screen Display.** Our old video component handled both the on-screen display (OSD) and video playback, but the NextGenVideo only does playback. The new component might prevent us from drawing an OSD by hogging the display resource.

4. **Latency.** Our two architecture drivers concern latency in the user interface and consistent smooth playback. Considering that both are changing with the new components, we are worried about slowdowns.

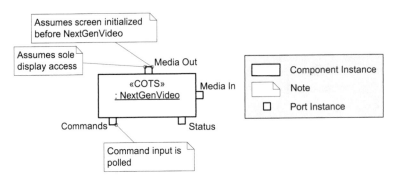

Figure 4.6: A boundary model of NextGenVideo component and its ports. Potential architectural mismatch areas are highlighted using UML notes.

These risks are interrelated: for example, how we solve the integration problem will affect the reliability and latency. We decide to investigate the integration first because if we cannot integrate the new components then we cannot start to analyze latency or reliability.

4.2.1   Integrating the new components

Since we know very little about the new components, we start doing some research on them. We are relieved to learn that the NextGenVideo component works out-of-the-box with the Cross Platform AV component. We continue directed research on the NextGenVideo component with the intent of understanding its boundary model and uncovering, as soon as possible, any facts that might indicate areas of architectural mismatch.

We start to take notes on the NextGenVideo component. The documentation describes four interfaces, which we model as ports[1]: Media In, Media Out, Commands, and Status. We will need to attach each of these ports to components in our system. We also collect some possibly troubling facts that we categorize as possible architectural mismatch: The NextGenVideo component does not initialize the display (it assumes that the display is already initialized), it assumes it is the only component using the display, and it polls for commands.

We also learn that its Media In interface comes with several example implementations including file and stream inputs, so we become less worried that we can connect it to our existing Media Buffer component using a shared memory connector. Although not strictly necessary, we decide to sketch out a graphical boundary model for the NextGenVideo component, shown in Figure 4.6, that uses UML notes to highlight

---

[1]In architecture models, components are required to use ports when they interact with things outside themselves. Ports on components are *not* the same as operating system ports, such as port 80 for web serving.

the possible architectural mismatch items. A similarly annotated module diagram would also work.

Armed with some knowledge about the COTS components, we decide to start designing a possible solution that integrates them into our system. We strongly prefer to work within the overall architecture previously shown in Figure 4.4. The Cross Platform AV and NextGenVideo components will be subcomponents within the Media Rendering / Playback component shown in that figure.

While hooking the NextGenVideo component up to the Cross Platform AV component should be easy, there are three additional ports to hook up, and our design must be able to detect and recover from a crash of the NextGenVideo component. We decide to build adapter components for each of the existing ports: a Command Adapter that reads from our message queue connector, a Status Adapter that writes to our message queue connector, and a Media Buffer Adapter that enables us to connect to the Media Buffer component. We sketch out our component assembly as shown in Figure 4.7.

This is just a proposed design and we need to validate it. The display must be set up before the NextGenVideo: the design can handle this by initializing the display when the Media Rendering / Playback component is created. It can pass this initialized display to the NextGenVideo component. The NextGenVideo component polls for commands: when the Command Adapter is polled, it can in turn ask the event queue for messages. The NextGenVideo has exclusive display access: this is still a potential problem, but we are not hitting it yet since our design does not yet handle the user interface overlay. So our design seems to accommodate the potential architecture mismatch concerns, at least from this high level.

Note the interesting binding on the Event Queue port. Normally a binding exists between just two ports, but here there are three. In the source code, there is an event queue connector that is written to by the Status Adapter and read from by the Command Adapter. Sometimes, as here, our architectural abstractions do not align neatly with the source code abstractions, as described in Section 16.1.

The problem of detecting crashes and restarting remains. We decide to watch the status updates coming from the NextGenVideo component and treat it as crashed or hung if the messages stop coming. This is a kind of heartbeat notification that the component is still running. Before starting a new instance, we will terminate the old process to be sure.

There are a lot of new components here, so we decide to write out a functionality scenario describing how they all work together. The scenario shown in Figure 4.8 traces a command coming into the Media Rendering / Playback component and the eventual detection of the NextGenVideo component crashing. This scenario helps us to understand how our design will work and can help us catch errors, but it is not time to start celebrating yet. Our design is plausible, but there are many issues that can

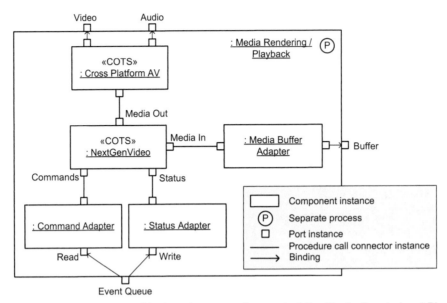

Figure 4.7: A component assembly that shows a refinement of the Media Rendering / Playback component instance, the same component instance previously shown in Figure 4.4. Also note the NextGenVideo component instance previously shown in Figure 4.6.

come up during the implementation that could derail it, so our next step to reduce risks is to prototype the design.

Our prototype shows that, indeed, playback works, we can detect when the NextGenVideo component crashes (for the prototype, we kill its process to simulate a crash), and we can cleanup and restart the component without affecting the overall Home Media Player system. Even better, we discover that we can detect the crash and restart playback in the same place within a second.

We have an easy time isolating the crash and restarting the video player because of our design decision to run each of the top-level components in its own process, a common architectural pattern in systems where reliability is important. This is an example of architecture-focused design in that our architecture choices are making something easy to accomplish.

Looking back on our risks, we decide that the integration and reliability risks are satisfactorily mitigated based on our modeling and prototyping. With a partial design and a prototype that demonstrates the integration of the NextGenVideo and the Cross Platform AV components, we have addressed two of the four risks. The two that remain are getting the on-screen display working and ensuring acceptable latency in the overall system.

<u>Name</u>: Detect that NextGenVideo component has crashed
<u>Initial state</u>: NextGenVideo is idle. The Media Buffer is initialized.
<u>Participants</u>: NextGenVideo, Command Adapter, Media Player Core
<u>Steps</u>:

1. The Media Player Core component sends a PLAY command to the Media Rendering / Playback component.
2. The NextGenVideo asks the Command Adapter for new commands.
3. The Command Adapter reads a PLAY message from the Event Queue port. It interprets the PLAY message, extracting the INPUT and POSITION parameters, performs necessary translations, and gives the new command to NextGenVideo.
4. The NextGenVideo (a) creates a new Media Buffer Adapter component connected to the Media In port based on the INPUT parameter, (b) opens the Media In port, and (c) begins playing the specified INPUT starting at the specified POSITION.
5. The NextGenVideo alternates between reading a frame of input data from the Media In port, writing a frame of output data to the Media Out port, reporting status on the Status port, and checking for new commands on the Commands port.
6. Some time later, the NextGenVideo crashes, and consequently stops reading commands and writing status.
7. Media Player Core component, failing to receive status updates, decides that the Media Rendering / Playback component has crashed.

Figure 4.8: A functionality scenario for video playback, which applies to the component assembly in Figure 4.7. The scenario is written out for your benefit, because a co-located team would probably just talk through this scenario while pointing at the component assembly that is sketched on a whiteboard.

4.2.2 On-screen display and latency

For video playback it was not a problem that the NextGenVideo component required exclusive access to the display, but now that we are hoping to show an on-screen display it is more troublesome. We go back to researching the Cross Platform AV component and find out that it supports virtual layers and transparency. We decide that we might be able to set up a layer, partially transparent, on top of the video layer and paint the on-screen display on that layer. This requires us to modify the design by adding an Overlay Renderer component, as shown in Figure 4.9. The new component gets its commands from the Command Adapter and paints the on-screen display.

For playback, we performed an initial validation of the design by writing out a functionality scenario. For the revised design we will just talk through the new behavior briefly. Since the NextGenVideo component has the main control loop, it occasionally polls the Command Adapter to find out if there are new commands. We must modify the Command Adapter to understand commands both for the NextGenVideo component as well as our new Overlay Renderer component and route the commands

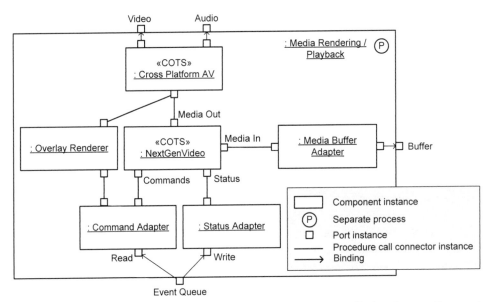

Figure 4.9: A revised component assembly (compare with Figure 4.4) showing a refinement of the Media Rendering / Playback component. Note the newly added Overlay Renderer component instance.

appropriately. We feel like we are bending the intended architecture here a bit, since the NextGenVideo is asking for its own commands, not asking the Command Adapter to look for on-screen display commands. We need to be careful about bending the architecture like this, as it is an example of *technical debt* which tends to accumulate. As before, validating the model helps us catch design errors but will not convince us that the risk is gone, so we build a prototype to ensure it works.

The one remaining risk is latency. Both of our architecture drivers (i.e., those requirements that are both high priority and difficult to implement) require low latency. It is possible to build latency models by assigning latencies to individual components and connectors and then analyzing various paths through the system. Since we do not yet know, for example, how fast our event queue connector dispatches messages or how long it takes our NextGenVideo component to decode a frame of video, we would be annotating our model with latency guesses and then analyzing those. Instead, since we already have a fairly complete prototype, it is easier to instrument it to record timings and measure the latency rather than estimating latency in a model. We are matching risks to techniques, and in this case the technique of measuring latency in the prototype is both more effective and less expensive than modeling.

4.2.3   Reflection

We were asked to integrate two new components into our system, NextGenVideo and Cross Platform AV, and we identified four risks: integration, reliability, on-screen display, and latency. As we designed a solution, we chose techniques that mitigated the risks and validated that the risks were indeed reduced, either by analyzing our model or by prototyping. We wanted to do just enough architecture and design work.

To address the risks of integration and reliability, we looked for architecture mismatch possibilities, created a boundary model of the NextGenVideo highlighting its ports and possible integration problems, and put it and the Cross Platform AV component into a component assembly. We validated the design using a functionality scenario followed by a prototype.

For the on-screen display, we returned to research and revised our component assembly with a plausible design, which we subsequently validated with a functionality scenario and prototyping. For the latency risk, however, we omitted all models and went directly to prototyping since that technique seemed most effective and efficient at reducing the risk.

In this chapter, the models were written out rather formally using neat diagrams. If this were an actual project, we could have simply sketched these on paper, or on a whiteboard. Often scenarios are not even written down, but instead discussed aloud while pointing at a sketched component assembly.

It is likely that skilled developers could have done all of this work without drawing any models. They appear to jump directly from problem to solution. This raises the question of how the developers decide what source code to write. Developers working on a problem must conceive of solutions in their heads before beginning to type, though perhaps they are not aware of how they arrive at solutions. This is similar to how experienced mathematicians skip over simple algebraic steps when transforming equations — they have internalized the process of manipulating the model.

4.3   Metadata consistency

We hope that third parties will be able to write plug-ins to extend the features of our Home Media Player, such as looking up lyrics for the currently playing song, browsing artist biographies, and finding related music. Plug-ins would relate the songs in our Home Media Player to websites that had the extra information. In readying our product to be shipped, our team is asked to investigate if third parties could indeed create plug-ins. We have designed an API for plug-in writers, but we are worried that our internal model for songs is much too primitive.

Each song in our system has what is known as metadata, that is, data that describes other data. So if a song file is the data, the metadata would include the song title and artist. We know that during our prototype we created the simplest model that would

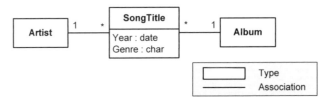

Figure 4.10: The information model based on ID3 tags that we had used up to now. It identifies three types (Artists, Song Titles, and Albums), how they relate to each other, and two attributes of the song title (Year and Genre).

work, but we also know that the websites that plug-in writers would connect to have richer and more expressive models. The risk we perceive is that although we have provided a song model API for plug-in writers, they will be unable to relate it to the complex models they find on the internet.

4.3.1 Prototyping and domain modeling

An easy and straightforward way to reduce this risk is to build prototype plug-ins for the examples we think up. However, ensuring all plug-ins will work is impossible since plug-in writers will want to do things we do not anticipate. There is another problem with prototyping, which is that writing web scrapers requires a lot of fussy effort. Conceptually, one just needs to read our song model and a corresponding web page. In practice, looking up the relevant web page, extracting the data, and stripping web markup is tedious. For our first product release we are hoping to simply know if plug-ins will be possible, rather than build several of them.

In this case, a cheaper alternative to prototyping is domain modeling. Prototyping a few scrapers will take a few days but domain modeling will take a few hours. Domain modeling enables us to look at the essential concepts and compare our song model with ones we find on the internet. On the other hand, domain modeling will not help us debug our API nor will we have any example plug-ins to entice third-party developers. Domain modeling includes modeling the concepts and the behavior of the domain, and omits references to particular technologies and data representations.

We are facing a domain risk and, by its nature, we cannot yet put our finger on a specific problem. Instead, we are worried that a problem might exist. This is an open-ended worry and we consequently might be tempted to engage in open-ended domain modeling, a variety of analysis paralysis. To guard against that, we choose to analyze three representative plug-ins that developers might want to build:

- A plug-in that shows lyrics for the current song.
- A plug-in that shows a biography of the current singer or songwriter.
- A plug-in that shows music that is related to the current song.

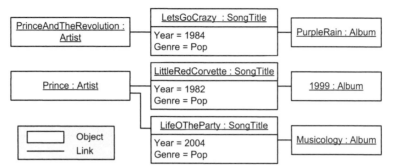

Figure 4.11: A snapshot that conforms to the information model shown in Figure 4.10. Where that diagram showed types (like Album), this one shows instances (Purple Rain, 1999, and Musicology).

We will collect some reasonable examples of songs, artists, etc. from the domain and represent them in our current domain model. Then we will do the same using domain models we find on the internet and look for differences and problems.

4.3.2 Our model and internet models

When we built our Home Media Player we used a simple model for songs. It was based on ID3 tags, which are metadata embedded in the song file itself, and includes the artist, song title, year, genre, and album. Figure 4.10 shows a graphical version of that information model.

Looking at the model, nothing jumps out as obviously wrong. Artists write songs that they collect into albums. Since we are unlikely to detect problems looking at this general model, we choose a concrete example from the domain to test the model. We choose to look at the artist Prince because he is a well-known artist, yet his music should challenge our model and reveal some complexity in the domain. We draw a snapshot showing a few of our favorite Prince songs, as shown in Figure 4.11. This is a legal snapshot based on our domain model and shows the album Purple Rain by Prince and the Revolution, and the albums 1999 and Musicology by Prince.

Looking at the snapshot, it is easy to see that we have a potential problem: the artist Prince was a member of the band Prince and the Revolution, but this fact cannot be expressed in the model. A human reading this model might guess that the two are related, but a computer interpreting the model would not.

Recalling the three plug-ins that we want to support, it seems like our model would support a plug-in that retrieved the lyrics of the song Little Red Corvette by Prince, since the model encodes the song title and artist. However, a plug-in might have some trouble retrieving a good biography unless the Prince and the Revolution biography were linked to Prince's biography. And our third plug-in that finds related music will

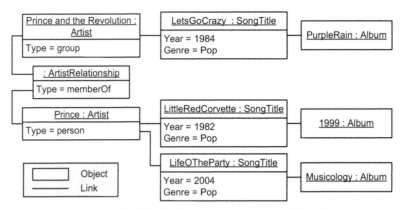

Figure 4.12: A snapshot using MusicBrainz information model, which adds a new type (ArtistRe-lationship) and adds an attribute to the Artist (named Type) compared to our original snapshot.

have trouble too. It could go to the internet, discover that Prince is related to Prince and the Revolution, but our Home Media Player would have no way to remember this since it cannot be represented in its simple model.

4.3.3 Researching other models

Discovering that our model for music is not expressive enough for the plug-ins we are investigating, we decide to learn about other models for music. Our research quickly shows there are two kinds of models, ones that focus on the song itself and ones that focus on a collection of songs. Examples of the song-based models include ID3 tags version 1 and 2, OGG tags, and FLAC tags, which are all designed to be embedded into the song file itself. Examples of database-based models include FreeDB, MusicBrainz, and Amazon. The database-based models are more expressive and include relationships between artists.

We want to know how MusicBrainz represents the situation in our snapshot. We learn more by reading what is available, including their database schema and their website. Their database schema reveals that in addition to the types (concepts) that we already have, there is an additional type called an ArtistRelationship that can exist between one Artist type and another. Furthermore, each Artist type can be either a group or a person. Consequently, MusicBrainz represents the same types differently, as shown in Figure 4.12.

Looking at the MusicBrainz website, we learn that Prince has used a number of pseudonyms. For a time, he used an unpronounceable symbol as his name and he is credited under a number of aliases. This is yet another challenge for our current domain model, since it cannot express the idea of pseudonyms or aliases.

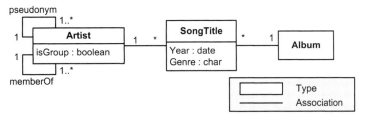

Figure 4.13: A revised information model for the music domain. Compared to the model in Figure 4.10, this one is more expressive because it adds a new attribute to Artist (isGroup) and two new associations (pseudonym and memberOf).

4.3.4 Design a new model

We have used domain modeling to identify some expressiveness limits that will hinder plug-in development, but we have not yet decided how to fix the problem. We could keep our current model, but that is limited. A better alternative is to adopt the full MusicBrainz model, or a similar one, but its complexity might deter third-parties from writing plug-ins. We decide to adopt some features of the MusicBrainz model into ours, specifically the ability to express relationships between artists such as pseudonyms and group membership, and to express group versus individual artists. Our revised domain model is shown in Figure 4.13.

We know that this model cannot express every wrinkle from the domain, but no model can. This model can express the snapshots we want it to and should support the development of plug-ins to retrieve lyrics, artist biographies, and related music. Since we only investigated three plug-ins, and did not build any, we cannot say that risk has been eliminated, but we were able to apply relatively little effort and improve our chances of success. We could continue on to build example plug-ins, reducing risk even further.

4.3.5 Reflection

A common risk when integrating IT systems is that one system views the world differently than the other, so they have difficulty communicating. To mitigate this risk, we build domain models representing how each system views the world and examine some concrete examples, which we represent as snapshots. We look for differences like a type existing in one model but not being expressible in the other.

For our Home Media Player, we identified the risk that third-parties would be unable to build plug-ins. We specifically worried that our model of music metadata was insufficiently rich to express the complex relationships that the plug-ins would discover on internet websites. Prototyping some plug-ins was an option but we chose to do some lightweight domain modeling to keep the effort down, since actually building working web scrapers can be quite time-consuming. However, we did want to avoid analysis paralysis and modeling the entire music domain, so we identified three plug-ins as representative examples and minimally modeled the domain to show their viability and, hence reduced our risks.

4.4 Conclusion

The primary goal of this chapter was to show the use of a risk-driven approach to software architecture. That approach consists of identifying risks, deciding the best set of techniques to mitigate the risks, and then evaluating the remaining risk. The chapter emphasized both "good enough" risk reduction (rather than striving for a complete risk elimination) and cost-effective techniques.

It is easy to read about a risk-driven approach and perceive it as banal platitudes — of course developers will work on the high risk areas and of course they will apply appropriate techniques. This chapter should demonstrate that the risk-driven approach goes beyond simply paying attention to risks and instead promotes risk to drive your use of architecture techniques.

The use of the risk-driven approach enabled an explicit choice about which techniques to apply in response to risks. As the chapter progressed, we investigated added developers, integration of components, and plug-in compatibility. We identified the risks of failure and chose appropriate mitigation techniques. The situations in this chapter were deliberately picked to highlight architecture techniques. In other cases, with different risks, we might just start coding.

At times during the chapter you may have disagreed with the choice of techniques, which indirectly points out a benefit to the risk-driven approach: it makes reasoning explicit. For example, while you may agree about the risks of plug-in incompatibility, you disagree about which techniques would best mitigate the risk, perhaps preferring to build prototypes instead of modeling the domain. Reasonable engineers will disagree on decisions like this, but now the disagreement resembles an engineering discussion rather than a methodology war. You could even create heuristics by attempting both approaches and collecting data over time.

Instead of applying architecture techniques until we ran out of them, until the documentation binder was complete, or until the project was canceled, we regularly re-evaluated the remaining risks and stopped when they had subsided. We had more modeling abilities up our sleeve but stopped short of building the most complete models possible. Notice that the amount of architecture work was not dependent on the guidance of a corporate design template or based on a percentage of the total project time. Instead, the stopping criteria was: is the risk substantially eliminated?

Besides the primary goal of demonstrating a risk-driven approach to architecture, the example has other benefits. Through the first section you saw how to generally document an architecture, including what others are likely to want to know. Architecture models, and the abstractions like components and connectors that underlie them, are crucial to understanding large, complex systems. You saw how a system could be understood increasingly well as we revealed views of it from the primary models and viewtypes. And you saw that architecture models showed some details while hiding others, which is an effective way of focusing attention on what you believe is important.

Another benefit was seeing that architecture modeling can be compatible with processes with short iterations, such as agile processes. None of the examples required weeks or even days of modeling effort to mitigate the risks. Architecture modeling by itself is insufficient — you must deliver systems, not models — but you can use architecture modeling to reduce risks before you start coding. A risk-driven approach to architecture is not a process in itself, but it is compatible with high ceremony or agile processes.

Chapter 5

Modeling Advice

This is the last chapter of first part of the book. This first part is about how you should approach architecture, what it is good for, and what you should expect from it. In the second part, we will shift to talking about the standard mechanics of modeling and abstraction, including ways of organizing models and techniques for solving problems. This chapter provides advice that augments your understanding of software architecture and the risk-driven approach. It encourages you to focus on risks, understand your architecture, and distribute that architecture knowledge to all developers. It identifies the dangers of making irrational architecture decisions, Big Design Up Front, and top-down design.

Software architecture will be helpful on your projects, but you deserve to be forewarned of the challenges that you will encounter. Using risk to drive your architecture decisions is a good idea, yet estimating risks is difficult. Evaluating alternative architectures is harder than you might expect, and you probably will be unable to reuse the models you build. Also, watch out for issues spanning engineering and management.

5.1 Focus on risks

Few books on software architecture explicitly advocate a process with lots of up-front design, so-called Big Design Up Front (BDUF), but it is difficult to read some of them and not infer that message. Broadly speaking, they lay out a large number of modeling and analysis techniques, many of which are expensive, and suggest that your project is risking its success if these techniques are not done.

This book has presented a risk-driven approach to software architecture that is related to the Spiral model of software development. It highlights that time spent addressing architecture risks must be traded off against other risks, such as time to market and customer acceptance. The key to making it work is the mapping between risks and techniques: if you can identify a set of risks, then you can choose a set of techniques to mitigate them. This is more efficient than prior approaches because you do not apply techniques that address non-risks for your project. You can do just enough architecture.

One benefit of this approach is that it explains why rational expert developers do different things in different situations. Agile software development, for example, has its origins on IT projects that often fail by moving too slowly to market or building systems customers did not want. The techniques employed in agile development are matched to these risks. Device driver developers write in C because they value performance and have relatively simple domains, while IT developers write in Java or C# because their domains are tricky and performance is comparatively less important than modifiability.

The risk-driven model of software architecture is process agnostic and therefore compatible with both BDUF and agile. Large, complex projects with many stakeholders will need to do more up-front architecture work, both for the team to agree on the risks, and to coordinate large numbers of developers. Agile projects may find their activities mostly unchanged, but now incorporate architecture risks into their work backlog.

In hindsight, the risk-driven model of software architecture may seem obvious, but one of the jobs of researchers is to mine the common sense of experts and extract the gold nuggets. More work still needs to be done to improve the mappings between risks and techniques, as the currently known mappings are just a start towards a complete body of knowledge on the subject.

5.2   Understand your architecture

At first glance, a sports game is just a bunch of players moving around, but coaches see and understand the action better than rookies can. They can categorize various offensive[1] and defensive strategies. They can see not just that a play succeeded, but understand if it was caused by a skillful offense or a mistake by the defense. They can predict the impact of a particular player missing the game and can compare and contrast the playing styles of different teams. The coaches, as experts, are taking in the same raw phenomena as others do, but they categorize and relate it better because they have built up a rich understanding about the game.

---

[1]Notice that an *offensive strategy* is an abstraction, and that its definition is much fuzzier than anything used in software architecture, yet that abstraction is consistently useful to coaches.

Experts in software architecture have similarly built up a rich understanding about software systems. They see how architectural choices resulted in a system that, for example, prioritized latency over modifiability. They can evaluate these choices and decide if they were rational. They use abstractions to partition the system and fit its complexity into their heads. They have studied architectural styles and know if a system's style aids in achieving its quality attributes. But understanding the architecture in no way prevents them from drilling down into the source code and choosing appropriate algorithms when that is the right way to solve a problem.

The core of architectural understanding is to be able to get at the "why" questions. Having the understanding does not mean you must follow a certain process, or program in a certain language, or write diagrams on paper. Understanding software architecture means that you have internalized the (admittedly incomplete and imperfect) knowledge and abstractions that have been built up, and that you can apply that understanding when building new systems or analyzing existing ones.

5.3 Distribute architecture skills

This book consciously uses the term *developer* instead of *architect* to emphasize that software architecture knowledge is important for more than one or two people on a team. Your software architecture is an engineering concern that is separable from the process your team follows and the job titles that are assigned. Many organizational structures work fine when the developers understand software architecture.

Imagine that you are the architect, or chief architect, responsible for a system. Would you prefer to be the only person on that team who appreciates the importance of the system's architecture? Each day would be a struggle to obtain information about the system so that you could build appropriate models, coupled with hassles in communicating your ideas to developers who would not understand what you are saying and could even resent your presence. Or would you instead prefer every developer to understand the architecture as well as you do?

Consider what happens when all developers have architecture skills. Your communication with developers is more efficient. They can answer your questions and relate them to the architecture models. They can take direction in the form of goals and, since they understand the desired quality attributes and tradeoffs, be trusted to make appropriate decisions. Since they are in the code every day, they can provide you with the essential information you need to build accurate models. Even small details in the code can be architecturally significant. There will always be local pressures to do something expedient, so the developers should understand when they should stick to the architecture, and when to raise a flag that it needs to change.

A skilled architect can exert great influence, but she is no antidote for unskilled and architecturally unaware developers who feed poor data into her models and are oblivious about when they are breaking architectural principles. Great engineering leaders invariably have a command of both the big picture and the details, so an architect who floats above the design and code is handicapped from the start.

You might be concerned that without an architect there would be chaos, and the system would grow incoherent without a single guiding voice. It is true that decisions must be made, and the team must act coherently, but these issues are separable from the job title of architect. A job title unrelated to architecture, such as *head engineer* or *technical lead*, would work equally well. Put another way, though it is important that the system use appropriate algorithms, there need not be a chief algorithmist to prevent chaos.

That said, having a job role for architects can be quite effective. Especially on larger systems, there are too many details for any one person to master them all, so some amount of specialization is appropriate. Some people on the team will emphasize architecture and know less about the day-to-day coding details, and others the reverse. But remember that centralizing or hoarding architecture knowledge is not the intention and would be counterproductive. The ideal is to have developers who are architecture-aware.

Here is a prediction: in a decade, it will seem equally foolhardy for a developer to ignore architecture as it is for a developer to ignore data structures today. There are good arguments for teaching software architecture to undergraduate students immediately after data structures, before compilers or operating systems, because they would be able to understand the architectural patterns seen in those systems and understand why each makes different design decisions and quality attributes tradeoffs. Few undergraduates go on to build compilers or operating systems, but almost all of them will use software architecture to build systems.

5.4   Make rational architecture choices

Design involves tradeoffs, so you cannot get every good quality imaginable. You should make *rational architecture choices*, meaning that your tradeoffs align with your quality attribute priorities. Performance is always nice to have, but if you value modifiability higher, then you should reject designs that yield performance at the expense of modifiability.

So, what does a rational architecture choice looks like? Decisions about how your system is designed should follow this pattern:

> <x> is a priority, so we chose design <y>, and accepted downside <z>.

An example is: Since avoiding vendor lock-in is a high priority, you choose to use a standard industry framework with multiple vendor implementations, even though using vendor-specific extensions would give you greater performance.

Spelled out clearly like this, it seems hard to imagine anyone making an irrational decision. Yet developers are human beings, not machines, and will behave imperfectly. Systems are large and complicated, and inconsistent choices may not be immediately apparent. In practice, quality attribute priorities are fuzzy and design rationales are rarely declared explicitly, which obscures irrational choices.

Here is an example of how good intentions can go awry. Imagine that a developer understands that this system's requirements prioritize maintainability over performance. But the developer has a background in high performance systems, so when designing the database schema he denormalizes some tables in order to make queries faster, with the tradeoff that maintenance is now harder. In a way, this design decision was more instinctive than reasoned, and there may never have been a moment when he consciously realized that the design contradicted the system's priorities. In another context, the higher-performance design would be laudable because performance is desirable. This is an example of an irrational architecture choice, however, performing a local optimization at the expense of overall priorities.

Developers on the same project will often disagree about design options. The disagreements can often be resolved, or at least reduced from a boil to a simmer, by exposing the decision making process. If the disagreement is simply that one developer thinks option A is better, and another thinks option B is better, it is hard to choose. When the rationale for each is expressed using the template, it may be clear that A helps usability, while B helps testability. This does not immediately resolve the disagreement, since both usability and testability are desirable, but now the question is which quality is a higher priority for the project. It casts the problem as an engineering or requirements decision, not as a judgment about who is the better designer, and can help take egos out of the dispute.

Designing software is a big optimization problem. Constraints, desires, known-working patterns, designers' prejudices, and comfort areas are all jumbled together. Uncertainty fogs truth. Developers try to create designs that best satisfy this jumble. Since this design optimization is messy, two developers are unlikely to produce the same design. However, despite subjective evaluations, any acceptable design should follow from rational architectural choices[2], where you accept that you cannot have everything, so you insist that design decisions follow your prioritized desires.

5.5 Avoid Big Design Up Front

In *Big Design Up Front* (BDUF), the early weeks or months of a project are primarily spent designing instead of prototyping or building. It is a pejorative term coined by

---

[2]David Garlan's software architecture class emphasizes that developers should prioritize the desired quality attributes and make consistent architecture choices. I call these *rational architecture choices*, but credit for the idea goes to him.

people, like agile advocates, who are concerned about *analysis paralysis*, a situation where a project spends too much time designing and not enough time building. BDUF is associated more with waterfall processes than spiral processes (both discussed in Section 3.9).

The waterfall process model is a linear series of steps that lead to delivery of the system (Royce, 1970). Common steps include requirements, design, implementation, and testing. Teams try to finish the current step before proceeding to the next. Going back to the previous step is allowed in order to fix mistakes, but otherwise discouraged. While waterfall processes are commonly seen in practice, few experts recommend them.

In contrast, the spiral process model of software development instructs engineers to build the system incrementally, starting from the highest risk items (Boehm, 1988). Each turn of the spiral takes the team through all steps of software development, such as requirements, design, implementation, and testing. The spiral model is the basis of most modern processes, include agile processes and the Rational Unified Process.

So, what could go wrong with doing all the design in advance? The dangers with BDUF include that you work on non-problems, you work inefficiently on paper compared to writing code, you fully work out designs that end up abandoned, and you take so long that the project is canceled. Your judgment at the moment can be faulty, since you can work on intricate designs, convinced that they are relevant and your effort is well-placed, but when you look back you realize that it would have been more efficient to interleave prototyping with design.

BDUF has a few variants, including *Design Until Perfect*. Although the original description of the waterfall process allowed backtracking to previous stages, in practice teams often resist backtracking and try to perfect the current stage before proceeding. Organizational processes may require *sign-offs* after each waterfall stage, which further discourages re-work.

Another variant is *Modeling For Modeling's Sake*, where a team creates lots of models, in great detail, because they know how to build the models, not because the models are helping. It may feel like progress since they see improvements in the models, but what they need is improvements in the system.

Despite the dangers of BDUF, it is sometimes the best option, especially on larger projects or ones with demanding quality needs. For example, space systems have high technical risks, and radiation machines have high safety demands, so time spent on careful design may pay off. Still, it is best to be wary of BDUF and move on to prototyping or implementation once the critical risks have been addressed.

5.6   Avoid top-down design

Top-down design is the process of refining a high-level specification of an element (component, module, etc.) into a detailed design by decomposing the element into smaller pieces and specifying those pieces by allocating responsibilities. Alternatives to top-down design include bottom-up design and hybrids. Section 11.3 discusses how the smaller pieces relate to the higher-level element, and suggest additional design strategies, such as following an architectural style.

The temptation to start with a high level design and refine it is strong, but there are good reasons to avoid it. Lower levels may have strong patterns that you may violate through ignorance. If you persist with your top-down design, small problems may recur because your design is ill suited to the lower level patterns. Similarly, it is difficult to exploit existing COTS components and modules for reuse since you will not uncover them until later.

Top-down designs can ossify via Conway's Law into organizational structures. Initial decompositions can become permanent decompositions because it is difficult to change the team structures.

The systematic top-down approach denies the reality that developers have flashes of insight that enable them to design elegant solutions. These insights are not limited to top-level entities, and instead span from the very detailed to the very abstract. Developers may notice an opportunity to use a low-level framework feature, like a command queue, to enable a top-level quality attribute. It is difficult to plan for flashes of insight but important to be ready to take advantage of them.

5.7   Remaining challenges

So far this book has been a rah-rah supporter of software architecture. However, any honest advocate has the responsibility to disclose not only what works well, but also the known limitations and problems.

Not everything about software architecture is easy and straightforward, and it is better to know about problems in advance so that you can be on the lookout for them. The following sections describe a number of difficulties that you may encounter when applying the techniques and advice from this book. A similar list of challenges, except relating to the standard architecture abstractions, is described in the second half of the book in Section 16.1.

Estimating risks. Risk can be used to steer you to appropriate architecture activities and can help you decide when to stop modeling and begin coding. While this is better than simply guessing how much architecture work is enough, it is not a paint-by-numbers solution, as you have two hard jobs:

- **Risk identification**. It is difficult to identify risks, so you may be blindsided by an unforeseen risk. Checklists can help by sharing and preserving previously identified risks.

- **Risk prioritization**. After you have identified a risk, you must weigh its importance. If you guess too high, you will be swamped with a long list of risks and will have a hard time deciding which to address first. If you guess too low, you may plow ahead into implementation too early, and your architecture may be unsuited to handling the omitted risks.

Engineers will have different opinions of risks and priorities, so you may find yourself trusting one engineer's estimates over another's, which is a return to subjective decision making. And even if you are accurate in identifying and prioritizing risks, it is no guarantee that you will be able to successfully mitigate them. You should look at the risk-driven model as an improvement over other alternatives, but not without its own difficulties.

Evaluating alternative architectures. The architecture of your system has a big impact on its ability to satisfy quality attribute requirements, so you will likely want to consider several different alternative architectures. Seen from a distance, evaluating alternative architectures is as simple as building and evaluating a few models. You build a model of each alternative, then you evaluate how each helps or hurts the architecture drivers and quality attributes that you identified.

In practice, evaluating alternatives is more difficult than this because the devil lives in the details, and your model may not include those details. Of course you could build detailed architectural models for each design, but that is expensive, so you (rightly) hesitate to do that.

This is the inherent tension: you are hesitant to spend much time adding details to models you have not committed to, but you may not discover problems with those designs until you investigate their details. Perhaps the specifics of external API's will invalidate your assumptions, or perhaps a prototype will reveal that the performance model needs more attention.

Evaluating alternative architectures requires more crystal ball gazing than you should be comfortable with. You must make decisions based on sketchy data and incomplete models. Undoubtedly you knew this lesson already, but you should not think that choosing between design alternatives will be easy after you learn notations and techniques for architecture modeling.

Reusing models. Software developers have been reusing code since the invention of the subroutine in the 1950s. Perhaps the pinnacle of code reuse today is the object-oriented framework, but there is the perpetual hope that developers can reuse ideas beyond code, such as designs and other models. This is practical today only in small doses, such as named design patterns and architectural styles.

The reason models are not more reusable is inherent in their nature: Models omit details. A model built to answer one question can safely omit many details, often the details that are essential to answer a different question. In other contexts this is obvious: a scheduling model for trains cannot be reused as their financial depreciation model, since the scheduling model would omit details like the purchase price of the train.

One of my favorite jokes to tell kids goes like this:

> Tell a kid, "You are the bus driver," then proceed to describe how many people get on and off at various stops, then end with, "... and at the last stop everyone gets off. What is the bus driver's name?"

The joke works because the kids start building a model of passengers on the bus and forget about who the bus driver is. They build a model to solve one problem, the passenger count, and are stymied when I ask a question they did not expect.

If you build a model of a component one day, then later decide to use the component in a different setting, for example a concurrent one, your model will probably not answer the questions you now want to ask, such as if the code is thread-safe. Generally, a model built for one purpose will not work for another purpose.

Issues spanning engineering and management. It is unlikely that your organization's management will pay much attention to lower-level design decisions like the indentation style in your code, but they are likely to be interested in the functionality and qualities of your system. Sometimes, when deciding the architecture for your system, you will face a choice that can either be solved by engineering or by management. For example, a distributed system might be cheaper to build if you can assume that each site will support the software that runs there, or you could design it for central administration at a greater cost. The decision regarding system administrators is likely to be made by management, not engineers, and other similar situations occur at the architectural level of design.

5.8 Features and risk: a story

At the close of the first part of this book, it is appropriate to take stock of the risk-driven model of architecture and compare it to pure feature-driven development. This book's message is not that risk is the only thing you should focus on, but rather that risk is important, and it can help you decide how much design work you should do.

The following story discusses my (true) efforts to make relatively small architectural changes to an application, one that had been built with a priority on features. As you read the story, notice how architecture influences my redesign of the application.

Remote control phone application. I have a smartphone, so I went looking for an application that would let me control my home media player (like the one in Chapter 4) from my mobile phone. On the internet, I found an open-source application with many features. Looking at earlier versions of the application revealed that adding new features had been a priority. When I ran the application, however, I found two problems.

- **Diagnostics**. At first the application would not talk to my media center, yet it was hard for me to diagnose why. A code investigation revealed that the library used to communicate with the server failed to report many connectivity problems, instead lumping them into a single error code.

- **Slow user interface**. Navigating through the screens of the application was slow. Even backing up a page caused a noticeable lag. I discovered that neither the application nor the communication library was caching the server responses, yet these responses changed slowly or not at all (such as album art or the list of songs on an album).

After looking at the code, I realized that both problems could be fixed by revising or replacing the communication library. In a minor way, the application had an unsuitable architecture, at least according to my quality attribute priorities.

Design options. Users of this application might, like me, have connection problems, and it was easy to make these easier to diagnose. It just required the communication library to detect and report distinct error conditions. However, because of the existing interface choices, this required changes to existing API's.

The slow user interface could be improved by reducing the number of server requests, since each request took tens of milliseconds. The current application was doing no caching and re-querying the server whenever it needed data. A design option on the other extreme would be to cache everything. However, the phone has limited storage space, so I would have to trade off storage space with latency reductions. Like with the diagnostics, adding caching was difficult to accomplish without changing the API's.

Even if the developers had consciously decided to defer caching and error handling, it would have been better if they had built API's to accommodate such changes. In an ideal world, I would have been able to revise the communications library and hand it back to the original developers, who could drop it in place to resolve the problems.

The original application used a traditional client-server architecture, where the phone was the client and the media center was the server. However, it is worth considering other architectural styles and their implications. In my house, there are often music files on various computers. A peer-to-peer architecture might have been more appropriate, one where any peer could play music from any other. In fact, we could imagine streaming the music from the "cloud" to any device, including back to the phone.

Approach. Looking back, how was it possible to approach the problem from an architectural standpoint? First, I explicitly considered failures — specifically failures related to quality attributes like debug-ability, usability (latency), and modifiability. Second, I generated design options and evaluated them with respect to the failures. For the usability failure, it was even possible to start understanding the solution space and its general tradeoffs. Finally, I looked at the overall architectural style (client-server) and considered if it was matched to the problem at hand.

The order of these activities is less important than the thinking that accompanies them. Notice the attention paid to risks, quality attributes, failures, design options, and architectural styles, and compare that with a purely feature-focused approach.

Conclusion. Many people will advise you to focus entirely on features. They base their advice on having seen too many projects waste time on features and infrastructure that, in the end, were unnecessary. But if Aristotle were still alive, he would remind us that virtues are not absolute, and instead exist between excess and deficiency. You can have too much of a good thing and focusing exclusively on features is too much.

The architecture of a system can mitigate engineering risks, primarily quality attribute risks. Software architecture researchers were not the first to suggest that quality attributes (or quality attribute requirements, or the "-ities") are worthy of your attention, but they have reinforced that message and have connected quality attributes with architecture choices. When thinking about a system's architecture and design, you should consider the failure risks that the system faces.

The risk-driven model helps you do just enough architecture. Your primary focus could still be on features, but appropriate attention is placed on risks, quality attributes, and architecture. Architecture should not be equated with Big Design Up Front and, as seen in this story, some time spent thinking about the architecture can help you choose designs that mitigate failure risks.

Part II

Architecture Modeling

Chapter 6

Engineers Use Models

The first part of this book was about software architecture and risk. It advised you to build models of your architecture, models that were just good enough to mitigate your risks. But it did not say *how* to build those models or what was in them, so this part of the book describes the software architecture concepts and notations you will need. Do not be afraid of the detailed architecture models you will find in this part of the book. The intent is not to turn you into an ivory tower architect or a generator of shelfware. We start with a chapter that describes how models are used in engineering.

When I was in high school, I asked my father for help with my calculus homework. I was surprised to learn that, despite his working as an engineer since college, his calculus knowledge was rusty and he rarely used it. He also told me that his company only hired engineers who knew calculus — not because they needed to apply calculus on the job, but because their engineering training that included calculus gave them the ability to solve problems using abstraction and models.

Some simple problems can be solved directly, without abstraction. When confronted with a complex problem, engineers map that problem into an abstract model (such as a calculus equation), solve the problem within the model, then translate that solution back into a real world solution. For engineers, it is this ability to solve problems using abstract models is that is essential.

When an engineer solves a problem using a model, the overall process is the same regardless of the type of model. As shown in Figure 6.1, an engineer's goal is to move from a real world problem to a real world solution. Simple problems can be solved directly, without abstraction, and an engineer can move directly across the gray arrow. The problems that engineers get paid to solve, however, are harder and

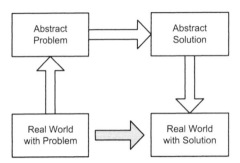

Figure 6.1: A commuting diagram, popularized in software engineering by Mary Shaw. Simple problems can be solved directly (gray arrow). Complex problems are solved by using abstractions, the long way around the diagram.

require the longer path via abstractions. The real world problem is represented in the abstract model, solved in that modeling domain, then that solution is mapped into a real-world solution. This overall process is the same whether your model is a calculus equation, an accounting ledger, or an architecture model.

6.1   Scale and complexity require abstraction

Software developers, as engineers, instinctively reach for abstractions when their problems are large or complex. When developers are reasoning about a small number of classes in a program, they can inspect and reason about those classes directly. When that number rises, they can calm the rising chaos by using design patterns to explain clumps of collaborating classes. But at some point the number of classes is sufficiently large that developers reach for even larger abstractions to make sense of the program. It is not a question of their being forced into new abstractions; it is a matter of using the ones suited for the scale or complexity of the problem.

Abstractions can also be a more efficient way to learn about a system than direct inspection of source code. Imagine that one developer wants to explain a system he already understands to another developer. If they had a long time, they could both read and discuss lots of source code, perhaps hundreds of thousands of lines. But if they only had a few hours, then sketching out a model of the system would be more effective.

It is one thing to say that developers sketch a model on a whiteboard, and quite another to describe exactly what they should sketch. What do those diagrams look like, and what are the abstractions that they represent? This second part of the book describes a set of abstractions that are suitable for modeling the architecture of software systems.

6.2 Abstractions provide insight and leverage

You will surely recall from your math classes a story problem such as the following:

> Two trains are 3000m apart and headed towards each other on the same track. One is traveling 10m/s, the other 20m/s. When will they meet?

When your teacher introduced such problems, you already knew some algebra, so you could have solved a problem if it were stated as 10x + 20x = 3000. The teacher's intent with the story problem was for you to learn how to map the story into an algebraic model and back again, just like in Figure 6.1. To solve the problem, you had to learn to build a model that included the details that were relevant to the question being asked. The model provided insight into the essential problem and algebra provided leverage to solve it. The domain of trains gave you no particular insight or leverage, but an algebraic model did.

Ideally, software architecture would be solvable and universal just like algebra. Architecture modeling is rarely as simple as the train problem, but architecture models can provide insight and leverage. With an appropriate model, you can do things like find possible intrusion vectors, identify bottlenecks, and estimate latency. This is important because developers need to reason about more than just a system's features; they need to reason about its qualities too.

6.3 Reasoning about system qualities

I recently attended a lecture about building scalable websites. The presenter discussed technology X, his inability to make technology X run quickly, and his successful switch to technology Y. He described the compactness of the new language used in technology Y, the improvement in the interfaces, its extensibility, and finally presented the much improved throughput numbers for his website.

Under all these details, however, there was a nugget of insight to be found, which was that technology X stored data in a hierarchy and technology Y stored it flat. Both used relational databases, but a web page request in technology X required, on average, twenty database queries to retrieve the hierarchical data, while technology Y required just one. Substantially all of the throughput differences between technology X and Y could be traced to that single difference. When evaluating throughput, you could ignore technology Y's qualities except for the data representation choice. But how can you arrive at that conclusion?

To reason about system properties, you must have a model in your head that helps you organize and make sense of the details, something like the sketch (i.e., *cartoon*) in Figure 6.2. That model it so simplified that it works for both technologies X and Y, but it is sufficient to analyze the details that are known. Every web request that comes in

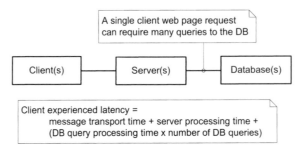

Figure 6.2: An informal sketch (a cartoon) of the web system. Sometimes you will keep models like this in your head, other times you will sketch them on paper or a whiteboard. The second part of this book discusses standard models and notations for describing your software architecture.

will require some message transport time, some processing on the server, and some number of queries to the database. If you assign some plausible numbers to these variables, such as 10ms for message transport time, 10ms for the server processing time, and 25ms for the time to query the database once, it is clear that the twenty database queries are going to slow the system down. This model ignores factors like caching and queueing, but even this simple model turns a pile of facts into problem that can be analyzed.

Architecture models are a good way to understand and address thorny issues because they can cut through the extraneous detail and help you focus on the essential parts and relationships, make predictions, and evaluate alternatives. If you were running a website on technology X, code tweaking would not fix the throughput problem. Your success would depend on sifting through the clutter of details to discover how the data representation in technology X hindered throughput.

6.4   Models elide details

When you reasoned about when two trains will meet, you safely elided the color of the trains and many other details. When you reasoned about the performance of a website, you elided details like the programming language. Models, by their nature, elide details. "Essentially, all models are wrong, but some are useful." (Box and Draper, 1987)

To create a useful model, you must choose to include the right details while sweeping others under the rug. Including irrelevant details adds clutter, making the model harder for you to reason about. The introduction to this book discussed modeling a driving route from New York to Los Angeles using highways. Which details should you include in a model to solve that problem? Some roads have signposts made of wood, others concrete, and others metal. That choice can be safely omitted from

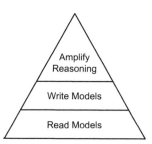

Figure 6.3: Everyone who works with models must be able to read them. Some people will be able to write models, but the goal of designers should be to use models to amplify their reasoning abilities.

your model when you search for the shortest route. However, the shortest route may include a road smaller than a highway, so your model should include those smaller roads, or else your model may lead you to a wrong answer.

You should be aware of the tension between complete models and usable models. Sometimes a complete model of a problem is too difficult to reason about, yet simplifying that model can lead you to wrong (or suboptimal) answers. For example, if your model only includes highways, you may not find the shortest route. On the other hand, if your model includes every vaguely flat and drivable surface (parking lots, front yards, fire roads) then your model will be huge and therefore harder to solve. Building a useful model usually involves making tradeoffs like this.

6.5 Models can amplify reasoning

The same model can be used by different people for different purposes. There are three basic levels of modeling skill: reading models, writing models, and amplifying reasoning with models. As shown graphically in Figure 6.3, the ability to accurately *read a model* is the most common, and it is a prerequisite for the others. For example, the buyers of a custom-designed house need to be able to read the house blueprints so that they can speak up when the designs do not match their desires. An analogous situation occurs with custom software development between the stakeholders and the software developers.

Fewer people must be able to *write a model*, which involves making sure its documented form, or syntax, is correct. A house design originates in a designer's head and it is written down as blueprints so that it can be shared with the house's stakeholders (the various people who need to agree to the design). Note that the roles of model designer and model writer may be distinct. For example, draftsmen are model-writing specialists who are usually not the designer.

During the design of a house, a house designer employs a model as a tool that *amplifies his reasoning,* enabling him to design more complex houses than he would with just his mind and memory. He must coordinate many details and it is easy to make mistakes. During design, he has questions that must be answered, such as, "Does opening a door block a cabinet?" and, "How much drywall is needed in the bedroom?" Errors are likely if he keeps all the details in his head. When he instead creates a model, he has less of a memory burden, can use standard representations that make errors easier to detect, and can predict how the house will perform. His use of a model to amplify his reasoning abilities is different than simply being able to read a model that others have presented; he uses the model to help him design better. In software design, experienced designers know how to build models to enable analysis, to make errors easier to detect, and to discover truths that are not immediately obvious.

6.6   Question first and model second

Different models are good for different things. A model that helps you predict response time will probably not help you find security holes. So it is best to follow this simple rule: *question first and model second.* That is, know what questions you want the model to answer before you build it. That way you will have an easier time choosing its abstraction level and what details it includes.

This is one of those rules that looks straightforward but it is easy to violate. If you have ever done any work around your house, you may have heard a similar rule: *measure twice and cut once.* I have broken that rule many times, and each time I find myself muttering the rule under my breath. I am also a fan of its corollary, told to me by an old friend, "No matter how many times I cut it, it doesn't get any longer!"

You may get lucky and cut it the right length, but why not just measure it again? Similarly, you may get lucky and build a model that does what you want, but why not decide what questions it should answer first? That way the model will be sure to help you.

6.7   Conclusion

Engineers use models to solve large or complex problems. To do so, they take the long path around the commuting diagram, creating an abstract model of a problem, solving it using the model, then mapping back into the real world. An abstract model provides insight into the essential problem, allowing your human problem solving abilities to work better. Additionally, a model may provide particular leverage on solving the problem, just as you saw algebra providing leverage to solve the train problem.

A model helps you to organize the facts and details about your system. You saw an example of a website built from two different technologies with a variety of differing details. A simple model enabled you to organize those details and see that a single detail, the hierarchical vs. flat data storage, accounted for the performance difference between the two technologies.

An essential ingredient in modeling is choosing which details it will include and exclude. A model with too many details can obscure the essential problem and inhibit your reasoning. Be aware, however, that you may have to accept the imperfect reasoning that comes with a smaller model, since a more complete model may be too big or complex to reason about.

Some people, such as stakeholders, only need to read a model. For example, a house buyer needs to be able to read blueprints well enough to make an informed purchasing decision. Draftsmen can write a syntactically correct model. But, as a software developer, your goal is to use models to amplify your reasoning abilities. If you had never been taught math formally, you could likely still reason about simple problems. That education instilled a model of mathematics that enables you to solve much harder problems.

Whenever you build a model, you are in effect deciding *not* to build other models, such as models that have more performance details or ones that ignore security. The only way you can choose a suitable model is to know, in advance, which questions you need that model to answer. Otherwise you may build an insufficient or bloated model. A corollary is that whenever you build a model, you should carefully choose its level of abstraction.

6.8 Further reading

The idea of using models to solve problems is central to all engineering. This book's use of the commuting diagram to emphasize models comes from Mary Shaw (Shaw and Garlan, 1996).

Some people asked to build an architecture model will have an easier time of it than others, perhaps in the same way that some people have a particular facility for art or mathematics. My experience with architectural skills transfer shows a wide range of aptitude across software developers (Fairbanks, 2003). If you find yourself overseeing training or skills transfer involving models, keep these three levels in mind (reading models, writing models, amplifying reasoning) when choosing a curriculum.

Chapter 7

Conceptual Model of Software Architecture

In this book's introduction, you read a story about a coach and a rookie watching the same game. They both saw the same things happening on the field, but despite the rookie's eyes being younger and sharper, the coach was better at understanding and evaluating the action. As a software developer, you would like to understand and evaluate software as effectively as the coach understands the game. This and subsequent chapters will help you build up a mental representation of how software architecture works so that when you see software you will understand it better and will design it better.

The idea of using models, however, is often wrongly conflated with the choice of software process (i.e., waterfall) and has been associated with analysis paralysis. This book is not advocating building lots of written models (i.e., documentation) up front, so it is best to knock down a few strawmen arguments or misunderstandings:

- **Every project should document its architecture: False**. You should make plans before going on a road trip, but do you plan your commute to work in the morning? Models help you solve problems and mitigate risks, but while some problems are best solved with models, others can be solved directly.

- **Architecture documents should be comprehensive: False**. You may decide to build a broad architecture document, or even a comprehensive one, but only in some circumstances — perhaps to communicate a design with others. Most often you can model just the parts that relate to your risks, so a project with scalability risks would build a narrow model focusing on scalability.

- **Design should always precede coding: False**. In one sense this is true, because code does not flow from your fingers until you have thought about what you will build. But it is false to believe that a design phase (in the software process sense) must precede coding. In fact, early coding may help you discover the hardest problems.

So you should set these strawmen ideas aside. The real reason to use software architecture models is because they help you perform like the coach, not the rookie. If you are not already at the coach level, you want to get there as soon as possible. The standard architecture models represent a condensed body of knowledge that enables you to efficiently learn about software architecture and design. Afterwards, you will find that having a standard model frees your mind to focus on the problem at hand rather than on inventing an new kind of model for each problem.

Conceptual models accelerate learning. If you want to become as effective as a coach, you could simply work on software and wait until you are old. Eventually, all software developers learn something about architecture, even if they sneak up on that knowledge indirectly. It just takes practice, practice, practice at building systems. There are several problems with that approach, however. First, not all old software developers are the most effective ones. Second, the approach takes decades. And third, your understanding of architecture will be idiosyncratic, so you will have a hard time communicating with others, and vice versa.

Consider another path, one where you see farther by standing on the shoulders of others. Perhaps we are still waiting for the Isaac Newton of software engineering, but there is plenty to learn from those who have built software before us. Not only have they given us tangible things like compilers and databases, they have given us a set of abstractions for thinking about programs. Some of these abstractions have been built into our programming languages — functions, classes, modules, etc. Others likely will be, such as components, ports, and connectors[1].

Some people are born brilliant, but for those of us who are not, how effective is standing on the shoulders of those who came before us? Consider this: you are probably a better mathematician than all but a handful of the people in the 17th century. Then, as now, math virtuosos had talent and practiced hard, but today you have the benefit of centuries of compacted understanding. By the time you leave high school, you solve math problems that required a virtuoso a few hundred years ago. And before that, the virtuosos of the 17th century had the benefit of someone else inventing the positional number system and the concept of zero. As you consider

---

[1] Research languages like ArchJava have already added these concepts to Java.

the two paths, remember that you can and should do both: learn the condensed understanding of architecture and then practice, practice, practice.

Conceptual models free the mind. A condensed understanding can take the form of a conceptual model. The coach's conceptual model includes things like offense and defense strategies, positions, and plays. When he watches the movement of players on the field, he is categorizing what he sees according to his conceptual model. He sees the motion of a player as more than that — it is an element of a play, which is part of a strategy. The rookie, with his limited conceptual model, sees less of this.

Conceptual models accelerate progress in many fields. If you ever took physics, you may have forgotten most of the equations you learned, but you will still conceive of forces acting on bodies. Your physics teacher's lessons were designed to instill that conceptual model. Similarly, if you have ever studied design patterns, you cannot help but recognize those patterns in programs you encounter.

A conceptual model can save you time through faster recognition and consistency, and amplify your reasoning. Alfred Whitehead, said "By relieving the brain of all unnecessary work, a good notation sets it free to concentrate on more advanced problems, and in effect increases the mental power of the race." (Whitehead, 1911) This applies equally to conceptual models. As mentioned in the introduction, Alan Kay has observed that a "point of view is worth 80 IQ points," continuing to say that the primary reason we are better engineers than in Roman times is because we have better problem representations (Kay, 1989).

There is a general consensus on the essential elements and techniques for architecture modeling, though different authors emphasize different parts. For example, the Software Engineering Institute (SEI) emphasizes techniques for quality attribute modeling (Bass, Clements and Kazman, 2003; Clements et al., 2010). The Unified Modeling Language (UML) camp emphasizes techniques for functional modeling (D'Souza and Wills, 1998; Cheesman and Daniels, 2000). The conceptual model in this book integrates both quality attribute and functional models.

Chapter goals and organization. The goal of this part of the book is to provide you with a conceptual model of software architecture, one that enables you to quickly make sense of the software you see and reason about the software you design. The conceptual model includes a set of abstractions, standard ways of organizing models, and know-how. You will never become good at anything without talent and practice, but you can accelerate your progress by building up a mental conceptual model.

This chapter shows you how to partition your architecture into three primary models: the domain, design, and code. It relates these models using designation and refinement relationships. Within each model, details are shown using views. The three chapters that follow this one examine the domain, design, and code models in more detail. An example system for a website called Yinzer runs throughout. A *Yinzer* is a slang term for someone from Pittsburgh, home of Carnegie Mellon University, and is derived from *yinz*, which is Pittsburgh dialect equivalent to *y'all*.

> Yinzer offers its members online business social networking and job advertisement services in the Pittsburgh area. Members can add other members as business contacts, post advertisements for jobs, recommend a contact for a job, and receive email notifications about matching jobs.

Subsequent chapters cover other details on modeling and give advice about how to use models effectively.

7.1   Canonical model structure

Once you start building models, there are lots of bits and pieces to keep track of. If you see a UML class diagram for the Yinzer system that shows a Job Advertisement associated with a Company, you want to know what it represents: is it things from the real world, your design, or perhaps even your database schema? You need an organization that helps you sort those bits into the right places and to make sense of the whole thing.

The *canonical model structure* presented here provides you with a standard way to organize and relate the facts you encounter and the models you build. You will not always build models that cover the whole canonical model structure, but most projects over time will have bits and pieces of models that follow the canonical structure.

7.1.1   Overview

The essence of the *canonical model structure* is simple: Its models range from abstract to concrete, and it uses views to drill down into the details of each model.

There are three primary models: the domain model, the design model, and the code model, as seen in Figure 7.1. The canonical model structure has the most abstract model (the domain) at the top and the most concrete (the code) at the bottom. The *designation* and *refinement* relationships ensure that the models correspond, yet enable them to differ in their level of abstraction.

Each of the three primary models (the domain, design, and code models) are like databases in that they are comprehensive, but are usually too large and detailed to work on directly. (More on this shortly, in Section 7.4). *Views* allow you to select just a subset of the details from a model. For example, you can select just the details about a single component or just the dependencies between modules. You have no doubt worked with views before, such as a data dictionary or a system context diagram. Views allow you to relate these lists and diagrams back to the canonical model structure. Organizing the models in the canonical structure aids categorization and simplification.

The canonical model structure categorizes different kinds of facts into different models. Facts about the domain, design, and code go into their own models. When you encounter a domain fact like "billing cycles are 30 days," a design fact like "font resources must always be explicitly de-allocated," or an implementation fact like "the customer address is stored in a varchar(80) field," it is easy to sort these details into an existing mental model.

The canonical model structure shrinks the size of each problem. When you want to reason about a domain problem you are undistracted by code details, and vice versa, which makes each easier to reason about.

Let's first take a look at the domain, design, and code models before turning our attention to the relationships between them.

7.2 Domain, design, and code models

The *domain model* describes enduring truths about the domain; the *design model* describes the system you will build; and the *code model* describes the system source code. If something is "just true" then it probably goes in the domain model; if something is a design decision or a mechanism you design then it probably goes in the design model; and if something is written in a programming language, or is a model at that same level of abstraction, then it goes in the code model. Figure 7.1 shows the three models graphically and summarizes the contents of each.

Domain model. The domain model expresses enduring truths about the world that are relevant to your system. For the Yinzer system, some relevant truths would include definitions of important types like Ads and Contacts, relationships between those types, and behaviors that describe how the types and relationships change over time. In general, the domain is not under your control, so you cannot decide that weeks have six days or that you have a birthday party every week.

Design model. In contrast, the design is largely under your control. The system to be built does not appear in the domain model, but it makes its appearance in the design model. The design model is a partial set of design commitments. That is, you leave undecided some (usually low-level) details about how the design will work, deferring them until the code model.

The design model is composed of recursively nested *boundary models* and *internals models*. A boundary model and an internals model describe the same thing (like a component or a module), but the boundary model only mentions the publicly visible interface, while the internals model also describes the internal design.

Code model. The code model is either the source code implementation of the system or a model that is equivalent. It could be the actual Java code or the result of

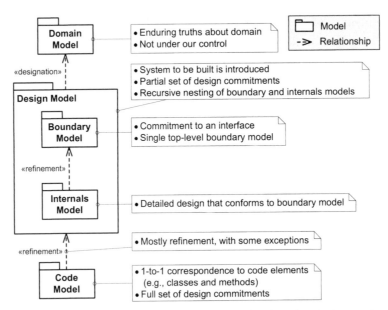

Figure 7.1: The canonical model structure that organizes the domain, design, and code models. The design model contains a top-level boundary model and recursively nested internals models.

running a code-to-UML tool, but its important feature is that has a full set of design commitments.

Design models often omit descriptions of low-risk parts knowing that the design is sufficient so long as the developer understands the overall design and architecture. But where the design model has an incomplete set of design commitments, the code model has a complete set, or at least a sufficiently complete set to execute on a machine.

7.3   Designation and refinement relationships

You no doubt have an intuitive sense of how the domain relates to the design and how the design relates to the code. Because this chapter seeks to divide up models and relate them, it is a good idea to examine these relationships carefully so that you can fully understand them.

Designation. The *designation* relationship enables you to say that similar things in different models should correspond. Using the Yinzer example, the domain model describes domain truths, such as people building a network of contacts and companies posting ads. Using the designation relationship, these truths carry over into the design, as seen in Figure 7.2.

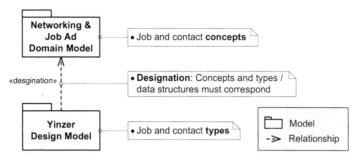

Figure 7.2: The designation relationship ensures that types you choose from the domain correspond to types or data structures in your design.

You have leeway in your design but it should not violate domain truths. You can designate that selected types from the domain must correspond to types and data structures from the design. Things that you do not designate are unconstrained.

While in practice the designation relationship is rarely written down precisely, it would be a mapping that defined the correspondence between the domain elements (e.g., Advertisement and Job types) and the design elements (e.g., Advertisement and Job types and data structures).

Perhaps surprisingly, the design is rarely 100% consistent with the domain because systems often use a simplified or constrained version the domain types. For example, the system may not realize that the same person reads email at two different email addresses, and so might consider them two different people. Or the system may restrict domain types, such as limiting the number of contacts a person can have in the system. But when correspondence with the domain is broken, bugs often follow. The designation relationship is covered in more detail in Section 13.6.

Refinement. *Refinement* is a relationship between a low-detail and a high-detail model of the same thing. It is used to relate a boundary model with an internals model, since they are both models of the same thing, but vary in the details that they expose. Refinement is useful because it lets you decompose your design into smaller pieces. Perhaps the Yinzer system is made up of a client and a server piece, and the server is made up of several smaller pieces. Refinement can be used to assemble these parts into a whole, and vice versa. The mechanics of refinement are discussed in depth in Section 13.7.

Refinement is also used to relate the design model with the code model, but there it is not so straightforward. The structural elements in the design model map neatly to the structural elements in the code model. For example, a module in the design maps to packages in the code, and a component in the design maps to a set of classes in the code.

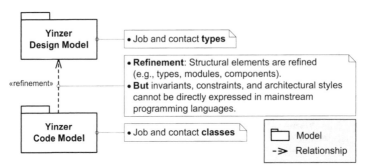

Figure 7.3: The refinement relationship ensures that types you choose from the domain correspond to types or data structures in your design. Be aware that there are elements in the design (invariants, constraints, styles) that cannot be expressed in programming languages.

However, as shown in Figure 7.3, other parts of the design model are absent in the code model: invariants, constraints, and architectural styles. Essentially no mainstream programming languages can directly express the constraints from the design model. It is true that constraints such as "all web requests must complete within 1 second," or "adhere to the pipe-and-filter style" can be *respected* by the code but they cannot be directly *expressed*. This gap between design and code models is discussed in more depth in Section 10.1.

7.4   Views of a master model

In your head, you understand how any number of systems work and carry around models that describe them, such as models of your neighborhood or how you manage your household. From time to time, you sketch out excerpts of those models, such as a map for a friend showing him how to get to that great restaurant, or you write down a list of groceries. These excerpts are consistent with that comprehensive model from your head. For example, you could have written out a full map for your friend, but presumably the one you drew is accurate so far as it goes, and is sufficient to get him there. And your grocery list represents the difference between your eating plans and the contents of your refrigerator.

The domain, design, and code models are comprehensive models like these. They are jam-packed full of details since, conceptually at least, they contain everything that you know about those topics. It would be difficult or impossible to write down all those details, and even keeping them straight in your head is difficult. So, if you want to use a model to reason about security, scalability, or any other reason, you need to winnow down the details so that you can see the relevant factors clearly. This is done with *views*.

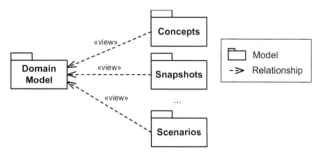

Figure 7.4: The domain model acts as a master model containing all details. Views show selected details from the master model. Because they are all views of the same master model, all of the views are consistent with each other.

Definition. A view, also called a *projection*, shows a defined subset of a model's details, possibly with a transformation. The domain, design, and code models each have many standard views. Views of the domain model include lists of types, lists of relationships between them, and scenarios that show how the types and relationships change over time (see Figure 7.4). Design views include the system context diagram and the deployment diagram. You can invent new views as appropriate.

Philippe Kruchten, in his paper on 4+1 views of architecture, showed that it is impractical to use a single diagram to express everything about your architecture and design (Kruchten, 1995). He explained that you need distinct architectural views because each has its own abstractions, notation, concerns, stakeholders, and patterns. Each view can use an appropriate notation and focus on a single concern, which makes it easy to understand. Together, the views comprise a full architecture model, and each view presents a subset of the details from that full model.

View consistency. Each view (or diagram) you create of a domain, design, or code model shows a single perspective on that model, exposing some details and hiding others. The diagrams are not isolated parts of the model, like drawers in a cabinet. Instead, they are live projections of the model and the views are consistent with each other. So if the model changes, the views do too. House blueprints are views of a house (or its design) so you expect them to be consistent with each other.

For example, imagine that you have two views of the domain model: a list of types in the networking and job advertisement domain (such as Ads, Jobs, and Contacts), and a scenario (a story) describing them. We will describe scenarios in more detail soon, but for now consider it a story told about how the domain types interact over time. If you were to revise the scenario to reference a new domain type, like a declined invitation to join a contact network, you would expect to see that type in the list of defined types. If it is not there, it is a bug in your domain model.

Master models. The domain, design, and code models are each conceptually a single *master model*. Every view you draw must be consistent with that master model. Think of it this way: when you revised the scenario to refer to a new type, your understanding of the master model was revised. Since any other view is derived from the master model, it should reflect your new understanding. Disregarding pragmatics for a moment, all of the diagrams you build should be consistent at all times with each other because that is the way that you, in your mind, understand the domain to work. Pragmatically, however, while you are building models there will be times when they are inconsistent with each other, but you strive to eliminate those bugs.

To reinforce the idea of unified and consistent models, it may be helpful to imagine a programming environment where all of these elements fit together and are typechecked. In that programming environment, a scenario that tried to refer to a type that was not defined in the master model would yield a type checking error.

Discussing views formally makes them sound difficult, but in reality people can use them with almost no effort. For example, you can imagine your bookcase as it is now, or imagine it with only the red books, or imagine it with the red books rotated so that you can see the cover instead of the spine. Each of these is a view of your master model of the bookcase. Notice that while you have never written down a model of your bookcase, you nonetheless have one in your head that you can manipulate. One of the challenges in software development is ensuring that developers, subject matter experts, and others all have the same master model in their heads.

Examples of master models. Master models are a helpful concept because they explain what your views refer to, but you have options regarding what the master model represents. The most straightforward example of a master model is an already existing system. You can create many views of an existing system. Consider your neighborhood as an example of an existing system. You do not have a complete model of your neighborhood written down anywhere, but you do have the neighborhood itself. Views of the neighborhood can be tested against the neighborhood to see if they are consistent with that master model.

Another example of a master model is a system that will be built. Unlike your neighborhood, this system does not yet exist, so it is a bit trickier to build views of it and ensure the views are consistent. Yet somehow things tend to work out OK. You might embark on a project to renovate a room in your house without writing down any explicit models, but you must have a master model in your head in some form. That model includes details about what should happen when (for example, demolition happens *before* painting) and cost estimates. That model in your head is likely incomplete, so views of it will necessarily be incomplete too.

Here are some concrete examples of master models of software systems. The master model may be the system you previously built or a system you plan to build. It can be a combination of the two, such as an existing system with planned additions.

Or it could be even more complex, such as a model of the system as you expect it to look at three-month intervals over the next few years.

Limiting size and focusing attention. You use views in modeling to limit the size of the diagrams and to focus attention. Imagine how confusing a medium-sized domain model would be if you tried to show all the types, definitions, behaviors, etc., on the same diagram. You may have seen the giant printouts of corporate database schemas taped to a wall somewhere and seen people trying to use them by putting a finger in one place and tracing the lines to other parts of the diagram. Views avoid that.

7.5 Other ways to organize models

The canonical model structure from this chapter consists of a domain model, a design model, and a code model. This basic organization of models has a long history, visible in the Syntropy software development process (Cook and Daniels, 1994), though it probably traces back even further.

Other authors have proposed similar model structures, and while there are some differences in their organizations and nomenclature, there is a core similarity shared by all. With only a little bit of squinting, one can identify the domain, design (boundary and internals), and code models. Figure 7.5 is a summary that maps this book's model names to some of those found elsewhere.

Despite the broad strokes of similarity between authors, there are differences. The one concept that does not align well across authors is *requirements*, because it can mean different things to different people. Requirements models could overlap with business models, domain models, boundary models, or internals models.

7.6 Business modeling

There is a kind of model not found in this book's canonical model structure: *business models*. Business models describe what a business or organization does and why it does it. Different businesses in the same domain will have different strategies, capabilities, organizations, processes, and goals and therefore different business models.

Domain modeling is related to *business modeling*, which includes not only facts but also decisions and goals that organizations must make. Someone at some point decides what the organization does and the processes it follows. Some of the processes are partly or fully automated with software. The goals and decisions of an organization can be influenced by the software that you build and buy.

So why include domain models but not business models in this book? This book includes domain modeling because misunderstanding the domain is a common cause of failure in IT projects. Misunderstanding business processes can also cause failures, but those are rarely engineering failures.

	Business Model	Domain Model	Design Model		Code Model
			Boundary Model	Internals Model	
Bosch			System context	Component design	Code
Cheesman & Daniels		Business concept	Type specs	Component architecture	Code
D'Souza (MAp)	Business architecture	Domain	Blackbox	Whitebox	Code
Software Engineering Institute (SEI)			Requirements	Architecture	Code
Jackson		Domain	Domain + machine	Machine	
RUP	Business modeling	Business modeling	Requirements	Analysis & design	Code
Syntropy		Essential	Specification	Implementation	Code

Figure 7.5: A table summarizing the models proposed by various authors and how they map to the business, domain, design (boundary, internals), and code models found in this book.

7.7   Use of UML

This book uses Unified Modeling Language (UML) notation because it is ubiquitous and its addition of architectural notation in UML 2.0 has brought it visually closer to special purpose architecture languages. This book deviates from strict UML in a few places. Any remaining deviations from UML are inadvertent.

- In UML, connectors can be solid lines or ball-and-socket style. They are distinguished using stereotypes to indicate their types. In this book, connectors are shown using a variety of line styles, which is a more compact way to convey their types and can be less cluttered.

- In UML, a port's type is shown with a text label near it. This book uses that style, but it sometimes clutters the diagram, in which case ports are shaded and defined in a legend. Not all UML tools allow shading or coloring of ports.

7.8 Conclusion

Once you begin to build models of your system, you realize that understanding and tracking lots of little models is hard, but building a single gigantic model is impractical. The strategy proposed in this chapter is to build small models that fit into a canonical model structure. If you understand the canonical structure then you will understand where each model fits in.

The first big idea was to use designation and refinement to create models that differ in their abstraction. The primary models are the domain model, design model, and code model, and they range from abstract to concrete. The second big idea was to use *views* to zoom in on the details of a model. Since the views are all projections of a single master model, their details are consistent (or are intended to be). In order to hierarchically nest design models, you use refinement to relate boundary and internals models.

Coaches see and understand more than rookies not because they have sharper eyes, but because they have a conceptual model that helps them categorize what they are seeing. This chapter describes the entire canonical model structure in detail, but do not let this alarm you. In practice you would rarely, if ever, create every possible model and view. Once you have internalized these ideas, they will help you to understand where a given detail, diagram, and model fits. As shown in the case study (Chapter 4) and the chapter on the risk-driven model (Chapter 3), following a risk-driven approach to architecture encourages you to build a subset of models, ones that help you reduce risks you have identified. This chapter, and subsequent ones, provides detailed descriptions to help you can internalize the models and thus be better at building software, not to encourage you towards analysis paralysis.

7.9 Further reading

This book is a synthesis of the architectural modeling approaches invented by other authors. It has three primary influences. The first is the work on modeling components in UML from D'Souza and Wills (1998) and Cheesman and Daniels (2000), which focus primarily on modeling functionality. The second is the quality attribute centric approach from the Software Engineering Institute (Bass, Clements and Kazman, 2003; Clements et al., 2010) and Carnegie Mellon University (Shaw and Garlan, 1996). The third is the agile software development community (Boehm and Turner, 2003; Ambler, 2002) which encourages efficient software development practices.

There are several good books that describe the general concepts of software architecture. Bass, Clements and Kazman (2003), describes a quality-attribute centric view of software architecture and provides case studies of applying their techniques. Taylor, Medvidović and Dashofy (2009) is a more modern treatment and is logically organized like a textbook. Shaw and Garlan (1996) is becoming dated but is the best book for understanding the promise of software architecture. Clements et al. (2010) is an excellent reference book for architecture concepts and notations (and also has a useful appendix on using UML as an architecture description language). These books rarely venture down into objects and design, but D'Souza and Wills (1998) and Cheesman and Daniels (2000) do, showing how architecture fits into object-oriented design.

Probably more than any other book, Bass, Clements and Kazman (2003) has shaped the way the field thinks about software architecture, shifting the focus away from functionality and towards quality attributes. It describes not only the theory but also processes for analyzing architectures and discovering quality attribute requirements. The book also contains a great discussion of the orthogonality of functionality and quality attributes.

Rozanski and Woods (2005) offer perhaps the most complete treatment of how to understand and use multiple views in software architecture. It also contains valuable checklists relating to several standard concerns.

The simplest pragmatic approach to component-based development is found in Cheesman and Daniels (2000). They lay out an organizational structure for models using UML and treat components as abstract data types with strict encapsulation boundaries. A similar approach, but with greater detail, is found in D'Souza and Wills (1998). Both emphasize detailed specifications, such as pre- and post-conditions, as a way to catch errors during design. This book de-emphasizes pre- and post-conditions because on most projects they are too expensive, but the mindset they encourage is excellent.

The best book at articulating a vision of software engineering that includes software architecture is probably Shaw and Garlan (1996). While reading it, it is difficult not to share their enthusiasm for how architecture can help our field.

The nuts and bolts of architectural modeling, including pitfalls, are well described by Clements et al. (2010). One of the book's goals is to teach readers how to document the models in a documentation package, which can be important on large projects.

To date, the most comprehensive treatment of software architecture is by Taylor, Medvidović and Dashofy (2009) in their textbook on software architecture. It covers real-world examples of software architecture as well as research developments on formalisms and analysis.

Developers working in the field of Information Technology (IT) will be well served by Ian Gorton's treatment of software architecture, as his book covers not only the basics of software architecture, but also the common technologies in IT, such as Enterprise Java Beans (EJB), Message-Oriented Middleware (MOM), and Service Oriented Architecture (SOA) (Gorton, 2006).

Using abstraction to organize a stack of models is an old technique. It is used in the Syntropy object oriented design method (Cook and Daniels, 1994) and is central to Cheesman and Daniels (2000), Fowler (2003a), and D'Souza and Wills (1998).

Many authors have suggested ways of organizing and relating architecture models. Jan Bosch models the system context, the archetypes, and the main components (Bosch, 2000). John Cheesman and John Daniels propose building a model of the requirements (a business information model and a scenario model) and a model of the system specification (a business type model, interface specifications, component specifications, and the component architecture) (Cheesman and Daniels, 2000). Desmond D'Souza, in MAp, suggests modeling the business architecture, the domain, and the design as a blackbox and a whitebox (D'Souza, 2006). David Garlan conceives as architecture being a bridge between the requirements and the implementation (Garlan, 2003). Michael Jackson suggests modeling the domain, the domain with the machine, and the machine (Jackson, 1995). Jackson's primary focus is on system requirements engineering, not design, but his specifications overlap well with design. The Rational Unified Process (RUP) does not advocate specific models, but suggests activities for business modeling, requirements, and analysis & design (Kruchten, 2003).

Every developer should be familiar with the 4+1 architecture views paper (Kruchten, 1995), but also be aware that it is just one of many different sets of views that have been proposed for architecture, such as the Siemens Four Views (Hofmeister, Nord and Soni, 2000).

You should also be aware of the IEEE standard description of software architecture, IEEE 1471-2000 (Society, 2000). In it, you will find most of the same concepts as in this book. It has a few additions and differences worth noting. While it uses *views*, it treats them as requirements from the *viewpoint* of a *stakeholder* focused on a particular *concern*, rather than as projections of a consistent master model, what it would call an *architecture description*. It also describes the *environment* the system inhabits, its *mission*, and *library viewpoints* (which are reusable viewpoint definitions).

Authors are increasingly paying attention to business process modeling in addition to domain modeling. Martin Ould provides a practical process for modeling business processes (Ould, 1995). Desmond D'Souza describes how to connect business processes to software architecture by connecting business goals to system goals (D'Souza, 2006).

The relationship between software architecture (specifically enterprise architecture) and business strategy is covered in Ross, Weill and Robertson (2006). As software developers, we perhaps assume that the natural future state should be that all systems can inter-operate. The surprising thesis of the book is that the level of integration should relate to the chosen business strategy.

Chapter 8

The Domain Model

A domain model expresses enduring truths about a domain, for example, that customers have contact phone numbers. Domain models are also called concept models, conceptual models, or abstract models, but the idea is the same: to express the details of the domain that are not related to the system's implementation. For the domain of the Yinzer system, the enduring concepts include advertisements, jobs, contacts, and employment.

The purest kind of knowledge to express in a domain model concerns truth from nature rather than a construction of mankind, but even the concept of advertisements would fail to clear that hurdle. Domain models also include knowledge that, so far as your project is concerned, will always be so. This could include the idea that companies have jobs that they advertise. If there was a standard format for job postings then a domain model might include it, but you should be wary of the slippery slope because, as you begin to introduce technical details, it becomes harder to decide what is an enduring truth and what is a design choice.

You may be wary of domain modeling, so this chapter starts out by providing some anecdotes about real situations where such models have been helpful. It covers the mechanics of building domain models that cover state and behavior. And it briefly covers the difference between domain modeling and the more expansive topic of business modeling.

Domain modeling provides a way to gain insights that are essential to the design process. In particular, domain models help you to answer questions that are unrelated to your design, such as what comprises a person's network of contacts. Domain models, because they are free of design details and can be drawn with simple notation, are an effective way to interact with subject matter experts, whose eyes would glaze over at the sight of your technical designs. A domain model can form the basis of a *ubiquitous language* that is shared by developers and subject matter experts.

Domain models will be more or less useful to you depending on what kind of system you build. Systems in IT domains tend to have complex domains that their developers have not yet mastered. Web developers or device driver writers might have relatively simple domains but have complex performance or scalability requirements, so domain models are often less useful to them. However, regardless of what kind of system you build, you will sooner or later run across a problem that domain models can help you with.

8.1   How the domain relates to architecture

It may not be immediately obvious that domain modeling is relevant to software architecture, or even if it is relevant, that you should spend any time doing it. Common objections include:

- You already know your domain.

- The domain is too simple to bother modeling it.

- The domain is irrelevant to your architecture choices.

- It is someone else's job to do requirements.

- The best way to learn the domain is incrementally, as you write code.

- Domain modeling is an open-ended analysis paralysis activity.

These are reasonable concerns and, at times, they are good reasons to avoid domain modeling. But before you flip forward to the next chapter, consider these two true stories and how they relate to the objections.

Cell phone contact list. I recently started using a so-called smart phone that not only places calls but also connects to the internet, sends and receives emails, and runs programs. It has a single contact list that contains all of the people I have phone numbers or email addresses for. Furthermore, this contact list is synchronized with a web server, so the phone's contact list is always updated. So far, so good.

The phone is not the only thing using my contact list — it is shared with my email program on my computer. Every time I send an email to a new person, that person is added to the shared contact list. Can you guess what happens next?

The first time I went to make a call, I discovered that I had to scroll through 1400 contacts to find my friend's phone number. Many of those on the list had no phone numbers, but since this is a smart phone, I could click on their entry and send them an email (or call them, or send a text message).

There are many ways you can categorize this problem, including as a user interface problem or an integration problem. But leave yourself open to the idea that the developers, in their efforts to solve the problem of missing phone numbers, had misunderstood the domain. Is my list of email contacts really the same list as my phone contacts? And how do people decide what numbers go onto their phone's contact list?

Consider this: do you have every phone number for everyone you know in your mobile phone? Or do you follow a different scheme and keep a subset on the phone, such as personal contacts plus a few important work contacts? That was my old scheme. Keeping a full list of work contacts could be convenient but it could also be trouble. Imagine my embarrassment if I were to sync my contact list with a complete work address book, then were to accidentally call Ken Smith (someone from work who I hardly know) instead of Ken Creel (my good friend) and say "Whassup?" — or worse.

User entitlements. The second story is more pedestrian and takes us away from judging the size of my circle of friends and phone etiquette. I was working to integrate several applications at a financial company and one option was to purchase a vendor product that handled user entitlements. An *entitlement* is simply permission for a user (or login) to perform an action, such as the ability to create new database tables or access the third floor of the building. As computer users, we would like to think that we understand this domain rather well, since we bump into it every time we log on or find a folder that is write-protected.

There were various profiles of users inside the company, such as clerks, and standard sets of entitlements for those profiles. Looking across the company, it became clear that there were two kinds of systems: ones that supported *active profiles* and others that supported *template profiles*. With active profiles, if you were to add a new entitlement to the clerk profile, all clerks in the company would then have that entitlement. With template profiles, that new entitlement would only be applied to newly hired clerks, leaving existing clerks who had been stamped with the old template unchanged.

It should be clear that I needed to know which vendor products supported either active or template profiles so that a suitable architecture could be designed. Furthermore, depending on the answer, the vendor product could be incompatible. The vendors could answer detailed questions regarding messaging formats and server hardware requirements, but it was an enormous challenge to discover their domain assumptions, including their handling of these profiles and whether the entitlements could be organized hierarchically.

Concerns revisited. Let's return to the list of concerns about domain modeling and examine them in light of these two stories.

- **You already know your domain.** Undoubtedly this is often true, though it is less often true in "boring" business domains than in "sexy" internet and systems domains, where developers enjoy learning about the domain.

- **The domain is too simple to bother modeling it.** Domains are rarely much simpler than a list of names with phone numbers and email addresses. But, at least for the way I use a mobile phone, the software caused trouble by being inconsistent with the domain. Admittedly, it may not have been obvious that trouble was imminent until after the email and phone contact lists were merged.

- **The domain is irrelevant to your architecture choices.** The domain differences between the vendor entitlement management products show that systems can be incompatible because of domain differences. While the domain influences your architecture, it is a mistake to believe that your architecture is latent in the domain, waiting for you to discover it.

- **It is someone else's job to do requirements.** Maybe, but that person may not have your vantage point on how the domain can cause architecture problems, or you may need to assist them with the domain models.

- **The best way to learn the domain is incrementally, as you write code.** Learning the domain by writing code is indeed a good way to learn it, but there are cases when this is impossible or impractical. In the example of the entitlement product selection, a team of developers and (paid) consultants from the vendor performed a proof of concept integration, but even that took weeks. In that case it was overwhelmingly cost-effective to model on paper first, and the questions generated during domain modeling helped inform the integration test.

- **Domain modeling is an open-ended analysis paralysis activity.** This is a real danger. You could start modeling the domain of contact lists for phones and end up building a model of why people become friends. You want to model just enough of the domain.

If analysis paralysis is a real danger, how can you avoid it?

Avoiding analysis paralysis. To avoid analysis paralysis, you must limit how much domain modeling you will do. One technique is to decide what questions you want the model to answer before you build the model. That way, once the model can answer the questions, you can stop modeling. But what questions should you ask?

In general, the list of interesting questions to ask about the domain is quite large. But the domain influences the architecture in limited ways, which cuts down on the possible questions. You want to avoid domain misunderstandings that would translate into an architectural failure, which means asking questions about failure risks. Two common risks are usability and interoperability.

In the mobile phone story, the developers combined two contact lists that were previously separate. They allowed the email program and my phone to inter-operate via the shared contact list, but people with lots of contacts have reduced usability. The problem of interoperability arose in the entitlement story also, since we tried to buy an entitlement system that would connect to existing systems.

Another technique to avoid analysis paralysis is to decide how deep and how broad your domain model will be. Consider the entitlement system example. Regarding depth, we could have selected a single system and looked at every kind of entitlement it handled. Regarding breadth, we could have surveyed every kind of system in the company that handles entitlements, or we could survey a sample. Again, you would choose to go deep or wide (or both) depending on where you perceive the risk.

In the end, to avoid analysis paralysis, you must recognize when additional domain modeling is providing no additional value. Indeed, the choice is more difficult than that, because you want to stop domain modeling when it provides less value than another activity, such as prototyping.

The following sections discuss how to create domain models so that, when appropriate, you can dig into the domain and discover problems. Domain models cover both state and behavior, so these sections describe how to use information models, snapshots, navigation, invariants, and scenarios. The example that runs throughout is the Yinzer system that provides social networking and job advertisement services.

8.2 Information model

The easiest and most valuable part of a domain model is a list of *types* and their definitions, as seen in Figure 8.1. It describes the things that exist in the domain of job advertisements and business networking and, if you are careful about writing the definitions, it also describes the *relationships* between those types. Even if you are a domain expert, writing definitions like these may be hard — what exactly is a Job? — but the fact that it is hard means that you are working to clarify the concepts. If you are not a domain expert, nailing down such definitions is a great way to start learning the domain.

An *information model* can also be drawn graphically, as seen in Figure 8.2. Compared to the textual version, it has the immediate benefit that the relationships between the types are explicitly expressed as *associations*. As seen in the diagram, a Person is associated with many Contacts, the set of which is called a Network, and a Contact exists between two People. These graphical models use Unified Modeling

Type	Definition
Advertisement (Ad)	An Ad is a solicitation to find a Person to employ in a Job at a Company.
Company	A Company is an employer that offers Jobs to People.
Contact	A Contact is a relationship between two People that indicates that they know each other.
Employment	Employment is a relationship indicating that the Person is or was employed at a Job at the Company.
Job	A Job is a role at a Company where a Person works.
Job Match	A Job Match is a relationship between a Job and a Person indicating that the Person may be suitable for the Job.
Person	Someone who can be employed.

Figure 8.1: A textual information model for the job ad and business networking domain. The Yinzer system's design and implementation will need to be consistent with this model of the domain.

Language (UML) class diagram syntax, with UML classes representing types. You can stereotype the UML classes with «type» if it is not clear from the context or the legend.

The system to be built does not appear in the information model, or anywhere else in your domain model. The information model does not imply a design: an Advertisement is not a data structure and so it makes no sense to ask if a Person or a Contact can navigate a pointer to the other. The intent of the information model is to describe a part of the world, not the design. Subject matter experts can analyze your information model and find mistakes.

Advice on UML use. UML is a rich language but it is in your best interests to restrict your use of its notations, especially in domain models that are often shared with non-developers. In domain modeling, you should limit your models to use a simple subset of UML model elements: classes (stereotyped as types), objects (type instances), associations, links, multiplicities, and role names. This discourages you from obsessing about modeling domain wrinkles and ensures that the model can be read by subject matter experts. If you need to express important domain subtleties it is better to write them textually in a note on the diagram instead of assuming the reader knows the difference between a filled or empty diamond in your model.

Although they do not appear in Figure 8.2, attributes on the classes (types) are fine in moderation and with the understanding that they do not represent stored data. For example, the Employment type could have begin and end dates or a Job Match

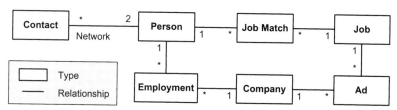

Figure 8.2: An information model for the job advertisement and business networking domain, shown graphically using a UML class diagram.

type could have a suitability rating. Use the UML *generalization* relationship (which shows that one type is the supertype of another) sparingly because it causes trouble for non-programmers like subject matter experts (SME's).

8.3 Navigation and invariants

Information models provide the vocabulary to be used in other parts of the domain model. *Invariants*, or constraints, express predicates that must always be true. Some invariants are already expressed through the multiplicities in the graphical model. For example, based on the multiplicities in the model above, a Contact happens between exactly two People. You might additionally decide that, in the domain, a Person's Network cannot have duplicates. You could write this invariant using plain text (i.e., "A Person cannot have a Contact to the same Person multiple times") on the information model in a UML *note* or in a separate document. Notice that the invariant refers to types in the model: Person, Network, and Contacts.

The idea that you can traverse across associations in the model is called *navigation* (D'Souza and Wills, 1998). If you put your finger on the Person type, you can follow an association down to the Contact type. Since there is a "*" at the end of that association, it means that the Person has zero to many Contacts. The word Network on that association is called a *role*, which provides a convenient way for you to refer to the collection of Contacts. A Contact has two People and the invariant says those should always be two different people.

If the invariant had been written more carefully, it could even have referred directly to the associations between types and you could use navigation to check it. Object Constraint Language (OCL) can be used to precisely express the navigation (Warmer and Kleppe, 2003). It could have been written as the OCL invariant:

> context Person
> inv: network.person->asSet()->size() = network->size() + 1

This OCL expresses that the number of People connected in your Network is equal to the number of Contacts in your Network, plus one (the one represents you).

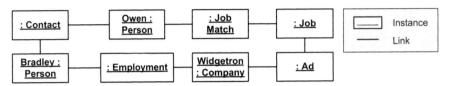

Figure 8.3: A snapshot (i.e., instance diagram) of the information model for the job advertisement and business networking domain. Notice that some instances are named (Bradley and Widgetron) and the rest are anonymous.

Unless you are hoping to have a computer read and check this OCL, it is unlikely to be cost-effective to write it. However, it is a great aid to thinking clearly and precisely. As you write a natural language invariant, you can think whether it could be formalized; if it is a bit imprecise then you tighten up the natural language. This is an example of a broader theme throughout architecture modeling: knowing how to formalize something yields higher quality models, even when you do not actually apply the formalism.

8.4   Snapshots

It is easy to make mistakes when thinking about information models because they refer to general types, not concrete instances. For example the information model talks about a Person, not Bradley, and a Company, not Widgetron. You can draw a *snapshot*, or *instance diagram*, which shows instances, not types, as seen in Figure 8.3.

Notice that each *instance* in the snapshot corresponds to a type in the information model, just as each *link* corresponds to an association. The anonymous Contact instance is linked to the Person instance named Bradley and the Person instance named Owen, which is consistent with the information model where a Contact exists between exactly two People. Notice also the notation for snapshots: the text is underlined and a colon separates the instance name from the type name. An instance can be anonymous, like the Contact instance is in the diagram. This relationship between types and instances, a *classification* relationship, is the same one that exists between classes and objects in object-oriented programming.

You can avoid making mistakes in your information models by thinking about the snapshots you want to allow or disallow. You might draw a snapshot where Bradley is linked to a Contact, and then back to him. Looking at the snapshot, you would decide you want to disallow that, and would write the invariant mentioned above about not being in your own Network. The information model here is rather simple, but remember the trick of sketching out a snapshot as your information model becomes complex.

Name: Owen becomes employed at Widgetron
Initial state: Bradley is employed at the Widgetron Company
Actors: Owen, Bradley
Steps:
1.   Owen and Bradley meet at a professional conference, exchange business cards, and become part of each other's Network of Contacts.
2.   Bradley's company, Widgetron, posts an Ad for a software developer Job.
3.   Bradley matches Owen to the Job.
4.   Owen is hired by Widgetron for the software developer Job.

Figure 8.4: A functionality scenario for the job advertisement and business networking domain. It starts in the initial state, involves the list of actors (Owen and Bradley), and describes four steps that correspond to changes in the information model. Other things may happen, but if they do not cause a change to the model, then you should generally not include them in the scenario.

8.5   Functionality scenarios

A snapshot expresses how the instances in the model might be linked at an instant in time and the information model expresses all the possible snapshots. What you cannot yet express is how the domain might change from one snapshot to another. *Functionality scenarios*, also called simply *scenarios*, like the one in Figure 8.4 express a series of events that cause changes to the information model.

A functionality scenario uses the vocabulary defined in the information model, like Ads and Contacts. Each scenario starts in an initial state that is written out textually in the scenario. That initial state could equivalently be drawn out as a snapshot. Each step in the scenario changes the model. If you were to draw out a snapshot of the state of the model, it would be different after each step. For example, after the first step in the scenario from Figure 8.4, the snapshot will contain a new Contact instance linking Owen and Bradley.

It is important to focus on changes to your model that happen with each step in the scenario. This focus encourages tight scenarios: It may be the case that after step 2, Bradley telephones Owen to tell him about the Job opportunity or that Owen sends his fancy suit to the cleaners, but the model does not talk about these types so you leave them out of the scenario. However, if you decide that these are important, you should add them to the information model. Thinking about before and after snapshots for each step in the scenario ensures a tight correspondence between types and behavior.

Since this is a domain model, Owen and Bradley represent real people, not computer records. Their Network of Contacts is real and could be either a stack of business cards or just memories. This is the essential difference between domain models and design models: elements in the domain model represent the real things and happenings, while elements in the design model represent computer records or computer hardware.

A scenario describes a single possible path rather than generalizing many paths. In practice, writing just a couple scenarios can be effective in describing a domain, but sometimes you will want a general model. UML *activity diagrams* and UML *state diagrams* can be used to describe generalized behaviors, but they require more effort to build than scenarios.

Scenarios, like snapshots, are easy to make because they deal with concrete instances rather than general types. This is doubly good news because you will have better luck engaging subject matter experts with scenarios than you will with generalized domain models.

8.6   Conclusion

Separating the domain from the design has several benefits. Many questions arise that are unrelated to the design, for example, whether current employees of a company should receive a company's job ads. That is an interesting question, but its answer will not pop out when you model your database schema or design your class hierarchy. Domain models are effective at investigating such questions because they are free of extrinsic design details. Another good reason to keep domain models separate from code models is that SME's can teach you about the domain but are uninterested in your programming language and data structures. Sometimes different experts will use different terms for the same types, and you can use a domain model to drive the team to use a single vocabulary, sometimes called ubiquitous language (Evans, 2003).

By building a domain model, you will come to understand your domain better. For example, a domain model encourages you to ask questions like: if I am in your network of contacts, must you be in my network? People on your team may initially have different answers to these questions, but the team needs to develop a shared understanding of how things work in the domain, or else bugs in the design and code are inevitable.

A real domain has essentially unlimited richness. A model of that domain is a simplification and must make choices about what it includes and excludes. You must accept that a domain model will describe some things and not others. For example, perhaps an Ad in the real world can describe more than one Job but the model limits it to describing a single Job. When building a domain model you must decide how wide and deep it is, roughly corresponding to the number of types and how many wrinkles and special cases it handles.

Even though the information model is a simplification, it is precise, and you can use it to answer questions. For example, you could answer which Contacts are in Bradley's Network, or what Companies Owen has worked for. However, you need decide in advance what questions you need the model to answer and stop modeling once it can answer them. The questions you want it to answer are related to the risks you are worried about, particularly interoperability and usability. For example, two sub-teams on your project may need a shared understanding of the contact network so that their software will inter-operate. If you find yourself modeling a part of the domain, stop and ask if not understanding it is likely to lead to failure.

8.7 Further reading

The domain modeling in this book is based on the domain models from Catalysis (D'Souza and Wills, 1998). Catalysis domain models have the ability to be substantially more detailed and complex than what is shown here.

Functionality scenarios are similar to use cases (more about that is found in Section 12.6). Cockburn (2000) is my favorite book on use cases because it is succinct, provides guidance on how to structure use cases, and advises you when to stop writing them.

Chapter 9

The Design Model

You have begun the transformation of yourself from rookie to coach by learning about the canonical model structure consisting of domain, design, and code models. In the previous chapter you saw the first of the three primary models, the domain model, which models facts about the world that your system lives in. This chapter covers the second primary model, the design model, which models the design of your system. Where the domain model contained advertisements, jobs, and contact networks, the design model will show how your system is designed such that it can manipulate computer representations of those types. You have little control over the facts in the domain, but you have great control over your system's design. Using your knowledge about the domain and your design skills, you design a system that will exist in harmony with domain facts. This chapter enriches your mental conceptual model of architecture, showing you how to organize a system design using views, encapsulation, and nesting.

When you reason about software architecture, you will spend most of your time thinking about the design model, so it should be no surprise that it is expressive and deep. To avoid drowning you in details, this chapter provides a readable overview of the design model, showing an example of the Yinzer system design and corresponding models. As you read this chapter, your attention should be on how the different models fit together to describe the system. Subsequent chapters dig into additional details on the model elements and relationships and how to use them. This chapter concludes with a discussion of viewtypes, dynamic architecture, and architecture description languages.

9.1   Design model

As we discussed in Section 7.4, the domain, design, and code models are all comprehensive models with every possible detail in them, something called *master models*.
So the *design model* is a master model containing every last detail about the design.
The idea of a master model is a convenient abstraction because it explains how all
the diagrams you draw are related to each other.

In practice, however, almost no one builds a complete and comprehensive design
model. But if you did, you would find that its comprehensiveness would make it
impractical to use directly. Models amplify your reasoning by focusing your attention
on salient details, so a master model with all details would not be very effective.

What you want is to keep that comprehensive design model in your head, but
still have the ability to sketch out diagrams that show a limited number of details,
ones that you can reason about effectively. You must insist that those diagrams be
consistent with your master model. To reconcile these competing demands, you can
use a combination of views, encapsulation, and nesting.

- **Views**. A view is a projection of a model that reveals selected details. We will
  use views to selectively narrow our focus of the comprehensive design model.

- **Encapsulation**. Encapsulation separates the interface of an element from its implementation. We will use the term *boundary model* to refer to a model element's
  interface since the term *interface* is commonly used to refer to a programming
  language construct (e.g., Java interfaces). The implementation is called the *internals model*. Both the boundary model and the internals model describe the
  same thing, but the boundary model omits any details of what the element looks
  like on the inside.

- **Nesting**. Most elements in your models have sub-structure. An internals model
  of an element consists of smaller elements. Each of these elements can be described by a boundary model, and the implementation of those elements can be
  described by an internals model. Consequently, a single element can be decomposed into a tree of nested boundary and internals models.

Through the use of views, encapsulation, and nesting, you can build models that show
only the details you need to reason about a problem. And since you understand the
relationships involved, you can relate these models back to your design model, which
acts as a master model with full details.

The design model is related to the domain model by a *designation* relationship (see
Figure 9.1). That is, selected facts about the domain are designated to be also true in
the design. So for the Yinzer domain, you would designate the existence of Ads, Jobs,
and Contact Networks to also exist in the design of the Yinzer system. The design

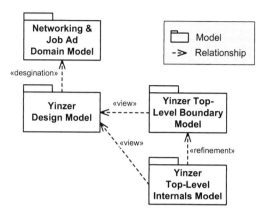

Figure 9.1: The Yinzer top-level internals model and its relationships with the design model and boundary model. Both the boundary and internals models are views of the design model, since they show selected details from it. An internals model refines a boundary model (in this case the entire Yinzer system), showing the same thing in more detail.

model is also related to the code model, but as you will see later, the relationship is a bit more complex, mostly resembling *refinement*.

9.2 Boundary model

The boundary model is what outsiders can see of the system (or an element in the system), which includes its behavior, interchange data, and quality attributes. The boundary is a commitment to an interface but not to implementation details. The boundary model describes what a user needs to know to understand how a system works. It is an encapsulated view of the system that hides internal details, so when developers change the internal design, users are undisturbed.

The design model has a single *top-level boundary model* that describes the system and how it interacts with the domain. Figure 9.1 shows the top-level boundary model for the Yinzer system. The Yinzer design model contains all design details, so you can build a view of it that shows the Yinzer system interface (i.e., the Yinzer top-level boundary model) or a view that shows that interface plus implementation details (i.e., the Yinzer top-level internals model). You know those views must be consistent with each other because they are views of the same Yinzer design model.

9.3 Internals model

The *internals model* is another view of the design model, one that reveals the details that are omitted from the boundary model. Figure 9.1 shows both the boundary and internals models as views of the design model. While both the boundary and internals models are views of the design model, they are also related to each other by a *refinement* relationship. The internals model describes the same thing as the boundary model and adds more details, which is the definition of a refinement relationship.

Crucially, anything that is true in the boundary model must be true in the internals model. So, any commitments made in the boundary model must be upheld in the internals model. If the boundary model says that the Yinzer system will be online 99.5% of the time and will be deployable on Linux systems, then that must be true of the internals model also.

Both the boundary and internals models are described using the same elements, such as scenarios, components, connectors, ports, responsibilities, modules, classes, interfaces, environmental elements, and tradeoffs. Some things in the internals model are elaborated, such as the component assembly and scenarios.

9.4   Quality attributes

Like most teenage boys, during high school I assembled looms that my mother sold in her weaving store. She sold looms made from wood and cotton, so when you wove fabric with them you heard organic noises like thumping and whooshing. Other brands of looms used metal in places, which is much more durable but makes clanging noises. Both kinds of looms were equally good at making fabric, but they differed in durability and the noise they made.

Software systems have the same distinction between their functionality and other qualities. Some systems are faster, others are more modifiable, and others are highly secure. Before proceeding to the next section, which provides an example of the Yinzer system, let's pause to consider those other qualities, called *quality attributes*, sometimes called just QA's, which describe observable properties of a system.

Software architecture experts tend to focus more on quality attributes than functionality. This is not because functionality is unimportant, but because many designs could achieve the same functionality with differing qualities. Quality attributes are mostly orthogonal[1] to functionality but there is some interaction between the two. Quality attributes tend to be *emergent* in that there is no one place in the code with the responsibility for security, modifiability, latency, or deployability (for example). These qualities instead emerge from the architecture and design.

In an ideal world, all of your systems would maximize every quality attribute, but in practice you have to prioritize some qualities over others. Telephone switches are required to provide dial tone within 40ms and to have 99.999% uptime or else the operator may face fines. In order to meet those quality attribute requirements,

---

[1]For example, in sports, most of the time the choice of ball color is independent of the game, but green golf balls are probably a bad idea.

the software developers might have to prioritize latency and availability over code maintainability and another qualities. Banking software might prioritize security over latency.

The next section walks you through a description of the Yinzer system's design. The walkthrough does not contain full details on each element, relationship, and diagram, but these can be found in Chapters 12 and 13.

9.5   Walkthrough of Yinzer design

To give you an overview of how the design model can be organized, this section walks through various views of the Yinzer system. For the most part, the diagrams and elements are the same in both the boundary and internals model, but you will see that they are used slightly differently. It begins with views of the boundary model and moves on to the internals model.

Two views are particularly effective at giving an overview of the system: the use case diagram and the system context diagram. The use case diagram is good at showing functionality (the use cases) while the system context diagram is good for showing other systems that interact with Yinzer.

Next, several abstractions are introduced, including components, ports, connectors, responsibilities, design decisions, modules, quality attribute scenarios, architecture drivers, and tradeoffs.

Finally, the walkthrough covers the internals model. It shows a component assembly of the internal design of the Yinzer system, and augments the functionality scenario from the boundary to show how each step is accomplished. The importance of constraints and architectural styles are also shown.

9.5.1   Use cases and functionality scenarios

The UML *use case diagram* provides a compact, graphical overview of the functionality of a system and the actors and systems that it interacts with. Figure 9.2 shows the Yinzer system, several use cases, and the Yinzer Member, Non-Member, and Timer actors that use the system. The Timer actor is special and indicates that those use cases run at particular times each day as batch jobs.

Each *use case* describes a general capability of the system, not a specific example of that capability in use. The Invite Contact use case, for instance, describes how a Yinzer Member, generally, could invite someone to become part of his Network of Contacts. Contrast this with a step in a functionality scenario, where you would see a specific Yinzer Member, such as Alan, enacting a use case.

Use case diagrams show what the system can do, but they do not impose sequencing constraints on the use cases. You might guess that the Invite Contact use case would occur before the Accept Invitation use case, but that is just a guess. The easiest

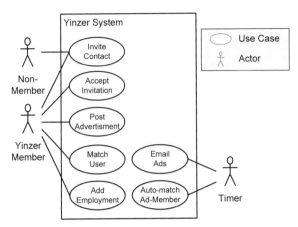

Figure 9.2: A use case diagram for the Yinzer system. It is effective at presenting a broad overview of the Yinzer system's functionality.

way to describe a sequence of events is to use a functionality scenario, just like you did in the domain model. Figure 9.3 shows a functionality scenario of how Kevin takes a Job at Widgetron.

You may want to flip back to Figure 8.4 to compare this scenario with the scenario in the domain model. When you were modeling the domain, there was no Yinzer system, so it was impossible to talk about a Member using it as a web application, or the system generating an email, but now you can. You have made some commitments, like using links in emails (step 2), but have left other design options open. Note also that in the domain you talked about People, while here in the design you talk about Yinzer Members. This is because the Yinzer system does not exist in the domain, so you could not differentiate Yinzer Members from everyone else.

Notice that each step in the scenario corresponds to an invocation of a use case. Step 1 corresponds to the Invite Contact use case and step 2 corresponds to the Accept Invitation use case. Where the use case model expresses the possible use cases, a functionality scenario expresses a specific trace or path of use case invocations. Between a use case model and some functionality scenarios you can describe both what behavior is generally available and concrete examples of it.

What you have not described is the set of all legal paths that exercise the use cases. In the scenario, Invite Contact occurs before Accept Invitation, but is this always true? You cannot tell from just the use case diagram and scenarios. If it is important to you, you can create a UML activity diagram that shows all legal paths that exercise the use cases.

Unless the scenario is intended to describe the user interface, it is best to write it so that several possible user interfaces are possible. For example, in step 1 of the

Name: Kevin takes a job at Widgetron
Initial state: Alan and Own are Members of Yinzer; Kevin is not. Alan works at Widgetron.
Actors: Alan, Kevin, Owen
Steps:
1. Alan invites Kevin to be a Contact in his Network. / The system sends Kevin an email.
2. Kevin clicks a link in his email, joins Yinzer, and accepts Alan's invitation to be a Contact.
3. Widgetron posts an Ad for a Job for a software developer. / The system auto-matches Owen to the Job, sending him an email.
4. Alan sees the Ad and matches Kevin to the Job. / The system sends Kevin an email.
5. Kevin takes the job and changes his Yinzer profile to add his employment at Widgetron.

Figure 9.3: A functionality scenario for the Yinzer system. Its steps refer to the boundary model (e.g., the Yinzer System component in Figure 9.4), so you only see the actors using the system, not the internal components collaborating.

scenario, Alan invites Kevin to be a Contact, but it is not specified how exactly this is done: how many steps does that take, is there a list of Members to choose from, or does he begin typing their names and the system auto-completes? This keeps the scenario sufficiently general to allow changes to the user interface and makes the scenario easier to understand. You will need to commit to the user interface because it has architectural impacts, but adding those details to this use case would add clutter and reduce its clarity.

9.5.2 System context

The *system context diagram*, as seen in Figure 9.4, is similar to the use case diagram in that it provides an overview of the system and the actors / systems it interacts with. The biggest difference is that functionality is much more visible in the use case diagram, while the system context diagram more clearly shows the *connectors*, which represent channels of communication to external systems. Both the system to be built and external systems are shown with *ports*, which segment the interface of a system into smaller chunks of related functions. As seen in the example, the system context diagram can reveal details about the technology used, such as Web, SMTP, and IMAP connections. A system context diagram is a special case of a *component assembly* diagram.

Notice that the Yinzer Member's browser is connected to two different port instances on the Yinzer system: the Contacts and the Job/Advertisement port instances. Rather than provide a single port with every web operation, this design divides the Yinzer functions across the ports.

Because of this increase in precision, the system context diagram encourages a more literal depiction of interactions. Notice that in the use case diagram, the Yinzer

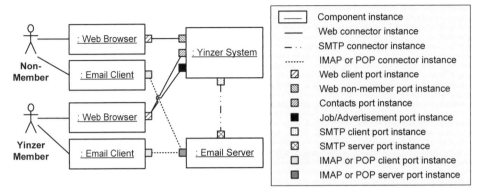

Figure 9.4: A system context diagram for the Yinzer system that shows the Yinzer System component instance and all the external systems it connects to.

Member is shown interacting with the system, but here the interaction is intermediated by a Web Browser and an Email Client. The system must communicate via ports, so once you decide that a port serves web requests, it is more likely that you will put a Web Browser at the other end of that connection instead of directly connecting it to the Yinzer Member.

9.5.3 Components

Each of the boxes in the system context diagram is a *component instance* (an instantiated *component type*). This book uses the definition of a component from Clements et al. (2010), which states that "Components [are] the principal computation elements and data stores that execute in a system." Components may only communicate, directly or indirectly, using ports and connectors.

When you draw diagrams that show component instances, you should show all of the ports and connectors. This practice is strongly encouraged as you can imagine the frustration of analyzing a diagram and making conclusions, only to later learn that there were other interactions that were omitted from the diagram. By constraining how the components communicate and insisting that your diagrams show all the communication paths, you stand a fighting chance of understanding a system from its diagrams. This idea is discussed further in Section 13.7.1. If you need to draw a simplified diagram that omits connections or components, put a note on the diagram so that this is clear to readers.

The system context diagram shows the system as it would exist at *runtime*, connected to other systems that you represent as component instances. In this example, there are six component instances: a single instance of the Yinzer System, two different Web Browser instances, two different Email Client instances, and an instance of an Email Server. Notice that even if the two Web Browser component instances were running exactly the same code you could still differentiate their instances. Indeed, the Yinzer System must distinguish the instances because one browser is being served web pages for a Yinzer Member, while the other is being served web pages for a Non-Member, even though both web browsers have the same *component type*.

The relationship between a component type and a component instance is the same as the relationship between a class and an object. You can read the declaration of a class or a component type in the source code, and you find class instances (i.e., objects) and component instances at runtime.

You already saw the use of invariants in the domain model and you can use them to constrain how the component instances are arranged. You could, for example, write an invariant that required the Member's Web Browser to support HTML 4.01 or higher.

9.5.4 Ports and connectors

As seen in Figure 9.4, The Yinzer System communicates via four *ports*: one that answers web requests for Yinzer Non-Members, one that answers web requests about the job network, one that answers web requests about advertisements, and one that sends out emails. Three ports provide services (the web ports) and one requires a service (the email port). Essentially all programming languages let you express that some code *provides* a service but notice that the Yinzer System *requires* a compatible SMTP server for email. Not every port can be categorized as either a provides-port or a requires-port, but many can be, so your diagrams should include that distinction when reasonable.

In contrast to a use case diagram, a system context diagram localizes each use case to a port on the Yinzer System component. The Contacts port supports the Invite Contact, Accept Invitation, and Add Employment use cases. The Job/Advertisements port supports the Post Advertisement and Match User use cases. The Non-Member port supports parts of the Invite Contact use case.

Ports interact via *connectors*, which are pathways of runtime interaction between two or more components. The system is shown using web connectors, SMTP connectors, and IMAP / POP connectors. Other, more general, connectors include procedure calls, events, pipes, shared memory, and batch transfers.

Like a scenario shows just one of many possible behavior paths of the system, the system context diagram[2] shows just one of many possible configurations of the system. Over time, the number and identity of Yinzer Members and Non-Members connecting to the system changes, and the system context diagram would change correspondingly.

---

[2]Chapter 12 will describe how to draw a component assembly using component types instead of instances.

You can assign *properties* to any element in your models, but they are most commonly seen on connectors. You might want to use a property to declare the throughput of the connector, or its reliability. For example, the SMTP connector might have the following properties: 1000 emails / second, encrypted, synchronous.

9.5.5   Design decisions

When you look at the design for a system, it can be hard to tell which parts are there because of important, reasoned decisions. Other parts are just acceptable designs that fill space between the important decisions that the developers agonized over.

Consider, for example, Figure 9.4 that shows the context diagram for the Yinzer system with the Yinzer member using a web browser to use the system, which appears to be a client-server system with a thin client. Perhaps the big decision was to build a client-server system, and the choice of using a thin client instead of a thick one was just one of several acceptable alternatives.

There is some debate among architecture experts about the best way to describe a system. Some believe it is best expressed as a set of views. Others believe it is best expressed as a set of design decisions. For the most part, this book follows the views approach but encourages you to document your important design decisions too. What is undisputed is that highlighting the most important design decisions provides insight into what you spent time designing, and is an effective way to describe your architecture.

9.5.6   Modules

The Yinzer system is constructed with source code that you can organize into *modules*, or packages. You can use the UML package element, which graphically looks like a folder, to represent a module in your diagrams. Figure 9.5 shows the modules for the Yinzer system boundary. This set of modules aligns well with the architecture abstractions, which makes it easy for someone reading the code to infer the architecture. The idea of architecturally-evident code is elaborated in Section 10.3.

There is a module for each of the ports because users of the system need to know how that port works in order to use the system. Each port will interact with external systems so the datatypes that are exchanged must be revealed. Both of the Web Ports will be exchanging HTML and HTTP data. The SMTP Client Port will be exchanging SMTP data in emails. If the datatypes you exchange with other systems were proprietary, revealing their structure would be essential, but since HTML, HTTP, and SMTP are defined standards, you could omit their definition here. The Yinzer System module is also shown, but is marked as private because in the system boundary you do not want to reveal the implementation details of the system, only the necessary interface elements.

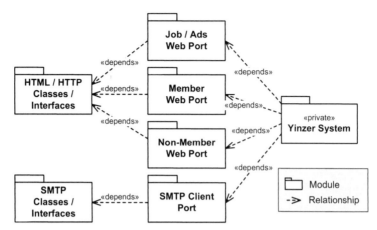

Figure 9.5: A view of the Yinzer boundary model that shows the externally-visible modules and dependencies. The organization of the modules foreshadows the architecturally-evident coding style described in Section 10.3.

Inside of each module you would expect to see the source code artifacts, like classes, interfaces, and headers. The details would vary by the chosen programming language, so for example in C you would expect .h header files, and in Java you would expect to see interfaces and classes.

The modules are related to each other by the *dependency* relationship. A dependency between two modules means that one module may need to change when the other module does.

9.5.7 Deployment

The Yinzer system will be deployed onto hardware and the hardware's configuration will impact how the system performs. Figure 9.6 shows the component instances for the system deployed both at a primary and backup data center, which are examples of *environmental elements*, or sometimes simply called *nodes*. The figure also shows that the user's PC is connected to the data center by the internet, and that the primary data center is connected to the backup via an intranet, which are examples of *communication channels* (sometimes called *links*, but note that the term "link" means something else in snapshots).

This diagram shows how running component instances are allocated to hardware, for example that the User PC hardware is running an instance of the Web Browser software. It could also show how source code is allocated. If, for example, you had an AJAX style web application that required code to run on the user's PC, you could have showed a module deployed onto that environmental element.

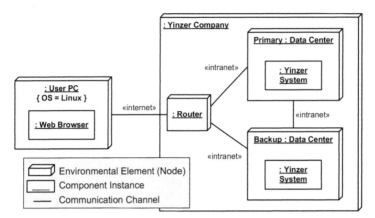

Figure 9.6: A view from the allocation viewtype showing environmental elements (User PC's, Routers, and Data Centers) and communication channels (the internet and intranet links) of the Yinzer system. It also shows component instances that are hosted on the hardware.

Functionality scenarios can be used in understanding behavior related to deployed hardware and software. For example, a scenario could describe the sequence of actions taken to migrate software to a new server, or what happens during backups. Oftentimes getting software running from scratch can be difficult, as can upgrading existing software. You can express how the installation or upgrade of software should proceed through a scenario that describes the steps.

9.5.8   Quality attribute scenarios and architecture drivers

The easiest way you can communicate your thoughts about quality attributes is to prioritize several of them for your system. For the Yinzer system, you might prioritize them this way:

scalability > modifiability > security > usability

Such a ranking is trivially easy to write down and distribute throughout your team. It may simply inform everyone, or it might stimulate discussion about the priorities, but either way it will guide design and coding choices the team makes every day.

A more explicit yet still lightweight technique of describing quality attribute requirements is to write them as *quality attribute scenarios*. A QA scenario can be described using a six-part template consisting of the source, stimulus, environment, response, and response measure (Bass, Clements and Kazman, 2003). Using this template helps the requirement to be clear and testable. Figure 9.7 shows a single QA scenario for the Yinzer system. Most systems are likely to have a handful of QA scenarios.

Source	Yinzer Member
Stimulus	Request web page from Yinzer server
Environment	Normal operations
Artifact	Entire system
Response	Server replies with web page
Response Measure	Web page sent out by Yinzer system within 1 second
Full QA scenario	A Yinzer Member clicks on a link in his Web Browser; it sends a request to the Yinzer system, which sends out a web page as a reply within 1 second

Figure 9.7: An example of a full quality attribute scenario for the Yinzer System. You may omit some sections, but you should strive to write falsifiable scenarios.

QA scenarios[3] work great for obviously measurable qualities like latency, and less well for qualities like maintainability and usability. For example, you could write a quality attribute scenario saying that a developer must be able to switch the database vendor within one week. This would presumably inspire decisions like using vanilla SQL rather than vendor extensions, but it is hard to know how long a hypothetical modification will take. This modifiability scenario is easy to describe, but others can be much more difficult.

You can investigate the suitability of your architecture by introducing *prioritization* to your quality attribute scenarios. To do so, you require that each quality attribute scenario is rated both by stakeholders and by developers. Both rate the quality attribute scenario on a { High, Medium, Low } scale, with stakeholders rating its importance and developers rating how hard it will be to achieve. This yields a tuple such as (High importance, Medium difficulty), usually shortened to just (H, M).

Some quality attribute scenarios will be easy: the ones rated (H, L). And others are likely to be deferred or watered down: the ones rated (L, H). But others, usually the ones rated (H, H), are both important and hard to achieve, so developers will need to pay considerable attention to them as the system is designed. Such quality attribute scenarios are known as *architecture drivers* (Bass, Clements and Kazman, 2003) because developers will use them as test cases when creating and evaluating architecture options. Architectural decisions, such as the use of a 3-tier style, will make achieving the architectural drivers easier or harder. The list of architectural

---

[3]The term *scenario* has been used by different software architecture authors to mean different things. Rather than invent new terminology, this book refers to *functionality scenarios* and *quality attribute scenarios* to distinguish the two ideas. You may shorten the terms to *scenario* and *QA scenario* because they otherwise can be rather long.

drivers is usually small, and may include particularly difficult scenarios as well. Note that the idea of architecture drivers and the rating system come from the ATAM technique, described in Section 15.6.

9.5.9 Tradeoffs

You would like your system to be ideal in every quality attribute dimension: perfectly secure, perfectly usable, and unbelievably fast. But getting more of one quality attribute generally means getting less of another one, meaning that there is a *tradeoff* between them. Achieving more security in your system may hinder usability. The Yinzer system sends Non-Members an email with a link back to the Yinzer website. Anyone who clicks on this link can see the event details, but the link has a large random number in it so it would be hard to guess. You can imagine designs that are more secure, but they would likely be harder to use.

Some tradeoffs apply to all systems, such as the tradeoff between usability and security. Other tradeoffs originate in the domain of the system. Consider the Yinzer domain where companies must describe the required job skills in an advertisement, but those requirements could be structured (e.g., a taxonomy of skills) or freeform (e.g., a block of text). If they are structured, the job of matching seekers to jobs is easier algorithmically but harder on users. If they are freeform, then users are relieved of work, but the mechanism to match jobs with seekers will entail more guesswork. Finding domain tradeoffs is like finding a nugget of gold in a stream: it is a valuable insight that can be quickly conveyed to others not yet expert in the domain. Tradeoffs influence what will be easy or hard for your system to achieve.

That concludes the walkthrough of the boundary model. We now shift to describing the internals model, which still describes the Yinzer system, but now you will see how it is implemented behind its interface.

9.5.10 Component assembly

A *component assembly* shows a specific configuration of component instances. You have already seen one special case of a component assembly: the system context diagram from Figure 9.4. In general, a component assembly can show any collection of components, ports, and connectors, but the system context diagram is constrained to show the system and its connections to other systems. In the internals model, you use component assemblies to show the internal designs of components.

In the Yinzer system context diagram, you already saw that a component called the Yinzer System exists and it has four ports: Non-Member, Contacts, Job/Ads, and SMTP Client. The Yinzer System internals model is required to have the same four ports, but it reveals details about the inside of the Yinzer System component. Figure 9.8 shows four internal components: Contacts, Advertisements, Users, and Emails.

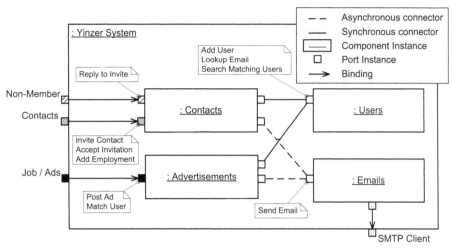

Figure 9.8: A component assembly of Yinzer System from the internals model. It shows the same Yinzer System component instance shown in Figure 9.4, but also reveals its refinement into four internal component instances and shows the bindings between external and internal ports.

This component assembly is logically nested inside of the Yinzer System component instance from the system context diagram. The outer box on the component assembly is labeled in the top left corner indicating that it is an instance of the Yinzer System.

The component assembly shows *bindings* between the external ports on the Yinzer System and the internal ports, those on Contacts, Advertisements, and Emails. A binding between an external and internal port means that any interactions with the external port are handled by the internal port. A binding is not a connector and no work is done in a binding. Bindings exist to maintain encapsulation, since you want to tell external systems about the Job/Ads port but hide the existence of the Advertisements component. When binding ports, the easiest case is if the two ports are identical, but the internal port must at least be compatible with the external port (e.g., be a subtype), so it could for example provide additional operations that are not visible on the external port.

In a Java program, users of a class often depend on an interface that the class supports, rather than depending on the class directly. You are seeing a similar situation here with components. Users of a component depend on ports rather than the component itself. This gives the developer flexibility because it enables substitution and evolution by hiding the internals of the component.

You may have noticed some differences in the style of Figure 9.8 compared to earlier figures. Here, UML notes are used to describe the responsibilities of the ports, which is an alternative to detailed legends like those in Figure 9.4. This style has the advantage that you can see exactly what operations are on each port, but it would be impractical if there were long lists of operations.

Boundary models and internals models follow a recursive pattern. In the system context diagram, you saw that the Yinzer System component existed, but you only knew about its boundary, not its insides. Here, in the internals model, you see the insides of the Yinzer System and discover that you can only see the boundary of the Contacts, Advertisements, Users, and Emails components, but not their insides. You could continue refining and show internals models for each of those components. At a point of your choosing, you stop refining and show or build the actual implementation, which might be classes, procedures, functions, etc.

9.5.11   Two-level functionality scenarios

Functionality scenarios were used previously in the domain model and in the boundary models and they work similarly here, in the internals model. The important difference is that you can now show how the internal components collaborate. One way to do this is to start with a boundary model scenario and elaborate it with inter-component interactions that can only be seen in the internals model. Figure 9.9 shows how the steps from the boundary model scenario in Figure 9.3, labeled with numbers, are elaborated across the internals model components, labeled with letters.

9.5.12   Responsibilities

Models, especially graphical ones, use short names to refer to complex parts. For example, the three words in "Guest Web Port" provide a minimal explanation about what that port does. It is easy for two developers to think that they agree on a design but discover later that they had different assumptions about what the responsibilities of the Guest Web Port.

Fortunately, listing the *responsibilities* of a port or other architectural element is inexpensive and effective. It follows the concept of responsibility-driven design (Wirfs-Brock, Wilkerson and Wiener, 1990) and mirrors the use of Class Responsibility and Collaborator (CRC) cards in object-oriented design (Beck and Cunningham, 1989). Responsibilities are easily written down in a table or can be put on diagrams as UML notes.

9.5.13   Constraints as guide rails

Software developers are constrained by the requirements from the domain and may have technical solution constraints too, but they also voluntarily impose additional *constraints* on their designs. This seems counter-intuitive since it is already hard to create a system, and adding restrictions would seem to make it harder, but developers voluntarily constrain their designs so they can control a risk or enable a quality of the

Name: Kevin takes a job at Widgetron
Initial state: Alan and Owen are Members of Yinzer; Kevin is not. Alan works at Widgetron.
Actors: Alan, Kevin, Owen
Steps:

1. Alan invites Kevin to be a Contact in his Network. / The system sends Kevin an email.
    a) Contacts component looks up Kevin's email address with Users component. Kevin is not found as a Yinzer user.
    b) Contacts component composes an email to Kevin inviting him to join Yinzer and Alan's network and asks Email component to send it.
2. Kevin clicks a link in his email, joins Yinzer, and accepts Alan's invitation to be a Contact.
    a) Kevin, by clicking link in the email, uses his browser to go to the Yinzer website (via its Non-Member port) and replies to the invite.
    b) Contacts component adds Kevin as a user of the Yinzer system with no contacts.
    c) Contacts component registers Kevin and Alan as contacts of each other.
3. Widgetron posts an Ad for a Job for a software developer. / The system auto-matches Owen to the Job, sending him an email.
    a) Advertisements component extracts relevant features of the Ad.
    b) Advertisements component searches the Users for matches, yielding Owen.
    c) Advertisements component composes an email to Owen informing him of the Ad and asks Email component to send it.
4. Alan sees the Ad and matches Kevin to the Job. / The system sends Kevin an email.
    a) Alan uses the Advertisements component to match Kevin with the Ad.
    b) Advertisements component composes an email to Kevin informing him of the Ad and Alan's recommendation.
5. Kevin takes the job and changes his Yinzer profile to add his employment at Widgetron.
    a) Kevin uses the Contacts component to update his profile.

Figure 9.9: Yinzer System internal functionality scenario that starts with the numbered steps of the boundary functionality scenario from Figure 9.3 and elaborates how the components of the internals model accomplish them (the lettered sub-steps).

system. Such constraints act as *guide rails*, channeling the system in the desired direction.

Imagine a system that must run on a small computer. A developer might assign RAM budgets to various components to ensure that the system will fit in memory. Or consider a system that will be ported to run on other operating systems. A developer might insulate the system from operating system (OS) details that will vary, restricting what calls the system can make. Consider: if developers did not constrain their system by assigning RAM budgets or limiting OS calls, how would they know that the system could fit on a small machine or could be ported to another OS?

Constraints are necessary in order to analyze a system: *No constraints means no analysis.* Without constraints you have a pile of code that could do anything: it could exceed RAM budgets, depend on a particular OS, circumvent the cache coherency policy, neglect to release locks, or violate access restrictions. During design, developers reason about how an assembled collection of parts acts as a system. They constrain what the parts of the system must do and must not do. The constraints enable them to know that the sum of the parts will behave as intended.

The design of the Yinzer system uses constraints to ensure that its quality attribute scenarios can be fulfilled. Sending an email can easily take several seconds as remote servers are contacted and the message is delivered, yet the quality attribute scenario requires the web pages to keep one-second response time. The design uses asynchronous connectors between the web facing components and the Email component to queue outgoing emails so that the web facing components are not waiting while the email is delivered.

9.5.14 Architectural styles

Sometimes a set of constraints occurs regularly enough that it is useful to name it as a pattern. These patterns are called *architectural styles* and are defined as "a specialization of element and relation types, together with a set of constraints on how they can be used." (Clements et al., 2010). Architectural styles restrict the design in order to give the developer control over a risk or to enable a quality attribute.

Consider the Apache web server, a system that is intended to be open for plug-in extensions. Apache is designed so that new code can be inserted into a chain of filters that process web requests or responses, what is called a pipe-and-filter architectural style. One of the characteristics of the pipe-and-filter style is that each filter does an isolated job, and so it is easy to add filters to the pipeline. Apache chose an architectural style that made it easier to achieve its goal of modification by third party developers. Notice that the architectural style not only constrained the design, it provided a vocabulary to talk about these particular kinds of components and connectors, naming them filters and pipes.

Most architectural styles apply to the component and connector types and the topologies of the component assemblies. This provides control over the runtime behavior and qualities of the system. Styles can also apply to modules (e.g., in the layered style) and environmental elements.

This completes the walkthrough of the design model for the Yinzer system. It provided an overview of the common models used in the design. Most of the elements and diagrams that were used to describe the boundary model, such as design decisions, tradeoffs, and use case diagrams, can also be used on internals models. The remaining chapters in the book will provide additional information on how to use the ideas covered here.

9.6 Viewtypes

Looking back on all the views, you can see patterns in how they are organized. Some views are easy to reconcile with each other, while others are not. For example, it is easy to reconcile the Yinzer functionality scenario with its component assembly, and you could imagine merging these views together into a single view without much difficulty.

But other views are hard to reconcile with the source code view, such as a view of the instantiated objects or components. You would have to scour the source code and mentally animate it to imagine which component instances will appear at runtime, and in which configurations. Put another way, if you have the source code in one hand and a component assembly in the other, it will take you a while to determine if that code could possibly create that configuration of component instances at runtime. While it was easy to reconcile the functionality scenario and component assembly views, there is no obvious way to reconcile module and runtime views. What you would like to do is group together the views that are easy to reconcile.

9.6.1 Viewtype definition

This grouping is accomplished through the idea of viewtypes. A *viewtype* is a set, or category, of views that can be easily reconciled with each other (Clements et al., 2010). The views that cannot be reconciled belong to different viewtypes. In software architecture, viewtypes[4] apply to any design or code model, including the top-level boundary model and any nested internals or boundary models.

It is an unfortunate fact that you cannot easily reconcile every view of a software system. Clearly, in some sense all of the views must be reconcilable, if only in your head, because you build systems that conform to all of the views. A good way of thinking about reconciling views it is to consider someone else's design, not your own, and how hard it is to find flaws and inconsistencies between their views.

9.6.2 Standard architectural viewtypes

The three standard viewtypes in software architecture are the module viewtype, the runtime viewtype, and the allocation viewtype. The *module viewtype* contains views of the elements you can see at compile-time. It includes artifacts like source code and configuration files. Definitions of component types, connector types, and port types are also in the module viewtype, along with definitions of classes and interfaces.

---

[4]The term *viewtype* should not be confused with the term *viewpoint*, which is the view of a system from a single perspective, such as the view of a single stakeholder. A viewtype contains a group of similar views and categorizes views so you can answer the question "what type (i.e., category) of view is this?"

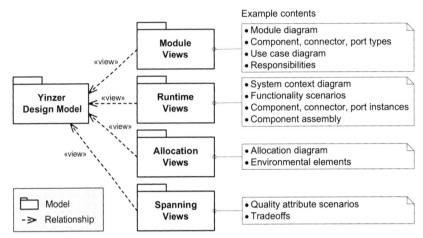

Figure 9.10: The Yinzer design model acts as a master model that (conceptually) contains all design details, so it is too big to use directly. Views show a selected subset of its details, possibly transforming them. Views are categorized into the three standard viewtypes (module, runtime, and allocation viewtypes) plus spanning views.

The *runtime viewtype*, also called the *component and connector (C&C) viewtype*, contains views of elements that you can see at runtime. It includes artifacts like functionality scenarios, responsibility lists, and the component assemblies. Instances of components, connectors, and ports are in the runtime viewtype, as are objects (class instances).

The *allocation viewtype* contains views of elements related to the deployment of the software onto hardware. It includes deployment diagrams, descriptions of environmental elements like servers, and descriptions of communication channels like ethernet links. It may also include geographical elements, so that you can describe two servers in different cities.

Figure 9.10 shows a graphical summary of the three viewtypes with a non-exhaustive list of the contents of each viewtype. It shows one additional viewtype, the *spanning viewtype*, which contains views that cross over between two or more viewtypes, because not everything will fit neatly into the categories. Here is an example of a tradeoff that spans viewtypes. You decide to denormalize a database schema (described in the module viewtype) in order to achieve greater transaction throughput (described in the runtime viewtype) so you describe that tradeoff in the spanning viewtype. Four viewtypes, and some example contents often found in the viewtypes, are summarized in Figure 9.11.

Viewtype	Example viewtype contents
Module Viewtype	Modules, layers, dependencies, responsibilities (like CRC), database schemas, interfaces, classes, component types, connector types
Runtime Viewtype	Object instances, component instances, connector instances, behavior models (state machines, scenarios), responsibilities (instance-based)
Allocation Viewtype	Deployed software, geography, computation nodes
Spanning	Tradeoffs (quality attribute, business, other), functionality scenarios, quality attribute scenarios

Figure 9.11: The three standard viewtypes (module, runtime, and allocation viewtypes) plus spanning views. Views within a viewtype are easy to reconcile with each other, but hard to reconcile with views from other viewtypes.

9.6.3 Types and instances in different viewtypes

A viewtype contains views that are easy to reconcile with each other, while the views in different viewtypes are difficult to reconcile. Source code directly expresses classes, interfaces, modules, and (if you squint) component types, so they are easy to reconcile and are all part of the module viewtype. On the other hand, when you look at a view of component types, it is not obvious what component instances will appear, so types and instances are different viewtypes.

As a result, component *types* exist in the module viewtype and component *instances* exist in the runtime viewtype. It may be surprising to hear this, so to understand it better, it is helpful to consider the parallel with classes and objects. When you look at source code, you can trivially see what classes exist because you define them directly in a programming language. Conversely, you cannot directly see class instances (i.e., objects) because they are not created until the program runs.

9.6.4 Reasoning across viewtypes

The divide between the module and runtime viewtype has been noted for quite some time. In 1968, Edsger Dijkstra, using slightly different terminology, expressed clearly how hard it is to understand how code will behave at runtime by looking at its source code, and gives advice on how to minimize the problem (Dijkstra, 1968):

> [O]ur intellectual powers are rather geared to master static relations and ... our powers to visualize processes evolving in time are relatively poorly developed. For that reason we should do (as wise programmers aware of

our limitations) our utmost best to shorten the conceptual gap between the static program and the dynamic process, to make the correspondence between the program (spread out in text space) and the process (spread out in time) as trivial as possible.

The generalized point is that reasoning across viewtypes is difficult, whether it is module to runtime, or runtime to allocation. As a consequence, you should do two things. First, you should take Dijkstra's advice and build in a style that makes the runtime viewtype easier to imagine when you examine things in the module viewtype. Section 10.3 describes an architecturally-evident coding style, which is a way of structuring your programs so that other people can see the architectural elements and envision what they look like at runtime.

Second, you should reason from an appropriate viewtype. Each viewtype has an affinity for certain kinds of questions, as discussed in Section 3.5. Asking questions about how many instances exist and how they are communicating to each other are best answered by looking at a runtime view. With some difficulty and inaccuracy, you can look at source code, mentally animate it, and answer those questions, but they are straightforward to answer in the runtime viewtype.

9.6.5   Stitching together viewtypes

While providing separate views for various concerns is helpful in understanding each concern in isolation, it leaves open the problem of understanding the architecture as a whole. The "+1" in Philippe Kruchten's 4+1 architectural views is for functionality scenarios that weave through the other four views.

Scenarios cut across viewtype boundaries so that they can stitch together the otherwise disjoint views. Most scenarios describe a sequence of events within a single viewtype, such as a sequence of actions that the system performs at runtime. But some scenarios span viewtypes, such as how a system responds at runtime to a change in its physical deployment, or how a web server like Apache can initialize its (runtime) component instances based on a (module viewtype) configuration file.

Tradeoffs can span viewtypes also. Modifiability is primarily concerned with the module viewtype and performance with the runtime viewtype, but a tradeoff between them would span the two viewtypes. By separating out distinct views of your architecture, you have divided the problem, and by using scenarios and tradeoffs you conquer it by showing how the views relate to describe the whole architecture.

9.6.6   Advice on completeness

If you are trying to explain your system to someone, it is a good idea to include a representative view from each viewtype. Otherwise, what is obvious to you as the developer (e.g., that the system is deployed on one computer) may not be clear to others. Thinking about each viewtype also helps avoid tunnel vision during design, ensuring that you have at least considered where the software will be deployed, for example.

So far you have seen diagrams representing the system at runtime but they showed just one instant in time. However, many systems change their runtime configuration as they execute. The next section discusses dynamic architecture models.

9.7 Dynamic architecture models

Developers are comfortable building systems where the configuration of objects (class instances) changes at runtime. However, because components are larger than objects, their runtime configurations tend to change less, if they change at all. Developers try to minimize runtime architectural changes because it is easier to analyze a single static configuration than all of the possibilities that come with runtime reconfigurations. Some designs require changes at runtime, however, such as peer-to-peer voice chat systems that reconfigure themselves continually as computers join or leave the network.

Many systems change their configuration of components only during startup and shutdown and have a stable configuration of components for the rest of their lifetime. When you show a component assembly, you are usually showing this *steady state configuration* of the system. You must be aware that this is a simplification of the truth because errors can easily occur when you do not think about the dynamics of startup and shutdown.

There are a few ways to make it easier to envision the runtime configuration from the source code. One is to follow an architecturally-evident coding style, discussed in Section 10.3. Another is to move the configuration out of the source code, which must be executed, and instead put it into a declarative configuration file. Many frameworks require this, such as Apache Struts (Holmes, 2006), Enterprise Java Beans (Monson-Haefel, 2001), and NASA/JPL's MDS (Ingham et al., 2005). While it is possible to statically analyze source code, it is a difficult task, but analyzing a declarative configuration file is easy.

Dynamic architecture models, which describe how an architecture changes at runtime, are an open research area. When possible, you should avoid designs where the architecture changes at runtime for two reasons. First, static architectures are easier for developers to understand, which should lead to better modifiability and fewer bugs introduced. And second, static architectures are easier to analyze for quality attributes. Sometimes the nature of the problem or quality attribute requirements will force you to use a dynamic architecture. When that happens, you will find yourself out on the leading edge of software engineering with less support from empirical data, modeling concepts, and engineering techniques.

9.8 Architecture description languages

When you draw a diagram, you are actually using a modeling *language*, such as UML, the Unified Modeling Language. Architecture description languages generally have poor support for dynamic architectures, but they do have adequate support for static architectures.

When you draw a diagram, you probably do not think of it as a language, or imagine representing the same information in a textual language, but they are equivalent. A simple language might say that you can have any number of alternating *a*'s and *b*'s, and express it like this: *(ab)**. Similarly, your architecture diagram might say that you can have any number of clients and servers, so long as a server has no more than 10 clients.

When you choose a tool to draw architecture diagrams, you are embracing a set of constraints imposed by an architecture language. If you use a general purpose drawing tool then you have almost no constraints, though readers may wonder about the semantics (meaning) of the purple triangle on your diagram. Choosing a tool that draws UML diagrams, or one that supports another *architecture description language* (ADL), constrains you to use the elements in that language, such as rectangles that represent components (but no purple triangles).

The formality of the language constrains your expressions, for better or for worse. After using an architecture description language for a while, you will think about system design in terms of component types, connector instances, source code modules, etc., because these are the concepts in the formalism and perhaps enforced by your drawing tool. This is good because these concepts are endorsed by the software engineering community as being helpful, but it can be frustrating when your language cannot express your ideas.

Using a tool that constrains your syntax is no guarantee that your designs make sense. Noam Chomsky famously illustrated this principle with a syntactically correct sentence that makes no sense: "Colorless green ideas sleep furiously." (Chomsky, 2002). A tool will guarantee that your diagrams conform to the language constraints (syntax), but not that they have meaning (semantics).

Another option is to use a general purpose drawing tool and use self-discipline to draw diagrams that conform to a language, say UML. When you are starting out, however, it is best to use a tool that supports the language directly, since its constraints act like training wheels on a bicycle until you are ready to ride on your own. You may dismiss this idea, thinking that you do not need such help. But I have taught architecture to plenty of bright people (such as you) and I see, over and over, those bright folks creating gibberish diagrams with both syntactic and semantic mistakes until they "learn to ride the bike" and solidify their conceptual model of architecture.

This book's pragmatic advice is to use UML for architecture models unless there are strong arguments against it. Unlike other ADLs, UML has modern tool support from many vendors and the biggest base of developers who know how to read it. It is not without problems, but it works well enough and there is plenty of advice on how to use it effectively. While there is likely an ADL out there that better suits your needs, it will have tool support from a single vendor at most, and few developers will know how to read your models. UML has the additional benefit that it works for domain, design, and code models, so you will not have to switch languages.

9.9 Conclusion

The software architecture canonical model structure is based on three primary models: the domain, design, and code models. Each of these is treated as a master model with a full set of details. You avoid becoming lost in the details because views allow you to reveal or hide selected details.

This conceptual model is helpful because software projects require you to process and organize many bits of information. One bit might be the legal protocol for interacting with a credit card processing system. Another bit might be the dependencies in the module build system. And yet another bit might be quirks on how a legacy system represents international addresses. Working on a system means integrating details like these into a model that relates them and enables you to design a solution.

This chapter provided more detail about the conceptual model of software architecture. It provided information to help you partition your design into manageable pieces, knowledge about how to solve problems, and a set of architectural abstractions, such as components, that you can use to reason about your software. You will probably never build a complete design model. Instead, you chop up the design model into smaller pieces using views, encapsulation, and nesting.

An internals model is a refinement of a boundary model. Both are views of the design model but they differ in the details they reveal. Anything that is true in the boundary model must be true in the internals model. Any commitments made in the boundary model (such as the number and type of ports, QA scenarios) must be upheld in the internals model. Because the design model is related to the domain model by designation, selected facts about the domain are designated to be also true in the design.

Both the boundary and internals models are described using the same elements, such as scenarios, components, connectors, ports, responsibilities, modules, classes, interfaces, environmental elements, and tradeoffs. Some of these are elaborated in the internals model, such as the component assembly and functionality scenarios.

A viewtype is a set, or category, of views that can be easily reconciled with each other. The three standard viewtypes, or categories of views, are the module viewtype, the runtime viewtype, and the allocation viewtype. The module view contains tangible artifacts and definitions that developers can manipulate, such as classes, interfaces, and component types. The runtime viewtype contains instances like objects, component instances, and connector instances. The arrangement of the instances can change at runtime and there may be multiple instances of a class or component type. The allocation viewtype describes how elements from the module and runtime viewtypes are deployed to hardware and locations.

You should pay attention to both what your software does (its functionality) as well as how it does it (its quality attributes). The two are mostly independent, so two different systems can do the same thing, but one might be fast while the other is secure. Architecture experts tend to focus attention on quality attributes because the architecture has a big impact on them.

Most of your models will show a static configuration of elements, but some architectures are dynamic and change at runtime. It is difficult to reason about dynamic architectures and there is limited tool and analysis support. Most architecture description languages, such as UML, support static architectures but have limited support for dynamicism.

9.10   Further reading

The suggested design views in this chapter show you how to bridge functionality and quality attributes in architecture models. Bosch (2000) covers some of this ground by making the point that you can initially partition a system based on functionality then tweak it to achieve the desired quality attributes. (More details on decomposition strategies are found in Section 11.3).

The functional modeling approach in this chapter is inspired by Catalysis (D'Souza and Wills, 1998). The Catalysis software process uses refinement extensively to enable zooming in on details and zooming out to see the essential problems. In so doing, it cleans up the distinction between use cases, scenarios, and operations, showing them all to be actions at different levels of refinement. This chapter's approach to quality attribute modeling is inspired by work at the SEI, including Bass, Clements and Kazman (2003) and Clements et al. (2010).

Architectural styles can be looked at as simply architectural patterns, but their potential to be much more is evident when they are formalized as they are in the Acme language (Garlan, Monroe and Wile, 2000) and the Acme Studio tool (Garlan and Schmerl, 2009). The insight has probably occurred in other contexts, but David Garlan's course on software architecture (Garlan, 2003) describes how constraints and styles are necessary tools of an architect and without them there can be no analysis. Chapter 14 of this book provides a detailed look at architectural styles.

If you do decide to use a modeling language besides UML, the thorough comparison found in the Taylor, Medvidović, and Dashofy software architecture book will be helpful (Taylor, Medvidović and Dashofy, 2009).

Chapter 10

The Code Model

Source code is both the end deliverable and the medium in which solutions are expressed. Architecture models are not the end deliverable, so they are useful only when they can be related to the code. Consequently, it is important to understand the relationship between architecture models and code.

At first glance, that relationship may seem straightforward. For example, a model that talks about modules or components is easy to relate to the corresponding code elements. But models can also include ideas that are hard to relate, such as, "A lock must be held before every access to this data." You can relate that architectural idea to code, but it is not a straightforward structural correspondence. There is a *gap* between architecture models and code.

You will learn about three topics in this chapter. The first is the differences between architecture models and code. The second is ways to handle their inevitable divergence. And the third is a style of programming, an *architecturally-evident coding style*, that embeds hints about your architecture into your code to reduce the amount of *design intent* that is lost.

10.1 Model-code gap

To begin understanding the differences between architecture models and code, it is helpful to start with an inventory of what each of them contains. Figure 10.1 summarizes the kinds of elements you commonly find in architecture models and in source code. As you scrutinize the lists of elements, you can notice differences in their vocab-

Location	Examples of elements
Architecture model	Modules, components, connectors, ports, component assemblies, styles, invariants, responsibility allocations, design decisions, rationales, protocols, quality attributes, and models (e.g., security policies, concurrency models)
Source code	Packages, classes, methods, variables, functions, procedures, statements

Figure 10.1: A summary of the kinds of elements commonly found in architecture models and in source code. There are differences in vocabulary, abstraction, design commitments, and presence of intensional/extensional elements.

ulary, abstraction, design commitments, and presence of general/enumerated (i.e., intensional/extensional) statements. Let's take a look at each of those differences.

Vocabulary.   A simple comparison of the lists of elements in architecture models and source code reveals that they use different vocabulary to talk about the same things. For example, architecture models contain *modules* while source code contains *packages*, which is a nomenclature difference, but in essence the same thing.

Other vocabulary differences exist because architecture models and code express distinct ideas. Consider a thought experiment where you express your architecture model in UML and you also automatically generate a UML model of your source code. When you compare these two UML models, you will find differences. For example, your source code model does not express the component types or instances found in your architecture model. While method call connectors and event bus connectors both show up in your architecture model, only method calls are seen in your source code model. The architecture model and source code have different vocabulary because each expresses ideas the other does not.

Abstraction.   Architecture models tend to be more abstract than source code in two ways. First, a single element in an architecture model often aggregates multiple elements in source code. For example, a component type in an architecture model may map to a dozen classes in the source code. Similarly, an architecture model may show a client or a server, each corresponding to many classes or procedures.

Second, when they describe the same element, architecture models generally describe that element with fewer details than source code does. An architecture model may stop its descriptions once it reaches the level of modules and components, but source code continues the detail through classes, methods, and instance variables. If you imagine a gradient on which you place different kinds of elements, architecture models contain the more abstract elements, source code contains the less abstract elements, and the two overlap by both including some of the elements in the middle of the gradient.

Intensional / Extensional	Architecture model element	Mapping into source code
Extensional (defined by enumerated instances)	Modules, components, connectors, ports, component assemblies	These correspond neatly to elements in the source code, though often at a higher level of abstraction (e.g., one component corresponds to multiple classes)
Intensional (quantified across all instances)	Styles, invariants, responsibility allocations, design decisions, rationales, protocols, quality attributes, and models	Source code will conform to these, but they are not directly expressed in the code. Architecture model has general rules, code has examples.

Figure 10.2: Tabulation of various architectural elements and how they map into code. Extensional elements in the architecture map fairly cleanly to code elements, but intensional elements do not.

Design commitments. Another difference is that architecture models and source code do not both contain the same design commitments. An architecture model may commit to the use of some technologies (e.g., AJAX and REST) but source code goes much farther and commits to how those technologies are implemented. Architecture and design models can make a partial commitment, but source code must make a full commitment, or at least enough of a commitment to be executable. For example, it may be sufficient in an architecture model to state a quality attribute scenario that account lookups happen with 0.25s, but source code will describe the data structures and algorithms necessary to make that happen.

Intensional-extensional. Perhaps the biggest difference between architecture models and source code is that architecture models contain a mixture of intensional and extensional elements, while code has only extensional elements. *Intensional* elements are those that are universally quantified, such as "All filters communicate via pipes," while *extensional* elements are enumerated, such as "The system is composed of a client, an order processor, and an order storage components." Figure 10.2 lists which architecture elements are intensional and extensional.

The distinction between intensional and extensional elements in architecture and code, identified by Amnon Eden and Rick Kazman (Eden and Kazman, 2003), is important because it explains which parts of the architecture model will be harder to map into the source code. Since source code is extensional, extensional elements of the architecture model, like components and component assemblies, are easy to map into the source code. Recall the component type from the Yinzer system design model that was called Contacts. That component would correspond to several classes in the source code. You can even imagine minor changes to the programming language

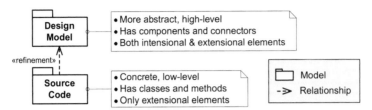

Figure 10.3: Extensional elements in the design model have a refinement relationship to the source code. Intensional elements do not, since they are rarely expressible in the source code, and contribute to the model-code gap.

to let you express components directly. For example, ArchJava adds architectural elements like components and ports to Java (Aldrich, Chambers and Notkin, 2002).

Conversely, it is hard to relate intensional elements, like design decisions, styles, and invariants to the (extensional) source code. Intensional elements establish general rules that apply to all elements, but standard programming languages cannot directly express these rules. Though source code cannot express the rules, it should respect the rules. So, for example, if your architecture model has a design decision (an intensional element) that says to avoid using vendor-specific API's, you cannot express that rule in your C++ source code, but none of your code should use those API's. When you look at source code, you cannot see the design intent of the intensional elements, but the code should respect that design intent.

Model-code gap. Your architecture models and your source code will not show the same things. The difference between them is the *model-code gap*. Your architecture models include some abstract concepts, like components, that your programming language does not, but could. Beyond that, architecture models include intensional elements, like design decisions and constraints, that cannot be expressed in procedural source code at all.

Consequently, the relationship between the architecture model and source code is complicated. It is mostly a refinement relationship, where the extensional elements in the architecture model are refined into extensional elements in source code. This is shown in Figure 10.3. However, intensional elements are not refined into corresponding elements in source code.

Upon learning about the model-code gap, your first instinct may be to avoid it. But reflecting on the origins of the gap gives little hope of a general solution in the short term: architecture models help you reason about complexity and scale because they are abstract and intensional; source code executes on machines because it is concrete and extensional.

Attempts to avoid the gap. People react differently when they hear about the model-code gap. Some see the difficulty as an opportunity to retreat to known ground by avoiding architectural abstractions entirely. However, this would be just one step away from the big ball of mud architecture (Section 14.7). Your ability to handle complexity and scale would be greatly diminished because architecture abstractions exist to give you a handle complexity and scale. While there are difficulties in using the abstractions, managing a sea of classes is probably more difficult.

If you cannot avoid the abstraction gap then you must manage it. There are two primary ways to manage the gap: mechanically and by hand. Mechanically, it may be possible to write in a higher-level, N-th generation language and generate the source code. This is the technique of application builder/generators and Model Driven Engineering (MDE) (Selic, 2003b). By generating code, the gap between the architecture models and the higher-level language is reduced or even eliminated compared to writing normal source code. In a few domains this approach is practical, but the grand vision of MDE is not yet ready for mainstream use.

The other way to manage the abstraction gap is by hand, which means that developers must understand both the architecture models and the code, then ensure they are consistent. The model-code gap contains some accidental complexity that can be helped by aligning architectural elements with programming language elements and representing architectural concepts in the code. Section 10.3 will discuss how to do this using an architecturally-evident coding style. But even after removing the accidental complexity of misalignment, you will need to periodically synchronize your models with your code, as discussed in the next section.

10.2 Managing consistency

Whether you start with source code and build a model, or do the reverse, you must manage two representations of your solution. Initially, the code and models might correspond perfectly, but over time they tend to diverge. Code evolves as features are added and bugs are fixed. Models evolve in response to challenges or planning needs. Divergence happens when the evolution of one or the other yields inconsistencies.

Some inconsistencies between code and models are tolerable, but it depends on the nature of the inconsistency. Perhaps your model describes online performance. Some code you add will not disrupt that model, such as code for an offline statistical analysis feature. In contrast, a seemingly trivial change to multithreaded code can break your concurrency model. Generally, though, you will want to avoid inconsistencies between model and code and there are several ways to do this, summarized in Figure 10.4.

Ignore divergence. One of the most common ways to handle model - code inconsistencies is to simply ignore them. Oftentimes developers can use an outdated model

Strategy	Description
Ignore divergence	Perhaps use an outdated model and remember what has changed.
Ad hoc modeling	Keep the model in your head and re-create it as necessary.
Only high-level models	The most fundamental parts of your architecture change slowly, so you can keep models of only them.
Sync at lifecycle milestone	Reconcile code and models at end of iteration, deployment, or other milestone.
Sync at crisis	Reconcile code and models when something goes wrong, or design review. Surprisingly common.
Constant sync	Expensive and uncommon.

Figure 10.4: Architecture models and source code tend to diverge over time as each evolves. This table summarizes of the strategies for handling the divergence.

but simply remember the ways in which the code has diverged from the model. During presentations, a diagram might be presented with the caveat that it is out of date and the audience is told about the changes.

A variant of this is to plan to use the models only during initial design phases when there is no source code and then to focus attention on the code once it exists. Ignoring the divergence is surprisingly common in practice, and often describes what actually happens despite intentions stated to the contrary.

Ad hoc modeling. Models are created on-the-fly as needed by developers, possibly only on whiteboards. Developers must keep the architecture in their heads and be ready to recreate it for communication or collaboration purposes. They might sketch out the current architecture and their proposed changes, or draw a zoomed in view of a selected part. Teams following agile development are more likely to be doing this, especially if their background includes architectural or UML modeling experience.

Only high-level models. Generally speaking, the more general or abstract the models are, the greater their ability to accommodate changes in the code. For example, an architecture model that only describes a client and server is quite resilient to code changes. A project may choose to keep high-level diagrams updated and use ad hoc modeling for details, which minimizes the documentation burden yet keeps around some diagrams for new developers or to communicate with other teams. This technique is common in practice.

Tools	The use of a tool or higher-level programming language can reduce gaps and divergence, and can lower the synchronizing effort.
Detail level	Higher detail models will incur divergence faster and require more synchronizing effort.
Tolerance	You should understand your project's tolerance for deviations — when do the models need to accurately reflect the code and who will be using them?

Figure 10.5: How can you choose an appropriate model-code synchronization strategy? These three ideas distilled from the list of model-code synchronization strategies can help.

Sync at lifecycle milestone. Developers may evolve the code for some amount of time but wait until the end of an iteration, stage, or release before updating the models. In practice, teams may have good intentions of synchronizing at a milestone, yet defer it endlessly.

Sync at crisis. While the name is amusing, it is common to see teams ignore models until they are in dire need, at which point they furiously update or recreate them. This dire need could be a design problem, a collaboration problem, or perhaps a design review. They may look for tools to recover or reverse-engineer the design and architecture of a system, but their effectiveness is limited because mainstream programming languages cannot express the high-level design intent found in architecture models, as discussed in the previous section.

Constant synchronization. Some teams choose to keep their models and code synchronized at all times, but it requires a lot of effort. It can be appropriate if the project is following a process where coding and design strictly alternate, or if the project is the focus of great external attention. Because of the effort involved, it is relatively uncommon in practice unless only high-level architecture models are maintained, or a tool is used to render UML diagrams of the source code.

How to choose. Which of these strategies is right for your project? Recall why you are using models: to solve problems. The models themselves are not what your customer is asking you to build, so you should focus on how they help you build software even when they become out of date. A security model may be useless if it does not closely match the code, but a model listing your architecture drivers probably retains value even when a bit stale. Figure 10.5 lists three ideas about the use of tools, model detail level, and tolerance for divergence that can help you choose an appropriate strategy.

10.3 Architecturally-evident coding style

The remainder of this chapter discusses the idea of embedding hints about your architecture in the source code, what is called an *architecturally-evident coding style*. Before explaining how that is done, it is important to discuss why it is a good idea.

The minimum requirements for a program are that it runs and does something useful. The code might be a tangle, but if it runs and does something useful then someone will find it acceptable. In general, this is much too low of a standard, primarily because tangled code is hard to maintain. If you write code that works, but you can barely understand it, then it will take a lot of effort to evolve that code.

Consequently, almost all developers use standard control flow constructs and give variables descriptive names, such as "totalExpenses" instead of just "t". These are clues and hints you leave in the code so that someone who reads it later (which includes you) will make the right inferences about your design intent. The computer and compiler do not care what the variable is called, or if control flow is a maze of GOTO statements, but developers do. We take it for granted today, but a few generations ago programmers argued about using standard control flow in programs, though you do still hear some developers complain about descriptive variable names.

A similar but more current elaboration of this idea concerns object-oriented coding style. In a language like C# or Java, you could write programs using a single class and a single intricate method. Doing so would deviate from standard object-oriented practice, however, which is to mirror the types from the program's domain in the source code classes. A program that manipulates addresses and accounts would be expected to have corresponding Address and Account classes. The key idea is that the program's author has a mental model of how the domain works, and so maintenance becomes easier because the code respects and reveals that model.

Developers can go further by embedding clues about other models, such as their architecture model. They can embed hints about the system's architectural style, constraints, components, properties, and so on. Developers maintaining the code would have an easier time if this model were easily inferred from the code, just like the domain model.

When programming in an architecturally-evident coding style, developers embed hints about the system's architectural model, a kind of *design intent*, into the source code. They go beyond what is minimally necessary for the program to work and follow the *model-in-code principle*. This preservation of architectural design intent has several benefits: It can prevent future code evolution problems, aid project efficiency by reducing the time developers spend inferring intent from code, lower the documentation burden by keeping intent in the code instead of documents or diagrams, and improve ramp-up time for new developers.

The sections that follow dig into the details you will want to know about the architecturally-evident coding style, such as how you can embed design intent in code, what exactly the model-in-code principle is, and what kind of architectural design intent is helpful to express. An informal catalog of patterns for expressing architectural design intent is presented, and the chapter wraps up with an example of using the architecturally-evident coding style on a system to process emails.

10.4 Expressing design intent in code

You can think of a program as a solution to a problem. Like any solution, it is certainly better to have a solution than not, but even better than the solution alone is to add the knowledge that led to its creation. The solution alone, whether it is a car, a proof, a toothbrush, or a computer program does not contain all of the knowledge held by its creator.

A solution is like a path through a maze: it will successfully guide you from start to finish but it does not tell you why other paths were not chosen. The solution must express the *what* but not necessarily the *why*. From the solution, you can infer some of that knowledge, but not all of it.

Consequently, when you read source code, you do not understand the problem as completely as the original developer did. That gap in understanding is the *design intent* that is lost, the understanding and intentions of the original developer that are not present in the solution.

There is hope, however, because when you read source code you *infer* some amount of the design intent. You have flashes of insight and say, "Aha, I see now why this is so." Most of the time, source code is written merely to express the solution, but it can be written such that it helps a reader infer the design intent by inspiring those flashes of insight.

Deliberately dropping hints. An effective way to convey design intent is found in Kent Beck's book on Smalltalk best practices (Beck, 1996). His Intention Revealing Message (i.e., method name) pattern says to give methods names that not only reveal what they do, but also why they are doing it.

For example, a program's design intent might be to highlight double-clicked text by displaying it with reversed colors. The most straightforward way to do this would be to put code that reverses the text colors into the double-click event handler, but the pattern recommends going beyond this. The event handler should invoke a new method called highlightText that would reverse the text colors. By doing so, the developer expresses that the intent of reversing the video is to achieve the highlighting. The bureaucratic overhead of maintaining an additional method is negligible and it avoids writing comments that may grow stale over time.

Design by contract. Other examples of expressing intent are more explicit. Bertrand Meyer popularized the concept of *design by contract* where method pre- and post-conditions as well as object invariants are inserted into the source code and checked by automated tools (Meyer, 2000). By relying on a method's contract, clients can safely ignore any internal implementation and treat the method, or the entire object, as a black box.

Most developers follow a lightweight version of design by contract where methods are short, have a succinct purpose, and have a name that conveys their purpose. You have surely seen code that rejects this practice, such as methods with ambiguous names like "doSomeStuff" or method implementations that contain surprises unanticipated from the implicit contract implied by their names. When design by contract is rejected, readers have to "open the box" and deal with more complexity.

Soft mechanisms. You can categorize the hints and clues in source code as either soft or hard mechanisms. *Soft mechanisms* rely on human interpretation for them to be effective, as in the class naming examples above. If you do not speak Greek, reading Java code with Greek class, method, and variable names in it might be just as hard as reading disassembled Java code. Code comments are another example of a soft mechanism.

Hard mechanisms. The second category is *hard mechanisms,* which are machine-checkable. Usually some amount of correctness or self-consistency can be analyzed. Most times there is no objective or global idea of correctness, but rather correctness of source code with respect to some stated design intent. For example, there is no objectively right or wrong answer about whether X and Y can communicate, but if you declare the design intent that they should not, then that intent could be checked.

Code organization, such as the inheritance hierarchy or co-locating related functionality in the same module, class, or method, might seem like a hard mechanism. But the compiler would be just as happy if that same code were reorganized, so it is a soft mechanism that relies on the reader to draw the right inferences.

Pre- and post-conditions, invariants, and assertions are all hard mechanisms. The type system in most languages enforces information hiding and compatibility. Modules and packages usually have visibility constraints. Virtual methods, class hierarchies, and interfaces can all be used to enforce design intent. Some design patterns can enforce intent too, such as using the Facade pattern to limit access. Going beyond mainstream programming languages, you can create more expressive languages, use pre-compilers, or combine annotations with analysis to express and enforce design intent.

10.5 Model-in-code principle

One kind of design intent that you would like to communicate to readers is the models that you use, including domain models and architecture models. If you provide hints and embed parts of the model into the source code, design intent will be easier to recover, or may not be lost at all. This idea can be expressed as the *model-in-code principle*:

> Expressing a model in source code helps comprehension and evolution.

A corollary of this principle is that expressing a model in code necessarily involves doing more work than is strictly necessary for the solution to work. Every solution provides some hints about the domain and the knowledge necessary to create the solution, but the big idea is to express more than is necessary for the solution to work. Objects in the source code do not care what they represent, if they are encapsulated, if they are used as simple data structures, etc., so you can use them in stylized ways to reduce the amount of design intent that is lost.

Domain models in code. The standard way of conveying design intent in object-oriented programming is to mirror your understanding of domain types and relationships in the class structure of your program (Booch et al., 2007). The domain model, whether it is written down or exists in the heads of its developers, may include accounts and addresses as types, so the source code would similarly have Accounts and Addresses as classes. Since developers who read the program often already have an understanding of the domain, they will have some intuition about how the classes in the program work. They will have an easier time choosing where to add new code because they can allocate responsibilities to classes that correspond to domain types. They can also predict how the original developer allocated responsibilities. A new developer could learn about the domain simply by reading about Accounts and Addresses in the source code.

A stricter version of embedding the domain model in the source code is found in *domain driven design* (Evans, 2003). It is compatible with the model-in-code principle but goes further by encouraging an agile development process and discouraging expressing domain models on paper.

Since there are not controlled experiments to test the model-in-code principle, perhaps the most compelling supporting evidence is its continued popularity with developers. Starting with the Simula language in the late 1960's (Holmevik, 1994), object-oriented languages have been designed to facilitate mirroring the domain model in the source code. Software developers are continually reflecting on the state of their craft and the idea has not been thrown out yet.

There are some logical arguments why it is helpful to embed your domain model in your code. One is that the nouns in the domain change more slowly than the verbs.

Mirroring the nouns in the domain will lead to less churn than mirroring the verbs in the domain, as functional or procedural programs do, but it is hard to demonstrate that the verbs change more quickly. Another argument is straightforward, that developers reading the code can infer the domain types, which directly helps comprehension and should help evolvability.

Technical debt and divergence.   One consequence of expressing models in code is a curse with a hidden blessing. The curse is divergence: the developers' current best understanding of the model can diverge from the model expressed in the source code. The less accurate the model in the source code is, the less useful it is, so developers toil to minimize the divergence. Ward Cunningham refers to this divergence as *technical debt* and defines it as the accumulated misalignment of code with respect to the current understanding of the problem (Cunningham, 1992; Fowler, 2009). Most examples of technical debt that have been offered relate to domain model misalignment, but other examples, like failing to upgrading to a new database version, broaden the idea to other kinds of design, including architecture.

Divergence and technical debt are inevitable with or without models expressed in the code, so the hidden blessing is that divergence is easier to identify and fix when models are expressed in the code. Rather than a gut feeling that the code is becoming uglier, you can compare the model with the code and identify exactly which parts are in need of repair.

Although this discussion has focused on domain models in the code, the model-in-code principle is not specific to domain models. Developers who can see the architecture in the code are more likely to comprehend it and less likely to accidentally break its styles or constraints. Most architectural elements change relatively slowly, including the large-grained components, the connectors, and the styles in use. And expressing the architecture elements can greatly simplify the mapping between module and runtime views of the system.

10.6   What to express

Now that you have seen that code can fail to express your design intent and you have heard about the model-in-code principle that suggests embedding your model in your code, what is the architectural design intent that you want to see in the code? What do your architecture models reveal that is normally difficult to discover from code? We will look at these questions from the perspective of the module, runtime, and allocation viewtypes.

Module viewtype.   Source code is itself in the module viewtype, so code expresses most elements from the module viewtype rather well. One exception is that most languages lack a full-featured module system. Most languages cannot express the dependencies between modules that are important parts of the architecture model. Programming languages often have relatively simple module visibility restrictions that can force you to break encapsulation. Some languages, such as C, express modules only via the directory structure where source files are saved, assuming that one directory means one module.

Programming languages let you declare data structures and classes but not the larger architectural elements like component, connector, and port types. It is difficult to see what set of classes makes up a component or connector type. Classes and interfaces can express what services are provided, but not what services are required. While you can talk about the dependencies code has, it is usually awkward or impossible to express those dependencies in the code itself.

Protocols for interaction are an obvious concern that is visible in architecture models but that has no first-class representation in source code. Code comments are often used to discuss legal calling sequences. Protocols can be expressed using annotations, which are increasingly common in object-oriented languages. Annotations are also being used to express other architectural properties.

Runtime viewtype. The entire runtime viewtype is hard to envision from looking at source code because you must read through the code and mentally animate the runtime instances. This mental animation is made harder with branching, looping, and input parameters. When relevant code is not co-located, it is easy to overlook places where new components are instantiated or where connections are made.

A runtime view of a system can look like a sea of objects. Boundaries between components are hard to discern because the code does not let you declare anything larger than a class. Connectors are hard to see too because identical communication mechanisms, such as method calls or the Observer design pattern, are used both within and between components. Connectors may have no runtime representation at all. Communication between components does not happen just at ports, but often from any number of objects inside the components.

Architecture constraints and styles, as intensional elements, are exceptionally difficult to see in the source code. Architectural constraints and styles often refer to components and connectors rather than objects, so inferring them is doubly hard. First, components and connectors must be identified from the sea of objects, and second, the rules governing their runtime arrangement must be inferred.

While protocols are a common source of trouble, they have no representation in the module or runtime views. Even when legal protocol transitions are written as comments, the protocol itself has no representation either in the module view or in the runtime view. That means that when a reader mentally animates the code, he must envision both the protocol and its current state, even though neither has an explicit representation.

Allocation viewtype.   The runtime viewtype is merely difficult to infer from source code, but it is usually impossible to infer the allocation viewtype. Natural language is used to describe how code should be deployed, if it is written down at all. Often code is deployed in one large chunk on a single machine, but not always. The kind of machine and the network properties will impact the system's performance, and in cases it may be possible to express these properties in the code.

10.7   Patterns for expressing design intent in code

Now that you have seen some opportunities for expressing architectural design intent in the source code, we turn to specific patterns for doing so. This section provides a set of patterns that can be used to express architecture models in code. These patterns assume the use of a mainstream statically-typed object-oriented language such as Java, C++, or C#. Other categories of languages can use similar patterns, but may also have other opportunities to express design intent.

This set of patterns describes how you can include code that, while unnecessary for the program to function correctly, provides hints about the architecture to readers and maintainers of the code. While these patterns have a bureaucratic overhead in that they add more lines of code, none of them has a significant runtime performance or space overhead.

To understand the patterns, it is useful to understand the reification pattern. The general object-oriented pattern called *reification* says that you create an object to represent a concept. For example, the concept of an event could be implemented as a method call, but using reification you would create an event object. As you will see, a common strategy in this set of patterns is to make your architecture abstractions evident in the source code by reifying them as objects, superclasses, or annotations.

Component types.   Component types are bigger than classes but programming language provides nothing bigger, so you can reify a component as a class. There are a number of things you can do to make these component classes visible. You can do it simply with a naming convention, such as naming a class FooComponent. You can additionally provide an empty abstract superclass or interface called Component that serves to tag your intended component classes. This pattern is similar to the Java Serializable interface, which also has no methods but serves as a marker.

In a normal object-oriented system, it is difficult to identify the components because there are so many classes. Since most integrated development environments (IDEs) will let you search or browse subclasses, it will be easy to identify the set of components in the system by looking for subclasses of Component.

The component class can have instance variables that refer to the component's ports and/or connectors. Objects inside the component could have an instance variable referencing the component object. When these objects need to communicate

Design Intent	Patterns
Component types	Create class to represent the component, possibly with abstract superclass or interface as tag, possibly with naming convention: class FooComponent, possibly with instance variables to identify ports, possibly with component invariants as methods
	Align module and component names, possibly with sub-modules
Connector types	Create class to represent the connector, possibly with abstract superclass or interface as tag, possibly with naming convention: class FooConnector
Port types	Create interface to represent provided port
	Create class to represent provided or required ports, possibly with abstract superclass or interface as tag, possibly with naming convention: RequiredFooPort
Protocols	Use port class and State design pattern
	Use external tool, annotations, and static analysis
Properties	Use annotations and static analysis
	Use naming pattern: AsynchronousSend
Styles and patterns	Use naming pattern: FeatureExtractFilter
	Place style superclasses in named package
Invariants & constraints	Bake invariant into API
	Use assert statements or modeling language (e.g., JML)
	Use comments
Module dependencies	Use existing language support or comments
	Use external tool, annotations, and static analysis
Module access restrictions	Use naming pattern: InternalFoo
	Hoist using component framework (e.g., OSGi)
Runtime structure	Co-locate component creation, attachment, initiation
	Hoist setup phase, possibly into declarative form

Figure 10.6: A summary of the patterns to express design intent in source code.

with other components, they could ask the component object for the appropriate port or connector, such as myComponent.getOutputPort(). Communication between objects inside the component would be as usual.

Having an explicit component class provides a place to put checks that span the component, such as initialization checks. The component class also provides a place to put comments, possibly including comments about invariants that span the component, or methods that check that the invariants hold.

Connector types.   The concept of a connector is quite general. Examples include method calls, event dispatches, and shared variables. In the source code, you might use these mechanisms to communicate between components or simply between objects inside a single component. To highlight that communication is between components, you can reify the connector type as an class. As with components, you can simply name the connector EventBroadcastConnector, or you can use an abstract class or interface named Component.

When two components want to communicate, they would create an instance of the connector class then invoke methods on it. What happens inside the connector depends on what kind of connector it is, but it might send messages across the network, write to a shared variable, enqueue a message, or simply invoke another method.

One advantage to having an explicit connector is that you can move some responsibilities out of the components and their constituent classes. For example, using shared memory without an explicit connector means that the component is responsible for safe concurrent access to the memory. With an explicit connector, this responsibility can be moved to the connector, leaving the component a bit simpler. It also opens up the possibility of later changing the type of connector, for example swapping a local connector for a distributed one.

Having an explicit connector means that arbitrary classes inside of a component should not be communicating outside of the component, and should instead route their communication through the connector. This restriction should make the code easier to read later on and should make debugging protocol errors easier because all messages flow through one place.

Port types.   Object-oriented languages can describe the methods a class provides, so you can use object-oriented mechanisms like abstract superclasses in C++ or interfaces in Java to express a component's provided behavior. Your component class could implement these interfaces to express its provided interface.

But you may also want to describe what the component requires from its environment. Since there is no corresponding object-oriented mechanism to do that, you can create an object that represents a port and name it something like InventoryPort. As with component and connector types, you may also use a superclass or interface called a Port. Your component class will have an instance variable that refers to this port, such as requiredInventoryPort, and outgoing communication can be sent out the port and then on to a connector.

You can also make port objects that represent the provided behavior. These will behave similarly to the Facade design pattern (Gamma et al., 1995).

Protocols. Having an explicit port or connector gives you a place to express protocols. The port object or connector object could be written to check or enforce the protocol at runtime, logging protocol violations or even rejecting messages that would break the protocol. One possible choice is to use the State design pattern to implement the protocol (Gamma et al., 1995). Another option is to use an instance variable to track the protocol state. The state of the protocol could then be queried at runtime by objects in the component.

Another choice would be to use annotations to express the protocol and use static analysis to check that the source code will always conform to the protocol.

A lightweight option is to just document the protocol for human readers, perhaps as JavaDoc comments, on a port class. This option at least centralizes communication to flow through a single place and provides a natural place to document the protocol in comments.

Properties. In architecture models, you may place properties on many kinds of elements. For example, a connector may be synchronous or asynchronous, A module may depend on the language features introduced in Java 5, and a component may require 50MB of memory when running.

One way of expressing these properties is to use annotations in the source code, which works with languages like Java and C#. Annotations can be placed on elements that are first class in a programming language, which would include objects and methods. The more architectural elements that you reify, the more places you have available to place annotations.

Another option, and one that works with all languages, is to encode the properties into the names, such as a method named asynchronousSendMessage. This option is unwieldy with multiple properties encoded into a single method name and may not work if the method names are previously constrained by an interface definition.

Styles and patterns. The design patterns book (Gamma et al., 1995) makes the point that standardizing the vocabulary of patterns enables developers to communicate more efficiently. Code that includes the name "visitor" is a strong hint that the Visitor design pattern is being used.

Since styles are kinds of patterns, you can use the same kinds of hints to make them visible. A developer reading code that mentions a pipes and filters or clients and servers has been given a strong hint as to the architectural style being used. Styles have constraints on how the pieces can be put together, and if you use annotations you may be able to write tests or analysis that checks that the constraints are satisfied.

You can strengthen the hint by providing superclasses or interfaces to represent the elements of the style, such as pipes and filters. By placing these superclasses in a package with an appropriate name, like infrastructure.pipeAndFilterStyle, you make the connection to the style quite apparent.

Invariants and constraints. When source code breaks an invariant, the effects may not show up locally and debugging becomes difficult. One way to avoid problems is to bake the invariant into the API. For example, in a hash table data structure, the API may require that a key and a value are added at the same time, preserving the invariant that there are no keys without values and vice versa. Enforcement using an API often ensures the invariant, but does not make the invariant visible.

There are ways make the invariant visible. Code comments are an option, but unsatisfactory because they may not be read, may become out of date, and are local while invariants may span many objects. Developers can embed the invariants into the code with assert() statements or use a constraint modeling language like JML or Spec#. Unfortunately, these methods often have difficulty expressing invariants that span objects, which are the norm with architectural invariants.

Programming languages require precision, but some invariants are difficult to express precisely. One example is the constraint that filters in a pipe-and-filter system should process incrementally rather than in batch. What we want to avoid is one call to open the output port, one call to write all the data, and one call to close the port. But is it incremental enough if it writes just twice? Should it write once for every read from the input port? The problem here is the definition of "incrementally" is a bit fuzzy, but presumably you would know it when you see it.

Module dependencies. While module dependencies are one of the most common constraints that teams think about, programming languages can make expressing them quite difficult. Most mainstream languages have no good mechanism to express dependencies like "module A should not depend on module B." Comments can be used, but even then there is often no obvious place to put them. Java 7 is scheduled to include support for modules, which includes expressing module dependencies. Today, external tools exist to express and check dependencies (Sutherland, 2008).

Support for modules may be present outside of the language, however. In .NET (Fay, 2003), code can be bundled together into assemblies that express dependencies on other assemblies. Enterprise Java Beans (Monson-Haefel, 2001) in Java are similarly bundled into web archive files.

Module access restrictions. Modules are used both to group code together and to enforce encapsulation boundaries. Almost all module systems (like Java packages) allow you to mark contents as public or private, but they have limits so developers may be forced to reveal details they would prefer to keep private. It is possible to use soft mechanisms to hint at the private parts, for example the way the Eclipse framework names packages like InternalFoo. Smalltalk did not originally have any enforcement of public or private methods, but private methods were placed in a category named Private.

Soft mechanisms like these work well when the developers realize what the hints mean but they cannot catch accidental encapsulation violations. Hard mechanisms for enforcing visibility include hoisting the problem into a framework like OSGi (see Section 2.8) that will enforce visibility, or using the improved module systems defined in upcoming JSRs.

Module-component alignment. In the source code there is no requirement that you align modules (i.e., groups of code) with components (i.e., a group of code you intend to instantiate at runtime). You could define a component to consist of code from scattered modules, a little bit of code from this module and a little bit from that one. It is clearer, however, if you align the modules and components so that components are made up of whole modules, rather than fractions of them.

Since you have control over the module hierarchy, you can usually package the modules so that their boundaries line up with component boundaries. You can go further by creating one module (or package, or folder) that contains sub-modules for each component, and another module that contains the data interchange types that will flow between components. This pattern is frustrated by reused modules because you cannot place them into the module hierarchy as you choose.

Module to runtime mapping. Figuring out which component instances will exist at runtime and how they will be connected is difficult to do by reading source code. If your architecture is static (i.e., it goes through a setup phase and then does not change), then you can make the task of understanding easier by co-locating the code that does the setup. The setup usually consists of three parts: creating instances of components and connectors, attaching the components via connectors, and initiating processing. While some systems can simply start, other systems will have a complex initiation sequence, and scattering it makes the code hard to understand.

The setup phase is often hoisted (Section 2.8) because it can be standardized. In non-hoisted setup, procedural code executes and results in a configured set of component and connector instances. In hoisted setup, however, bootstrap code reads a declarative file that describes the configuration; it then performs the creation, hook-up, and initiation, accordingly. This can greatly simplify the job of understanding the system's runtime configuration, since a developer no longer has to mentally animate procedural code, and can instead read a declarative file. Examples of frameworks that hoist the setup include Struts, Enterprise Java Beans, and OSGi / Eclipse.

Not all architectures are static, however. A voice-over-IP application may rely on a network of nodes that is constantly shifting as computers join and depart. In dynamic architectures like this, understanding the architectural style helps you understand the system's runtime configuration. The style may limit the number of nodes that your computer may connect to, or it may preferentially connect to supernodes. Instead of thinking that "anything can happen," you know how the style constrains the possible runtime configurations.

To understand dynamic architectures better, you can make the language of dynamism as simple as possible. For example, you can limit the architecture changes to adding / removing nodes and connecting / disconnecting nodes, rather than fancier operations. Constraint checking should be as clear as possible. By simplifying, you stand a chance of understanding how the architecture can change, and therefore what kinds of configurations may arise.

Anti-pattern: Buried treasure.   While most of the other advice is on what you should do, this is advice on what to avoid. It is easy to subvert the other good practices by burying treasure in inappropriate places. Responsibility-driven design asks you to allocate responsibilities to parts of your design, but you should avoid hinting at one thing while doing another (Wirfs-Brock, Wilkerson and Wiener, 1990). For example, most developers reading source code will assume that a getX() method will have no side effects and a method named launchSpaceShuttle() will do the obvious thing. If you signal to the reader that you have allocated a responsibility, you should follow through in the details.

A corollary of this is that if you suspect a reader might be surprised by what will happen, then avoid that surprise by hinting at the effects. Sometimes simply renaming methods will yield clarity, other times you may need to refactor the design.

Notes on component frameworks. The patterns above can be applied directly in the programming language, but another way to express architecture elements is to use a organizing framework that structures the code. Where the patterns above embed architecture elements into the source code, these frameworks group classes and package them into modules using a separate language, usually described in a *manifest file*. The frameworks often have a runtime presence so that they may manage the modules while the system is running.

The OSGi framework, for example, defines *bundles* (i.e., modules), services, a registry, a bundle life-cycle, security, and a standardized execution environment (OSGi Alliance, 2009). Its bundles are simply JAR files (Java ARchives) with a manifest file that describes the purpose of each file. The manifest describes the bundle name, version, and its required and provided dependencies. The manifest file is written in a simple proprietary language, so it requires no changes to the Java source code.

Microsoft .NET provides similar features with *assemblies*. The manifest file in an assembly describes the assembly name, version, the set of source code files, and the assembly's required and provided dependencies.

If you use a component framework like OSGi, .NET, Java Enterprise Edition (Java EE), or similar, it will likely conflict with using many of the architecturally-evident coding patterns from this chapter. In some ways, the declarative nature of the manifest files is an improvement over the more subtle hints provided via the patterns, and the frameworks generally provide other benefits related to runtime management of

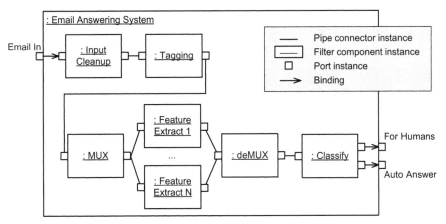

Figure 10.7: A component assembly for the Email Answering System. It accepts an email on the Email In port, categorizes it, then emits it either from the For Humans port or the Auto Answer port.

code, often allowing a system to load new modules at runtime. On the other hand, these frameworks may constrain the kinds of systems that can be built. For example, Java EE supports N-tier systems well, but not the pipe-and-filter or peer-to-peer styles.

Limits. Even if you follow all the advice here, your code will be missing design intent. You have already seen that invariants are difficult to express, especially when they span many objects or components. Architectural decisions are also hard to make evident: the source code has every detail necessary for the program to run, but your architecture may have made commitments to only a few decisions. When evolving your code, it is difficult to disentangle those commitments from the parts that are meant to be open to changes. Signaling responsibilities is also difficult. Code evolution usually involves adding new features and developers must make choices about where best to put the new code.

10.8   Walkthrough of an email processing system

It is useful to have a concrete example so that you can see how to make architecture models visible in code, so this section will apply the patterns to a system designed to process emails. The system will read the emails and, if it is sufficiently confident that it understands the request, it will answer the email itself. If it does not understand the email then it will leave it for a human to handle. A system like this might be helpful in a company that receives many repetitive emails, such as requests for shipment tracking numbers.

The processing of incoming emails flows through several stages of processing, as shown in Figure 10.7. The first stage is to clean up the original text, for example removing HTML and other markup, yielding a purely textual message. From that, the text is marked up to indicate the subject, sender, paragraphs, sentences, words, account numbers, names, and tracking numbers. Then several feature analyzers are given a chance to recognize salient features in the message. These analyzers can be quite computationally intensive. Finally, the combined results from the feature analyzers are fed into a classifier that decides if it understands the message and either provides a response email or admits defeat. The system has been implemented using a pipe-and-filter architectural style (see Section 14.8) because of the overall flow and to enable parallel processing of the feature analyzers.

This system could be implemented as one big procedure with the structure of a flowchart, or it could be implemented in an object-oriented style. Instead, it is implemented using an architecturally-evident coding style. The example shows how you can reveal your module structure by organizing your packages, make component and connector types visible, and even help readers anticipate the runtime structure of the system.

Package structure. Source code is itself in the module viewtype. It is not a challenge to discover what code exists because you can simply look at it. As a codebase grows larger, however, its organization becomes increasingly important. You can structure the set of packages and modules to provide hints about the architecture. Figure 10.8 shows the package structure for the email system. Its top-level organization makes clear what is shared infrastructure relating to the pipe-and-filter style, and what is the specific system. Inside the system, the package organization makes it easy to find individual components and the datatypes that flow between them. Although it is not shown, you would expect to find the components package subdivided to reveal each component in the system.

The package organization is helpful in revealing the architecture, but it has limits. You might hope to co-locate all the code for a component in a single package, but this is usually impractical. The Pipe class, for example, uses a LinkedBlockingQueue from the java.util.concurrent package in the standard Java libraries, so you must refer to that package instead of including it in the infrastructure package directly. The more code sharing there is, the harder it will be to use the package structure to reveal what code makes up a component.

Furthermore, the package hierarchy cannot reveal dependencies, so to discover the dependency on the java.util.concurrent package you would have to read the source files in the package. Additionally, there is no way to express desired constraints across packages. For example, you cannot express that the system.components package may depend on the system.interchange package, but not the reverse, so a developer evolving the code could accidentally add such a dependency.

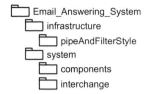

Figure 10.8: The package structure for the Email Answering System. It is organized so that the module structure is apparent from the directory structure, but module dependencies cannot be inferred.

Visible component types.   Some of the source code in the email processing system will have a runtime presence as one or more component instances, such as the tagging or classifying component instances from the system. Other code exists as functions to be used (such as a statistical analysis package), and has no runtime instances. The source code should reveal not only the modules (e.g., that statistical analysis package), but also the component types (e.g., the tagging component).

Figure 10.9 shows the source code for a Filter class. The Filter class exists so that someone reading the code is aware that you are using the pipe-and-filter style. Another option would have been to simply add "filter" to the names of other classes, such as TaggingFilter, but having an explicit class has other advantages. Most modern development environments (IDEs) have the ability to display a class hierarchy, so you could display a view of all subclasses of the Filter class, showing at a glance all of the filters you have defined.

Note that the Filter class is a subclass of the Component class. This is another hint to readers of the code that you are defining a component. You are embedding your understanding of the architecture, specifically that some of the code is there to implement components, and that a filter is a kind of component. The Component class has an empty implementation, so it is just a hint to developers, and does not provide any reusable code.

The Filter class, in contrast, does provide code. It takes advantage of using Filter as a superclass to do some architecture hoisting (Section 2.8), standardizing and simplifying the handling of concurrency in the system. Each filter runs in its own thread, incrementally processing its inputs. The Filter class sets up a Template pattern, requiring subclasses to implement the virtual work() method to do their processing.

Ideally, this implementation would enforce the constraint that filters process incrementally, not in a single batch, but it is difficult to see how to enforce this constraint. It would also be helpful to ensure that filters communicate only through pipes, but again it is difficult to express this constraint in the code. You can write comments describing the constraints, and the Filter class provides a good place to put the comments. Finally, Java allows a class to have only a single superclass. In this system,

```
1   package infrastructure.pipeAndFilterStyle;
2   import infrastructure.Component;
3   /**
4    * This class defines a skeletal filter that reads data from
5    * one or more input ports and writes data to one or more output
6    * ports.  Subclasses should override the work() method to
7    * implement the functionality of their filter.
8    */
9   abstract public class Filter extends Component implements Runnable {
10      /**
11       * This run() method is invoked when the thread starts.
12       * It runs until the abstract work() method terminates,
13       * or the thread is interrupted.
14       */
15      public void run() {
16          try {
17              this.work();
18          } catch (Exception e) {
19              System.exit(1);
20          }
21      }
22      /**
23       * Template method --- subclasses must implement
24       * Read available data from input ports and incrementally
25       * write processed data to output ports.
26       */
27      abstract protected void work() throws InterruptedException;
28  }
```

Figure 10.9: Source code for the Filter class. Every filter in the system is a subclass of this one, which establishes a Template method pattern for subclasses to complete.

it was possible to use Filter as a superclass, but in other systems that may not be possible. Another option is to use Java interfaces since a class can implement many interfaces, but this would not allow you to hoist concurrency concerns.

Visible connector types.   If components can be difficult to see in the source code, then connectors are almost invisible. The most common connector, a procedure call, is impossible to differentiate from regular messages being sent between the smallest of objects. So it is arguably more important for you to provide hints about connectors, since they make inter-component communication visible.

Figure 10.10 shows the source code that implements a pipe connector. Similar to the Filter component, the pipe is its own class that is a subclass of an empty Connector class. You could use your IDE to show all subclasses of Connector, which will let you know the kinds of connectors available in the system.

Unlike the abstract Filter class, the Pipe class provides a concrete implementation

```
1   package infrastructure.pipeAndFilterStyle;
2   import infrastructure.Connector;
3   import java.util.concurrent.*;
4   /**
5    * Implements a pipe to be used as-is, not subclassed like
6    * the Filter superclass. Reads from the pipe will block if
7    * no data is available. Writers should invoke close(), which
8    *    a) prevents future writes to the pipe
9    *    b) lets the reader know that no more data is coming
10   */
11  public final class Pipe<T> extends Connector {
12      private BlockingQueue<T> myPipe = new LinkedBlockingQueue<T>();
13      private boolean isClosed = false;
14
15      public T blockingRead() throws InterruptedException {
16          if ( myPipe.isEmpty() ) return null;
17          T t = myPipe.take();
18          return t;
19      }
20      public void blockingWrite(T t) throws InterruptedException {
21          if ( isClosed() ) throw new IllegalStateException();
22          myPipe.put( t );
23      }
24      public void close() throws InterruptedException {
25          this.isClosed = true;
26      }
27      public boolean isClosed() {
28          return isClosed ;
29      }
30      public boolean isClosedAndEmpty() {
31          if ( isClosed() && myPipe.isEmpty() ) return true;
32          else return false;
33      }
34  }
```

Figure 10.10: The source code for the Pipe class. Unlike the Filter class, it provides the final, non-subclassable implementation of a pipe. It provides a safe concurrent queue that can be used by any Filter.

of a pipe and is not designed to be subclassed. It uses a thread-safe BlockingQueue from java.util.concurrent to enqueue and dequeue messages. As long as filters exclusively use this pipe class to communicate with other filters, the filters can mostly ignore concurrency and not have problems, which was the intention of architecturally hoisting the concurrency concern into the Pipe and Filter infrastructure classes. (Note that since this connector implementation does not clone the sent messages, the sender could interfere with the receiver if it held a reference and mutated the message object after sending).

The Pipe class has a simple API consisting of reading, writing, and closing. The class will throw an exception if reads or writes occur after the pipe has been closed. The state of the protocol is explicitly represented in the isClosed boolean field. While the system does have explicit components and connectors in the source code, it has omitted explicit ports. If the protocol had been more complex, or if a component had to track the state of connections to multiple components, it would have been reasonable to have explicit ports.

The Pipe class shows one additional kind of hint: it reveals properties. The read and write calls are not asynchronous, so the caller may block if there is no message ready to read, or if the pipe is full. Consequently, the methods are named blockingRead and blockingWrite. This hint works well because it highlights just one property, the synchronous nature of the call, so but it would work less well with many properties, such as a blockingFooBarBazRead.

Easy mapping to runtime viewtype.   So far the code has provided hints to make elements of the module viewtype more visible: modules, component types, and connector types. As you saw before in Section 9.6.4, envisioning how a system will behave at runtime by looking at its code can be quite difficult. You can make that mapping from module viewtype to runtime viewtype easier by following conventions in the source code.

Figure 10.11 shows an excerpt from the source code that instantiates the components and connectors for the system. This system has a static component assembly, that is, its configuration of components and connectors does not change as the program runs (see Section 9.7 on static and dynamic architectures). If you co-locate all of the initialization and setup code, then a developer reading that code can directly see what instances are created and how they are arranged.

While this example shows an example of hoisting the concurrency concern, the program itself is in control of instantiating its components and connectors. Other systems hoist this concern too, such as Apache Struts, which uses a configuration file to declare the servlets it should instantiate. So, this example cannot ensure that this is the only place where components are instantiated or connections are made.

Reflection on example.   Looking back on this example, you can see that the code embeds concepts from the architecture model. Not all of the architecture model is expressed and there are still opportunities for a new developer to accidentally violate intended constraints, but there are plenty of hints to guide him in the right direction also. For example, the code clearly expresses the use of the pipe-and-filter architectural style. This style is well-suited to the demands of the problem and enables easy parallelization of the computationally intensive feature extraction stages.

Concurrency is always a tricky problem. The code simplifies the problem by solving it once and applying that solution consistently: filters only interact via thread-safe pipes. In the system here, your worries do not ramp up as the number of threads in-

```
1  ...
2  public static void main(String[] args) {
3      createPipes();
4      createFilters();
5      startFilters();
6      ...
7  }
8  protected static void createPipes() {
9      pipeCleanupToTagging = new Pipe<EmailMessage>( );
10     pipeTaggingToMux = new Pipe<EmailMessage>( );
11     ...
12 }
13 protected static void createFilters() {
14     filterCleanup = new InputCleanupFilter();
15     filterTagging = new TaggingFilter();
16     ...
17 }
18 protected static void startFilters() {
19     filterCleanup.run();
20     filterTagging.run();
21     ...
22 }
```

Figure 10.11: Arbitrary source code can create and reconfigure new component instances at any time, but readers of the code will have difficulty imagining the runtime structure. Instead, as seen here, you can co-locate the code that creates components, and similarly co-locate their configuration, which makes it easy for readers.

creases. The filters are constrained by the style to always read from their inputs and write to their outputs, a simplification that makes reasoning about many threads possible. Compare this solution with an unconstrained system with hundreds of threads, one where you would be right to worry about concurrency problems.

The system embodies architecture-focused design (see Section 2.7), since it consciously relies on the architectural design to solve the concurrency problem. It does not address problems locally, nor does its thread safety arise accidentally. It hoists the concurrency problem into actual running code in the infrastructure package, rather than just a design. In practice, this would allow a developer working on a filter to focus exclusively on the job of the filter, rather than also worrying about concurrency.

10.9 Conclusion

While architecture models may take many forms, including drawings on paper, whiteboard sketches, or simply verbal communication between developers, models lose their value when they no longer correspond to the source code. Developers face the challenge of overcoming the model-code gap between what the models express and what the source code expresses. It exists because models and code have different vocabularies, express ideas at different levels of abstraction, have different levels of design commitments, and most importantly differ in their use of intensional and extensional elements.

Once you recognize that a gap exists, you are confronted with the challenge of managing it, because the models and code tend to diverge over time. Teams may follow various strategies to manage the divergence, but some key insights are: that tool and programming language choices can reduce gaps and therefore divergence, that higher detail models will diverge faster than lower detail models, and that projects will vary in their tolerance for divergence.

Design intent is lost during the transition between design and code. Currently, developers avoid losing design intent by expressing hints in the code, including using intention revealing names, and applying the concepts of design by contract. The model-in-code principle says that expressing a model in the system's code helps comprehension and evolvability. Developers already mirror their understanding of the domain in the code they write by creating classes that correspond to types in the domain. Making the domain model evident in the code goes beyond what is strictly necessary for a solution to work, but developers do it to aid code comprehension and to make future code changes easier. They use a combination of hard and soft mechanisms to communicate the model.

An architecturally-evident coding style seeks to minimize the amount of lost architectural design intent. Making the architecture model evident in the code has the same advantages as making the domain model evident. The architecture model represents hard-won knowledge that developers should strive to maintain as they write code. This chapter provided a set of patterns that can be used to encode architectural elements in object-oriented languages like C++, Java, and C#.

You must make judgment calls about whether or not to apply these patterns and choose which parts of your architecture model to express in the code. For example, the email processing example did not represent the ports in the code because they would add bureaucracy to the code without much benefit. In another system, it might be rather important to express ports, perhaps because the protocols are complex and ports are a natural place to represent those protocols.

Chapter 11

Encapsulation and Partitioning

The choices made by software developers have a big impact on the qualities of the software. This chapter discusses one of the biggest choices that developers must make: how they partition the software into smaller pieces, and what the interfaces to those pieces look like.

Most systems are organized into a hierarchy of modules or components. If you build this hierarchy well, it will tell a story to whoever looks at it, and it will be easy to understand. This chapter presents several strategies for partitioning components or modules. Not all interfaces are effectively encapsulated, and an interface description is more than a list of operation signatures. This chapter presents a method for describing the minimal set of abstractions necessary to understand how operations work. A theme that runs through the chapter is that partitioning and encapsulation are tied closely to comprehensibility.

11.1   Story at many levels

Invariably, large systems will have lots of interacting parts. Unless great care was taken in their design, they will be hard to understand. For example, if you look at old machines, like the ones in London's National Museum of Science and Industry, you will see many parts intricately interconnected. After staring at these machines for a long time, you can begin to understand how they work, but the understanding does not come easily. If you look at their modern equivalents, you will see that they are better structured and that their constituent parts are encapsulated.

Both the old machines and the new ones work, so the benefit is *cognitive*, not technical. The systems themselves do not care if they are elegantly designed or inscrutable, but developers who work with them do. Developers prefer systems that are well-organized, not ones that are a sea of classes, modules, or components that make their heads swim.

The question is: how can you build systems that are comprehensible? The usual answer is to structure the system using a hierarchical nesting of parts. Yet this is only part of the solution, since a hierarchically nested system may still be hard to understand. For example, what if a system has many components, but just one level of nesting? Or if its modules are haphazard groupings of functions? Or if modules and components have poor encapsulation boundaries that couple them tightly and reveal their implementations?

To be comprehensible, your software should be structured so that it reveals a *story at many levels*. Each level of nesting tells a story about how those parts interact. A developer who was unfamiliar with the system could be dropped in at any level and still make sense of it, rather than being swamped.

Constructing the story. No simple process or set of rules will always yield a system that is comprehensible and tells a story at many levels, but here are a few general guidelines that will steer you in the right direction.

1. Create levels of abstraction by hierarchically nesting elements (primarily modules, components, and environmental elements).
2. Limit the number of elements at any level.
3. Give each element a coherent purpose.
4. Ensure that each element is encapsulated and does not reveal unnecessary internal details.

If you do this at every level of nesting, developers will see a reasonable number of elements and will infer a story about how they work together. For example, in the Yinzer example, there were just four components (see Figure 9.8). You can infer how they collaborate to solve a problem, and with the provided scenario it is even easier. You should expect that each of those components will have subcomponents or objects within it, but if those components or objects also follow the guidelines above, then you could understand them too. The result is a story at many levels.

Note that maintaining multiple levels of nesting is a bureaucratic burden. You must trade off the cognitive benefit of maintaining a story at many levels with the maintenance costs. While each project will strike its own balance, here are some rough heuristics.

At a particular level of abstraction, a reasonable number of elements is likely between 5 and 50, with 50 being quite large. So, most components should be composed of 5 to 50 sub-components (or classes), and most modules should have between 5 and 50 sub-modules (or files). When you approach 50 elements, consider refactoring to bring the number back down. Similarly, if you find you have very few elements, consider refactoring to "eliminate middle management" by combining levels.

Benefits and difficulties. Architecture models enable you to tell a story at a higher level of abstraction. When the first programs were written, the invention of sub-routines allowed developers to tell a story of a master and servant routines. The master task could be understood at an abstract level without reading each of the sub-routines. The invention of modules, structured programming, and object-oriented programming enabled stories to be told with increasingly large codebases. The story from the subroutine level was still there, but it was augmented with a story about what each module did. The concepts in software architecture allow you to tell a story about larger chunks — for example, that this is a 3-tier system with one tier behind a security firewall.

Having a story at many levels provides several benefits. First, developers are more able to cope with *scale* and can reason about modules, components, or environmental elements in huge systems. This is increasingly important as internet-scale systems are constructed by composing existing systems. Second, developers are confronted with less *complexity*. Large systems entail lots of moving pieces, but the story at many levels restricts how much complexity has to be comprehended at any given moment. Developers treat subcomponents as black boxes and must reason only about the components at the current level. Being "dropped into the code" at any level is possible. These benefits are cognitive, not technical, as they benefit developers and their ability to maintain the system.

There is some cost, however. Maintaining a story at many levels is a bit like gardening, since as the system evolves the story needs maintenance to keep it up. Beyond the upkeep, it requires effective encapsulation, which is difficult and is a kind of deferred gratification.

11.2 Hierarchy and partitioning

Creating a story at many levels is a beneficial way to structure a system. It relies on the idea of *partitioning*, which is the division of a system into disjoint pieces. For example, a spacecraft can be partitioned into the payload and launch vehicle, and software might be partitioned into a client and a server. The whole system and its constituent parts are related, sometimes being called *hierarchical nesting* or *hierarchical decomposition*. The relationship between the parts and the whole is referred to as a *partition* relationship, and is described in more detail in Section 13.2.

Non-hierarchical systems. As helpful as partitioning is, every once and a while you will come across a problem that resists your efforts to decompose it. Each time you try to partition it a different way, you find something that gives you trouble.

Daniel Dvorak gives an example of such trouble: he compares using a hard disk in a server room with using it on a spacecraft (Dvorak, 2002). Turning on a hard disk drive always requires power, creates heat, and applies torque to the disk drive enclosure. When it is in a server room you can safely ignore these effects and treat the hard drive as a hierarchically encapsulated piece of a computer. If you place that same disk in a spacecraft, however, you will find that those effects cannot be encapsulated. The drive will sap scarce power from other devices, heat up one part of the spacecraft inappropriately, and torque the spacecraft to change its course. His point is that not every system can be hierarchically decomposed, with subcomponents treated as encapsulated black boxes.

Seeing the challenges on a spacecraft makes it easy to appreciate how powerful the idea of hierarchy is. Because hierarchical nesting is so effective, almost all systems use it, whether they are natural systems or engineered ones.

Top-down design. Just because the parts in your system are hierarchically nested does not imply that you should build them following a top-down process. Although it may be your first instinct when you hear about hierarchical decomposition, design rarely proceeds top-down. Just because an internals model is more detailed than a boundary model does not mean you cannot build it first. Many different processes will end up with a hierarchically nested set of components and modules.

Even if you do begin with top-down design, as you dig in you will likely find some details that force you to revise your earlier design decisions. A common path is to work both top-down and bottom-up at the same time and reconcile the designs. Top-down design is an architecture anti-pattern discussed in Section 5.6.

Dominant decomposition. Every library organizes its books on the shelves. Some order the books by topic so that you can browse nearby related books. Others order the books by size so that space is efficiently used. The trouble is that a single organizational system must be chosen — the books can be organized by topic, by color, by size, by author, or any other concern, but this single concern becomes the *dominant decomposition*.

Consequently, problems related to that dominant concern will be easier to solve, but problems related to other concerns will be harder. For example, if you organize books by their size, then it will be easy to find the tallest books but harder to find ones by a specific author. This problem of one concern dominating others is referred to as the *tyranny of the dominant decomposition* (Tarr et al., 1999).

When you decompose your system into modules and components, you are imposing an organization on it, just like the librarians did to their libraries. Most systems

Decomposition Strategy	Elements
Functionality	Clumps of related functions
Archetypes	Salient types from domain
Architectural style	Named elements from style
Attribute Driven Design	Tactics from table
Ports	An element corresponding to each port
Orthogonal abstraction	Elements from another domain, e.g., math or graph theory
Jigsaw puzzle	Existing elements, plus new ones as glue

Figure 11.1: A summary of decomposition strategies for components and modules. Design rarely proceeds top-down and just because an internals model is more detailed than a boundary model does not mean you cannot build it first.

choose functionality as their dominant concern, but you find some systems where other concerns are dominant. You may have never consciously thought about your strategies for decomposing a module or component into smaller pieces. The next section surveys several strategies that will make you consciously aware of which strategies are available, and enable you to choose a strategy that best fits your problem.

11.3 Decomposition strategies

At the end of your project, you will have created modules and components with internal structure. They will be made up of other modules and components, and eventually objects. But how do you decide on those subdivisions and internal structures? Most developers would say they depend on their intuition rather than following any prescribed strategy. Studying the strategies of experienced developers will accelerate your progress and generally raise the quality of your designs.

Sometimes there is little choice in the decomposition, because a framework forces design choices, or because company style guidelines require a certain design, but other times your choice is relatively unconstrained. To illustrate different strategies, the examples that follow continue with the Yinzer example. The decomposition strategies that follow are summarized in Figure 11.1.

11.3.1 Functionality

Decomposing a system based on functionality is perhaps the most obvious strategy. To do so, you inventory the required functionality and clump together related functions. For the Yinzer system, consider the following two options that clump together functionality into components:

1. Website, Database, Email, Business Networking, Job Advertisements
2. Member Operations, Non-Member Operations

Both clumpings seem reasonable but yield different design challenges. The first option consolidates infrastructure into three components — Website, Database, and Email — which would mean that they are shared by the Business Networking and Job Advertisements components. The second option would make such sharing harder, since Member or Non-Member Operations would crosscut the infrastructure functions. Presumably both Member and Non-Member Operations would be further decomposed into subcomponents.

Choosing functionality as the dominant concern is usually compatible with achieving required quality attributes, except in extreme cases. Imagine that the Yinzer system's first priority was scalability. Arguably either decomposition is compatible with scalability, though perhaps the second, by not reusing a single database, lends itself to easier scalability.

11.3.2   Archetypes

The allocation of responsibility can be aided by identifying what Jan Bosch calls *archetypes* (Bosch, 2000) or what John Cheesman and John Daniels call *core types* (Cheesman and Daniels, 2000). Archetypes / core types are salient types from the domain, such as a Contact, Advertisement, User, or Email. Notice that this is the decomposition strategy originally used in Figure 9.8.

Characteristics of an archetype include having an independent existence and having few mandatory associations to other types. So, could the concept of a Job Match (the pairing of a person to a job) be an archetype? Probably not, since it is not very long lived and is strongly dependent on an Advertisement.

As with a functional decomposition, archetypes are usually compatible with achieving required quality attributes, except in extreme cases.

11.3.3   Architectural style

A system can be decomposed so that its components are elements defined by an architectural style. A system in the pipe-and-filter style would have components that were filters and connectors that were pipes, each suitably specialized for the system. Section 10.3 shows an example of a pipe-and-filter system where that style is used to build a system that answers emails.

It is common to initially decompose a system based on an architectural style, then to decompose one of those components using a different style. For example, you could

1. Choose the module to decompose
2. Refine the module
   a) Choose the architecture drivers
   b) Choose or invent a suitable architecture pattern
   c) Create modules and allocate responsibilities
   d) Define module interfaces
   e) Verify functionality scenarios and QA scenarios
3. Repeat for every module

Figure 11.2: A synopsis of the SEI's Attribute Driven Design process, which guides you to tactics that address your quality attribute drivers.

build the Yinzer system using a 3-tier style, with a User Interface tier, a Business Logic tier, and a Persistence tier. The Business Logic tier could be decomposed according to functionality, perhaps with Job Ad and Business Networking subcomponents.

Choosing an architectural style as the dominant concern is highly effective at achieving quality attribute goals because each style has known qualities that it promotes, such as modifiability with the pipe-and-filter style.

11.3.4 Quality attributes and Attribute Driven Design (ADD)

Small systems usually focus their attention on functionality, while larger systems must pay more attention to achieving quality attributes. The larger the system is, the more likely it is that subcomponents will have stringent quality attribute requirements. The Attribute Driven Design (ADD) process from the Software Engineering Institute describes how quality attributes can be used to drive recursive design of modules (Bass, Clements and Kazman, 2003). Figure 11.2 shows a sketch of the ADD process. Note that the process is defined for modules, but it is straightforward to apply it to components.

The core idea of ADD is to first decide which quality attributes are the most important for this component, expressed as quality attribute scenarios, then choose a pattern or design that is suited to achieving those qualities. The patterns used in ADD could include architectural styles, design patterns, or domain-specific patterns known by the developer.

The critical difference between simple decomposition based on architectural styles and ADD is the reliance on a table that maps quality attributes to *tactics*. Section 3.4 briefly mentions tactics, describing them as a kind of pattern bigger than a design pattern and smaller than an architectural style. Examples of tactics include: Ping/Echo, Active Redundancy, Runtime Registration, Authenticate Users, and Intrusion Detection (Bass, Clements and Kazman, 2003). The table of tactics maps from a quality attribute to some general tactics and then to several specialized tactics. Using the table, a developer can go from the architecture driver that is known to a set of specialized tactics that should enable that driver.

11.3.5   Ports

Every component has ports, which are used to communicate with other components. Since each port represents a distinct grouping of functionality or responsibility, it can be reasonable to provide a component to handle that port's interactions, or to act as a mediator (Gamma et al., 1995) to other components. Creating components corresponding to each port is rarely a complete solution and developers must add other components.

For the Yinzer example, you could create components corresponding to each of the four ports: Non-Member, Contacts, Job/Ads, and SMTP Client. This choice might be a good one if you were concerned about security and wanted to segregate access by members and non-members. Alternately, it could help provide different service levels to different kinds of users, such as free and paying users.

11.3.6   Orthogonal abstraction

A powerful but often overlooked strategy is to recast the responsibilities of a component into a different domain, such as a domain where an algorithmic formalism can help (D'Souza and Wills, 1998; Bosch, 2000). For example, a system that handles work orders could be cast into a directed graph of dependencies and processed by a component like the MAKE program, or computer graphics operations can be cast as matrix operations that are much faster to compute. Arguably the map-reduce architectural style (see Section 14.14) is the recasting of a data processing problem into a particular distributed computing abstraction.

Some domains have a stable set of abstractions that have been devised by experts in the field, for example the domains of compilers or databases. In these domains it makes sense to take advantage of that domain-specific knowledge and consider using these abstractions as the basis for your decomposition. The abstractions may reveal underlying truths that are not evident from a superficial investigation of the domain, or using the abstractions may enable a higher performance implementation.

When this strategy is relevant it can be a big win. However, applying it is dependent on a flash of insight that connects the current domain with another, more fully investigated domain. The Yinzer system has no obvious connection to an orthogonal abstraction, or perhaps the right flash of insight has simply yet to strike.

11.3.7 Jigsaw puzzle

Sometimes you have several sub-components already, and the desire to reuse them drives your design. You might have a relational database, an existing vendor component, and some code from a previous project that can be repackaged. You can assemble these pieces to get partial coverage of the required features and qualities, and you add some new code, perhaps in the form of connectors or adapters, to complete the job. This kind of design can be like assembling a puzzle where the pieces were not originally from the same set.

11.3.8 Choosing a decomposition

For most systems, choosing any decomposition will work acceptably, but if you choose one that is suitable for your quality attribute requirements then your job will be easier. The architectural style and ADD approaches are most directly connected to quality attribute requirements.

Looking back at these approaches, you can see a pattern emerge. Several of these approaches choose an architectural element and make it the dominant concern: quality attributes, functionality, architectural style, and ports. Sometimes it is best to choose an orthogonal abstraction from the problem domain, and other times existing COTS components will be such compelling candidates for reuse that they drive the internal design.

11.4 Effective encapsulation

Encapsulation is closely related to decomposition. Where decomposition insists that the problem be broken down into smaller problems, *encapsulation* says that the solution to the smaller problem should be partially hidden. If you use a toaster, you probably do not care if the heating elements are metal or ceramic, only that the toast comes out according to the dial setting. If the toaster required you to be aware of the required voltage on the metal or ceramic element heating elements, you would consider that a failure to encapsulate its implementation choices. Sadly, programs with poorly encapsulated parts are quite common.

An effective API of a module or component should hide implementation details and provide the user with a simplified understanding of what each API operation does. For example, if you have a collection with a sort() operation, you may not know the data structure used to hold the collection or the algorithm used to sort, but you must know that the collection consists of possibly unordered elements, and that after the sort() operation is invoked it consists of ordered elements. Effective encapsulation enables users to comprehend the API, as well as hiding implementation details from them.

Cognitive burden reduction. Architecture needs encapsulation because encapsulation reduces complexity. For example, you may appreciate that a radio is doing many difficult tasks in tuning in signals and presenting them clearly, but your mind only has to deal with an on/off button and channel selector. You could learn a more complicated interface, like the interface to old crystal radios, but the tradeoff is that you would have less time to learn other things.

As the complexity and scale of systems grows, encapsulation helps you treat parts as black boxes whose internals you do not need to understand, as long as you understand their interfaces. Encapsulation saves you time and conserves your mental resources, but only when the encapsulation is effective.

Encapsulation failure. I once worked at a company where they changed our timesheet process. Before the change, we would submit timesheets only when we used vacation time. But, at the urging of the accounting department, the process was changed so that we submitted a form each week that allocated hours to various accounts, such as normal working, vacation, and holidays. We were sent to an hour of training on how to fill out the forms. It was sufficiently complicated that whenever I took vacation I had to go back and read the directions on how to debit and credit the various accounts.

The lesson of this story is that not all encapsulation is effective. The accounting department had designed a system that was arguably encapsulated because the software developers did not actually have to do the work of the accountants nor did they have access to the accounts. But the encapsulation was ineffective because the interface leaked abstractions. It exposed the abstractions used by the accountants (i.e., the debiting and crediting of accounts), which made the accountants' jobs easier at the expense of every employee. This probably sounds similar to APIs you have used in the past — thin veneers over the implementation that were easy for the module developers to present, but that forced you to engage in details and abstractions that seemed to be unnecessary distractions.

The accounting example shows that encapsulation is not simply binary, so it is unhelpful to talk about an "encapsulated component." Instead, you must distinguish between *effective encapsulation* and poor encapsulation. Perhaps an interface hides some details, but are they the details that you want to hide? And given what you want to hide, is the interface as small as possible? Effective encapsulation is beneficial but requires good judgment.

Parnas modules. As a thought experiment, imagine that a module's operations were simple getters and setters for the data structures inside the module. In some sense that interface would be encapsulated, but it would be ineffective at hiding any design secrets or choices. You would have great difficulty changing the internal data structures, or possibly even the algorithms, without disturbing your users.

In 1972, David Parnas wrote a paper on how to create stable modules that exhibit effective encapsulation (Parnas, 2001). The essence of his approach is that you should ensure that the details likely to change are hidden inside the module, and that changes to those details will not influence the module's interface. Imagine that you are considering two design alternatives, A and B. Parnas suggests that you design the modules and interfaces so that both alternatives are possible to implement with the same API. You are hiding your design secret, which is whether you used design A or B. That secret should be encapsulated behind the interface, so you retain the option to change your mind without the change rippling out to users.

A *Parnas module* hides a secret to minimize coupling, rather than just grouping together related code. However, consider how rarely this advice is followed in practice: in a 3-tier system, how many modules must change when a new attribute is added to an item (e.g., an order or customer) appearing in the UI and database? Instead of creating Parnas modules, other criteria are used for modularizing code, such as relatedness, architectural style, authorship, or deployment needs.

Judgment and risk. Effective encapsulation is hard to achieve: Parnas' good advice is often violated to serve other goals, and the accountants who designed the time-keeping system thought they had effectively encapsulated their system. So how can anyone achieve effective encapsulation?

Ideally, every module and component would have a well-encapsulated interface, but the effort to build good API's is expensive. Some API's will be used by external users of the module, while others will be used only by the team that built the module. You may choose to spend more effort on the external-facing API's because the consequences for making mistakes there are higher: users could become dependent on details of the implementation or fail to understand how the API works.

Your architecture may drive you to partition the system in a certain way, and to encapsulate some implementation details instead of others. For example, if you are considering the possibility of moving a module or component to a different machine, you may design an API so that the connector can be local or remote. If you anticipate that developers beyond your team will add components to your system, you may choose to make the plug-in API for them well-encapsulated.

To get effective encapsulation, you must anticipate how you and others will use the module in the future, and consider implementation options that you want to keep open. Such crystal ball gazing is difficult, error-prone, and expensive. Keeping options open takes effort and usually complicates the design.

Here again, the idea of using risk to drive architecture is applicable. Sometimes it would be a big risk to expose data structures, or have an API that is hard to use, such as in a published Windows API. On the other hand, it may be OK if some module API's end up with ineffective encapsulation, perhaps those that are not user-facing or are cheap to refactor. The next section describes a somewhat expensive process for creating encapsulated API's, so you will need to use your judgment and risk estimates to decide when it is worth the effort.

11.5   Building an encapsulated interface

Encapsulation requires that a module or component's boundary, or interface, is described separately from its internals. This section describes how to create a component interface based on the idea of abstract data types. It first describes how an abstract data type of a stack works, then extends this idea to components.

11.5.1   Stack abstract data type

When people talk about abstract data types (ADT's) they usually use a stack. Furthermore, they used to provide the real world example of the spring-loaded stacks of cafeteria plates, but I have not seen one of those in a long time. A stack is a simple data type that can be accessed only from the top, not the middle or bottom. You can *push* an item onto the top of the stack and *pop* an item from the top of the stack. Sometimes there is an operation to *peek* at what is on top without removing it.

There are two useful and related benefits of ADT's. The first benefit is that you can invent and analyze algorithms that depend only on ADT's instead of a concrete source code implementation. That way you can show that an algorithm runs in $O(\log n)$ time without depending on any particular implementation. Most developers do not invent or analyze new algorithms, but they do use encapsulation, which is the second benefit. Encapsulation is the idea that a developer reveals an interface to use a mechanism but hides the insides that implement it.

The simple way to specify an interface would be to provide method signatures for the methods. Here are signatures for push and pop:

> void **push**(Object o)
> Object **pop**( )

With signatures like these it is easy to see what must be passed in as parameters and what will come back out as return values. What is surprisingly missing is the stack itself. Perhaps you can deduce what these methods do because you have previously been exposed to stack ADT's before, but if this were a new ADT then it is unlikely you would understand how it works.

It is possible to make these signatures more clear by providing pre- and post-condition specifications. Pre-conditions state what must be true in order for the method to complete successfully. Post-conditions state what will be true when the method completes. Here is an example of how you can augment the signatures, yielding an *action specification*:

void **push**(Object o)
>   **pre-condition**: stack is not full
>   **post-condition**: stack is unchanged except that o is on the top of the stack

Object **pop**( )
>   **pre-condition**: stack is not empty
>   **post-condition**: stack is unchanged except that the returned object is the one that was previously, and no longer, on the top of the stack

While these specifications may be incomplete and not perfectly precise, they are an improvement compared to the simple signatures. The stack is explicitly mentioned, the success case behavior of push (when the stack is not full) and pop (when the stack is not empty) are described in the post-conditions.

A user of a stack needs a mental model of what the push and pop operations do, even if the details of how they do it are hidden. That mental model includes at least these concepts: the stack exists, the stack is unchangeable except at its top, the stack can be full, and the stack can be empty. The conceptual model includes both information and behavior because the push and pop methods manipulate the state of the stack.

Reflecting on this stack ADT, three big ideas emerge:

1. The model of information and behavior should be self-consistent. The behavior specifications must refer to the information specifications. When methods are invoked they transform the information from one legal state to another.

2. The model should be minimally sufficient for clients. The clients should not need to understand more details than are necessary.

3. So long as the implementation is consistent with the model, the implementation can vary arbitrarily. You could, for example, implement the stack as an array, a linked list, a database, or a distributed memory cache so long as it behaves like the model.

11.5.2   Modules and components as ADT's

The boundary model of a module or component has a lot in common with an abstract data type. Both describe an encapsulation boundary behind which an implementation is hidden. When you create models of modules, the interfaces are defined with Java interfaces or C .h files. When you create models of components, the interfaces are defined with ports. Just as you can create an interface model for users of the stack

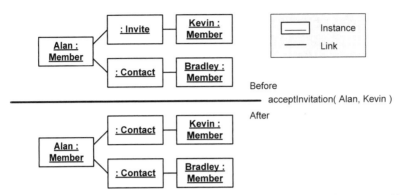

Figure 11.3: Snapshots showing the state of the model before and after Kevin accepts Alan's Invite to be part of each other's Contact Network. Note that the Invite instance in the first snapshot is replaced by a Contact instance in the second snapshot.

ADT, you can create an interface model for users of a Yinzer port. The example looks at a single action but the process is the same if there were multiple actions.

Consider the action from the Yinzer system where a member accepts an invitation to be part of another member's contact network. The method signature for the action might look like this:

> void **acceptInvitation**(Member requestor, Member requestee)

Note that the concept of an invitation is not seen as a parameter. An alternative signature would be to make the invitation object a parameter. Either way, the mental model of the user must include the idea of invitations. As with the stack ADT, pre- and post-conditions are added, like this:

> void **acceptInvitation**(Member requestor, Member requestee)
> **pre-condition**: invitation exists with requestor and requestee
> **post-condition**: the invitation no longer exists and the requestor
> and requestee are in each other's network of contacts

This describes the behavior of the Yinzer system, but only hints at the mental model a user needs. You can build an explicit type model that shows how they relate to each other by focusing on the terms referred to in the return values, parameters, and pre- and post-conditions. You could try to draw that type model now but, instead, first create some snapshots that you can use to test the type model. At this early stage they are more helpful because they are concrete. Figure 11.3 shows a pair of snapshots, the first showing that Alan has invited Kevin to join his contact network, and the second showing Alan and Kevin as Contacts of each other after the acceptInvitation action.

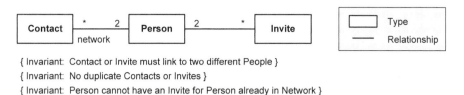

{ Invariant: Contact or Invite must link to two different People }
{ Invariant: No duplicate Contacts or Invites }
{ Invariant: Person cannot have an Invite for Person already in Network }

Figure 11.4: A minimally sufficient type model to support the Accept Invitation action. Notice that the graphical notation is not sufficient to express all the needed constraints, hence the invariants as notes.

You should use the pair of snapshots as a guide to help you create an accurate type model. Figure 11.4 shows a type model that is consistent with the snapshots. Notice that it has a few invariants to prevent some snapshots you do not want, snapshots that would otherwise be permitted by the graphical part of the model.

This is not the only possible model — you could have devised other snapshots and type models that are consistent with the action and pre- and post-conditions. For example, you could have eliminated the Invite type and added a boolean attribute to Contact indicating if it was a pending invitation or an accepted contact. Either model would work for the users and still allow developers to build arbitrary implementations in the internals model.

If this Yinzer port had more actions, then you would follow the process again to elaborate the type model. The result is a model that describes what a user of the port needs to know to use the provided actions. You have seen this process for ADT's and ports, but the idea is the same for describing methods on objects, or describing functions in modules.

Here is the process in a nutshell:

1. Select a port on the component (or an object, module, etc.).
2. For each action (or method, function, etc.) on that port, write out its signature and pre- and post-conditions.
3. Sketch one or more snapshot pairs showing how the instances would change as a result of the action (possibly reusing your functionality scenarios to help build the snapshots).
4. Generalize the snapshot pairs into a type model.

Following this process hides internal details yet reveals how to use the interface. In short, it gives you effective encapsulation. The resulting type model should be minimally sufficient to describe the behavior of the port, but does not describe how the internals of the component are implemented. It should also be self-consistent in that there are no terms used in the action descriptions that are undefined in the type model, and vice versa.

11.6   Conclusion

When you build software, you will make choices about how the system is divided up into smaller parts. You will almost always design it as a hierarchically nested set of parts. The choices you make regarding partitioning and encapsulation will have a big impact on the system's qualities. Invariably, you will be faced with partitioning choices that make some features or qualities easier to achieve, but others harder to achieve.

If you follow a particular style of hierarchical structure, then your system can be understood as a story at many levels. Other developers will be able to infer how it works and will not be swamped with too many objects, modules, or components at any given level of abstraction.

Your designs will have a dominant concern that organizes their decomposition. This chapter discussed several partitioning strategies: Functionality, Archetypes, Architectural style, Attribute Driven Design, Ports, Orthogonal abstraction, and Jigsaw puzzle. Although these might seem to imply that you should follow a top-down design path, it is more effective to work both top-down and bottom-up and reconcile the problems you discover.

Each part that is divided up will have an interface, and that interface should hide some of the details of the internal implementation. As the story about the accounting timesheets demonstrated, not all encapsulation is effective, and inappropriate abstractions can leak out across API boundaries. Parnas modules are one antidote. Parnas advocated keeping design secrets behind module interfaces such that you can choose between your design alternatives without that change being visible to clients.

The biggest benefit of encapsulation is that it reduces the cognitive burden of other developers. They can treat the component or module as a black box and not look beyond its interface. Effective encapsulation also contributes to comprehensibility, because simpler interfaces are easier to understand.

But there is no free lunch since building encapsulated interfaces takes effort. This chapter presented a process for building a full description of interfaces that includes the operation signatures, their pre- and post-conditions, and the type model necessary to understand what the operations do. You will need to apply your judgment to decide when such effort is justified. However, once you internalize this idea, you will see and analyze API's differently, and may not need to go through the full process to get the benefit.

11.7   Further reading

The idea of abstract data types is an old one, dating back to the early 1970s with the CLU and Alphard programming languages (Liskov, 1987; Shaw, 1981). The application of those ideas to components is described in D'Souza and Wills (1998) and D'Souza (2006), including using minimal type models to describe port operations based on pre- and post-conditions, and the use of snapshot pairs to drive the creation of the type model.

This chapter has deliberately conflated two distinct forms of abstraction, ADT's and objects, which are from a theoretical perspective quite different. William Cook's essay on the topic highlights the differences (Cook, 2009).

Subjects, aspects, and multi-dimensional separation of concerns were introduced to programming languages starting in the 1990s. Two papers that have high relevance to architectural modeling are Harrison and Ossher (1993) and Tarr et al. (1999), since they discuss the general problem of dividing a system into elements and the impact of the dominant decomposition.

Herb Simon noticed that the distinction between the inside and outside of a system may not be a purely human invention, as it occurs commonly as emergent organization patterns in nature (Simon, 1981). Many biological systems observe a nested hierarchy like architecture models do.

Chapter 12

Model Elements

This chapter describes the vocabulary of elements that are needed to produce architecture models, elements like modules, components, connectors, ports, roles, quality attributes, rationales, environment elements, scenarios, invariants, tradeoffs, and styles. This is the core set of elements that is needed for architecture modeling, and this core set is broadly supported both in industry and academics. The set of elements here is not comprehensive, as many views exist with specialized elements.

Chapter 9 discussed these same elements, but in less detail. The primary goal of that chapter was to make the conceptual model of architecture clear, and digging into details of the elements would have distracted from big picture understanding. This chapter probes the corner cases, compares and contrasts related elements, and provides advice on usage. As a result, you will notice some duplication as this chapter reviews those ideas, but the advantage is that you can come back to this chapter as a reference. You can safely skip over this chapter on your first read and come back later.

The diagrams here conform to UML syntax, or are quite close. This book recommends against digging too deep into the intricacies of UML for fear that only UML experts will understand subtle distinctions, such as the shape of arrowheads or the slant of the font. If you need to make subtle distinctions, remind readers of the syntax in the diagram legend.

Examples that run throughout this chapter will primarily use the canonical Library Problem (Wing, 1988) because of its widely understood domain, and to show you another example. The library in this problem statement is rather simple: It allows librarians to check out and return copies of books, add copies to the library, list books by author or subject, list the copies checked out by a borrower, and list the borrower who last checked out a copy. Borrowers (library patrons) can use the web to list the books they have checked out.

12.1 Allocation elements

Software runs on hardware, and that hardware must be located somewhere: in a server closet, in a data center, in the accounting department, or on a satellite. Allocation diagrams like Figure 9.6 show where modules and component instances are deployed. Such diagrams can help you reason about failures related to location, such as security breaches and reliability.

Software engineering authors are in broad agreement about what should be in allocation models and diagrams, but there is little agreement on what the elements should be called. UML refers to places where software can be deployed as *nodes* and refers to the communication channels between nodes as *connections* (Booch, Rumbaugh and Jacobson, 2005). SEI authors refer to both as *environmental elements* (Bass, Clements and Kazman, 2003). And a recent textbook refers to them as *hardware hosts* and *network links* (Taylor, Medvidović and Dashofy, 2009). The term *node* is rather general, the term *connection* is easy to confuse with *connector*, and the term *host* does not really fit for some hardware, like routers. So this book uses the terms *environmental elements* and *communication channels*, as clumsy as they are.

Examples of elements that can be allocated include the executable code for the user interface, the executable code for the database, and the configuration files that define the database schema. Notice that these examples include both component instances and modules. These elements are deployed onto environmental elements. The most obvious environmental element is hardware, such as an individual laptop or a server farm. Environmental elements can be nested within each other, so you can show that the server farm has hundreds of server computers inside of it.

In addition to hardware, it is expedient to treat human and political entities as environmental elements. That way you can draw a diagram showing a server farm (hardware) with subdivisions for the accounting department's servers and the finance department's servers. Strictly speaking, you cannot deploy software onto the accounting department. However, think of it as a shortcut that is equivalent to annotating some servers with a property saying they are owned by the accounting department. If you are mindful that you are taking a shortcut, and realize that accountants themselves do not run the software (computers do), this is a timesaving shortcut.

Properties on the environmental elements, modules, and components can be used for other purposes, such as indicating compatibility. A component might require 2GB of memory or access to the internet from the hardware it runs on. These constraints and capabilities can be expressed as properties of the elements and could even be

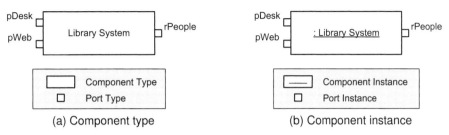

(a) Component type   (b) Component instance

Figure 12.1: A component type and instance. Notice that component instances are underlined and have a colon, optionally preceded by the instance name.

checked by a tool. Even without tools, properties give you a place to express these constraints so that other developers can see them.

12.2   Components

Components, the workhorse abstraction of software architecture, are defined as "the principal computation elements and data stores that execute in a system" (Clements et al., 2010). Components communicate only via connectors, and connectors themselves can do substantial work.

This section discusses several topics relating to components, including: component types and component instances, the relationship between modules and components, the use of subcomponents, uncertainties and ambiguities that exist in component modeling, and Component-Based Development (CBD). The next section discusses components as they are used in component assemblies.

Types and instances. Components follow the same type-instance relationship, *generalization*, as classes and objects do. In object-oriented programming languages today, you define classes in the programming language and see objects at runtime. If you had a programming language that supported components directly, you would declare *component types* in that language and you would see their *component instances* at runtime. Classes and component types are defined in the module viewtype, since you see them directly in the source code; objects and component instances are seen in the runtime viewtype, since you do not see them until runtime.

The distinction should now be clear between a component type and a component instance, but you will hear people say just "component" without distinguishing. They usually mean a component instance, but it is best to ask when it is unclear. Unlike classes, which usually have many object instances, component types are often instantiated only once in a system.

	Components	Modules
Exist in module viewtype	Types: Yes; Instances: No	Yes
Exist at runtime	Types: No; Instances: Yes	Rarely
Multiple instances	Often	Rarely
Used for encapsulation	Yes	Yes
Communicates via	Ports and connectors	Interfaces

Figure 12.2: A table showing some features that highlight the differences between components and modules. Both modules and component types are composed of source code, but you rarely instantiate a module (you would only have one instance of a math library, for example) but multiple instances of components are common.

Here is an example that highlights the differences between component types and instances. Imagine that the Library System is designed with mirrored database servers in case of problems. That design would have at least two component instances for the database, with one of them ready to take over if the other fails. Both database component instances do the same job, namely they store information about the library, so they are of the same component type and run the same executable program. Notice, however, that you can tell the two instances apart even though they run the same code and hold the same data, so the instances are said to have *identity*.

Figure 12.1 shows how component types and instances are depicted in diagrams. You can distinguish a type from an instance because the instance is always underlined and has a colon before type name. In the example, the component type is "Library System" and the instance has no name, so it is called an *anonymous instance*. Notice that in isolation you cannot visually distinguish a port type from a port instance, but you can tell based on what it is attached to.

Compared with modules. Components are composed of the same things as modules (such as source code and configuration files), but the intention is that you will see instances of components at runtime. Those component instances will interact with each other in constrained, well-understood ways via ports and connectors. Compare this with a module, which is a collection of implementation artifacts (classes, interfaces, etc.) that may have been grouped together for arbitrary reasons (e.g., math functions, legacy Fortran routines, data interchange types, or code authored elsewhere), that is rarely instantiated at runtime, and that has no constraints on how it interacts with other modules. Figure 12.2 summarizes some important differences between them.

You may wonder why there are both modules and components: Is a component not an instance of a module? Said another way, is it true that class:object :: module:component? While this would clean up the conceptual model, and is sometimes true, it is not true for many modules. Plenty of modules are never instantiated, such as math modules, nor does it make much sense to think of them as having runtime existence or structure.

However, a well-organized module can closely resemble a component type. Imagine a system with a user interface module and a backend module. The developer of this system has organized the modules so that they correspond to what will be instantiated at runtime. While this is good practice, it is not always possible, and therefore the concepts of components and modules must be separate because they will not always line up as well as they do in this example. It may help you to think of a component as a special case of a module, one that you intend to instantiate at runtime (often more than once), and one that interacts with other such modules in a constrained way.

Subcomponents and implementation. Every system will have at least one component, which is the system itself. It is good practice to have additional components nested within the system because then each component is individually easier to understand and reason about, as discussed in Section 11.1. A nested component can be referred to as a *subcomponent*, but it is a matter of perspective — your component is perhaps someone else's subcomponent.

This nesting can be repeated many times but does not continue forever. At some point of your choosing, the nesting stops and the component is implemented, not with more components, but with classes, functions, procedures, etc. Many factors enter into the decision of how many components a system should have and how many levels of nested components to use, including the size of the components, the availability of off-the-shelf components for inclusion, and natural division points such as differing source code languages or physical deployment locations. Ultimately a developer makes a judgment call, one that becomes easier with experience. As a general rule, it is rare to see subcomponents implemented with a single class or just a few lines of code.

Uncertainties and ambiguities. At some point, what was meant by *object* and *class* was up for debate and many alternatives were proposed. Today, mainstream languages have codified generally agreed definitions for them. Since you cannot yet define component types and instances in programming languages, there is still substantial room for uncertainties and ambiguities between people who use the terms. Here are a few areas of common misunderstandings.

- **Types and instances.** Not everyone who talks about components is careful enough to distinguish component types from instances. It is easy to conflate them because components are often instantiated just once. A system might have just one user interface, one business logic component, and one database. In this case there are three component types and three component instances, one for each component type. In object-oriented programming, a class with a single instance is unusual, but seen often enough that the pattern has been named the Singleton design pattern (Gamma et al., 1995). Components are generally much larger than classes, so instantiating them just once is common.

- **Just *component*.** It is best to be careful and say either *component type* or *component instance*, not just *component*. Saying *component instance* takes a long time and has a lot of syllables, so sometimes it is (understandably) shortened to just *component*. Depending on the context, you may be able to take this shortcut too, but be aware of your audience and choose accordingly.

- **Files and databases.** Some things are obviously components, like big chunks of running code, but other things are not so clear. Is a file a component? Single files or the filesystem are often represented as components so that you can show clearly that your other components interact with them. Otherwise, someone reading a diagram may be surprised to later learn that a component reads or writes files, since other communication is shown clearly. What about a database? Databases are always represented as components, but the type of a database should never be "Oracle" or even simply "Database." Instead, its type depends on how you have configured it for its purpose, for example an InventoryDB, or PayrollDB.

- **Modules and components.** Keep in mind that although this book describes a conceptual model of architecture that has distinct meanings for modules and components, you will find many people using the terms interchangeably.

CBD and a component marketplace. In the 1990s, many people talked about a future component marketplace, something that was central to component-based development (CBD). The idea was that the software industry would embrace development of components to be sold individually as products to be used by software developers, rather than selling them assembled into an end-user product (Heineman and Councill, 2001). Parallels were drawn with the computer hardware market, where some companies sell complete computers while others sell components that are assembled into computers. So far, the market for components has been small. For example, databases are sold as components, but they are the exception rather than the rule.

While a component marketplace has not flourished, plenty of software applications have CBD underpinnings and scripting languages have programmatic access to their core functions, independent of their GUIs. Furthermore, many companies internally produce components that are used by other teams inside the company.

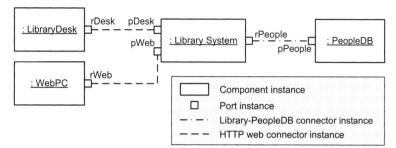

Figure 12.3: A system context diagram of the Library System. A system context diagram is a kind of component assembly that shows the system to be built (here, the Library System) and the external systems it connects to. The Library System component instance shown here is refined in Figure 12.4.

The idea of components as something packaged for sale in a market is different than the architectural definition of components in this book. Clemens Szyperski provided a definition of components that emphasizes the fully-packaged nature: "A software component is a unit of composition with contractually specified interfaces and explicit context dependencies only. A software component can be deployed independently and is subject to composition by third parties." (Szyperski, 2002) It is probably easiest to think of such *CBD components* as a special case of *architecture components* since every CBD component would satisfy the definition of component, but not vice versa.

12.3 Component assemblies

A *component assembly*, also known as a *component and connector diagram* or simply as a *runtime diagram*, shows an assembly of component, port, and connector instances or types. Their arrangement is the component design and different arrangements will yield different qualities.

System context diagram. A *system context diagram* is a component assembly that focuses on the system being designed. It shows that system as a component instance and also includes external systems that the system connects to. Figure 12.3 shows a system context diagram of the Library System.

Refinement. Another way to use a component assembly is to use it to *refine* another component, showing its internal design. Figure 12.4 shows how we can refine the Library System component from Figure 12.3 to show how it is implemented with subcomponents. The component assembly consists of the five internal components,

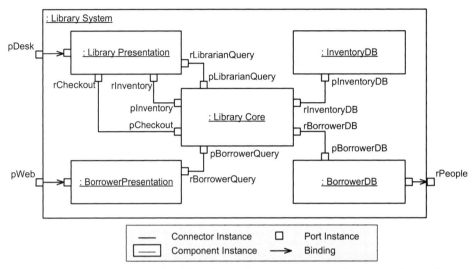

Figure 12.4: A component assembly of the Library System component instance. External ports are bound to internal ones. It is the same component instance seen in Figure 12.3 and this diagram additionally shows its internal details.

shown as anonymous component instances, and the connector instances between them.

Notice that the diagram shows the Library System as a component instance that wraps around the component assembly. This wraparound component is referred to as the *external* or *enclosing* component and it its name should be shown, often in the upper left or right corner. Using *bindings*, ports on the external component are bound to compatible or identical ports on internal components. In this case, notice that the three ports of the Library System component have been bound to ports on the internal components.

This refinement can continue to nest recursively. For example, you could take the Borrower Presentation component from Figure 12.4 and build a component assembly showing its refinement. The outer box (the enclosing component) would be labeled "<u>: Borrower Presentation</u>" and it would have the two ports on Borrower Presentation bound to internal subcomponents.

Refinement semantics. When you use a component assembly to refine an existing component, the component assembly must conform to the enclosing component's specification, which includes its port definitions, quality attribute scenarios, and invariants. This internal design may go beyond what was specified by adding additional functionality, or exceeding the specified performance invariants, but it cannot do worse.

During refinement, you could in theory add any detail — but you risk angering the reader of your diagram if you do something unexpected. For example, if you show a component with two ports but later reveal, in the refinement, the existence of previously unmentioned third port then a reader would be justifiably surprised.

Refinement always insists that the high-detail model of the component be compatible with the low-detail version. The conservative rules followed (called *closed semantics* and discussed further in Section 13.7.1) go further to prevent surprises. The rules are:

- The number and types of ports are unchanged
- The externally-visible constraints and behavior (e.g., invariants, quality attribute scenarios) are unchanged

Sticking with closed refinement semantics is usually the best choice, but sometimes it is difficult since real components may have dozens of ports. Showing all those ports may work against the desire to show a high-level diagram that is simple and clear. For example, a component might have ports for administration, logging, and other technical details that could be elided from diagrams used as "big picture" introductions.

The simple solution to this dilemma is to omit the ports, but to put a note on the diagram saying that some ports have been omitted. That way a reader will not be surprised when encountering a more detailed diagram that shows those ports, nor will the reader try to draw any conclusions based on the absence of those ports.

When you follow these rules, you prevent a reader from becoming surprised and saying, "Hey, where did that come from?" You should encounter no surprise when you look at examples of component refinement in this book, such as the refinement between the Library System component in Figure 12.3 and Figure 12.4, because they follow this set of rules that limit what can change and what new details can be introduced.

Expressiveness. Some component assemblies are more expressive than others. If you refer back to Figure 4.4, you will notice that it clearly shows the different types of connectors used, while Figure 12.4 does not. If you have different types of ports or connectors, it is a good idea to distinguish them visually and add them to the diagram's legend. An alternative and more compact way to describe the ports is to label each port's type on the diagram, as seen in Figure 12.4, and separately provide a specification for each port type.

Understanding the design. A component assembly does not describe everything about how the internals of a component work. The component assembly refers to component, connector, and port types, so each of these needs to be understood by the person reading the diagram. Understanding a component, connector, or port

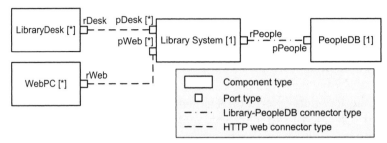

Figure 12.5: System context diagram of the Library System, as in Figure 12.3, with component types instead of instances. This diagram says that there can be only one instance of the Library System and PeopleDB components. There can be multiple instances of the LibraryDesk and WebPC components and their connections to the Library System terminate on unique (not shared) ports.

type means understanding its properties, invariants, responsibilities, type model, and behavior model.

Said another way, the system context diagram in Figure 12.3 is just the beginning of what a reader needs to know to understand the design. That diagram would need to be accompanied, either verbally or on paper, by descriptions of the ports, invariants, styles, quality attribute scenarios, design decisions, etc., that go along with the design. A component assembly is a great way to introduce a design, but it is not in itself sufficient to understand it.

Snapshot of a dynamic architecture. Almost every system has a dynamic architecture, meaning that its configuration of components changes during runtime. Most systems quickly converge on a steady-state configuration that is stable for most of its runtime, so you may simply think of them as static, but during startup and shutdown there are changes. A component assembly usually shows a single runtime configuration of the instances and it is usually the steady-state system configuration. But it could alternately show types instead of instances, as discussed next.

Be aware that if you want to analyze the system's startup or shutdown behavior, looking at its steady-state configuration will be insufficient, and you will need to use multiple component assemblies that represent its configuration at different times. Also, to analyze a fully dynamic architecture you will also need many component assemblies.

Using component types. The system context diagram in Figure 12.3 and its refinement shown in Figure 12.4 are both drawn using component, connector, and port *instances*. Using instances instead of types makes those diagrams exceptionally easy to read and understand. However, those diagrams represent just one of the many possible configurations that you wish to allow. The system has just one Library System component instance and one PeopleDB component instance, but it can have many Library Desk and Web PC component instances, yet this is not clear from the system context diagram.

A component assembly that uses *types* instead of instances can show this. Figure 12.5 is a system context diagram for the Library System but it uses component, connector, and port types instead of instances. Notice too that it has numbers on it representing the multiplicities of the components and ports that are allowed.

Most of the time when you are drawing component assemblies you will want to stick to instances because the diagram is so clear, but sometimes you may wish to draw them with types. If you are struggling to create a component assembly with types, recall that it is OK to draw one with instances and add a note describing your intentions. For the system context diagram, it might be simplest to use the diagram with instances and add a note saying, "The Library System and PeopleDB components have just one instance; the Library Desk and Web PC components can have many instances, each with an unshared pDesk or pWeb port."

12.4   Connectors

Components are the principal computation elements and data stores, and they only communicate via their ports. The port on one component is attached to the port on another component by a *connector*, defined as "a runtime pathway of interaction between two or more components" (Clements et al., 2010). Connectors are shown in most diagrams that show components, including Figure 12.4 in this chapter.

Following the pattern you saw with components, you find *connector types* in the module viewtype and *connector instances* in the runtime viewtype. As with components, you should similarly assume that people mean "connector instances" when they simply say "connectors," but it is better to ask and be sure.

The importance of connectors. It is easy to underestimate connectors, perhaps because the most common one is a local method call, or perhaps because they are shown on models as a simple line, rather than as a box like components are. Connectors, more so than components, drive architectural styles (Shaw and Garlan, 1996; D'Souza and Wills, 1998). Most styles allow components to do arbitrary computations, but restrict what the connectors can do and their topology. Connectors dictate that clients can call servers but not the reverse. Connectors ensure that two copies of a database component are replicated and ready in case of failover. Connectors either enable or prevent a COTS component from integrating with your existing systems.

Connectors enable components to communicate, but this should not be interpreted as a less important job. Connectors do real work and often that real work is the communication that must happen.

Connector type	Notes
Local procedure call	Most common connector when components are all in the same memory space.
Remote procedure call	Concrete examples include SOAP and HTTP requests. Both local and remote procedure call connectors are kinds of request-reply connectors.
SQL or other datastore	Declarative language used to load/store data.
Pipe	Simple producer-consumer relationships between components.
Shared memory	Fast but complex communication.
Event broadcast	Consumers depend only on events, not on producers.
Enterprise bus	Standardizes intra-application communication for assembly of large systems.
Data drop	Distribution mechanism for shared data from single source.
Incremental replication	Handles state synchronization.

Figure 12.6: A tabulation of some common connector types and notes about them.

Often the value of an application is in its connectors, rather than its components. An architect at a large financial institution put it to me like this: Several programs may do a given job, but differ in how well they inter-operate with other programs. It may take longer to build the connectors than the component itself.

Real work can be done in connectors. Connectors can convert, transform, or translate datatypes between components. They can adapt protocols and mediate between a collection of components. They can broadcast events, possibly cleaning up duplicate events or prioritizing important ones. Significantly, they can do the work that enables quality attributes, such as encryption, compression, synchronization / replication, and thread-safe communication. It is hard to imagine systems achieving qualities like reliability, durability, latency, and auditability if their connectors are not contributing.

Common types. The concept of a connector is quite general, and encompasses the common ways to communicate, including procedure calls and events, as well as more complex mechanisms like pipes, batch transfers, and incremental replicators. It also covers indirect means of communicating such as interrupts and shared memory. Some example implementations of connectors include remote procedure calls, the rsync program, SOAP over HTTP, and enterprise service buses. Figure 12.6 shows a list of common types of connectors. Complex connectors are often built using simpler ones.

Connector substitutability. Academic experts on architecture insist that connectors are first-class elements of an architecture in the same way that components are. You should already be comfortable that a component has an interface, defined by its ports, and that you could swap it for another component that supports that same interface.

If connectors are first-class elements in your architecture language, can you swap them too? For example, if your components are communicating via pipe connectors, can you swap the pipes for an event bus without affecting the clients of the connector? In architecture models the answer is yes, but often this property is lost in the translation into code. Source code that implements components often implements an interface and clients depend on that interface. However, source code that implements connectors rarely implements an interface, so clients depend on a specific connector implementation. Examples of this include clients knowing that they are putting events onto an event bus, or making remote method calls.

Maintaining substitutability of connectors in the implementation is a choice that developers must make. A component may be able to provide users better error handling and reporting, for example, if it knows that it is using a remote procedure call instead of a local one.

However, most systems would benefit from substitutable connectors. Increasingly, no system is an island, and standalone systems today are integrated into a larger system tomorrow. As will be discussed in Section 10.3, giving connectors first-class status in the code is easy and has little performance impact. Most communication in code happens inside components, which would be unchanged. But when communication happens between components, as in the connection between a client and a server, it is worthwhile considering making the connector first class and substitutable, which lets you change its implementation without disturbing those who use it.

Choosing suitable connectors. In principle, you could use any kind of connector between your components, but in practice you will have preferences for one kind of connector or another. For example, it might be inefficient to use an event bus when simple method calls would work, or it might be complicated to use shared memory communication with lots of threads, but you could imagine making them work. Once you put all of these seemingly dissimilar means of communication in the category called "connector," it is easier to focus on the problem of choosing a suitable type of connector.

When connectors are treated as first-class elements of your architecture language, it is easier to see that your choice of connector, much like your choice of architecture, can be appropriate or inappropriate. You may assume by default that all connectors are local method calls, and indeed they are often the best choice, but they cannot be used when communication spans machines or processes. Nor are they the necessarily best choice when you need to analyze a system or ensure an emergent property. Method calls are a low-level connector, and as such will give you little leverage on

Property	Notes
Connector name	If you cannot think of a descriptive name, you can use the names of the components on either end.
Roles	Each role should be named and its port compatibility should be clear.
Topology	Most connectors are binary, but some are ternary or N-way.
Functionality	Connectors can do data conversions, fix or patch data for consistency (such as quoting special characters or closing dangling HTML tags), or encrypt and decrypt streams.
Type model	As with ports, connectors have a domain that users must understand. When documenting the type model, be clear if the types are conceptual or data interchange types. If the model is graphical, the latter can be stereotyped with «interchange».
Behavior model	Many connectors are simply open or closed, but if they have a more complex protocol it can be documented graphically using a UML state diagram (or similar) or textually.
Other properties	May include reliability, performance, resource requirements, security, implementation technology, standards.

Figure 12.7: Example properties of a connector. A diagram rarely shows every property you might care about for a connector. Consider these common properties when describing a connector.

the problem to be solved compared to a connector with more smarts.

In the library example, each connector has a domain-specific job to do, such as communicating checkin and checkout requests from the Library Desk to the Library System. You must match the requirements of that domain-specific job with a connector type that provides appropriate qualities and features. For example, if you chose a local procedure call connector or a shared memory connector then the Library Desk and Library System components would need to be on the same machine. If you chose a pipe then it would be easy to transform the stream of input, but you would need a separate connector for any return values that go back to the Library Desk. Asynchronous event connectors make it easier to balance incoming events across many machines, but usually entail complexity to handle responses that come back at an unknown time in the future.

Chapter 2 described how, at macro-scale, architecture choices yield systems with different qualities (throughput, usability, modifiability, etc.). Here at micro-scale, you see that connector choices yield different qualities too.

Connector name	LibrarySystem-PeopleDB Connector
Roles	rPeople, compatible with rPeople port pPeople, compatible with pPeople port
Topology	Binary
Other properties	Protocol: SQL Transport: TCP/IP Throughput: 10,000 person records/sec Synchronous
Functionality	TBD
Type model	A row from the PERSON table in the pPeople role contains ... A Person class in the rPeople role contains ...
Behavior model	The connector starts in the CLOSED state, transitions to the OPEN state after a call to open(), then to the CLOSED state after a call to close().

Figure 12.8: A description of the LibrarySystem-PeopleDB connector between the Library System component and the People Database component from Figure 12.3.

Properties. Like other architecture elements, connectors have properties. Common properties of connectors include performance (throughput and latency), security, reliability, synchronous / asynchronous delivery, delivery guarantees, compression, and buffering.

Diagrams rarely have enough space to show all of the connector's relevant details, so details are usually provided elsewhere. When you are explaining a connector to someone else, think about explaining the common connector properties described ·in Figure 12.7. An example of documenting the connector between the Library System and an external database containing records of people (the connector shown in Figure 12.3), is shown in Figure 12.8.

When connectors are shown on diagrams, ensure that the type of each connector is evident. When there are only a few connector types, changing the line style (thick, thin, dashed, etc.) is effective, but with more types it is clearer to use the UML stereotype to indicate the connector's type.

It is tempting to annotate diagrams to indicate technology properties of the connectors, and it is easy to do this in a first draft. But then you will want to add another property, perhaps indicating the throughput of different connectors, and then which connectors are synchronous versus asynchronous. There are two solutions to this property overload: first, either omit properties from the diagram and rely on a legend or external descriptions, and second, have multiple versions of the diagram, each an-

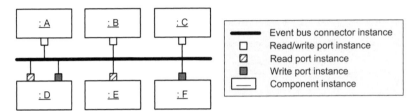

Figure 12.9: An example component assembly showing an event bus instance connecting several component instances, which can have a read port, a write port, or both. Note that in diagrams like this, where all instances are connected to a bus, you cannot tell which ones are intended to communicate with each other.

notated for different purposes. For example, you might have one diagram annotated to show properties relevant to throughput, while another diagram is annotated to help you with security.

It is also tempting to put arrows on connectors, but this can cause confusion as to what the arrow means, as described in Section 15.4.

Roles. The end of a connector that attaches to a port is called a *role*. For a connector to successfully attach to a port, the role and the port must be compatible. Roles are rarely shown in graphical diagrams (i.e., just the port and the connector are visible), though an example is shown in Figure 12.11 because it shows the refinement of a connector, and therefore must show the connector's roles.

Intuitively, you know that you cannot attach any connector to any port, which means that you are mentally type-checking the connector's role with the port. Architecture Description Languages (ADL's) formalize this intuition and let you declare ports and roles so that compatibility can be explicitly checked.

N-way and bus connectors. Most connectors are *binary*, meaning that they have two roles. A binary connector enables two components to communicate. *N-way (or N-ary) connectors* have three or more roles, which enables N-way communication between many ports. The best-known example is a event bus, or publish-subscribe, connector. Since an event bus may connect many components, they are usually are shown in a slightly different notation than other components, as seen in Figure 12.9.

An event bus can be a boon for designers because it enables flexible reconfiguration of applications. Any component on the bus can potentially send messages to any other component on the bus. This flexibility is a liability when it comes to clear documentation, however. If you look at Figure 12.9, it is impossible to tell which components are communicating with each other and which are not. That is, while you can tell that it is possible that component A could communicate with component B, you do not know if it actually does.

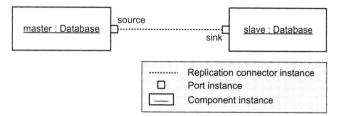

Figure 12.10: A component assembly showing a master and hot backup slave connected by a replication connector. Giving the connector a goal encourages you to think about the domain of replication and how it might fail.

A partial solution is to use differentiated read and write ports, as on the D, E, and F component instances, which yields some additional information, but still not who is talking to whom. A better remedy is to keep using the normal point-to-point style of diagrams, which are quite clear about which components are communicating and which are not, and put a note on the diagram saying that the connectors are actually the same shared event bus. Another good solution is to use multiple N-way connectors to indicate that a subset of the components are collaborating.

Goal connectors. It is useful to juxtapose two kinds of connectors. The first is the *micromanaged connector* that simply does a job you assign to it. If it fails, that is because you did not supervise it sufficiently. Its job is only to do what you told it to do. Micromanaged connectors do the simplest job possible and are simple connectors. The second kind of connector, a *goal connector*, has an assigned goal, or objective, that it is responsible for accomplishing. A developer who builds a goal connector must avoid failure by looking into the problem, discovering possible failure cases, and ensuring that the connector handles them. Goal connectors are usually complex as they have real domain work to do, and are responsible for seeing it completed.

Consider the seemingly simple task of keeping a hot backup copy of a component, ready for failover, seen in Figure 12.10. There must be communication between the master and slave, because the slave should maintain the same state as the master.

Your first thought may be to make a procedure call to the slave every time the master changes. That might work if the two components were co-located on the same machine, but backups are often kept on separate machines for reliability, so you may consider using remote procedure calls or events. But now there are more concerns: What if messages do not arrive? Is the latency between master and slave acceptable? Does the master process the replication synchronously or asynchronously? Does the data need to be compressed, or can you efficiently send deltas? Perhaps worst of all, are there transactional problems, where if a master fails in a transitional state you need to revert the slave back to the last known good state?

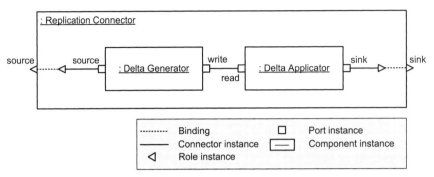

Figure 12.11: A refinement of the Replication Connector from Figure 12.10. It is more common to refine components than connectors, but large and complex connectors are composed of components on the inside.

By assigning a goal to this connector you reduce the chance that you treat it as a trivial mover of data. If the connector were made simpler, one or both of the components would be forced to assume additional responsibilities, diluting their cohesion and purpose. Assigning the synchronization goal to a connector simplifies your components, making them easier to build, maintain, and comprehend. It also simplifies your system description by raising its level of abstraction.

Domain connectors. Another way to encourage interesting connectors is use *domain connectors*. You do this by treating components as domains and assigning the job of bridging the domains to the connectors. Michael Jackson described a patient monitoring system where sensors on the patient reported body temperature and pulse; the system's job was to alert a nurse in case of emergency (Jackson, 2000). He showed that two different kinds of alarms were needed: one where the patient is suffering a heart attack, and another less urgent alarm where the patient has inadvertently removed the sensors.

Let's look at this example from the perspective of using connectors to bridge the domains. The first domain is that of collecting accurate sensor readings. There may be acquisition, digital to analog conversion, smoothing, signal transformation, and other work to be done in order to sense the patient's temperature and pulse. The second domain is that of alarms. There will be several severities of alarms and various ways of informing people. You might configure low severity alarms to blink a light, medium severity alarms to sound a local beeper, and high severity alarms to do all that plus sound a remote beeper.

Defining the domains this way, you might even be able to reuse these components in a different context other than patient monitoring, because each component handles a single domain, rather than knowing about the other component or about the patient monitoring system. The connector acts as an insulator, preventing domain details from one component seeping into the other.

Whenever two domain-specific components interact, you will need to write some code that understands both domains, whether that code is in one or both of the components, or in the connector. In this case, you need to write code that triggers a medium severity alarm if the patient has accidentally removed his sensors, and a high severity alarm if he is suffering a heart attack. If you place this code in either the sensing or alarm components then they will have a mixture of domains. You can instead place it in the connector, which at one end will take in sensor events and at the other end emit alarm events. It is impossible to avoid having code that knows about both sensors and alarms, but you can locate this code in the connector and thereby insulate the components.

Someone with the job of building the connector is more likely to create a good interface that describes the possible events that the connector will provide. The obvious interface recognizes heart rate and temperature events, but a developer of this connector is more likely to recognize that another event is needed: sensors disconnected. If you build a simple connector that provides the raw data to the monitoring component, it is easier to overlook the concept of disconnected sensors because you are unlikely to carefully consider the domain of the events. The insight here is that when you let the connectors do real work, you benefit both because you get simpler domains to work with, and because you may understand each domain better in isolation.

In this example the translation between the sensor domain and the alarm domain was rather simple, but in other cases it will be complex. Is it OK for a connector to be large and complex? Yes. You have already seen how a component can be refined to show its internal design, and the same refinement process can be used for connectors. In fact, connectors can be themselves implemented using components, as is described in more detail next. For example, an enterprise service bus guarantees properties like durability and in-order delivery, and that communication infrastructure is complex, so it is implemented using many distributed components and data stores.

Connectors should be treated as equals of components in software architecture. If you give them simple jobs then you do yourself a disservice, and likely pollute your components by hurting their cohesion and increasing coupling. Two concrete strategies are to assign goals to connectors and to use connectors to bridge domains.

Refinement. Connector refinement is essentially the same as component refinement. When you refine a component, you relate a boundary model of the component to an internals model of the component. Externally visible features from the boundary model are commitments that the internals model must uphold, things like the ports, invariants, and quality attribute scenarios.

Figure 12.11 shows the refinement of a replication connector, similar to the one

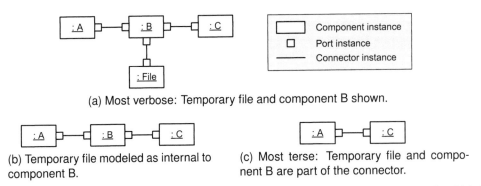

(a) Most verbose: Temporary file and component B shown.

(b) Temporary file modeled as internal to component B.

(c) Most terse: Temporary file and component B are part of the connector.

Figure 12.12: Different options for modeling a connection between components A and C, which is intermediated by component B and a temporary file.

originally shown in Figure 12.10. Recall that when a component is refined, the external ports must be the same (see Section 12.3). In connector refinement, it is the roles that must be the same. So where you earlier saw ports sticking out of the component assembly, here you see a source role and a sink role sticking out of the replication connector. A binding shows how the source role corresponds to a role on the inside of the subcomponent.

This figure is unlike any other in this book because it shows a connector with a dangling role, one not attached to a port. All of the other diagrams show connectors that are bound to ports, in which case the role is not shown graphically.

Modeling flexibility. Like components, connectors can do real work and you can reveal their internal implementations via refinement. This combination yields options for how you can model connectors. Consider, for example, the three alternatives shown in Figure 12.12 that all show components A and C communicating. In option (a), component B intermediates the connection and writes to a file. This model is consistent with the implementation of a durable event bus, one that does not lose messages even during a power failure. It can also be modeled as option (b), where the file is omitted. The file might still be used, but since it communicates only with B, you can choose to show it in the internals model for component B. And it can be modeled quite simply as in option (c), where both the file and component B are part of the internals model of the connector between A and C. It is important to note that the design is the same with all three modeling options, but (b) and (c) hide more details.

Choosing among modeling options like these is difficult, and without any context it is impossible to choose well. Recall that your architecture models are a bit like story problems in math. When you hear the story about the two trains traveling and are asked when they will meet, you abstract away details from your model that do not help you answer the question that is asked. That is, to decide which modeling option is best, focus on what questions the model must answer.

For example, if A and C are components you purchase, and you are to build B, it seems likely that you will choose a model that shows B explicitly. If you need to analyze your model for possible security threats, then you will want to see the intermediate file (and know if it can be tampered with). If you were analyzing the composition of components A and C using component B as an event bus, then you will hide both B and the file.

In the 1990's as object-oriented programming was becoming mainstream, developers would often joke about the nature of an object. "What is an object?" they would ask, then answer, "Anything you want!" Once you have done object-oriented programming for a while, the joke ceases to be funny because you develop an intuition for when something must be modeled as an object and when it can simply be an attribute of an existing object. The same shift will take place with architecture modeling as it becomes mainstream, and instead of joking about modeling flexibility, developers will build models that help answer their questions.

12.5   Design decisions

As developers design and build software, they make decisions about the design, and some decisions are bigger than others. That is, some decisions are pivotal. These pivotal *design decisions* shape the decisions from that point onward and constrain the design space. Such design decisions are not made lightly, and developers usually have an extensive rationale that underlies the decision.

Developers make decisions every day about the system's design and most of these provide little insight into the system. Only a handful of decisions are worthy of being considered pivotal design decisions. You should be wary of wasting time by expressing the less important decisions, whether you are writing them down or discussing them verbally.

Highlighting pivotal design decisions can help others understand why the system is the way it is. The rationale will connect the design decision to the forces that shape the system, including its functional requirements, quality attribute requirements, and tradeoffs present in the design space. Design decisions do not have a formal structure, but usually consist of a decision and a rationale. In the Library System example, a design decision could be:

> **Design decision:** The system will be built using Java because: the team has experience using with Java and a high-level and such a statically typed language can improve modifiability, which we value highly. C might be harder to evolve, its performance benefits are not a priority, and (potential) pointer bugs would hurt reliability.

Notice that the decision is interesting by itself, but provides insight via its connection to the forces that shape the system. Before hearing about the design decision, you might have been wondering why this team did not use your favorite language. Just knowing that the decision was to use Java does not answer your question. You may still disagree about their choice, but since you have the rationale, at least you know why the decision was made.

Writing down pivotal design decisions can help even when a design exists. Someone else looking at a design, or at code, cannot tell which decisions in the design are arbitrary and which are pivotal. Arbitrary decisions could be changed without fundamentally upsetting the design, pivotal ones cannot. Expressing the design decisions explicitly avoids loss of *design intent*, as is discussed in Section 10.4.

12.6   Functionality scenarios

Functionality scenarios describe the behavior of a system. In other architecture models, the system is described as a collection of components, modules, ports, interfaces, allocation elements, and so on. Functionality scenarios tell a story of how those elements can change over time and interact with each other. For example, a component assembly of the library system, like the ones shown earlier in Figures 12.3 and 12.4, only shows which component instances exist, not their behavior. A functionality scenario can describe how that component assembly model, or another model, changes over time. Functionality scenarios can be written textually, as in Figure 12.13, or they can be written graphically, as a UML sequence diagram.

Figure 12.13 shows an example functionality scenario of the life of a copy of Moby-Dick in a library. The scenario shows a single legal trace of behavior through a model, but it cannot describe every possible behavior. For example, this functionality scenario does not say what happens when borrowers lose the copy that they checked out.

Use cases are another popular way of describing behavior. They are largely equivalent to functionality scenarios, but there are some important differences. Use cases are activities that are high-level and visible to the users of the system. Use cases are often defined to be accomplishing a goal of an actor outside the system, so internal system activities would not count as use cases. Where functionality scenarios are a single trace of behavior, use cases can include variation steps that allow them to describe multiple traces. Because of these potential differences, this book uses the term *functionality scenario* to describe traces, but so long as you are clear about the possible misunderstandings, you may call them *use cases*.

Functionality scenarios and quality attribute (QA) scenarios, despite the similarity in names[1], are quite different. QA scenarios are similar to a single step in a functionality scenario. The term *quality attribute scenarios* comes from Bass, Clements

---

[1]This book refrains from changing existing terminology because it seems to be the lesser of the evils.

<u>Name</u>: End-to-end copy of Moby-Dick
<u>Initial state</u>: Larry is a Librarian; Bart is a Borrower
<u>Actors</u>: Larry, Bart
<u>Steps</u>:

1. Larry lists all Books about "fishing" / No matching books are found.
2. Larry adds a Copy of the Book "Moby-Dick" by Herman Melville to the Library. A record of the Book is also added.
3. Larry lists all Books by Herman Melville / "Moby-Dick" is returned.
4. Larry lists all Books about "fishing" / "Moby-Dick" is returned.
5. Larry (with Bart) checks out the Copy of "Moby-Dick" to Bart. Its due date is set to 6 September.
6. Larry lists who last checked out the Copy of "Moby-Dick" / Bart.
7. Larry lists the Copies currently checked out by Bart / Copy of "Moby-Dick".
8. Larry (with Bart) returns the Copy of "Moby-Dick" to the Library.
9. Larry removes the Copy of "Moby-Dick" from the Library.

Figure 12.13: An end-to-end functionality scenario showing the initial addition of a book copy to the library, it being checked out, and eventually removed from the library. It applies to the system context diagram for the Library System shown in Figure 12.3.

and Kazman (2003). The term *functionality scenarios* (or just *scenarios*) comes from D'Souza and Wills (1998), whose use of scenarios inspired the approach and techniques presented here. When it is clear from context, you can refer to functionality scenarios just as *scenarios*.

Structure. Functionality scenarios are easy to read because of their story-like quality, similar to fiction, but a useful scenario is non-fiction. It is structured and has checkable references to other models. Step 5 in the scenario above cannot be "Larry the librarian conjures elves from the computer system / the elves tie up Bart" because that (presumably) is not something the Library System can do, however fun it might be to build that system.

In this case, the story is about libraries and books, not elves. We know that because the other design models define the *vocabulary* we can use in this story, and those models talk about books, but not elves. The other design models further constrain the *actions* in the story: actions like adding copies and checking out copies, but not tying up library patrons. To achieve this connection with the other design models, a functionality scenario consists of the five parts shown in Figure 12.14: target model, scenario name, initial state, actors, and steps.

The meta-model of a functionality scenario is shown in Figure 12.15, and it formalizes the description above. It shows that each functionality scenario has one target model and a sequence of steps. Each step has an actor who initiates it and a single

Name	The scenario name can be anything that is helpfully descriptive.
Target model	The model that the scenario applies to. Functionality scenarios are often applied to component assemblies and port type models, but could apply to any model with elements that can change over time.
Initial state	The initial state describes the state of the model before the scenario starts. For example, the initial state could describe the contents of the library and the existing loans.
Actors	The list of actors who are involved in and initiate the scenario steps.
Steps	Steps consist of the following:

	Actor	Each step has an actor who initiates the step. Scheduled or timed events can be modeled as a timer actor.
	Action	Each step represents an invocation of an action that is defined on the target model. For example, Step 1 in the library scenario corresponds to a ListBooksAbout(topic) action.
	Referenced model elements	Each step may refer to model elements. For example, Step 5 in the library scenario refers to "Copy of Book" and "due date", which must be defined in the model.
	Return value	Each step has an optional return value, or response, which is described after a slash, as in Step 1 in the library scenario.

Figure 12.14: The parts of a functionality scenario. A functionality scenario refers to a target model, and consists of a scenario name, an initial state, a list of actors, and steps. Steps are broken down into the actor that initiates it, the action performed, references to model elements, and an optional return value.

action that is invoked. Each step transitions a model from a begin state to an end state. Actions belong to a model and reference some of the model's elements.

What is an *action*, exactly? Each model has ways that it can be changed, and actions are the mechanism for manipulating the model. For some models, the actions are obvious. When the scenario applies to modules with interfaces, actions are the operations that are defined on the interfaces. Component assemblies work similarly because ports define the behavior. But other times the action is less clearly defined and more abstract. For example, a scenario could discuss reconfiguring a router, which is a step done by a person. A developer compiling code could also be an action, or starting up a new data center. When the model already has clearly defined actions, it is easy to write precise scenarios, but when the model is less formal then writing a good scenario requires more discipline.

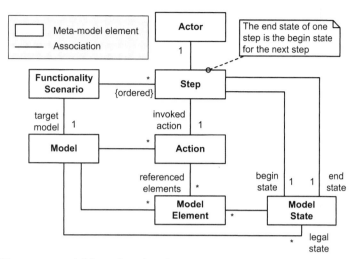

Figure 12.15: The meta-model for a functionality scenario. A functionality scenario is a behavior trace consisting of a sequence of steps. Each step is an occurrence of an action, initiated by an actor, and transitions the model from one legal state to another.

Two-level scenarios. Scenarios should be written at a consistent level of abstraction. Following a structure enforces this, because a scenario refers only to elements of the target model, which is itself presumably at a consistent level of abstraction. This is neat and tidy, but leads to the difficulty of understanding how scenarios at one level of abstraction relate to those at a different level. For example, a scenario for the Library System could refer to the system and its publicly visible operations (as in Figure 12.13), but not to the Library System's internal components. Separately, another scenario could be written that refers to the subcomponents inside the Library System.

To see how two scenarios at different levels of abstraction connect, the two can be merged and related. Figure 12.16 shows the first couple steps of the earlier scenario plus a second column that describes what happens to the internal subcomponents. The first column is the more abstract scenario that cannot see the subcomponents inside the Library System. The second column is the more detailed scenario that explains how the subcomponents accomplish the action described in the abstract scenario.

Generalizing functionality scenarios. A functionality scenario is just a trace, meaning that is it just one possible legal sequence involving the model, the actors, and the actions. You may need to build a general model that expresses every possible trace. For example, general models are useful for documenting or analyzing protocols between components. If you are publishing your component for use outside of your

Name: End-to-end copy of Moby-Dick
Initial state: Larry is a Librarian; Bart is a Borrower
Actors: Larry, Bart
Steps:

1. Larry lists all Books about "fishing" / No matching books are found.	Library Presentation (LP) extracts and sanitizes input from user form
	LP queries books about "fishing" from Library Core (LC)
	LC queries Inventory Database (ID) for all entries in Book table whose subject contains the substring "fishing". LC returns list of book objects to LP
	LP renders list of book objects as a result screen

2. Larry adds a Copy of the Book "Moby-Dick" by Herman Melville to the Library. A record of the Book is also added.	LP extracts and sanitizes input from user form
	LP adds book "Moby-Dick" to LC
	LC queries for existence of book "Moby-Dick" in ID. ID says no.
	LC inserts new book "Moby-Dick" into ID
	LC inserts new copy of book "Moby-Dick" into ID
	LP renders success screen

...

Figure 12.16: A fragment of a two-level functionality scenario, which elaborates the first two steps of the scenario from Figure 12.13. The right column references subcomponents of the Library System: The Library Presentation (LP), Library Core (LC), Inventory Database (ID).

group then you may want to provide documentation that goes beyond a few example scenarios.

There are many options for describing general behavior, including state diagrams, activity diagrams, and sequence diagrams. Note that sequence diagrams have traditionally been used to describe traces, but they can be augmented with annotations like "loop up to five times" to generalize the trace.

General behavior models can be difficult and expensive to build. Getting them somewhat right is easy, but 100% right, including exceptional paths, is hard. You may need them if you want to rigorously analyze a protocol or provide exact documentation. A general behavior model should be accompanied by at least one scenario, if only because of the analysis benefits from animating the scenario. This book recommends using scenarios when possible because they are cheap and effective in many situations, and because their story-like quality makes them approachable by both architecture experts and non-experts.

12.7 Invariants (constraints)

Invariants, also known as *constraints*, restrict the system, specifying either how it must be, or must not be. A defining characteristic of an architectural style is the constraints it places on the elements in a system. A pipe-and-filter style, for example, constrains the ordering of items in pipes and constrains the topology of how pipes and filters may be connected.

Developers impose guide rails (as constraints) on their designs so that they can understand them better. An unconstrained system can do anything, and therefore it is impossible to reason about what it may or may not do. Seemingly simple constraints like "Clients must not connect directly to the database, and must instead connect only to the business tier" enable developers to better reason about caching and performance. In short, no constraints = no analysis.

Invariants on class diagrams are written in UML notes, and can be written in Object Constraint Language (OCL) by putting the OCL expression inside curly braces. Architectural constraints are more often written down separately from diagrams as text. *Static invariants* deal with structure and *dynamic invariants* deal with behavior.

Static invariants. A static invariant is a restriction on the arrangement or quantity of instances (e.g., objects, component instances, connector instances) that can be created. An example of static invariants is that every truck must have an even number of wheels. In this case, you would have types that represent trucks and wheels, and the invariant restricts the how the instances of trucks and wheels are arranged. Another example static invariant is that every piece of data collected from a user must exist on at least two hard drives in separate server rooms. Static invariants can appear in many models and in different forms. In UML class diagrams, cardinalities on associations are static invariants, as are the ordering constraints like {sorted}.

Dynamic invariants. A dynamic invariant is a restriction on the behavior of instances. Examples of dynamic invariants include: only the print driver may send commands to the printer, every opening of a drawer is afterwards paired with a single closing of that drawer, or every ticket submitted by a user results in a response email being sent. In practice, you see many more static invariants documented because it is rather hard for humans to reason precisely about behavior.

12.8 Modules

A *module* is a collection of implementation artifacts, such as source code (classes, functions, procedures, rules, etc.), configuration files, and database schema definitions. They appear only in the module viewtype.

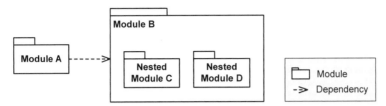

Figure 12.17: A UML module diagram where Module A depends on Module B, which contains nested modules C and D.

Modules can group together related code, revealing an interface but hiding the implementation. In this way they are similar to classes, but at a larger scale, since a module will usually contain many classes and other artifacts. The interface of a module is distinct from the interfaces of its contents.

Some languages provide explicit support for modules, so modules can be declared in the programming language. For example, modules in Ada are called packages and their interfaces are declared separately from the package body (i.e., implementation). Other languages have implicit support, such as C, where files that are conceptually in a package are simply placed in the same directory in the filesystem.

Modules have *properties* which apply to the implementation artifacts inside a module, such as what language they are written in, what standards they conform to, if they have been reviewed, if they have test harnesses, and what platform they work on. These properties can be shown on diagrams using UML stereotypes (e.g., «Java» or «encrypted»), or using your own notation that you define in the diagram legend. When representing the modules textually in a table or list, adding any number of properties is straightforward.

Modules can *provide* and *require* services. For example, a credit card billing module can provide payment services, but it requires a compatible credit card provider to complete its job.

A module can *depend* on another module, and there are many kinds of dependencies. Perhaps the most common dependency is that code from one module invokes code in another module. Another example of a dependency is that a class in one module can depend on a database schema in another module, because the fields of the class are persisted into the schema.

One module can be contained inside another, a relationship called *nesting*, or containment. Depending on its *visibility*, this may make the nested module and its contents inaccessible to other modules. Figure 12.17 shows a UML diagram with nesting and dependencies between modules. Modules selectively reveal their contents, so a module containing three classes might reveal some of the methods from one class, but none from the other two.

The architectural notion of modules is broader than what is available in most programming languages, so developers may have to apply programming idioms to implement the full notion of a module. For example, from an architectural perspective, every module has properties but few programming languages can express these properties directly, so programmers may express them in comments in the code.

Layers. A layered system organizes its modules such that lower *layers* act as virtual machines to higher layers. Dependencies are (almost) exclusively downward, where higher layers can use and depend on lower layers, but not the reverse. Layering is a specific style of organizing modules, and it is discussed in detail in Section 14.6. Not every system follows the layered style, yet you occasionally see diagrams where someone has attempted to force-fit it. In brief, every system has modules but not every system has layers.

12.9 Ports

All communication in or out of a component is done via *ports* on the component. All of the publicly available methods that a component supports, and all of the public events it responds to, will be specified in its ports. If a component sends a message to another component, writes to a database, or reads from the internet, it is through a port.

Operating systems also have the concept of ports, but there is no necessary connection between ports on components and ports in your operating system. You can choose to align the two concepts, so that there is a 1:1 relationship, or treat them as completely different things.

Ports reveal behavior through operations. Often clients must invoke operations in a particular sequence, a protocol. Ports can be stateful, in particular so that they can track the state of their protocols. Ports can also be annotated with properties. Ports are seen on many diagrams in this chapter, including Figures 12.3 and 12.4.

Provided and required ports. There is a range of options for how to specify ports. The easiest is to just name the port. A port can be categorized as *provided* or *required*, meaning that it provides services to other components, or that it depends on services from other components.

On diagrams, the color or shading of a port can indicate if it is provided or required, or the port name can be prefixed with a "p" or an "r", as seen in Figure 12.1. Provided and required ports often come in pairs, with the port on one side of connection providing a service and the other requiring it.

The simple provided / required dichotomy breaks down quickly when you look at real components, however, because most interactions are not purely provided or required. Furthermore, provided and required services are just one property of the port; others include which side originates communication, the primary direction of data flow, and qualities of the data itself like its format. Despite these issues, labeling ports as provided or required is often a useful, if coarse, designation.

Multiple port types. Although it is perfectly legal for a component type to have just one port type that exposes all of its operations, many component types have more than one port. Having just one port type requires you to route all communication through that one port type, so having multiple ports is desirable for several reasons:

- **Responsibilities**. As components become large, a single port would have enormous and varied responsibilities which would be better factored out into multiple ports that are smaller, simpler, and easier to understand.

- **Protocols**. Since ports can be stateful, using a single port may mean combining multiple state machines, which quickly creates a complex mess.

- **Coupling**. The component reveals a limited view of itself to each user, reducing coupling. In the Library System example (see Figure 12.3), the LibraryDesk has access to more operations than the WebPC does. Consequently, the coupling between the WebPC and the LibrarySystem is reduced. In particular, operations for the LibraryDesk can be changed without affecting the WebPC.

- **Usability**. Providing a smaller or simpler port has the benefit of simplifying what the user of each port has to understand.

- **Compatibility**. Each port has a type that can be checked for compatibility. A component might perform the same calculation, but provide results in JSON format from one port and in XML format from another port. The same component can offer different versions of the same interface so that legacy clients can be supported.

Informally, when a developer looks at a diagram or code and sees the human-readable names of port types, some knowledge about the system is conveyed (in the way described in Section 10.3 on an architecturally-evident coding style), so having multiple ports means more opportunity to convey knowledge and design intent.

Multiple port instances. A port type can have multiple instances. In the Library System, for example, many WebPC instances might be connected to the Library System. This yields options, as seen in Figure 12.18. In option (a), each component instance connects to a different port instance on the server. In option (b), all the component instances connect to a single port instance on the server. In option (c), each client and the server has a single port instance, but they use an N-way (in this case a 3-way) connector instead of binary connectors.

How do you choose whether or not to share a single port? It is easier to track a port's state with multiple port instances, and you should by default choose this

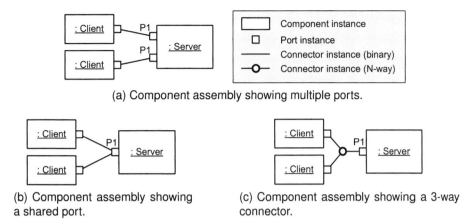

(a) Component assembly showing multiple ports.

(b) Component assembly showing a shared port.

(c) Component assembly showing a 3-way connector.

Figure 12.18: Component assemblies showing three options for handling multiple clients. The server can have (a) one port for each client or (b) one port shared by many clients, or (c) an N-way connector for many clients.

option. Shared ports are shortcut and can be a good choice when the connector protocol is stateless, like HTTP, and there is no security concern of data leaking across connectors. If clients are using distinct parts of an API, then sharing a port is a poor choice for coupling reasons, since changes made for one client will impact the other. You should also be aware that there is some semantic ambiguity, such as what happens when the component sends a message out a port: does it go to just one or all connected components?

How do you choose binary or N-way connectors? Again, security can influence the choice, since it is likely easier to secure a binary connector than events across a shared connector. An event bus is a special kind of N-way connector that gives designers the option to easily add and remove components while the set of events stays the same. Other kinds of N-way connectors are appropriate in special circumstances, such as querying multiple servers to get a consensus answer. They can also be used to reduce latency or distribute load by querying multiple servers. In general, if you see a component that must manage connections to multiple similar servers, consider if the connector could better handle some of those logistics.

Ports and interfaces. No mainstream programming languages support ports directly, though, as discussed in Section 10.3, you can adopt an architecturally-evident coding style to make them visible. Interfaces, on the other hand, are directly expressible. In programming languages, interfaces are usually just simple lists of operations. Ports and interfaces are similar in that clients depend on them rather than an implementation, but different in that it is unusual to think of interfaces as having instances

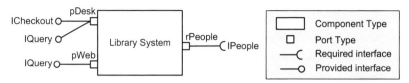

Figure 12.19: The Library System component shown with its two provided ports (pDesk and pWeb) and one required port (rPeople). These ports are shown with provided and required interfaces using UML ball-and-socket notation.

or state. Additionally, architecture models have the idea of required ports but few programming languages support the idea of required interfaces.

A port can support one or more interfaces. For example, the Library System has a pDesk port and it could support (i.e., provide) the ICheckout and IQuery interfaces, as shown in Figure 12.19. The figure also shows the rPeople port requiring the IPeople interface.

Stateful ports and protocols. Ports can have state, which usually happens because there is a protocol associated with them. Files, for example, support operations like open(), close(), read(), and write(), but clients cannot call those operations in any order they want to. A call to close() followed by a call to write() is likely to cause problems.

If the domain is unfamiliar to users, it may be worthwhile to write down the port's state machine. Figure 12.20 shows a Store component with one port, pCart, that provides shopping cart services. The port supports several operations: newCart(), addItem(Item), removeItem(Item), and checkout(). The figure shows these operations on a state machine that constrains their sequencing. This example is simplified and a more detailed one would include abandoned shopping carts that expire after some amount of time, removing items during checkout, etc. The more complex the state machine is, the more useful it is to write it down, either graphically, as in the figure, or textually.

If you have prioritized the risk of making protocol mistakes, then carefully modeling the protocol of ports is a good idea. If you work within an object-oriented framework, be sure that you understand the protocols of the callback methods, as this is an easy place to make mistakes that can crash your application.

Port type models. You can put multiple ports on a component for many reasons, but one important reason is to provide a simple and limited set of operations for a particular client. A component may support many operations and understand a complex domain, but a single port may expose just some of those operations and a simpler domain. The idea of effectively encapsulating a component through its ports is described in Section 11.4.

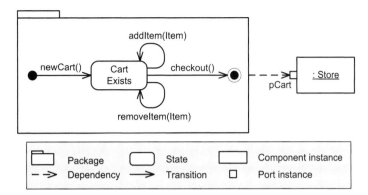

Figure 12.20: A state machine showing the protocol for using operations on a port. Users of the store's pCart port can invoke newCart() first, then addItem(Item) and removeItem(Item) any number of times, then checkout().

Figure 12.21 shows the Library Core component (shown earlier in Figure 12.4) and its four ports. It also shows the type model for the pInventory port. Clients using that port need to understand just three types: Library, Copy and Book. They do not need to understand other types that the Library Core reveals via other ports, including Loan and Borrower. Clients using the pInventory port need to understand if a Copy is removed from the Library or not, which is visible as an attribute is_removed on the Copy type, but clients do not need to know about other attributes of the Copy.

Notice that this figure shows the Library Core component annotated (stereotyped) with the UML icon for a component. UML uses the same diagram element (the classifier element) for both types and components, but there is little chance of confusion because you rarely see both on the same diagram. In Figure 12.21, the icon serves to disambiguate them since it has both types and components.

In most architecture models, the port's type model does not represent the datatypes that flow into and out of the port as parameters. When it does, you can stereotype the types with «interchange», meaning that this is a commitment to a data structure layout used for data interchange. See Section 15.8 for a discussion of the advantages and disadvantages of having an architecture model at exactly the API level.

Bindings and attachment. When you nest components inside of each other, you should be clear about how an external port maps to a port on the nested components, which you do with a *binding*. Figure 12.22 shows components B and C nested inside of component A, and a binding between port P1 on component A and port P1 on component B. The port on the subcomponent must be compatible with the port on the containing component, so in this case P2 must be compatible with P1. P2 could

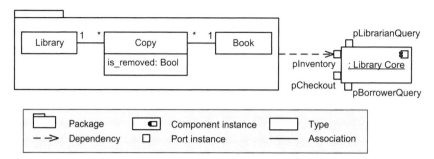

Figure 12.21: A type model showing the types used by one of the ports. The clients of a port need to understand just a subset of the component's full type model. The Library Core component instance was previously shown in Figure 12.4.

add more operations, but it must support all the operations on P1, and cannot change their meanings.

Generally, a binding is not a connector and no work can be done in a binding. Instead, a binding exists to preserve encapsulation. Users of component A do not even know that the subcomponents B and C exist, so they do not know that port P2 exists either.

Your source code implementations will often differ from the way the component assembly looks because your programming language probably has visibility restrictions (e.g., public and private modifiers in Java) that allow you to selectively hide and reveal elements. An implementation could reveal the interface corresponding to port P2 while hiding the implementation of components B and C. In that case, port P1 would have no runtime existence, so neither would the binding. You may think of a binding this way: A binding enables you to show which nested component's port is "sticking out" of the external component and visible to clients.

Two caveats are needed here. First, in UML, a *delegation connector* (i.e., a binding) is a subtype of a connector, though in its description it notes that it may or may not exist at runtime. Second, occasionally you will see work being done in a binding at runtime, such as selectively routing messages to several internal ports.

Ports can be *attached* to compatible roles on a connector. In Figure 12.22, port P3 is graphically shown as attached to the (graphically invisible) role on the connector. In contrast, port P1 is shown unattached.

12.10   Quality attributes

A quality attribute is a kind of extra-functional requirement, which are also called non-functional requirements and non-functional properties. The term *extra-functional* is preferred over *non-functional* because "extra" is more etymologically accurate than

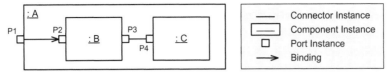

Figure 12.22: When a component is implemented with multiple nested components, external ports must be bound to internal ports. In this diagram, externally visible port P1 is bound to internal port P2, which must be compatible with port P1.

"non" in this context — these requirements go beyond functional requirements, not negate them. Most people would interpret a sign saying "non-functional" hanging on a water fountain to mean that it is broken, not that it is high throughput.

Understanding *quality attributes* is central to software architecture because a system's architecture will influence which qualities it can achieve. As with most things in engineering, it is easy to inhibit a quality, but hard to promote it. Seemingly trivial oversights can ruin a quality (e.g., security), but it takes careful planning to promote one.

Ideally, you would specify a testable condition for the quality you want, such as "Credit card transactions are authorized within 7 seconds 95% of the time." In practice, it is difficult to write good tests for some qualities, especially less quantitative ones like usability, security, modifiability, and portability. Section 12.11 discusses how to write testable quality attribute scenarios

Some quality attributes are best analyzed using a particular viewtype or view. My friend Tim once made this point vividly when he dropped a thick source code listing on the table and challenged anyone to find the one line of code that made the system run half as fast. Instead, he found it by looking at an execution trace (a runtime view), which quickly revealed the culprit.

Orthogonality to functionality. It may seem counter-intuitive initially, but functionality and quality attributes are mostly orthogonal concerns, meaning that they are independent of each other. You can convince yourself it is true by asking hypothetical questions: Can I build a specific system, such as a word processor, that is slow or fast? Secure or insecure? Testable or untestable? ... and so on for any quality attribute. Truly orthogonal concerns have no relationship to each other, like color and weight. Something can be red or blue, heavy or light, and there is no connection. However, size and weight are strongly related, as larger things tend to be heavier. Functionality and quality attributes are only mostly orthogonal because they do interact a bit. You could select a functional requirement and a quality requirement so that it is impossible to satisfy either, but not both, such as sorting a list faster than $O(n)$. But usually the design space is large, so functionality and quality attributes can vary independently.

Viewtype	Quality attributes	
Runtime	Performance	Latency
		Throughput
		Efficiency
		Scalability
	Dependability	Availability
		Reliability
		Safety
	Security	Confidentiality
		Integrity
		Availability
	Usability	Conceptual integrity / Consistency
Non-runtime (Module & Allocation)	Modifiability	Modularity
		Interoperabilty
		Portability
		Integratability
		Conceptual integrity / Consistency
		Extensibility
		Configurability
	Reusability	
	Supportability	
	Deployability	
	Testability	

Figure 12.23: A partial taxonomy of common quality attributes, also known as extra-functional requirements or "the -ities". Quality attributes are mostly orthogonal to functionality.

Taxonomy. Although it is possible to talk about quality attributes as broad categories, such as performance, you will usually need to be more specific within that category. For example, both throughput and latency are kinds of performance qualities, yet each is different. A new credit card processing system that increases throughput is desirable, but perhaps not if each authorization now has higher latency. Table 12.23 shows some common quality attributes organized by viewtype. Most of the quality attributes can be divided into finer-grained qualities. A larger taxonomy of quality attributes can be found in SEI technical reports (Barbacci et al., 1995; Firesmith, 2003).

Source	System stakeholder or developer
Stimulus	Wishes to change the PeopleDB
Environment	Design time
Artifact	Code
Response	PeopleDB replaced with no changes to LibrarySystem code
Response Measure	Within three days
Full QA scenario	A system stakeholder wishes to replace the PeopleDB with a compatible one; change is made within three days without changing the LibrarySystem code

Figure 12.24: An example of a full quality attribute scenario for the Library System. You may omit some sections, but you should strive to write falsifiable scenarios.

12.11 Quality attribute scenarios

Quality attribute scenarios concisely express extra-functional requirements. They are described in depth in (Bass, Clements and Kazman, 2003) and are an essential part of ATAM (Section 15.6.2) and the Attribute Driven Design process (Section 11.3.4).

Developers on most projects usually know the system's expected functions sufficiently well, but often they must infer or guess the quality attribute requirements. Since the architecture of a system strongly influences its throughput, security, and other quality attributes, developers who are not armed with QA scenarios or something equivalent are forced to choose an architecture based on their hunches, and stakeholders may not discover problems until quite late. Developers will build a good system, but there are different flavors of good: it may be a highly secure system instead of a highly usable system, or it may have excellent throughput instead of being easy to modify.

Structure. QA scenarios are like functionality scenarios in that they describe how the system should behave. Where functionality scenarios consist of a series of steps, each of which transforms the system, QA scenarios consist of a single step. At a minimum, a QA scenario describes a stimulus and a response. Examples of stimuli include users pressing buttons, intruders attacking the system, a batch job being submitted, and stakeholders requesting modifications. Responses include generated data, administrators notified of attacks, job completion, and changes integrated into the system.

The full structure of a QA scenario includes: source, stimulus, environment, artifact, response, and response measure. Figure 12.24 shows an example QA scenario from the Library System.

Falsifiability. Even when writing minimal QA scenarios, you should strive to make them falsifiable. If the QA scenario is not falsifiable then you cannot be sure that your system supports it (or that it does not). The system should be "user friendly" but who will be the judge of that? One of the best reasons to include a response measure is that it forces you to make the outcome falsifiable, and therefore testable.

Writing falsifiable QA scenarios is easy for quantitative quality attributes like throughput, but awkward and difficult for QA's like usability and modifiability. When you write a performance QA scenario you feel like it cuts to the essence of what the system should do, such as respond to 100 queries per second within 1 second 90% of the time, and always within 5 seconds. On the other hand, while you can write modifiability scenarios as above, they feel more like special cases rather then the essence. For example, it is easy to imagine a system that can handle three or four modifiability scenarios but be otherwise terribly difficult to evolve. Even though they are imperfect, a falsifiable QA scenario is better than "make it user friendly."

Finding scenarios. It is often said that the best way to appreciate your own culture is to travel to see other cultures. So it is with quality attributes. If you always develop IT systems then you will have internalized some prioritization of quality attributes, and your ranking is likely different from what Systems, Web, and Embedded developers have internalized. Looking at other kinds of systems will help you appreciate the qualities you are building in, and perhaps help you re-prioritize.

If you are not seeking QA scenarios then you will not find them, but any searching you do will reveal some of them. If your architecture is a big risk for the project then you should search diligently. Note that humans are better at criticizing a strawman than a blank sheet of paper, so you will likely elicit better responses from stakeholders by seeding them with your best QA scenario guesses and asking them to fix them. Structured processes like Quality Attribute Workshops (see Section 15.6.2) and the Architectural Tradeoff Analysis Method (see Section 15.6.2) are more formal ways of soliciting QA scenarios.

Architecture drivers. *Architecture drivers* are quality attribute scenarios that are both important to stakeholders and difficult to achieve. They can also be functionality scenarios. They represent the intersection of the most difficult scenarios and most important scenarios. As such, they are the scenarios that you should pay most attention to when designing your system.

Your architecture needs to support the demands placed on it, but often your system has so many requirements that it is hard to focus your thinking. By keeping the list of architecture drivers short, you can both focus your thinking and ensure that your architecture supports the hardest, most important demands on it.

Architecture drivers are selected from your existing lists of QA and functionality scenarios. Stakeholders rate each scenario by how important it is to them, usually on a High (H), Medium (M), Low (L) scale. Additionally, developers rate each scenario by how hard it will be to achieve. The result is a tuple like (H, M). Architecture drivers are usually the (H, H) tuples, scenarios that are both important to stakeholders and hard to build.

Architecture drivers are so named by the SEI authors of (Bass, Clements and Kazman, 2003) because they advocate using them to drive the architectural design process (as in Attribute Driven Design, Section 11.3.4). This book advocates using risk to help choose architecture activities, which is a similar goal, but not quite the same. The risk-driven model helps to answer the question, "What activities should my team do and when should we stop?" Architecture drivers are better at answering the related question, "What technical qualities must my architecture have?" There is overlap because some scenarios can be cast as risks, such as the risk that the system does not handle its transactional load. However, not every risk is clearly categorized as a scenario. For example, integration with a new framework might be a risk but is not obviously a QA or functionality scenario.

12.12 Responsibilities

As you design a system, you allocate responsibilities to system elements. You can allocate responsibilities to elements of any model in any viewtype. For example, a user interface module (module viewtype) may be responsible for rendering the user interface, a component instance (runtime viewtype) may be responsible for data on Colorado employees, and the Arlington facility (allocation viewtype) may be responsible for offsite backups. An element's responsibilities are often implied in its name.

System elements can have both functional and quality attribute responsibilities. Developers tend to think about the functional responsibilities first, but quality attribute responsibilities should not be overlooked. A database may be responsible for storing data on Colorado employees, but it may also be responsible for servicing queries within a half second, or for 99.99% uptime.

Chains of intentionality. Responsibility allocation is tied into the idea of a chain of architecture intentionality (see Section 2.1). Specifically, the chain of intentionality helps you decide which responsibilities you need to allocate to an element and which you can leave open to any reasonable implementation.

Here is an example that shows how the highest level architecture intentions flow through into responsibility allocations. Imagine that one of the system's architecture drivers is to handle queries within one second and you decided on a 3-tier architecture style with user interface, business logic, and persistence tiers. Because you need to ensure that queries are handled in one second, you assign performance budgets to each of the tiers and connectors such that the round-trip time will be safely less than one second. The performance budget on each element is a responsibility allocation that flows from the architecture driver.

In contrast, what you are *not* doing is assigning every element a responsibility for every quality attribute. In the example, the system did not have an architecture driver for security, so no security responsibilities are assigned. So, unless your chain of architecture intentionality has a reason to assign security responsibilities to a module, do not assign any. Of course, when you are looking at the details of a component and believe that it should have security responsibilities, yet you do not have an architecture driver for security, that is a clue that you might have missed an architecture driver.

Universal and enumerated responsibilities. Responsibility allocations are constraints, and the way that a responsibility is written (or thought about, or verbally communicated, etc.) determines how strong the constraint is. Responsibilities can be written as either universal or enumerated (i.e., *intensional* or *extensional*, as discussed in Section 10.1). Consider the following universal (intensional) responsibility allocation:

>   (a) All input validation should be done in the UI tier.

This responsibility is quantified across all elements and says that only the UI tier should be doing input validation. It is a general rule, so even as the system evolves to add new tiers, it still prohibits those tiers from doing input validation. Compare that universal responsibility allocation with this enumerated (extensional) one:

>   (b) The UI tier checks credit card checksums and integer ranges.

Perhaps today this covers all cases of input validation, so (a) and (b) seem equivalent. However, since (b) is an enumerated list, it does not say anything about what might happen tomorrow when a new tier is added. It provides no guidance on whether the next feature can implement its validation checks in a different tier.

The universal responsibility allocation is a stronger constraint, which may or may not be what you want. However, if you intend the stronger constraint, you should state it universally, as in (a), rather than leaving others to wonder if they should be inferring a pattern from an enumeration, as in (b).

12.13   Tradeoffs

Quality attributes often trade off with respect to each other. If you design a system so that its response time is as fast as possible, you may find yourself sacrificing modifiability, portability, or security. Sometimes these tradeoffs will be inherent in the problem, but more often they will be dependent on a particular design.

When you investigate your design space (the set of all possible designs that achieve the functional requirements), you will find designs that promote or inhibit the quality attributes in different amounts. You are confronted with a messy set of possible designs. When you discover a tradeoff, you have created clarity from the mess, and have simplified and condensed your understanding of the problem. You might find that, "Generally speaking, dependence on the platform (portability) trades off against speed. As we make the system faster, we have to use platform-specific APIs which make porting more difficult." These tradeoffs are nuggets of gold: a condensed insight into the problem you are working on.

Other things trade off besides quality attributes. At a more detailed level, design decisions may open up one set of features at the expense of another set. At a higher level, quality attributes may trade off against business decisions. For example, some companies are known for producing highly usable products with fewer features. Adding features might actually be undesirable because it adds complexity.

Tradeoffs are perhaps the most condensed knowledge about the system, so if anything about the system is documented it should be the tradeoffs. A new developer can gain insight into a system and its domain just by reading a short list of tradeoffs that shape its design space.

12.14   Conclusion

This chapter has covered the important model elements that you will use in architecture modeling. The elements are used on architecture models like system context diagrams, module diagrams, layer diagrams, allocation diagrams, and component assemblies. This chapter augments Chapter 7, which describes how the model elements can be put together into a canonical stack of models, and Chapter 9, which gives an overview of the design model. This chapter and the next are useful reference material, covering model elements and relationships, respectively.

You should certainly not strive to use every modeling technique in your architecture models. I once had to maintain some C++ code that had been written by someone who had just read a book on C++, so that code was full of multiple inheritance and other corners of the language. That is not what you want. Books have to spend more time on tricky concepts than on simple ones, but do not make the mistake of mirroring that emphasis in your system and models. They should be dominated by the straightforward concepts, like components and functionality scenarios. However, occasionally the best way to model an idea is with an N-way connector (or other tricky concept), and now you know how to do that.

Chapter 13

Model Relationships

Throughout this book, you have seen relationships between models. For example, the canonical model structure of domain, design, and code models uses the designation and refinement relationships. Refinement is also used to relate boundary models to internals models. Views are used everywhere. So far, these relationships have been described intuitively and informally.

At some point, however, you will want to know that the ground you are building on is more solid than that. This chapter adds precision to your understanding of the relationships but, in an effort to stay readable, it stops short of being fully formal. You can safely skip over this chapter on your first read and come back later.

A full understanding of model relationships will enrich your conceptual model of architecture and consequently your ability to detect bugs in your models. The conceptual model taught throughout this book makes some modeling choices, notably the use of closed refinement semantics and the use of master models instead of views-as-requirements. By the end of this chapter, you will understand why these were chosen and will be ready to read models that use different choices.

The modeling relationships are more general than software architecture or the Unified Modeling Language (UML), so you will see little of those here. Instead, the relationships are explained using an example of a house, for example relating the real house to its blueprints, and relating diagrams of its floorplan to a three-dimensional model of it.

The following sections discuss nine relationships between models, summarized in Figure 13.1: projection (view), partition, composition, classification, generalization, designation, refinement, binding, and dependency. The chapter concludes with an

Relationship	From-To	Description
Projection	Model-Model	Subset of details with optional transformation
Partition	Model-Models	Subdividing a model
Composition	Models-Model	Combining models
Classification	Type-Instance	Categorization of instances
Generalization	Supertype-Subtype	Subsuming relationship between categories
Designation	World/Model-Model	Correspondences between models
Refinement	Model-Model	Low-detail to high-detail
Binding	Model-Model	Conforming to a pattern
Dependency	Model-Model	Change to one may imply change to other

Figure 13.1: A summary of the relationships described in this chapter.

example showing how all the relationships can be used together. We begin with projection, the most commonly used relationship.

13.1   Projection (view) relationship

Cartographers have invented many projections of the Earth's curved surface onto a flat map. Each requires a mathematical function that maps (i.e., projects) a spherical surface onto a planar surface. Perhaps the best known is the Mercator projection, invented in 1569, which has the property that all lines of longitude and latitude intersect at right angles. On the Earth's surface, such intersections occur only at the equator, so as a consequence the Mercator projection exaggerates the size of land that is far from the equator. While falsely depicting Greenland as larger than Africa, this projection had the beneficial property that sailors wanting to get from one place to another can draw a line between the two and simply sail at that compass bearing. The Gall-Peters projection seeks to represent accurate sizes of countries but sacrifices the property of simple navigation.

A *projection*, which you can use interchangeably with the term *view*, can be informally thought of as what something looks like from a particular perspective. More formally, a projection shows a defined subset of a model's details, possibly transformed. A projection can remove details, such as a map that omits country boundaries. It can also transform the model, as seen in how the Mercator and Gall-Peters projections choose their transformations for easy navigation or accurate area. However, a projection cannot add information that does not already exist — it would be quite surprising to project the globe onto a piece of paper and discover a new continent.

Projections are used when creating blueprints of houses. While a three-dimensional house is being designed, two-dimensional drawings of the house are

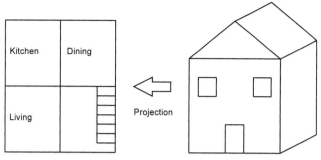

Figure 13.2: A two dimensional (2-D) floorplan view (i.e., a projection) of a three dimensional (3-D) house model.

produced. Each of these 2-D drawings is a projection of the entire house, as shown in Figure 13.2.

Consider a computer-aided design (CAD) program that stores an internal representation of your 3-D house plans and can compute any 2-D view that you ask. It may seem that this contradicts the rule that "projections cannot add information that does not already exist," because not every possible view already exists in the 3-D internal representation. But it is OK for the CAD program to transform its internal representation to show a view, which may require it to calculate and display a cross-section. What the rule prohibits is views that would be impossible to derive from the 3-D internal representation, such as a new room, or a garage.

Although you will use a lot of graphical views, some of the most useful are views textual or tabular. Figure 13.3 shows a view of the house that lists the costs. You could draw it graphically, but it would be easier and better to use a spreadsheet program.

13.1.1 Consistency across views

Having more than one view introduces a challenging problem: maintaining *consistency* across multiple views. If you use a 3-D CAD program to edit your 3-D objects, the problem of inconsistent views will not arise because the program mechanically computes the views for you, and presumably does not make mistakes. However, designers often work with 2-D views and use their own brains to keep the various views consistent.

My brother who constructs buildings encountered this problem on one of his projects. The front-facing view of the school he was building showed rainspouts, which he built as designed. Once he started grading the terrain using a top-down view of the grounds, however, he discovered that the design had the rainspouts exiting several feet below ground instead of at the surface. He had bulldozers on site

Roof	$17
Deck	$12
...	...
Driveway	$35
Total	$100

Figure 13.3: Many views are created ad hoc, like this table view of house construction costs.

when the inconsistency was detected — you would prefer to discover inconsistencies sooner.

View consistency is one of the harder problems in software architecture (see Section 16.1). You can use techniques to check consistency between particular parings of views, such as 2-D-floorplan to 2-D-side-view, but the number of specific pairings increases combinatorially with the number of views, so you should prefer general techniques when possible.

Since keeping views consistent is a difficult problem, you should insist on good reasons for using views at all. Views help you cope with two primary foes: complexity and scale. By showing a subset of the details of the full model, a view necessarily reduces the amount you need to comprehend. A view often highlights a single *concern* of the model, such as speed, airflow, or navigability. A specialist can use the view instead of the full model, for example as an electrician uses a wiring diagram to trace circuits. We will return to the issue of view consistency in Section 15.2.

13.1.2   A view of what?

Let's start with two views of a house, like the views in Figure 13.4. If you look at these two floorplans, you will notice that the staircases do not match up. The first floor view has the staircase on the right and the second floor view has it on the left. When you build multiple views, you will sooner or later encounter the problem of conflicting views.

But interpreting what the conflict means can be tricky because there are multiple interpretations. Perhaps the views are firm requirements, so a conflict means that the house is unbuildable until the requirements change. Or perhaps the designer made a design mistake and had not yet realized it. The following sections describe three interpretations of views: as requirements, as projections of a master model, and as projections of reality.

Views as requirements. One approach is to interpret each view as expressing requirements. The complete set of views represents the requirements for the system. For example, when designing the plans for a house, the architect may have insisted on locating the bathroom over the kitchen so that the water lines are aligned, and

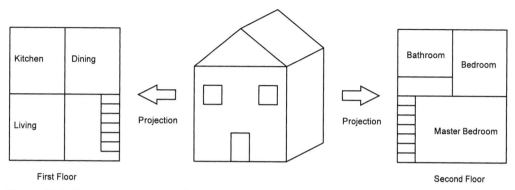

Figure 13.4: The same master model can have multiple views that focus your attention on different parts of the master model. The floorplan views put the staircase in different places, which raises the question: where does the error lie, in the views or in the main house model?

required the master bedroom to face east. He would create a view for each of these, constraining the house. The views could also come from different stakeholders, for example a view from the future owner constraining the house cost and another view from the city constraining the house size.

Let's refer to this approach as the *views-as-requirements* interpretation. Since each view expresses requirements for the solution, you should wonder if you can design a model (and subsequently build a house) that satisfies the requirements from all the views. In the case of Figure 13.4, solutions exist for each view, but not for the combined views. My friend Dean illustrates the challenge of conflicting requirements with the following example: "I want a 20-inch display that fits into my pocket."

Master model. Another way of approaching the problem of view consistency is to interpret each view as a projection of a complete design in the designer's head. Let's refer to this approach as the *master model* approach, because it assumes that the designer has a complete master model from which views could be mechanically derived. If the views are inconsistent, it is because the design is flawed. You would interpret the contradictions in the house floorplans as a flaw in the master model in the designer's head. We have all experienced the situation where we believe our plans or models are coherent until we try to put them into practice, at which time we discover latent errors.

The master model must contain all of the details needed to project the views and all the details needed to design the real artifact. In practice, designers often keep the master model in their heads and produce a selection of views. For example, designers often draw only 2-D views of a house, not a 3-D model. However, if you asked them, they could produce any 2-D view you desired from the master model in their heads.

Project reality. A third interpretation of views is that they are not projections of another model at all, but instead are projections of the real-world artifact. Using this interpretation, the floorplan blueprint of a house is either a projection of the to-be-built future house (using the views-as-requirements approach), or a projection of the actual house (using the master model approach). This interpretation combines the idea of projection and designation into one step, like the way that experienced mathematicians will skip over or combine steps in their work.

This book uses the *master model* approach and its diagrams show views that are projections of the master model. This way you avoid the possibility of creating a set of views for which there is no solution, and you keep the explicit step of showing correspondence between your models and the real world.

13.1.3   Views Aid Analysis

A well-chosen view can aid in analyzing a model, and this analysis is often informal and visual. If you are trying to schedule contractors to work on your house, you would start with a list of the contractors and their availability dates. Conflicts are not obvious if the list is unordered, but if you place them onto a timeline chart the conflicting appointments will jump out because your brain is good at detecting overlaps when shown like this. Leveraging our built-in skills as humans to do architecture analysis is discussed in more detail in Section 15.6.1.

Other analyses can be done algorithmically by computers. If your new house is subject to local taxes based upon its square footage, number of windows, and energy efficiency then a specialized view can be used to calculate the tax burden of various design options. Each specialist contractor you hire, such as heating or electrical, likely has specialized analyses they perform using a custom view of the house.

13.1.4   Grouping Views into Viewtypes

In Section 9.6, you learned that views can be grouped based on their similarity. All of the physical views of the house can be reconciled by using a detailed 3-D design. But you can also view your house from various legal perspectives: tax liabilities, mineral rights beneath the house, and whether or not you can keep chickens in the backyard. It is difficult to imagine how these fit into a 3-D physical model, but perhaps you could make a legal model of the neighborhood and reconcile the additional views there. These groupings of views are called *viewtypes*. A characteristic of a viewtype is that it is hard to reconcile it with another viewtype. In software architecture, the standard viewtypes are the module viewtype, runtime viewtype, and allocation viewtype.

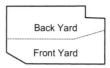

Figure 13.5: A partition divides a whole into non-overlapping parts. My father did not care how my brothers and I partitioned the yard, so long as we cut the grass.

13.2 Partition relationship

Growing up, one of the chores my brothers and I had to do was to cut the grass. There was a lot of it, and we were using a push-mower, so we would *partition* the chore into the front yard and the back yard and take turns cutting the parts. Between those two parts, the entire yard was covered. My father did not care how we divided our work as much as he cared about the whole yard being cut. Conveniently, this is a property of partitions: they must add up to the whole with no overlapping.

If you delight in corner cases, you may have thought, "If I define a view that only shows the front yard, and another view that only shows the back yard, wouldn't that be the same as a partition?" Indeed, those views would yield the same result as a partitioning. But every partition requires that the pieces comprise a complete set that covers the original without overlap, while a projection has no such requirement.

13.3 Composition relationship

Composition is almost the mirror opposite of partitioning. Where partitioning takes a model and describes how it can be divided into smaller models, composition takes smaller models and creates a larger model. The difference is that the parts combined through composition need not be the parts that made up the whole — so I could compose the front yard, the back yard, and the neighbor's yard (i.e., not part of the original partitioning of my yard) to make a huge yard. In modeling, this is quite useful when you have some parts of model you would like to share, for example shared datatypes used by both a frontend and backend.

13.4 Classification relationship

A *system of classification* allows you to pick up something and decide what category it belongs to. Using the definition originating with Plato, an ideal system of classification would have three properties (Bowker and Star, 1999). First, it would be unambiguous. Second, each thing would fit into one and only one category. And third, any item could be sorted into a category. Much like other ideas about ideals from Plato, like perfect geometric forms, you almost never see a classification system[1] that strictly conforms to these properties.

Despite Plato's rules, people are quite comfortable sorting things into multiple categories simultaneously. A drywall screw used in a house is in the categories of Fastener and also Magnetic. According to Plato, these cannot be part of the same system of classification because a thing must fall into just one category. You can solve this problem either by deciding that there are really two classification systems — one by function and one by electromagnetism — or by simply dropping the one-and-only-one category requirement.

This book uses the word *type* to refer to a category and *instance* to refer to the thing itself, and allows an instance to have multiple types. *Classification* is the relationship between a type and an instance. The classification relationship can apply to component types and instances, classes and objects, or other pairs of category and categorized thing.

You should resist the temptation to use the terms *class* and *type* interchangeably because it can cause confusion between the concept of classifying something (type) and the implementation of that concept in an object-oriented programming language (class). Note that in most object-oriented programming languages, an object has a single class, even if that class is derived from many other classes (multiple inheritance).

13.5   Generalization relationship

While classification describes how a type may categorize an instance, *generalization* describes how one type can subsume another. My house (an instance of a house) might be in the category of Modern Houses, but that means that my house is also of the type Eclectic House, as seen in Figure 13.6. It is also a (just plain) House, because House generalizes Eclectic House, which generalizes Modern House. The more general type is called the *supertype* and the less general type as the *subtype*.

The *Liskov substitution principle* (Liskov, 1987) provides an easy test for generalization: a subtype must be substitutable for its supertype. If a Modern House is a subtype of an Eclectic House, and you can sleep in an Eclectic House, then you can sleep in a Modern House. Note that in object-oriented programs you will encounter sub*classes* that do not pass this sub*typing* test.

---

[1]Another way to classify is to define a category with a *prototype* which exemplifies the category, and determine inclusion by similarity to that prototype. Empirical studies by Elanor Rosch indicate that this is likely how our brains work: we think that birds are small, quick moving, flying things that resemble sparrows. Ostriches and penguins make lousy birds and so it takes us longer to recognize them as belonging in the category Bird, but crows are pretty typical birds and robins are even more so. In this system of categorization, categorization is not boolean in or out, but rather degree of inclusion (Rosch and Lloyd, 1978).

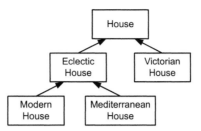

Figure 13.6: Generalization is the relationship between two types, such as the House and Victorian House types shown here. Using generalization, several types can be organized into a taxonomy.

Supertypes and subtypes can be organized into a hierarchy, called a *taxonomy*, shown in Figure 13.6. Common examples include geometric shapes and the Linnean taxonomy used to classify living things.

Taxonomies are unquestionably useful, but a few cautions are in order. A common experience is that the initial construction of a taxonomy is easy, but it becomes progressively more difficult as it approaches completeness. Taxonomies can become brittle over time because the instances being categorized change, and the way the taxonomy is used changes. Many useful categories crosscut established taxonomies; for example, birds, bugs, bats, and biplanes are Flying Things. A final caution is that taxonomies are subjective. Recall the drywall screws could be placed into a taxonomy organized by their purpose as fasteners, or one organized by what can be picked up with magnets.

We have been describing how one type can generalize another. It is also possible for one type to classify another. When you diagrammed sentences in school, categorizing parts of speech as nouns and verbs, you were classifying types. The types Modern House, Eclectic House, and House are related to each other by a generalization relationship, but they are all related to the type Noun by a classification relationship. In the field of models, this is referred to as *meta-modeling*. The UML has a defined meta-model called the Meta Object Facility that classifies all the UML boxes and lines.

13.6 Designation relationship

A *designation* allows you to bridge between two domains, for example between the real world and a problem domain model. A house made from bricks can keep you dry during a storm, while a box drawn with a pen on a piece of paper labeled House cannot. It is your intention, however, that the box in your domain model corresponds to the brick house in the real world. A designation identifies the two things and declares them to correspond. Designation can also show correspondence between two models, for example between a problem domain model and a design model.

You do not need to designate everything you put into the model. You should designate as few things as possible, what Michael Jackson refers to as a *narrow bridge* (Jackson, 1995). You can *define* the rest. So if you designate how your model house corresponds to your real house, you could define how the arrangement of walls in the house determines the square footage, or the taxes owed. You can think of the designations as a minimal set of variables you need to act as the base for your model, like some raw data you enter into a spreadsheet. The equations in your spreadsheet act as definitions, and they compute the rest of what you need based on the input data.

Designation is surprisingly common since computer systems are often used to keep track of what is happening in the real world. There must be a real thing and a computer representation of that real thing. Perhaps in the past you have had a difficult conversation with a clerk or customer service representative, trying to convince them that their designation relationship is wrong. Perhaps they believe that you live at your former address or owe them some money. Conflating the real thing and the designated thing in the model can be a source of errors.

13.7   Refinement relationship

Refinement is a relationship between a high- and low-detail representation of the same thing, as shown in Figure 13.7. A pencil-drawn picture of a house can be refined into a photo-realistic picture of a house. An alternate definition is that in refinement, all conclusions drawn from high level model are also true in low-level model.

Do not dwell on whether the high- or low-detail representation is created first, because refinement is the relationship between the two representations. You could start with the low-detail version (also called the *abstract* version) and add detail, or you could do the reverse, such as sketching a picture of your house. Either way you have two representations of the same thing, one high-detail, one low-detail.

The higher-detail representation is not always the more useful one. Consider the uses of an executive summary compared to the whole document, meeting minutes compared to a recording of the whole meeting, or an architecture model compared to a 10MLOC implementation.

Refinement maps.   If the two representations are of the same thing, there should be correspondences between elements in each. The roof in a sketch of a house corresponds to the roof seen in a painting. The collection of these correspondences is called a *refinement map*. The refinement map is not always written down because most correspondences are simple.

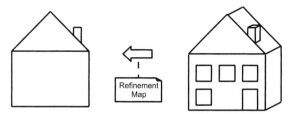

Figure 13.7: Refinement is a relationship between a high- and low-detail representation of the same thing. In this diagram, refinement is used to relate a high-detail representation of a house (the right one, with three dimensions) with a low-detail representation (the left one, with two dimensions). The higher-detail representation is not always the more useful one. A refinement map is rarely written down, but it relates the elements from one representation to the other.

13.7.1 Open and closed refinement semantics

If you build an abstract model, others who use it need to know what they can rely on. For example, if you show someone a diagram of a house, like the one at the left of Figure 13.7, that has no garage, can they assume that a more detailed model will not reveal a garage? You would like to be able to add details in the refined model, but also give some assurances to others about what new details you are allowed to introduce. You can communicate your intentions by committing to either open or closed refinement semantics.

- **Open semantics**. In refinement with *open semantics*, the refinement can introduce whatever new items it pleases. Adding a new garage or storey is fair game, as would be chicken coops and windmills.

- **Closed semantics**. In contrast, *closed semantics* restricts what kinds of new items can be introduced, often by listing the kinds of items that will not change.

In the house example, using closed semantics, you might categorically restrict the refinement so that no new garages or storeys are introduced. Things you do not mention in the list are OK to introduce, such as new windows or chimneys, so you still have an opportunity to add details. A common choice is to prohibit the addition of the kinds of items already shown in the low-detail model. For example, since the left side of Figure 13.7 shows a chimney, closed refinement semantics would prohibit the refinement from adding more chimneys, but since windows are not shown, any number of windows could be added. Figure 13.8 shows the house example with both open and closed semantics refinement.

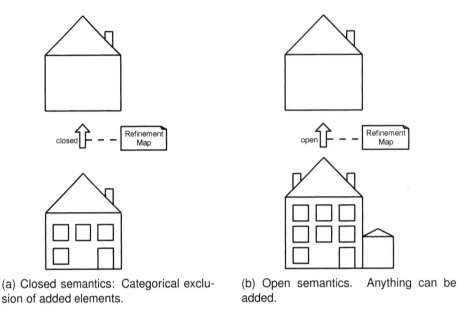

(a) Closed semantics: Categorical exclusion of added elements.

(b) Open semantics. Anything can be added.

Figure 13.8: The kind of refinement semantics determines what details can be introduced. In this example, the closed semantics categorically restricts the refinement so that no new garages, chimneys, or storeys are introduced. With open semantics, there are no such restrictions. In software architecture, it is best to follow closed semantics and prohibit new ports from being added.

13.7.2   Nesting

Two common uses of refinement in architecture models are nesting models within other models and zooming in or out from details. When you *nest*, you build a boundary model of an element (e.g., a component, module, environmental element) and an internals model of the same element. The relationship between them is refinement, because there are two models of the same thing with different levels of detail. Each model of the element has exactly the same interface/API, including operations, invariants, and quality attributes. They differ only in that the internals model shows more details; that is, it shows the internal design. Returning to the house example, you could use nesting to show two models of a house: one that included the rooms inside it and another that did not.

13.7.3   Zooming in/out from details

Another way you can use refinement is to stand off from details so that you can think about a more general, or abstract, version of the problem. When working on a story

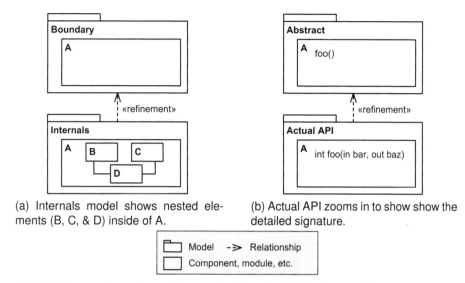

(a) Internals model shows nested elements (B, C, & D) inside of A.

(b) Actual API zooms in to show show the detailed signature.

Figure 13.9: Refinement can be used for nesting (showing hidden internal elements) and zooming (showing additional details).

problem where Barbara has five apples and Ralph has three apples, you realize that you can decide how many apples they have combined without thinking about apples at all. Refinement can be used to stand off from those details and see the essential problem clearly.

A famous example of standing off from the details concerns the bridges of Königsberg. The Pregel river runs through Königsberg and in 1735 there were seven bridges to and from two islands. People of Königsberg sought a path that crossed each bridge once and only once. Leonhard Euler demonstrated that there was no such path. He did this by abstracting away unnecessary details, such as the city being Königsberg and even that there were bridges, and in so doing he invented graph theory.

Figure 13.9 shows both nesting and zooming uses of refinement. On the left, it shows how the boundary model shows just a single component (or module, environmental element, etc.), while the internals model shows that component and its internal design with subcomponents B, C, and D. On the right, it shows refinement being used to relate two models, a zoomed-out model of component A and a zoomed-in model of the same component with a more detailed API.

The examples in this book use refinement to zoom out from details. You will notice that APIs on components and modules are more abstract than what you would expect in the source code, and that each step in the scenario is not quite detailed enough to be a method invocation.

13.7.4   Challenges and advantages

Whenever refinement is used, you will face some downsides because it omits details. The first is the risk that when you add in the full detail you will invalidate the design. Where Euler succeeded with zooming out, others find trouble. Josh Bloch discovered a bug that has existed in almost all Quicksort implementations for the past fifty years (Bloch, 2006). The problem is that an expression like $(x+y)/2$ in pseudocode yields the average, but the same expression in the implementation can overflow when the variables become large enough to overflow their number of bits of precision. The standard way to address this risk is to find out which missing details caused the problem, and add them back into your more abstract model. While your abstract model is now more detailed and complex, the old model was too zoomed-out to solve the problem, like a back of the envelope sketch used to plan a moon landing.

The second downside is that your abstract model cannot be used as API-level documentation, but nothing stops you from building that more detailed model if it is needed. In practice, API-level models are uncommon because they become outdated each time the code changes. Strategies for managing model-code consistency are discussed in Section 10.2.

The big advantage to using refinement is one that runs throughout this book: it can be used as a weapon to attack complexity and scale. Your mind is a limited size and it it hard to squeeze in a full understanding of a big and complex system. You will be able to build software systems that are larger and more intricate only if you can transform those bigger problems so they fit in your head. Refinement allows you to simplify complexity and compress scale so that they become tractable.

13.8   Binding relationship

Neighborhoods and houses follow patterns. For example, some neighborhoods have alleys where garages are behind the houses, while others lack alleys and so have garages facing front. Similarly, the architectural style of a house may dictate double-hung or sliding windows. At a smaller scale, electrical outlets follow the pattern set by electrical codes.

In all of these examples, a general pattern is established and individual elements are bound to the placeholders in the pattern. A *binding* relationship between two models pulls in the concepts from the source model and relates the placeholders with elements from the destination model.

Imagine you have a model (the source model) with a house and a garage. In this model, you are free to place the garage anywhere relative to the house. The garage could face the front, an alley, or perhaps the side. Next, imagine a pattern for neighborhoods where garages abut the house. The pattern would have three elements:

- a constraint saying the garage must abut the house
- a garage placeholder
- a house placeholder

When you bind this pattern to your source model, you bind the two placeholders to the house and garage, and now also have the "abut" constraint in the model. The result is a new model where the house must abut the garage.

Explicitly writing out the details of the binding can be tedious, but the intuition is clear. When you are binding in a *pattern* or a *style*, you must describe what-corresponds-to-what between the pattern and the source model. The resulting model includes all of the elements and constraints from both the pattern and the source model.

13.9   Dependency relationship

A *dependency* relationship exists when changes to one model may cause changes to another model. For example, you can express a dependency between an estimated price for constructing a house and the current prices of raw materials.

13.10   Using the relationships

Throughout this chapter, as each relationship was described, you have seen how the relationships were used in isolation, but their utility is clearer in context. Figure 13.10 shows most of the relationships in the context of plans for a house and garage. Each model is shown inside of an icon that resembles a folder.

At the right, the house and garage 2-D model is mapped into the real world using the *designation* relationship. That is, the house and garage in the real world are shown to correspond to the elements in the model. Next, the 2-D model is *partitioned* to show the garage and house separately. At the top, the garage model is related to the Rolling Door Style (a pattern) by *binding* its elements to those in the pattern. The model of the house is *refined* (using *closed semantics*) into a more detailed 3-D model. The 3-D house model is *projected* to show a view of the floorplan for the first floor. The floorplan view shows a room of type Kitchen, labeled R1; a room of type Living, labeled R2; and a room of type Dining, labeled R3. The relationship between R1 and Kitchen is a *classification*, a type-instance relationship, where the instance is called R1 and the type is Kitchen. And this floorplan model refers to a *taxonomy* of rooms, which shows that Kitchens, Dining Rooms, and Living Rooms are all kinds of Rooms.

It is easy to see how this diagram could be extended. If someone asks for more details on the garage, you could build a detailed model of the garage and relate it with refinement to the partition showing the garage. Similarly, additional projections could show views from different perspectives or enable analysis.

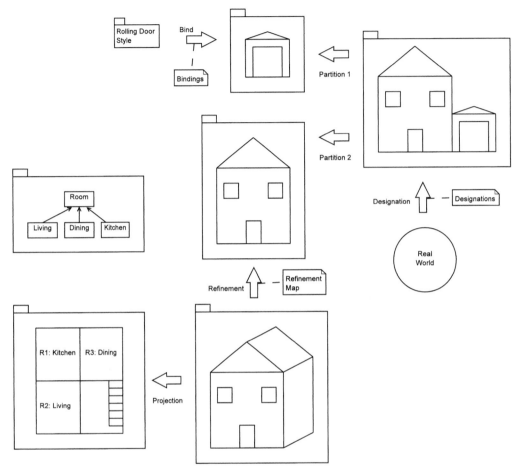

Figure 13.10: This summary diagram shows most of the relationships discussed in this chapter. The real world has correspondences to our full model, so it is a designation relationship. It is partitioned into a model of the garage and the house. The house model is refined to show details, then projected to show a view of one floor, which composes several room models.

13.11   Conclusion

This chapter has covered relationships that you will use in building models: projection (view), partition, composition, classification, generalization, designation, refinement, binding, and dependency. You have most likely already used these relationships informally. By shining some light on them specifically, you should now understand better what each is for and thereby avoid some modeling errors or confusion. You should understand that there are options you must choose: open or closed semantics, and master model or views-as-requirements.

The final example from Figure 13.10 shows a common occurrence: a collection of diagrams that relate to each other. Knowing the relationships from this chapter will help you put those diagrams together into a coherent and comprehensible model.

13.12   Further reading

Michael Jackson provides detailed discussions on a number of relationships including projection, partition, definition, and designation in Jackson (1995). Desmond D'Souza and Alan Wills base the Catalysis approach around the refinement relationship and discuss its use in analysis, design, and code. Refinement is a staple of architectural modeling, and Moriconi, Qian and Riemenschneider (1995) provide a formal treatment of correct architectural refinement.

Chapter 14

Architectural Styles

A *pattern* is a reusable solution to a recurring problem (Gamma et al., 1995). Patterns can be low-level and detailed, such as programming language *idioms*, at a moderate-level such as *design patterns* that express common object and class patterns, or at an even higher level. An *architectural style* is a kind of pattern that occurs at an architectural level and applies to architectural elements like components and modules. An architectural style defines a language consisting of elements and constraints.

An architectural style, often shortened to just *style*, defines a set of element types (such as modules, components, connectors, and ports) that can be used. A system that conforms to that style must use those types (and sometimes only those types), which restricts the design space. A style further defines a set of constraints that restrict how the types can be used, such as the system's runtime topology, dependencies between modules, direction of data flow across connectors, and visibility of components. A style may also define responsibilities for elements.

Some industry standards can be thought of as architectural styles. Enterprise Java Beans (EJB), for example, consists of a specification and several vendor implementations. It defines a set of elements, such as beans and the application container, and relationships between them.

Architectural styles were first recognized in the runtime viewtype, which still has the greatest variety of recognized styles, but the concept of style has been expanded to cover the module and allocation viewtypes also.

This chapter provides a modest catalog of architectural styles, most of which appear in catalogs published elsewhere. The descriptions here emphasize the connection between the constraints you impose and the system properties that you achieve as a result. Before jumping into the catalog, however, this chapter covers the advantages of architectural styles, the difference between the styles you see in practice (embodied styles) and the ones in the catalogs (Platonic styles), the connection between styles and architecture-focused design, and the distinction between architectural patterns and architectural styles.

14.1   Advantages

Constraints can act as guide rails (recall Section 2.2) that point a system where you want it to go. For example, to improve security in a web system, you may impose the constraint that all input must be sanitized.

   Working within a style's constraints can be difficult. The constraints that you (or someone else) imposed yesterday can be inappropriate today. Once a system is built within a style, it can require considerable effort to change to a different style. That might be OK if you could easily decide, in advance, which style was the best choice, but that is hard to do. Once you impose constraints, maintaining a system can be more difficult because you may have to seek out non-obvious designs just to stay within the style's constraints. So why should you consider imposing constraints or using a style?

Prefabricated set of constraints. You can think of a style as a prefabricated set of constraints with known benefits and drawbacks. Like anything prefabricated, you save yourself the work of designing and debugging it. It may not be perfectly tailored to your needs but it has the advantages of already existing and having known properties.

Consistency and understandability. The consistency brought about by the style's constraints can encourage clean evolution of the system, which can make maintenance easier. Rather than a bunch of arbitrarily different good ideas being implemented, you get a single good idea, consistently implemented.

Communication. Communication between developers is improved because the simple name of a style, like publish-subscribe, concisely conveys design intent to other developers. Just like with the named design patterns (e.g., Factory, Observer, and Strategy), developers who know the names can communicate much more efficiently.

Design reuse. When you use a style, you reuse a prefabricated set of constraints. As a result, any engineer writing in that style has the benefit of reusing the design knowledge of senior engineers who either invented or selected it. You can go further and push these style constraints into running code, called architecture hoisting. For example, the NASA/JPL Mission Data System (MDS) project designed a set of components and relationships that worked well to bridge their system engineering with their software engineering. They then they hoisted this style into an implementation that enforced the style constraints (Barrett et al., 2004). As a result, any engineer on the project was able to reuse the design knowledge of the senior engineers.

Ensure quality attributes. One problem with unconstrained, arbitrary code is that it can do anything. If you need the code to have a certain quality, such as maintainability, scalability, or security, you must constrain it. For example, a piece of software I regularly use has the ability to be extended with user-written plugins written in a scripting language. While I can download many of these plugins, they rarely work. Why? Because the software runs on several platforms, and yet the plugins are not constrained to use a cross-platform library. The unconstrained plugins invariably make a platform-specific reference, like C:\TEMP, which causes them to break on other platforms. In short, if the software wants plugins to run cross-platform, it must constrain what the plugin code can do.

Analyses. The other problem with unconstrained, arbitrary code is that you cannot analyze it. If you are asked to decide if a COTS system will integrate with yours, and that system has no constraints, then you will need to put on your deep wading boots and dig through the code. On the other hand, if you know that it uses the same architectural style as your system (perhaps client-server) and its messages are formatted using the same standard as yours, you should have an easier time deciding (i.e., analyzing). In short, no constraints means no analysis.

14.2   Platonic vs. embodied styles

If you have read the design patterns book (Gamma et al., 1995), you will have noticed that real code can vary from the ideal version of the pattern in the book. It should be no surprise, then, that architectural styles and patterns differ from the ideal too, and the variance can be quite large.

Patterns and styles serve several purposes. One purpose is explanatory, in that the name of the pattern communicates the overall design. Another purpose is to provide design qualities, such as the pipe-and-filter style enabling reconfiguration of the filters. A change to the pattern or style might still communicate the overall design, while diminishing its influence on design qualities. With that in mind, here are two polarized ways to think about architectural styles or patterns.

- **Platonic styles**. A *Platonic architectural style* is an idealization, so named for Platonic ideals like perfect circles. These are the kinds of styles and patterns you find in books and only rarely in source code.

- **Embodied styles**. An *embodied architectural style* is seen in real systems. It often violates the strict constraints found in Platonic styles. That violation often involves a big tradeoff: you can no longer rely on the style properties anymore, since those properties derive from the constraints. Sometimes embodied styles are also Platonic, as was the NASA/JPL Mission Data System (MDS) style.

A couple of examples should reinforce the difference between the two and highlight the tradeoffs. The pipe-and-filter architectural style imposes the constraint that filters only communicate via pipes and are otherwise independent. However, in practice, you will often encounter chains of pipes and filters where the first and/or the last filter violates the constraint. Sometimes the first filter reads data from somewhere other than a pipe, and sometimes the last filter exerts control over the entire chain. Do these violations impact the style's property, reconfigurability of filters? Probably, but just the first or last filter, and other filters can be reconfigured. Do these violations impact the explanatory value of the style name? Probably not.

A second example involves the client-server style. The Platonic style requires that servers be unaware of clients, as this yields coupling benefits: changes to the client will not impact the server. However, you may encounter embodied versions of the style where servers occasionally push data, unprompted, to the client. Depending on how this is implemented, it may result in a server that depends on the clients.

14.3   Constraints and architecture-focused design

Platonic architectural styles and architecture-focused design (see Section 2.7) are conceptually related. Recall that architecture-focused design means that you are re-lying on your architecture to reduce risks, achieve features, or ensure qualities: you are consciously depending on the architecture to achieve a goal. When following architecture-focused design, you could invent a novel architecture to achieve your goal, or you could employ an existing architectural style with its known effects on system qualities.

Relying on your architecture to ensure system qualities is related to Platonic and embodied styles. Strictly following the constraints in a Platonic architectural style yields known properties, which you are more likely to do with architecture-focused design. You may even choose to hoist (see Section 2.8) parts of the style to enforce its use.

In contrast, if you are following architecture-indifferent design (see Section 2.6) then you can use embodied styles, where the style constraints are not strictly fol-lowed. Despite deviations, the system may obtain some of the desired qualities. The named style will still serve as an inspiration or guide. It is not wrong to use an em-bodied style like this, but you should do it knowingly, as it would be foolhardy to violate a style's constraints yet still expect its benefits.

14.4 Patterns vs. styles

It can be helpful to distinguish *architectural patterns* from architectural styles, where patterns are at a smaller scale than styles. Patterns can appear anywhere in your design, and multiple patterns could appear in the same design. In contrast, a system usually has a single dominant architectural style. For example, if a system has a client-server style architecture, you would expect to see client and server components in the top-level design views. The system could also employ architecture patterns, such as the Representational State Transfer (REST) pattern to constrain the format of the messages exchanged by the clients and servers, or the directory pattern, so that clients can look up the server addresses.

The distinction between architectural styles and architectural patterns is not clear-cut and you will undoubtedly find examples where it is hard to differentiate them. As systems get larger, it is more common to see systems-of-systems, where a system that was freestanding is now incorporated into a larger system. If the original freestanding system had an architectural style, but it is now subordinate to the larger system's style, does that demote it to an architectural pattern? Probably. So instead of worrying about categorizing something as an idiom, a design pattern, an architectural pattern, or an architectural style, you can safely call them all patterns, and probably use the terms architectural pattern and architectural style as synonyms.

14.5 A catalog of styles

The following sections describe some of the most common architectural styles. These styles span the module, runtime, and allocation viewtypes. Architectural styles apply to your design and implementation models, but not your domain models (*analysis patterns* (Fowler, 1996) do apply to domain models). Most of these architectural styles have been described before and they are described here for two reasons. The first is to provide you with complete coverage of architectural topics, as you would otherwise wonder what those most common styles are. The second reason is to reinforce the connection between constraints and the resulting quality attributes.

Figure 14.1 provides a quick overview of the styles. It describes which viewtype each style applies to, its elements and relations, its constraints, and the quality attributes it promotes. The detailed textual descriptions in the following sections go into more depth and describe style variants and examples.

14.6 Layered style

The layered architectural style is perhaps the most common — so common that many developers assume that all systems are, or should be, layered. You may encounter

	Viewtype	Elements & Relations	Constraints / guide rails	Qualities Promoted
Layered	Module	Layers, uses relationship, callback channels	Can only use adjacent lower layers	Modifiability, portability, reusability
Big Ball of Mud	Module	None	None	None, but many inhibited
Pipe-and-Filter	Runtime	Pipe connector, filter component, read & write ports	Independent filters, incremental processing	Reconfigurability (modifiability), reusability
Batch-Sequential	Runtime	Stages (steps), jobs (batches)	Independent stages, non-incremental processing	Reusability, modifiability
Model-Centered (Shared Data)	Runtime	Model, view, and controller components; update and notify ports	Views and controllers interact only via the model	Modifiability, extensibility, concurrency
Publish-Subscribe	Runtime	Publish and subscribe ports, event bus connector	Event producers and consumers are oblivious	Maintainability, evolvability
Client-Server & N-Tier	Runtime	Client and server components, request-reply connectors	Asymmetrical relationship, server independence	Maintainability, evolvability, legacy integration
Peer-to-Peer	Runtime	Peer components, request-reply connectors	Egalitarian peer relationship, all nodes clients and servers	Availability, resiliency, scalability, extensibility
Map-Reduce	Runtime & allocation	Master, map, and reduce workers; local and global filesystem connectors	Divisible dataset amenable to map & reduce functions, allocation topology	Scalability, performance, availability
Mirrored, Farm, & Rack	Allocation	Varies	Varies	Varies: Performance, availability

Figure 14.1: A condensed summary of the architecture styles in this chapter. Refer to text for a full listing of elements, relationships, constraints, and quality attributes.

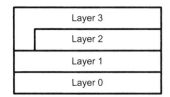

Figure 14.2: An example of the layered architectural style, part of the module viewtype. It consists of an ordered stack of layers that can only use the lower adjacent layer(s). Here, Layer 3 could use Layer 2 or Layer 1. Lower layers cannot use higher layers, except through callbacks.

systems that have been documented as layered, but the layers have been force-fit. It applies to source code elements, so it is part of the *module viewtype*.

Elements and constraints. The essential element of the layered style is a *layer* and the essential relationship is a *uses* relationship, a specialization of a dependency relationship. The layered style consists of a stack of layers where each layer acts as a *virtual machine* for the layers above it (see Figure 14.2) and their ordering forms a directed acyclic graph. In a simple layered style, a layer can use only the layer directly beneath it. This constraint means that subsequent lower layers are hidden, so a layer's interface defines a virtual machine for the layer above. Consider the Java Virtual Machine (JVM): programs that run on it cannot use subsequent lower layers and consequently are independent of the operating system and hardware.

Resulting qualities. The layered style's constraint leads directly to the quality attributes it promotes: *modifiability*, *portability*, and *reusability*. Since a layer depends only on the layer directly beneath it, subsequent layers can be swapped or emulated. Taller stacks of layers yield more opportunities for substitution at the possible expense of efficient execution (*performance*). For example, the Open System Interconnection (OSI) Reference Model defines a stack of layers for computer networking, but a naive layered implementation can be substantially slower than a non-layered one.

Variants. Variants of the layered style bend the constraint such that a layer may be able to skip down to lower layers. For example, the HornetQ message bus runs on the JVM and uses the Non-blocking Input/Output (NIO) library. However, when it detects that it is running on Linux, it uses the Kernel Asynchronous Input/Output (AIO) library, which improves performance. Notice that in this case it overcomes the performance liability yet maintains modifiability, portability, and reusability because it can fall back on the standard NIO library from the JVM.

Another variant you will see is *shared layers*, where every layer can use these shared, or *vertical*, layers. Such usage strains the definition of a layer to the breaking point, for how does a shared layer differ from an arbitrary, unconstrained module?

If you interpret these shared layers as a visual expediency to show dependence on a shared module, rather than as a different kind of layer, this variant makes more sense. For example, if every layer in your system depends on the C Standard Library (libc), and you thought it important to show on a diagram, you could show it as a shared layer.

Notes. The layered style can vary greatly from its Platonic form to its embodied form. The Platonic form, described above, derives clear quality attribute benefits from its constraint. However, in practice a layered style may violate its constraint, and you may see skipping of layers or lower layers using upper layers, which has the effect of negating the quality attribute benefits. Still, even in this relaxed form, layers may provide cognitive benefits to developers because the layers group modules into coherent functionality.

Lower layers can safely communicate with higher layers if they use a callback mechanism. Consider the common case of a user interface layer and a core functionality layer. The user interface may need to update its display based on what the core is doing, perhaps updating a progress bar based on the relative completion of a task. The core module could define a callback interface that reports the task status. To keep the layer ordering intact, the UI layer must initiate the callback, perhaps by asking the core to report its status and passing the UI layer as a parameter. The core layer does not know about or depend on the UI layer per se, since the UI layer implements a callback interface defined by the core layer.

The layered style is described in (Clements et al., 2010), (Buschmann et al., 1996), and (Shaw and Garlan, 1996).

14.7   Big ball of mud style

If the layered style is the most common targeted style, the *big ball of mud* style is perhaps the one most often actually achieved (Foote and Yoder, 2000). It is characterized by the absence of any evident structure, or perhaps vestiges of now-eroded structure. Also typical is promiscuous sharing of information, sometimes to the extent that data structures become effectively global. Although the module, runtime, or allocation organization can be a mess, it often starts in the module viewtype and spreads elsewhere. Repairs and maintenance are expedient and resemble crude patches rather than elegant refactorings. No effort is made to enforce any conceptual integrity or consistency. Technical debt is astronomically high.

Big balls of mud can happen as a result of throwaway code that persists longer than expected, often because it was useful and therefore maintained. Another factor is tradeoffs between short-term and long-term benefits. It may be in your short-term interest to make expedient patches rather than more expensive refactorings.

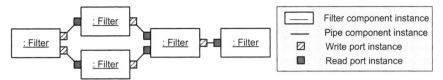

Figure 14.3: An example of the pipe-and-filter architectural style, part of the runtime viewtype, showing five filters and five pipes. Each filter must incrementally process its input and write its output. Consequently, several filters and pipes may be executing concurrently.

Unsurprisingly, such systems have poor *maintainability* and *extensibility*. It is tempting to dismiss the style as a pure anti-pattern, but Brian Foote and Joseph Yoder make the compelling argument that the style describes a *good enough* strategy of engineering (Bach, 1997), in the tradition of Richard Gabriel's *worse is better* argument (Gabriel, 1994). The authors note that "Not every backyard storage shack needs marble columns." (Foote and Yoder, 2000)

The forces that push systems to become big balls of mud have a peculiar stability in that once a system becomes a ball of mud, some developers find security and prestige in being the select few who can understand and evolve it, while those who detest the mud (and presumably could clean it up) run away. The result is that the ball of mud is rarely cleaned up.

14.8 Pipe-and-filter style

In the *pipe-and-filter* architectural style, data flows through pipes to filters that work on the data, similarly to the way that fluid could flow through pipes in a chemical processing plant. A key characteristic of the style is that the whole pipe-and-filter *network* is continually and incrementally processing data. This distinguishes it from the batch-sequential architectural style (see Section 14.9), in which each stage fully processes its data before handing it off to the next. An example of a pipe-and-filter system was seen in the linguistic processing system in Figure 10.7 and another example is seen in Figure 14.3. The pipe-and-filter style applies to runtime elements, so it is part of the *runtime viewtype*.

Elements and constraints. The pipe-and-filter style consist of four elements: *pipes*, *filters*, *read ports*, and *write ports*. When operating, a filter reads some input from one or more input ports, does some processing, and writes output to one or more output ports. It repeats this until it is time to stop. Filters can enrich, refine or transform the data, but pipes must only transport the data in one direction, without changes, and in order (Garlan, 2003). You can think of each filter as applying a *function* to its input.

In the simplest pipe-and-filter network, a linear one, data flows from a *source* through the pipes and filters until it reaches a *sink*. Sources and sinks are often files, but they can also be other stream sources or destinations. By having more than one input or output port, a network can become more complicated than just a straight line, but data still flows in one direction from the source(s) to the sink(s). Loops in the network are rare and often prohibited.

The pipe-and-filter style requires independent filters. Filters may not interact with each other, even indirectly, except through pipes, and cannot share state with each other. A filter cannot make assumptions about what happens upstream or downstream. To reinforce the idea of filter independence, you can think of a filter as a simple clerk in a locked room who receives message envelopes slipped under one door, processes them without referencing anything or anyone outside of the room, then slips another message envelope under another door.

A filter should incrementally read the input it receives and, as it processes that input, incrementally write its output. The intention of this constraint is to keep the entire pipe-and-filter network working at all times with data flowing through it, rather than having that data pile up in a filter, starving downstream filters. It is difficult to be precise about this constraint, however. For example, is it OK for a filter to read two input tokens and write the bigger of the two to its output? Probably, since it does not allow much data to pile up before it writes some incremental output. But this exception allows something that is arguably not very incremental: parsing. What about a filter that reads tokens until it recognizes an expression? That might allow quite a bit of data, perhaps all of it, to pile up before writing any output. You should evaluate this constraint in regards to your intentions with the pipe-and-filter network, as it might be either quite important or a rule that you can bend or break.

The correctness of the pipe-and-filter network should be deterministic with respect to concurrency. Whether or not your implementation is implemented with concurrency, a given input should always yield the same output.

Resulting qualities. The pipe-and-filter style enables late *(re-)composition* of a network. For example, in Linux, you can construct a pipe-and-filter network[1] on the command line, like this:

    cat "expenses.txt" | grep "^computer" | cut -f 2-

This would grab all lines in the file that begin with "computer" and output the remaining columns. There are many existing filters to choose from (such as grep and cut seen here), so users can create a network on the fly to compute the results they desire. This is an example of *modifiability* or *reconfigurability*. You may not even deliver a network, just a collection of pre-made filters for others to assemble. These

---

[1]Notice, however, that by piping the output through the *sort* filter breaks the style constraint for incremental computation, because *sort* must see the entire input stream before it can write its output.

filters would be *reused* by users. By working within this style, opportunities for *concurrency* are enhanced since each filter could run in its own thread or process. In general, pipe-and-filter networks are inappropriate for interactive applications.

Variants. Sometimes the network is constrained to be linear. Networks are usually directed acyclic graphs, but with care it is possible to introduce loops. Filters may either pull or push data from their input ports.

Notes. When implementing a pipe-and-filter network you will need to pay attention to how it should stop. You can terminate the network eternally, perhaps by killing off the processes, but how do you know that it is done processing? Sometimes the answer comes from the domain, such as when the input data (e.g., a file) has reached the end. Another alternative is to send an in-band token, along the pipe, that indicates the end of the stream. Yet another option is to close the pipes explicitly, and let filters test to see if the pipe is still open.

In the abstract, pipes are infinitely fast and big. But in practice pipes are usually implemented with a limited-size buffer that can fill up, which may impact performance of the system. There will also be performance differences if the filters are all in the same memory space or if they are on separate machines. CPU-bound networks may perform better if run on separate machines, but bandwidth-bound networks may run faster on a single machine.

It is worthwhile to distinguish two roles, possibly played by same developer, in order to clarify the meaning of filter independence. One role is that of a filter developer. When developing a filter, the developer can make no assumptions about upstream and downstream, or even the filter's role in the big picture, much like that clerk in the locked room. The second role is that of a pipe-and-filter network developer. This developer is responsible for assembling existing filters into a network that accomplishes the overall system goal, and has global knowledge about what is upstream and downstream of each filter.

The pipe-and-filter style is described in (Clements et al., 2010), (Taylor, Medvidović and Dashofy, 2009), (Buschmann et al., 1996), (Garlan, 2003), and (Shaw and Garlan, 1996).

14.9 Batch-sequential style

In the *batch-sequential* architectural style, data flows from stage to stage and is processed incrementally. However, in contrast to the pipe-and-filter style, each stage completes all of its processing before it writes its output. Data can flow between stages in a stream but is more often written to a file on disk. An example batch-sequential system is seen in Figure 14.4. The batch-sequential style applies to runtime elements, so it is part of the *runtime viewtype*.

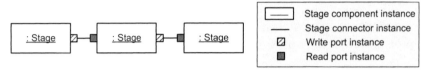

Figure 14.4: An example of the batch-sequential architectural style, part of the runtime viewtype, showing three stages. Each stage reads its entire input and writes its full output at one time, not incrementally. Consequently, each stage executes in sequence.

Elements and constraints. The processing components in a batch-sequential architecture are called a variety of different names, sometimes called *stages* or *steps*. There appears to be no standard name for the connectors between stages, probably because it is a leap of abstraction to see a file on disk as a connector. A single task that flows through the batch-sequential system is called a *batch* or a *job*. A stage has one or more read ports and write ports.

The batch-sequential style has similar constraints to the pipe-and-filter style. In particular, each stage is similarly independent. A stage depends on the data that it takes in, but not on the stages that come before it. Stages do not interact with each other except through the input and output streams or files. Stages fully process their input then terminate, after which the next stage does the same.

A batch-sequential system is most often a linear series of stages. No work is done in the connectors, which simply pass data unaltered from the write ports of the previous stage to the read ports of the next stage. A batch-sequential system is less commonly structured as a directed acyclic graph, but doing so creates opportunities for stages to run in parallel.

Resulting qualities. Batch-sequential systems promote the same quality attributes as the pipe-and-filter style, especially *modifiability* since stages are independent of each other. One difference is that where a pipe-and-filter system produces its output incrementally, a batch-sequential system's final output will be either absent or fully available, which will impact a system's *usability*. Another difference is that it has fewer opportunities for *concurrency* since the stages cannot be executed in parallel unless multiple jobs are flowing through the system. Batch systems are conceptually simpler since only one stage is running at a given time. They may also have greater *throughput*.

Notes. The batch-sequential style is described in (Taylor, Medvidović and Dashofy, 2009), (Garlan, 2003), and (Shaw and Garlan, 1996).

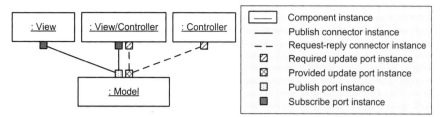

Figure 14.5: An example of the model-centered architectural style, part of the runtime viewtype, showing the Model, one component that receives updates about the model (the View), one component that updates the model (the Controller), and one component that does both (the View/Controller). The views and controllers do not interact with each other except through the model.

14.10 Model-centered style

In the *model-centered* architectural style, independent components interact with a central model (also called a *data store* or *repository*) instead of with each other. It is also known as the *repository style, shared-data style,* or *data-centered* style, It is renamed here because the the other names have caused developers to incorrectly infer that it requires a relational database, or similar. This style may use a relational database, but is more often used in-memory. An example is seen in Figure 14.5. This style applies to runtime elements, so it is part of the *runtime viewtype*.

For example, in a modern integrated development environment (IDE), a single central model represents the state of the edited program, including source code and parsed representation. This model is presented to the user with many views and controls. The view and control components are independent of each other, but all are dependent on the central model component. If the user edits the source code, this changes the central model. The central model notifies the compilation component of the source code change, prompting it to recompile and update the central model of the parsed code. That change to the central model is sent to the view that shows the lists of method names.

This architectural style is related to several design patterns, including the Document-View, Model-View-Controller (MVC), and Observer patterns (Gamma et al., 1995; Schmidt and Buschmann, 2003).

Elements and constraints. Every model-centered system has a *model* component and one or more *view, controller,* or *view-controller* components. The names for these components will vary depending on which variety of model-centered style is used. The types of connectors can similarly vary. If the model implements the Observer pattern then the connectors will notify the views of changes, but views could also poll the model. If a relational database is used, triggers can be used to cause update notifications.

Views and controllers depend only on the model, not on each other. There is a single shared model and many views and controllers. As in Model-View-Controller, special views and controllers may short-circuit and communicate directly, bypassing the model, but this tarnishes their independence with the benefit of better performance.

Resulting qualities. Model-centered systems are highly *modifiable* because of the independence of view and controller components from the model component and the minimal dependencies. Modifiability is also enhanced because the producer and consumer of information are decoupled. The system is *extensible* since unanticipated views and controllers are easy to add later. It can be easier to manage and persist state since it is centralized in the model component. *Concurrency* may be promoted since views and controllers can run in their own threads or processes, or even on different hardware.

Notes. Some example variants of this style are blackboards, tuple spaces, and continuous query databases. One important variation point is whether or not the model is structured in advance. Some variants make available a pile of unstructured data that is incrementally cleaned up by the views and controllers. Other variants make available structured data, but do not know how that data will be used by the views and controllers.

Because of its modifiability and extensibility, this style is useful when you do not know the future configuration of the system. The model-centered style is described in (Taylor, Medvidović and Dashofy, 2009), (Schmidt and Buschmann, 2003), (Clements et al., 2010), and (Shaw and Garlan, 1996).

14.11   Publish-subscribe style

In the *publish-subscribe* architectural style, also known as pub-sub or event-based, independent components publish events and subscribe to them. A publishing component is ignorant of the big-picture reason why an event is published, nor does a subscribing component know why or who published the event. To be sure, the developer who designs the system places publishers and subscribers deliberately, for example, one component publishes a "New Employee" event and another component subscribes to it and orders that new employee a computer. An example of a publish-subscribe system is seen in Figure 14.6. The publish-subscribe style applies to runtime elements, so it is part of the *runtime viewtype*.

Elements and constraints. The publish-subscribe style defines two kinds of ports, publish ports and subscribe ports, and one connector, an *event bus* (i.e., publish-subscribe) connector. Any kind of component can publish events (or subscribe to

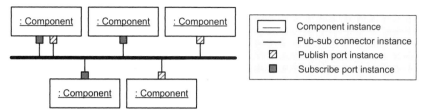

Figure 14.6: An example of the publish-subscribe architectural style, part of the runtime viewtype, showing five components attached to a publish-subscribe (pub-sub) connector using publish ports and subscribe ports. Subscribers depend only on the event, not on the publisher of the event, and publishers "fire and forget" the event, not depending on the response of other components.

them) so long as it uses a publish (or subscribe) port. The event bus is an N-way connector in that many ports can attach to it, rather than the usual binary connector that connects exactly two ports. Consequently, one component can publish an event and many components can subscribe to it. Notice that in this style the connector is the rock star, not the components, and that connector is responsible for quite a bit of work.

The event bus connector is responsible for delivering events. Components that publish events trust that events are delivered to subscribers, and subscribers trust that they receive events they subscribe to.

Subscribers depend only on the event, not on the publisher of the event. Subscribers are unaffected if the system developer replaces one event publisher with a compatible one, or splits its responsibilities across two publishers, so long as the same events are published.

Similarly, publishers are oblivious to event consumption. They must work equally well if their events are received or if no other component subscribes to them. You can imagine using an event bus to simulate a procedure call: one component publishes an event that is received by another and the response returns via a second event. This violates the obliviousness constraint since the first component is expecting a reply.

Resulting qualities. The biggest benefit of the publish-subscribe style is that it decouples producers and consumers of events. As a consequence, the system is more *maintainable* and *evolvable*. Consider the situation when a new component needs to do work based on an event. It can simply subscribe to that event and the system is otherwise unchanged. Specifically, the event publisher is unchanged. Similarly, a new event publisher can be added without affecting the system, and later a component (new or existing) can begin subscribing to those events.

The event bus adds a layer of indirection between producers and consumers. It can therefore hurt the system's *performance*. However, reusable resources may have better engineering (and performance tweaking) behind them than ad hoc but bespoke resources: consider the engineering behind a COTS relational database versus a bespoke file-based repository. An event bus implementation is something that you can buy and several open source implementations exist, so the performance handicap from the style may be offset by the comparative maturity of the event bus code.

Variants. Some publish-subscribe style variants require subscribers to register and deregister for events. Others use a declarative model where the subscriber simply states it should receive an event, for example using a programming language annotation or in a configuration file. This is related to another variation point: dynamic creation of event types, publishers, or subscribers. When the style variant allows such runtime changes, it is an example of a dynamic architecture (see Section 9.7).

Event busses vary in what properties they support. Some are *durable* in that they guarantee any message they accept will not be lost during a failure (e.g., power outage). They usually guarantee durability by writing all events to reliable storage, at least temporarily, but this comes with a *latency* tradeoff. They may also guarantee in-order delivery or prioritized delivery of events. Some may allow events to be batched together to avoid storms of similar events.

Publishers and subscribers define the vocabulary of the events. So, if a publisher puts out event A and a subscriber listens for event B, the vocabulary of the system consists of events A and B. The system may allow management of this vocabulary, for example translating event A into event B.

Notes. From a software maintenance and evolvability standpoint, the publish-subscribe style decouples event publishers from consumers, but do not confuse this with the system developer's knowledge and intentions. If you are designing a pub-sub system, you will deliberately introduce, say, a publisher of the "New Employee" event and a consumer of it. Be careful that this knowledge and intent is not lost in your diagrams. It is tempting to simply show an event bus with all of the components attached to it. In such a diagram, how can you tell who-talks-to-who? It only shows that anyone can talk to anyone.

The publish-subscribe style is described in (Clements et al., 2010) and (Shaw and Garlan, 1996). It is also described in (Taylor, Medvidović and Dashofy, 2009) as the *event-based* style, but be careful to note that they use the name *publish-subscribe* to describe a different style, what this book calls the *model-centered* style.

14.12   Client-server style & N-tier

In the *client-server* architectural style, clients request services from servers. The request is usually synchronous and across a request-reply connector, but can vary. There is an asymmetry between client and server in that the client can request that the server

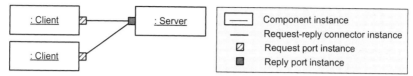

Figure 14.7: An example of the client-server architectural style, part of the runtime viewtype, showing a single server connected to two clients. Clients can initiate communication but the server cannot. The server does not know the identity of the clients until it is contacted.

do work, but not the reverse. An example of a client-server system is seen in Figure 14.7. This style applies to runtime elements, so it is part of the *runtime viewtype*.

Elements and constraints. The client-server style contains client and server components and, usually, a request-reply connector and ports. Clients can initiate communication but the server cannot. The server does not know the identity of the client until it is contacted, but clients must either know the identity of the server or know how to look up the server.

Variants. The client-server style has several variation points. Connectors may be synchronous or asynchronous, there may be limits on the number of clients or servers, connections may be stateless or stateful (i.e., sessions), and the system topology can be static or dynamic.

One variant of the style allows the server, after first being contacted by the client, to send the client subsequent updates. An example of this is the IMAP mail protocol where clients can contact the server and leave open a connector that provides them with updates as emails arrive on the server. Even in this variant, the server cannot contact the client without first being solicited, and the nature of the server to client communication is limited.

Another variant of the client-server style is the *N-tier* style. This style uses two or more instances of the client-server style to form a series of *tiers*, as seen in Figure 14.8. Requests must flow in a single direction across the system. A common case is a 3-tier system where a user interface tier acts as a client for the business logic tier server, which in turn acts as a client for the persistence tier server. In this style, tiers have exclusive functional responsibilities, so for example the user interface tier is exclusively responsible for user interaction and the persistence tier exclusively saves persistent data. The N-tier style has been described as a hybrid between the runtime and allocation viewtypes, since tiers are often (but not always) associated with different hardware. However, hardware could host two or more tiers. Definitions of *tiers* vary, but most agree that they are logical groupings of functions (like components) that can be allocated to hardware.

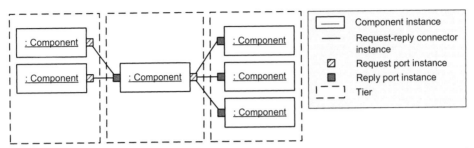

Figure 14.8: An example of the N-Tier architectural style, part of the runtime and allocation view-types, showing three tiers. Each tier has defined responsibilities, such as the first tier handling user interaction, the second tier handling business logic, and the third tier handling persistence. Tiers are usually allocated to specific hardware, but hardware may host multiple tiers.

Resulting qualities. The client-server style establishes an asymmetrical power relationship between the client and server in regards to who can initiate processing. However, the result is usually that the server ends up with more influence since it is providing the service. An organization can change a business process or rule by changing its implementation in one place, the server, rather than across the many clients, so *maintainability* is enhanced. This central control also aids *evolvability* of the system. The client-server style can also be used to *integrate* existing systems by creating a facade around the existing system and treating it as a server.

Notes. The client-server style is similar to the model-centered style, but the model-centered style has the additional constraint that the view and controller components do not interact. In practice, clients in a client-server system rarely interact, but the style does not prohibit it. The peer-to-peer style is also similar, except that it has no asymmetry between clients and servers — each peer can be either.

14.13   Peer-to-peer style

In the *peer-to-peer* architectural style, nodes communicate with each other as peers and hierarchical relationships are prohibited. Each node has the ability, but not obligation, to act both as a client and as a server. The result is a network of nodes operating as peers, where any node can request or provide services to any other node. The peer-to-peer style applies to runtime elements, so it is part of the *runtime viewtype*.

Elements and constraints.   The elements of the peer-to-peer style are similar to those of the client-server style. However, where the client-server connector (usually a request-reply connector) enforces a client role and a server role, a peer-to-peer connector has identical roles on either end that allow both requests and responses.

A peer-to-peer system is egalitarian where the client-server style is hierarchical. The ability to act as a server to any other node and make requests of any other node is required but it does not mean that every node must be fully connected to every other node. At any given time, a node is usually connected to a subset of the nodes, and connections may be added and removed as the system runs.

It is important to recognize that the peer-to-peer style is not simply a relaxation of the client-server asymmetry constraint, but a specific prohibition of that constraint, since the peer-to-peer style's qualities derive from the lack of asymmetry.

Resulting qualities. Peer-to-peer networks are often used to provide access to resources, such as files in a BitTorrent network, with redundant copies of the files held on multiple nodes. A node could request the file, or parts of it, from any of the nodes. Consequently, *availability* is promoted, since the file is still available even if one of the nodes goes offline. It also promotes *resiliency*, since failures of individual nodes are less likely to impair the system.

In contrast to client-server styles, a true peer-to-peer network has no single point of failure and no central infrastructure is needed. The network is highly *scalable* and *extensible*, as there are examples[2] of peer-to-peer networks that have grown to millions of nodes, including BitTorrent and Skype. These systems can grow in size after they are deployed without changing the code and without developer action.

Notes. Some of the strengths of peer-to-peer networks derive from the interconnectedness of the nodes, but this can be subverted if a clique of nodes is disjoint from the main network: an island. Avoiding islands may involve violating the strict interpretation of the guidelines, such as designating some well-known master nodes that can connect new nodes to the main network.

14.14 Map-reduce style

The *map-reduce* architectural style is appropriate for processing large datasets, such as those found in internet-scale systems like search engines or social networking sites (Dean and Ghemawat, 2004; Oreizy, Medvidović and Taylor, 2008). Conceptually simple programs, such as sorting or searching, would execute slowly on large datasets if a single computer were used. This style enables the computation to be spread across multiple computers. As the number of computers used increases, the likelihood that one of them will fail also increases, so this style enables recovery from such failures. The general arrangement of elements in a map-reduce system is seen in Figure 14.9. The map-reduce style applies to runtime elements but is also dependent

---

[2]Note that these specific examples are not pure peer-to-peer in that BitTorrent has trackers than facilitate peer exchanges and Skype has supernodes and other non-peer mechanisms to prevent islands in the network.

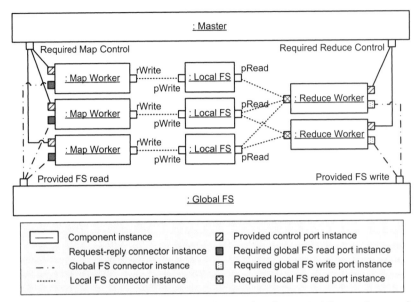

Figure 14.9: An example of the map-reduce architectural style, part of the runtime and allocation viewtypes, with three map workers and two reduce workers. A Master coordinates and distributes work to the map workers, who process a part of the input dataset that they read from the global filesystem (FS) and write to their local FS. Reduce workers read those results and combine them, writing their output to the global FS.

on a particular configuration of allocation elements to achieve its scalability, so it is part of both the *runtime* and *allocation viewtypes*.

The large dataset is split up into smaller datasets (called *splits*) and stored in a *global filesystem*. One or more of these datasets is processed (i.e., *mapped*) by a *map worker* component and the intermediate results are written to its *local filesystem*. The intermediate results and map workers are independent, so no map worker can read another's output. A *reduce worker* component reads the local results from multiple local filesystems and combines (i.e., *reduces*) the results to produce a complete final result, which is stored in the global filesystem. As with map workers, reduce workers are independent. Map workers and reduce workers execute on a set of computers, each with its own local filesystem. The master worker is responsible for instantiating the other workers and for allocating the splits to map workers. It also monitors the health of the workers and reschedules work when workers fail.

Developers working in this style only need to reason about the correctness of how a single machine is processing a single chunk of data. Lots of parallel computation is going on, but developers can safely ignore it, instead simply ensuring that any single map or reduce worker implements its function correctly.

Elements and constraints. A map-reduce system has a single master worker and multiple map worker and reduce worker components. The master worker communicates with the others with a worker controller connector. Map workers can write data to their local filesystem using a local filesystem connector, and reduce workers read data similarly. Both also use a global filesystem connector.

Much of this style is hoisted into a standard implementation library (or framework), so programmers are both shielded from its complexity and must abide by its constraints. To write a program, a developer must provide a map function and a reduce function. If the function that divides the original input set is ineffective creating equally hard chunks (e.g., size or complexity), some map workers will take longer to run than others, slowing down the overall system.

When deterministic map and reduce functions are used, the parallelized computation, even in when recovering from failures, is the same as a sequential one.

Resulting qualities. The primary quality attribute that map-reduce improves is *scalability*. Tasks that were impractical to compute with a single computer can be divided across many machines, improving the *performance*. Once a program is written to use the map-reduce style, it could run on a cluster of one, or one thousand, machines. Map-reduce also promotes *availability*, since it recovers from machine failures by rescheduling the work on another machine.

Notes. The performance of this style is heavily influenced by data locality. Intermediate results need to be kept close to the map and reduce worker components to avoid network bandwidth use. The global filesystem is often a distributed, redundant filesystem.

Map-reduce is often combined with the batch-sequential style, where output from one map-reduce job provides the input for the next. Each map-reduce job is a stage in the batch-sequential network. The combination of these two architectural styles (or patterns) can transform a problem that was not suitable for map-reduce into one that is.

Map-reduce is described as an architectural style in (Oreizy, Medvidović and Taylor, 2008), but the seminal paper is (Dean and Ghemawat, 2004). Hadoop, an open source implementation of map-reduce is described in (Hoff, 2008b) and (Apache Software Foundation, 2010).

14.15 Mirrored, rack, and farm styles

So far, the architectural styles have been from the module and runtime viewtypes. The styles from the allocation viewtype are more likely to be discussed by network engineers (or architects) than software architects. Here are some brief examples to give you a feel for what allocation styles look like.

Mirrored. In the *mirrored* style, identical hardware is duplicated and run in parallel. The government has historically regulated the landline telephone business and imposes uptime requirements. It is difficult to make a single computer (a telephone switch is just a computer with a lot of "peripherals" connected) sufficiently reliable, plus it may need to be offline to upgrade the software. Consequently, telephone switches are often built with two mirror image computers inside. Generally, they operate in lock-step, duplicating the effort, but if one fails then the other continues on its own. Software can up upgraded on one half separately from the other. Since each computer is equally reliable, the telephone switch *reliability* goes down, since there are twice as many computers that can now fail, but its *availability* goes up, since the likelihood that both simultaneously fail is lowered.

Rack. In the *rack* style, commodity server computers are stacked vertically to take up relatively little floor space. All of the computers in the rack are connected to the same network. That network in turn has one or more uplinks to the internet. The network connection for the rack is often faster, or less bandwidth constrained, than the uplink network, so it is faster for two computers on the same rack to communicate than two not on the same rack. Google has some of their original computer racks on display in their lobby and the rack is remarkable for its density: no cases, just computer motherboards and hard drives separated by cardboard. Even when using cases, the rack style is effective at increasing the *density* of computers in a server room and at providing a group of computers with *high bandwidth* between them.

Server farm. In the *server farm* style, many (usually identical) computers are located in the same room. The interconnection of the computers can vary and the farm may be composed of many racks. Farms are best understood in comparison to their alternative: dedicated, specially-configured computers tied to applications. Farms, in contrast, are thought of as a mass resource that can host any application. Note that applications may have restrictions on them so that they are suitable to run on a farm, such as being stateless. A farm is easily *scalable* by adding more of the same kind of hardware. Common uses of farms are for the user interface and middle tiers in 3-tier systems, where a farm of web servers handles the user interface and another farm handles the middle tier.

14.16   Conclusion

An architectural style is a kind of pattern that occurs at an architectural level and applies to architectural elements like components and modules. Patterns range in scope from idioms at the programming language level to styles at the architecture level. Architectural styles are patterns that dominate an architecture. They provide a known set of elements, relations, and constraints. The constraints restrict how the elements can be used, such as the system's runtime topology, the dependencies between its modules, the direction of data flow across its connectors, and the visibility of its components.

The use of styles encourages consistency and comprehensibility in your architecture, improves the density and accuracy of communication between developers, and promotes design reuse. Perhaps most importantly, through their constraints, they enable your architecture to promote or even guarantee quality attributes, and they promote your ability to analyze it.

The styles you have read about here are best thought of as Platonic ideals. When you look at actual systems, you are more likely to encounter embodied styles, ones that bend the style's strict constraints. If the constraints are bent too far, the style may lose its ability to provide desirable qualities.

Styles have a strong connection to architecture-focused design. Architecture-focused design means that you are consciously depending on the architecture to achieve a goal. One way to do that is to design a custom architecture tuned to the qualities you desire. Another way is to use an off-the-shelf architectural style that promotes those same qualities. When you are following architecture-focused design, you will gravitate towards Platonic styles, because bending the constraints puts the desired qualities at risk.

This chapter discussed architectural styles from the module, runtime, and allocation viewtypes. The module viewtype styles were layers and the big ball of mud. The runtime styles were pipe-and-filter, batch-sequential, model-centered, publish-subscribe, client-server, and peer-to-peer. The map-reduce and N-tier styles spanned the runtime and allocation viewtypes. And the mirrored, server farm, and rack styles were all from the allocation viewtype.

14.17 Further reading

Early writing on architectural styles includes Perry and Wolf (1992) and the perfectly titled "A Field Guide to Boxology" by Shaw and Clements (1997). Shaw and Garlan (1996) also covers architectural styles, including most of the ones included in this chapter, but also organizes them into categories, such as data flow styles. Clements et al. (2010) organizes these styles into viewtypes and provides a comprehensive accounting of the elements, relations, and constraints of each.

Architectural styles and patterns are both included in Buschmann et al. (1996), along with lower level design patterns and idioms. More recent writing on patterns and styles includes Taylor, Medvidović and Dashofy (2009) and the enterprise architecture patterns in Fowler (2002).

Chapter 15

Using Architecture Models

At some point you will have mastered the details of architecture models such that you can tell modules apart from components, can write perfect functional and quality attribute scenarios, and can recall every architectural style. But this is not your goal: you will want to go further and use models to make you a better engineer. You will use different views of your master model to highlight different details, yet still have them form a coherent picture of your architecture. You will want to build systems that are high performance, or secure, etc., so you will need to analyze the models you build.

This chapter provides guidance that goes beyond the syntax of drawing a model so that you can use your models productively. Compared to other chapters in the book, its topics range widely. It covers desirable model traits (like precision and accuracy), how to use views effectively, how to draw effective diagrams, when testing and proving are appropriate, how to analyze your architecture models, the dangers of architectural mismatch, how to plan for your user interface, models that describe existing systems versus models that prescribe future systems, and some hints about how to model existing systems.

15.1 Desirable model traits

What traits do good models have? What differentiates the insightful and useful model from another that is uninspired? This section discusses several desirable traits found in good models. Some are traits to strive for, such as low cost and a consistent level of detail. Other traits, such as accuracy and an ability to promote understanding, are essential. This list of desirable model traits incorporates ideas from David Garlan, Grady Booch, and Bran Selic, who have published similar lists.

Perhaps counter-intuitively, *completeness* is not always a desirable model trait. On occasion, you will build a complete model because one is needed by an analysis. As engineers, however, you must balance the cost of building the model against its benefit. That decision usually yields a compromise where models are incomplete yet still useful. The following sections discuss precision, accuracy, prediction, comprehension, detail, monothemacity, and cost as they relate to models.

15.1.1   Sufficiently precise

Here are caricatures of two popular approaches to modeling. The first caricature is of a sloppy model and the second is of a precise model.

- **The cartoon.** You have seen hundreds of these box and line diagrams projected during meetings to "give you a rough idea" of some design. When the model author is being honest, he may refer to these diagrams as *cartoons* to emphasize their lack of formality. However, all too often the author does not recognize the imprecision in the model. The sloppy model could have been created in a rush, or could be slickly produced with impressive 3-D effects. You may get dismissive replies if you ask questions like "What does it mean if two boxes are adjacent, or not?" or "Why are some lines blue and others red?" The most insidious kind of cartoon is one that looks sufficiently precise, but is not.

- **The blueprint.** The precise model is often based on a well-understood formalism, relying on set theory or Petri nets for semantics. The author exhorts you to understand that this is not a cartoon, and can be trusted. The model may explain some things in great detail to the exclusion of others, making you wonder if the author is searching for his keys[1] where the light is good, because some ideas are easier to formalize, or are better understood. The precise model takes a long time to build because anything good is worth the effort.

From these caricatures you may assume that both are bad and there is a better way. You would be only half right, since both can be good or bad depending on the context — you just need to know how to choose accordingly. One of the themes in this book is making engineering tradeoffs, and since your choice of model precision costs time (or money, or attention, etc.) you have to weigh its benefit against its cost.

The best way to choose the precision in your model is to decide, in advance, which questions the model must help you answer (as discussed in Section 6.6). Once

---

[1]This refers to an old joke: One man sees another searching for his car keys in the park underneath a lamp. He says, "Lucky you lost your keys over here." The other replies, "Actually I lost them over there, but the light is better over here."

you know the questions, you can choose the cheapest model that will answer the question. Often a sloppy model will suffice; other times only the most precise model can answer your questions. Beware of backwards justifications, where a precise model is generated and then questions put forth that only it can answer.

You may do your project a disservice if you choose the wrong level of precision. One way to do this is to be sufficiently vague in descriptions or designs so that reviewers do not object to them. One of the implicit questions your model must answer is, "Can a reviewer, stakeholder, or subject matter expert understand it well enough to identify flaws and provide feedback?"

If you do not know what questions you need your model to answer, your first impulse should be to avoid creating a model. However, if your lack of questions is because you are unfamiliar with the domain, you could build models according to the norm in your domain.

When you are building architectural models, the kind of project will influence the detail level in your models. For example, greenfield software development projects (i.e., those that build completely new software) have different risks than brownfield projects (i.e., those that extend an existing system).

15.1.2 Accurate

Accuracy in a model seems like an obviously desirable trait, because no one wants the errors implied by inaccurate model. However, a model may be accurate in some respects (e.g., it yields accurate performance estimates) but not in others (e.g., it gives poor cost estimates). Also, consider the model of Newtonian mechanics, which is useful in describing our normal observations, but is less accurate than quantum mechanics.

Accuracy is an broad term related to several distinct ideas, including consistency with the real world, consistency within the model, referential integrity, and falsifiability. A model that lacks these traits is unlikely to be useful, and may in fact be counterproductive if it leads you to false conclusions.

Consistency with the real world. When using a model, the basic process is to (1) map from the real world into your model, (2) do some work within the model, then (3) map the model output into conclusions about the real world (see Figure 6.1). *Consistency with the real world* requires that the model have designations from the real world that it uses as inputs (see Section 13.6), and also that the model's output agrees with the real world.

Self-consistency and referential integrity. *Self-consistency* requires that the model have no internal contradictions. An example of an internal contradiction was seen in Figure 13.4, where the first and second floor views of a house floorplan revealed a conflict about the staircase location. In addition to self-consistency, a model can have *referential integrity*, which means that the model only refers to elements in the model, and has no "dangling references" to things not mentioned in the model.

Falsifiability. *Falsifiability* requires that you are able to determine if the conclusions made in the model are true or false. Informal architecture models, sometimes called *marketecture* or *PowerPoint architecture* can fail to be falsifiable when they are so vague it is impossible to tell if they represent the real system or not. Open refinement semantics (see Section 7.3) make models difficult to falsify, because the refinement is free to change so many details that few things are certain.

15.1.3 Predictive

Engineers strive to build models that are *predictive* in that they can tell you something about the future. Predictions often anticipate behaviors, like "these processes will deadlock." Another kind of valuable prediction is one about constructability or suitability. It is better to know today that two components are incompatible than to find out during implementation. A model with no predictive power has little chance of reducing engineering risks.

In software architecture, it usually requires an expert modeler to produce a predictive model and the utility of the model depends on the skill of the person using it. As discussed in Section 6.5, many people can learn the syntax of a model and will be able to create one, but to choose which models to create, and to employ those models to amplify your analysis abilities requires a skilled and experienced engineer.

15.1.4 Promote comprehension

As with accuracy, to say that a model should *promote comprehension* seems to be obvious. A model that made a problem harder to understand would need to be balanced by quite a few other advantages.

Limiting details. The most obvious way a model can promote understanding is to exclude details. This way, a large problem is easier to fit into our limited-size minds. By excluding the right details, you effectively make the problem smaller.

Focusing attention. Another way to promote understanding is to focus attention. Herb Simon popularized the idea that while the world is growing increasingly complex, your attention is limited (Simon, 1981). A model can promote understanding by focusing your scarce attention on appropriate details in the problem. You will have already noticed that experts examining an artifact can quickly narrow their attention to salient details, something that is harder for non-experts.

In building a model and exposing select details, you can provide the reader with the benefit of your expertise through your selection of details. Contrast this with a computer-aided design (CAD) program that can mechanically generate an infinite number of views of a building design. The fact that you choose to present a particular view, for example the throughput and reliability of connectors, necessarily focuses the reader's attention on those details instead of others. If the model author acts like the CAD program and indiscriminately generates views, he has hindered the reader's comprehension.

Suitable format and notation. Not all models are equally easy to comprehend. It is usually the case that the essence of a model can be expressed in different forms and some forms will be easier to understand than others. It is possible that object-oriented programming has become popular because the abstraction of an object meshes more easily with most programmers' minds. Functional programming, for example, has many benefits, but it may be that most programmers reason about objects more easily than about functions.

Whether this theory is right or not, you should be wary of your own models and ensure that they are helping those who read them. If you find that a particular model always causes readers problems, you should investigate other equivalent models that are more easily understood. As discussed in Section 15.6.1, the human brain has a lot of hardware for special-purpose analyses, especially visual and linguistic ones, so it is prudent to choose models that take advantage of it.

Story at many levels. One way to promote comprehensibility of your models is to structure them as a *story at many levels* (see Section 11.1). Most complex things are designed to have internal structure so that a constituent piece can be understood separately from the whole and that the whole can be understood without knowing exactly how a piece accomplishes its job. The top-level of design should be comprehensible without opening subcomponents, and again each subcomponent should be comprehensible without opening its own subcomponents.

15.1.5 Consistent level of detail

A model with more detail is not always preferred to one with less detail. Instead, a model should strive for a *consistent level of detail*, rather than having some parts more detailed than others. Refinement can be used to selectively show more or less detail in a model. A model with a consistent level of detail can be refined to show additional detail in chosen parts.

A model with mixed levels of detail can be confusing to a reader because the differing detail may arise for different reasons. One interpretation is that the model is simply unfinished. Alternately, the model could be missing important details because those details are not known. Finally, the model could be deliberately eliding details because those details were unimportant. If you must create a model with an inconsistent level of detail, put a note on the model explaining the reason and you will reduce the reader's confusion.

Another reason to avoid mixing detail levels in a model is to avoid the phenomenon of "following the contours of the seabed." The reader should be allowed to absorb the additional details when the reader wants them, rather than when the model author wants to reveal them. A model that provides all available details will be deeper in some places than others. Most readers find it easier to first comprehend the big picture in a simpler model, and then later selectively explore the details as their need or curiosity guides them.

If you wish to show additional details concerning selected parts, build one model at a consistent level of detail, then build a refinement model that shows selected parts in greater detail, which yields a consistent level of detail, avoids confusion, and still provides additional detail as appropriate.

15.1.6   Monothematic views

The best and most useful models are produced through the deliberate inclusion and exclusion of information. When presenting a view of a model, it is best to use *monothematic views*, ones that selectively and consistently show categories of information from the model.

For example, a view could choose to show a component assembly annotated with the throughput of connectors. A monothematic view like this is suitable for analyzing throughput and its reader is undistracted by other categories of details like security and implementation language.

The name *monothematic* emphasizes the idea that a view consistently shows a single thing, but does not imply that only a single category of information is shown, so it is OK to show both throughput and reliability. What is discouraged is to inconsistently sprinkle in information, for example if some connectors are annotated to show their implementation technology and others are not. A view that has various categories of information similarly sprinkled on quickly becomes a mess.

15.1.7   Inexpensive

A central theme of this book is that effort spent on engineering should be aligned with perceived risks. It follows that an *inexpensive* model is easier to justify building. Models may have *detail knobs* that allow you to adjust their level of detail between rough sketches and intricate Swiss watches. Even better, the benefit curve often races ahead of the cost curve, so you should look for the least expensive model that addresses your risks. For example, creating a textual list of components and connectors requires very little effort, but is significantly more useful than having no model at all.

15.2   Working with views

We now shift our discussion from the desirable qualities of views to how best to work with them. If it were easier to reason about a system from the master model, or just one viewtype, or just one view, you would do that and forget about multiple views because they are a challenge to build and coordinate. However, a single model of even a medium-sized software system would be difficult to comprehend. It would be difficult to analyze too, since the salient details would be mixed in with extraneous ones.

Divide and conquer. As you have already seen, the solution to this problem is to keep the large model as a master model (see Section 13.1.2), but to show views of it that reveal only selected details. Conceptually, a system has just a single master model that has all details. You can slice it initially into three primary viewtypes and then further subdivide each of these into specific views. For example, a view might show just a component assembly or a single module. Slicing and dicing your master model into views that are easier to work with is an example of a *divide and conquer* strategy.

After knowing the basic strategy, some questions remain. Which views should you create? What problems are you likely to encounter with the divide and conquer strategy? And are there anti-patterns you should avoid?

A view for each concern. How do you choose which views to create? One answer is to build a view for each *concern*, where a concern is a dimension of the problem or system that you are interested in. For example, if you have an architecture driver related to security, you will probably get value from a view that reveals security details of your system.

Some engineering fields have a standard set of concerns. In the design of satellites, for example, the standard concerns are mechanisms, propulsion, thermal, stress, dynamics, and fluids/aerodynamics. Engineers specializing in thermal analysis draw specialized views of the satellite that help them solve heat-related problems and detect design errors. It is unlikely that the details needed for thermal analysis are the same as the details needed for stress analysis, hence the different views. Each engineering specialist gets a view that enhances or enables quantitative and qualitative analysis of his concern. In software, concerns often align with quality attributes and functionality.

Like engineers in other fields, most software developers learn specialized skills relating to concerns during their careers. Some developers are recognized as experts in security, for example, and others at telecommunications, but these skillsets are not as standardized as they are in other fields of engineering.

15.2.1 Problems you will encounter

In general, dividing up a big problem into smaller ones is a good strategy. You will, however, encounter difficulties because each view will have a narrow focus and because some problems live in between those narrow views.

Specialized views yield narrow focus. When you look at a collection of specialized, narrow views, it can be difficult to mentally synthesize those views together to envision the master model or the entire system. Your narrow views are much like the story of the three blind men describing an elephant, where one says the elephant is round and strong like a tree, another says it is flexible like a snake, and another says it is flat like a piece of paper. The challenge is to integrate the views back into an understanding of the whole elephant, rather than just understanding its leg, its trunk, and its ear.

When you are building views with the hope that your reader can reassemble them to understand the system, a partial solution is to include a view from each viewtype: module, runtime, and allocation.

Some problems live in between views. A narrow, specialized view excludes extraneous details so that you can focus on a particular concern. You gain leverage by creating such views, but there is a cost. If a view is monothematic and shows just one concern, where do you put knowledge about interactions between concerns? For example, there is a tradeoff in the design of an internal combustion engine: You can increase power by making the cylinders wider, but doing so reduces the space between the cylinders, which becomes a heat and stress problem. This tradeoff would not show up in a thermal-only view, or in a mechanical-only view.

In software systems, developers often learn a new domain each time they change projects, so such expert knowledge is unlikely to be known implicitly. One solution is to create mixed concern views, ones that show details relevant to two or more concerns, which allows you to write down the concern interactions that you discover, often as tradeoffs or invariants.

Inconsistency between views. When you create multiple views of your system, you open the door to inconsistencies between those views. This book uses the interpretation that there is a *master model* from which all views are projected. The master model approach says that inconsistencies can arise because the master model can have flaws, or because you made mistakes when drawing views of the master model. So, when you discover views that contradict, you need to trace that contradiction back to either a bug in the master model or a bug in the process by which you created the view.

Everything that views take apart must be put back together such that a system can be built. Consider an example from another engineering domain. If a thermal engineer's analysis reveals that one part of a satellite can become too hot, he rearranges the design of the subcomponents to compensate. It is essential that this update to the satellite propagates to every other view, otherwise the mechanical, electrical, and other engineers will be wasting time by working with out-of-date views. If the inconsistency is not caught, someone will start constructing the satellite only to discover it is unbuildable, perhaps because the views require its antenna to be in two places at once.

15.2.2 Anti-patterns you should avoid

Anti-patterns are ideas that are repeated by many people because they seem like good ideas, but in hindsight they can be seen as ideas to be avoided. When dealing with views, some developers become fond of a particular view, perhaps because it has helped them in the past, or they may try to create a single view that has every needed detail.

Anti-pattern: favorite view. Despite the need for various views to solve various problems, developers can become attached to their favorite "pet" views, even when they are inappropriate for the problem at hand. Perhaps their last project was organized into layers, so they gravitate to a layered module view, even if this project uses a peer-to-peer style.

Continuing to use a favorite view to reason about your system is usually possible, just more difficult than using a more appropriate view or viewtype. For example, developers can find protocol violations simply by looking at source code, but they would have an easier job if they used state models. Generally, you should use the views and viewtypes that are appropriate to your problem, rather than struggling with a favorite view.

Anti-pattern: one diagram to rule them all. Closely related to the idea of focusing on a single view is the attempt to make a single diagram serve all purposes: the *one diagram to rule them all*. This often occurs because the diagram[2] author does not yet realize that viewtypes are hard or impossible to reconcile and dutifully struggles to cram every detail onto a single diagram.

---

[2]The words diagram (a picture) and view (a projection of a model) can generally be used interchangeably. The word *diagram* is used here instead of *view* because this diagram does not necessarily adhere to the semantics we associate with views as projections of a master model.

Consequently, it can be impossible to tell if a line between two boxes represents a dependency between two modules or a runtime communication between two component instances. You may even notice the diagram author arguing that module dependencies (seen in a module view) and runtime communication (seen in a runtime component assembly) are the same thing.

As a result, a single diagram that tries to reveal code organization, runtime structures, and allocation to hardware becomes crowded and hard to understand. The diagram author may omit relevant details because they are hard to express, rather than drawing another diagram where they would fit easily.

15.3   Improving view quality

At this point you may be a bit worried about your ability to handle many views of your architecture. Perhaps you are even wondering if the divide and conquer strategy was such a good idea. Fortunately, there are techniques that help you manage those views, detect inconsistencies, and steer them to become consistent. Three techniques are discussed here: writing functionality scenarios, animating scenarios, and writing action specifications. The techniques on functionality scenarios augment the advice given in Section 12.6.

15.3.1   Functionality scenarios stitch together views

What views show in isolation, functionality scenarios reassemble into a whole, like a thread that connects separate pieces of cloth into a quilt. This insight is critical to Philippe Kruchten's 4+1 views of architecture (Kruchten, 1995), where the +1 view is scenarios that connect the other four views. A single scenario can refer to elements that appear in different views, and even different viewtypes, so scenarios help the reader to relate the pieces and understand the whole of the model.

In its most common use, a functionality scenario applies to a single model in a single view, such as applying to a domain model, a port, an allocation model, or a component assembly. However, it is easy to write a scenario that applies across models and even viewtypes. For example, a scenario for packaging and deploying source code would describe how it is compiled (module viewtype), tested (runtime viewtype), and distributed onto servers (allocation viewtype). Strictly speaking, a scenario applies to just one model, so when they are used to stitch together several views, those views must be of the same model, perhaps the master model.

Regardless of how casually you write them, functionality scenarios always have the advantage of reading like a story. However, if you take care in how you structure them, they are effective at tying together views. This section describes that structure and the rigor you should apply. As you grow to appreciate why the structure exists, it will feel less like a burden and more like an opportunity.

Informal dialogue. Here is an example of how you can keep your scenario tightly connected to your model. If you were working on the scenario for the library system (from Chapter 12), your inner dialogue, or perhaps even spoken dialogue if you are collaborating with someone else, might sound like this:

> OK, this step deals with how the borrower returns the copy. Is there an operation defined on the port for that? Yes, it's called Return(). So the borrower, Bart, will "return the copy of Moby-Dick" via the pDesk port. Actually that would be Bart and Larry, since only Larry the librarian can use the pDesk port. Then the system will need to match that up with the loan. Of course Bart doesn't know the loan ID, so the system will need to look the loan up and then change the loan's state from ... hmm, I haven't defined loan states yet.

This is just a snippet of dialogue but should give you an idea of how the writing of a scenario immerses you in the details of the target model. It might even feel a bit like writing code.

Checklist. As a reference, a checklist can be quite helpful in helping you learn to write a good scenario. Below is a checklist that can be used either while writing a scenario or when checking one after-the-fact.

- **Actor**. The actor that initiates each step should be clear, as should the recipient. To ensure this, always use the present tense, which will avoid linguistic constructions that hide the initiator, as in, "The copy is checked in." While you are thinking about the initiating actor, ensure it already knows about any data it must pass as a parameter. Also consider if the actor is allowed to initiate this action. The actor must also have a path of communication to the recipient, so a connector, dependency, or a communication channel may need to exist.

- **Action**. Each step should refer clearly to a single action defined on the target model. A good scenario has a single level of abstraction across steps. For example, if one step is, "Larry adds a copy of Moby-Dick to the library," another step should be at about that same level of detail, and not "Larry enters his username and password." Action names in the scenario should be as close as possible to the action name in the target model, but you can allow minor differences, especially if they improve readability.

- **References**. Scenario steps refer to model elements, such as parameters passed in or return values. The scenario should have no dangling references, so all references must be defined in the target model, including associations, attributes, and states (or other details relevant to the model type). However, the scenario should avoid referencing "things inside of things," so a scenario at the boundary of your system should not refer to subcomponents inside the system.

- **Target Model**. Each step should transform the target model from one legal configuration, or state, to another. An example of an illegal state would be a stack containing -1 items, or a loan that is not associated with a borrower. You should insist that each step causes a visible change to the target model. If it does not, you may need a more detailed model or a less detailed scenario. An exception to this is query operations, which rarely change the model. No step should cause invariants or constraints on the model to be broken.

- **Overall**. Does the scenario make sense overall? Has it skipped over any steps or difficulties? Does any actor in the scenario "just know" where something is, or "just know" which other object or actor to talk to, one that it should have to look up? Does it omit any difficult start-up or tear-down steps? As you write a scenario step, think, "is this exactly the right word; does it match the rest of the model?" You can also start with an empty target model and use the scenario to begin populating it, adding items as you mention them in the scenarios.

Scenarios without this careful attention to references are useful for understanding and documenting the design, but carefully structured scenarios help you while you write them to catch errors or omissions, and help you to think about how the views are stitched together to reveal the whole of the design.

15.3.2   Animating functionality scenarios

You have just learned how to write structured functionality scenarios such that you can catch problems. Your models will change after you write your scenarios, so you would like to be able to go back and re-check the scenarios. This section describes how to *animate scenarios* to check for problems in your models.

Developers often mentally animate programs in their minds in order to debug them. They walk through the program line-by-line and think about what impact each line of code will have and consider possibilities for bugs. The result is higher quality code with fewer bugs.

Animating scenarios is analogous to animating a program and often feels the same. Animating a scenario means that developers walk through a scenario and mentally animate it step-by-step. With each step, they imagine the changes that are taking place to the model. Animation promotes a close mental connection with the model, a perspective that helps you to catch inconsistencies and errors of omission.

The simplest version of animating a scenario is simple syntax and reference checking, but you can do much more. To do so requires you to use the scenario to examine your understanding of the system. Recall that at the pinnacle of the pyramid of modeling competence (from Figure 6.3). Developers use models to amplify their reasoning. Each step in the scenario can be used as a context from which to examine the system and see if it is reasonable and complete. The following are some questions that you can ask as you animate a scenario that will help you go beyond simple syntax checking.

- **Communication.** Does the actor have a choice about which port or connector to use? Should another port be added? Are the properties on the port or connector appropriate for the kind of message being sent (e.g., an insecure channel or a daily batch)? Does/should the actor know how to contact the recipient, or know how to choose the right recipient?

- **Before and after.** Should this action initiate any other messages? Is something returned or should it be? What should the state change of the model look like? Is this step dependent on something that must have happened before? Do the actors and the system have access to the data they are required to pass?

- **Beyond the scenario.** Is there a variant of this scenario step that would be more challenging to the system? Is there interesting behavior involved with startup, shutdown, empty collections, or deleting elements? How many scenarios are needed to give confidence in the system behavior? Is the behavior of each element reasonable given its allocated responsibilities?

These kinds of questions could be answered without a scenario, but the concrete context of the scenario can help uncover problems and can open up new avenues of thinking. These questions do not have right or wrong answers based on simple checks — do the connectors have *appropriate* properties? — so developers use scenarios to augment their analysis. When you animate scenarios across your model with the intention of detecting problems, you will find that reading through a single step is a rich mental activity that reinforces the interconnected nature of your models.

15.3.3 Writing action specifications

A third way to tie together your models is to use *action specifications*. Action specifications can tie together various views in much the same way that functionality scenarios can. Consider the action check_out_copy that describes how a borrower could check out a copy of a book from a library.

> void **check_out_copy** (Copy c, Borrower b)
> > **pre-condition**: c is not removed, c has no current loans
> > **post-condition**: new Loan l, linked to b and c, out = today, in = null, due = c.library.loanLength + today

Reading the action spec itself gives you some understanding of how the system must work: copies can be removed from the library, there are loans recorded, some loans are "current," loans identify the book and the copy, and there is a standard loan length.

You can use the action specifications to limit the size of your model by only including details that are required in the action specifications. You might be tempted to include the age of the book copy in the model, but if it is not mentioned or needed in any action spec then you would omit it from the model.

Action specifications make specific demands on other models. This spec requires that the following terms be defined: Copy, Borrower, Loan, and Library. Those terms have additional attributes: current loans, out, in, due, and loan length. And some states are referenced: removed books and current loans. A complete model would describe all of the states and transitions, and how the actions drive the state transitions. It should also describe how attributes relate to states, for example that a Copy has an attribute called isRemoved that corresponds to its state. You would also expect to see this action appear as a step in at least one use case.

Despite their utility, action specifications are time consuming and therefore expensive, so this book refrains from advocating that you regularly include them in your models. The idea underlying them, however, is that all the views of your model are interrelated, so knowing how action specifications work will improve your modeling ability. Even when you do not write down the spec, you may be thinking, "Have I defined all the terms I would need to satisfy the pre-conditions and post-conditions?"

15.4   Improving diagram quality

Here are two easy things you can do to improve your diagrams: include a legend and omit the arrowheads. I acquired both of these bugbears from David Garlan.

15.4.1   Put legends on diagrams

Unless it is on a whiteboard, diagrams always need legends. Consider this book: you have probably flipped through the pages and glanced at headings and diagrams. Even if the notational conventions were consistent, but stated only once on page 15, you would likely have difficulty understanding a diagram that you flip to on page 200. If you ever put together a packet that includes diagrams, people will flip through that too, and may well be confused without legends.

If you are using a standard notation, like UML, you can put an annotation on the diagram saying that, but realize that not everyone will recall the difference in UML arrows that distinguishes a dependency from subclassing. In any case, it is easy to copy a legend from an old diagram to the new one so that every diagram has one.

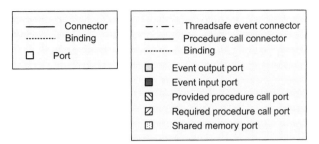

Figure 15.1: The legend on left is accurate, but minimal. The legend on the right provides insight into the mind of the designer and the abstractions employed.

Notice too that legends force you to be careful in your notation, since they summarize the elements and relations you are using in the figure. For example, if you start drawing some components with rounded corners, having to define them in the legend forces you to think about what they mean, and you may either decide that it is a significant distinction, or not.

Not all legends are, well, legendary. Consider the two in Figure 15.1. The one on the left has done the bare minimum job, like a kid who has told his mother that yes, he has cleaned his room. Even without seeing the diagram, the legend on the right is a glimpse into the architecture. It shows that the developer was not thinking of the lowest common denominator of interactions — component A connects to component B — but instead thinking about the nature of the communication, and possibly relying upon it to achieve qualities like performance or modifiability.

15.4.2 Avoid arrowheads on connectors

This book, like many books on software architecture, does not put arrowheads on the connectors. Why? Surely it is important to know that component A is the one that sends data to component B, and not the reverse. And it is important to know that B is the one that initiates the connection. And it is important to know that A can sever the connection. And so on. Sadly, there are many properties you would like to reveal in the diagram, yet only one arrowhead.

There are also semantic concerns: connector A requests data from B, who then replies with the bulk of the data transferred. Should the arrow point from A to B, because the first data transfer is from A, or from B to A because the bigger data transfer goes that direction?

The worst problem is that readers of the diagram tend to assume they know what the arrowhead means, but they can guess wrong. The alternative to arrows is to reveal some details using typographic differences in the ports and connectors, as you see in detailed legends. Remaining details are listed textually as properties of the ports and connectors. Few readers will jump to conclusions about port shading the way they do arrowheads, for example that a port shaded gray is an event output port, so they instead look at the legend to get the correct interpretation.

Using arrowheads is not right or wrong; it is a stylistic choice. However, if you do use arrowheads, you should use a legend to reveal what the arrowhead means.

15.5   Testing and proving

You are probably already aware of the difference between *testing* and *proving* but it is worth covering because of its importance in how you use your models. In short, testing can demonstrate the presence of bugs but not their absence. Depending on what kinds of questions you need your model to answer, either testing or proving may be appropriate.

Test models with good data.   If testing is appropriate, you still need the right data to feed into the model. Developers usually have a few concrete test cases "in their pockets" that they use to create candidate models. Models that cannot express the data in the test case must be revised or eliminated. For example, in the Home Media Player system example from Chapter 4, the model authors used the Prince songs to test the general model.

Once a model passes these pocket example tests, it should be evaluated on a broader set of concrete data. For example, I once built a model of security permissions using a few pocket examples. I then collected actual data from a broad range of groups in the company, covering different platforms and operating systems, and ensured the model worked on these also. Of course the model did not work perfectly, since real data throws unexpected curveballs.

Proving with analytic models.   Sometimes you need a model that has properties like isolation, freedom from deadlock, performance, or security. Usually these properties are emergent, and it is easier to reason about emergent properties in simpler models than in complex ones. You may need to simplify your model to give you leverage over the problem and to prove (or informally convince yourself) that you know what the emergent properties are. To prove properties, you probably need an *analytic* model instead of an *analogic* model, as discussed in Section 3.5. When using analysis tools to prove properties, most models will need to be transformed before being read by the tool, as discussed in the next section.

15.6   Analyzing architecture models

You may be under the impression that the benefit of expressing your architecture using a precise modeling language is that hairy, complex analysis programs can analyze your model and find problems that mere mortals cannot. Prepare yourself for a bit of an anticlimax because the primary analysis tool is between your ears. This section will describe some of those hairy and complex analysis programs, but its message is that your most valuable analysis tool is your brain plus clear models.

An appropriate view can obviate sophisticated analysis. Consider the humble calendar. If you want to know what day of the week December 26, 1965 falls on, you can flip to that calendar page and look at which column it falls under. In fact, you can do tricky operations on that date so easily, like finding the following Wednesday, that you hardly consider them computations. But consider what kind of program you would have to write, one that would have to compute leap years, etc., to answer similar questions and compare it to the answer that just pops out of a calendar view.

This section will survey some techniques you can use to analyze your designs and architectures. Many are applied as "back of the envelope" evaluations. They can still be quantitative and, when you are willing to invest the time, some of them can be formalized. We will start by looking at the informal techniques and move on to the formal ones.

15.6.1 Humans as architecture analysis machines

With computational analyses available, it is easy to overlook the option of analyzing models yourself. Human brains are remarkable at processing information, but quite dependent on the form of that information. Imagine trying to navigate from a map, but not a traditional 2D map. This "map" is an alphabetical listing of the street segments in the country. This representation would thwart a human, but a computer might actually find the task easier this way. That is because people have lots of visual processing capabilities that they use to find a route on a map. Maps are drawn to work with those human capabilities, for example by drawing major roads thicker than minor roads.

Architecture models can be built to similarly leverage our human capabilities. If you are searching for single points of failure in a system, you is going to have a hard time if you only look at the source code. However, the fact that all requests flow through a single load balancer would jump out when you look at an allocation view.

Standard viewtypes. But do the standard allocation, runtime, and module architecture viewtypes provide the right representations for humans to leverage their built-in analysis? There is no way to give a refutable answer to this question, but the general experience is that yes, the standard architecture views are good, but no, they are not ideal.

You should augment them with other views or viewtypes as needed. For example, Philippe Kruchten's 4+1 views includes a process view that is helpful if your system has multiple threads or processes. The standard architecture views are general-purpose, which gives them some leverage on almost all domains. The flip side to this is that they provide no domain-specific leverage. Consider again the calendar example. A calendar, as a domain-specific view, has the nice property that all the Mondays are in the same column, a domain-specific encoding that you would not get from the standard architecture views.

Flash vs. substance. The next time you are tempted to put a fancy gradient fill on an architecture model, stop and consider whether it aids or impedes comprehension. It may superficially glitz up the model and improve its boardroom-presentation appeal, but make sure it does not hurt anyone's ability to comprehend it because the human brain is usually the analysis machine.

15.6.2   Informal analysis techniques

Several informal techniques exist to analyze an architecture, including quality attribute workshops, architectural checklists, architecture and design reviews, and the Architectural Tradeoff Analysis Method.

Quality attribute workshops. Different analysis techniques work at different times in a project's lifecycle. *Quality attribute workshops* are a technique to discover and prioritize system quality attribute scenarios and are used before design begins (Barbacci et al., 2003). A workshop leader solicits stakeholders to write quality attribute scenarios where each scenario describes the system's measurable response to a stimulus. A simple scenario is "When the system receives a request, a response must be returned within 200ms." Quality attribute workshops provide a prioritized list of scenarios and can be used to identify risks. Some scenarios are very important to stakeholders, but not difficult for a system to achieve. When the scenarios are difficult to achieve, however, they help identify a risk of failure.

Architectural checklists. *Architecture checklists* are used during design or reviews to ensure that known risks are considered. Several general-purpose checklists exist that you can use as-is (Maranzano, 2005; Meier et al., 2003; Rozanski and Woods, 2005). Domain-specific checklists have the ability to catch even more specific problems, such as cross-site scripting vulnerabilities in web applications, something that would not appear on a general checklist.

Architecture and design reviews. An *architecture review* consists of a presentation of a proposed architecture, or design, to a group of reviewers who did not participate in the design (Maranzano, 2005). The review process provides the reviewers, who are domain experts and/or software architecture experts, an opportunity to identify potential risks or defects in the design. Participants have noted, however, that simply preparing for such reviews encourages them to scour their design for flaws so that most problems are caught before the actual review.

The reviewers may follow a risk-driven evaluation of the design, thinking of how the design might fail. They may suggest techniques to address the newly identified risks, and may identify techniques that could have been performed earlier.

Architectural Tradeoff Analysis Method. The *Architectural Tradeoff Analysis Method* (ATAM) is a kind of architecture review designed evaluate the suitability of a proposed architecture (Bass, Clements and Kazman, 2003). ATAM sessions must be performed after an architecture has been proposed since it investigates and discovers tradeoffs for a particular architecture. By knowing the quality attribute tradeoffs, developers have the opportunity to change the architecture, yielding a better set of tradeoffs.

ATAM also delivers a set of ways the architecture may not achieve the desired quality attribute scenarios, which are a particular kind of risk. ATAM sessions work best when both architecture experts and domain experts collaborate to identify risks. ATAM sessions can be both time consuming and expensive, making them difficult to apply on smaller projects, but the essential ideas of ATAM can be adapted to a lower-ceremony development process.

15.6.3 Formal analysis techniques

In addition to the informal techniques, there are quite a few formalisms and corresponding tools that can be used to check models. In most cases these tools will not work directly on your model or source code, so it must be transformed into a format that can be handled by the tool. First, we will take a look at the transformation process then proceed on to discuss specific analyses, formalisms, and tools.

Transforming models for analysis. The exact process for analyzing your architectural model using a particular tool will depend on each, but it is possible to make some generalizations. What follows is a sketch of the basic process for the round trip to get an answer from a tool that includes transforming your model into a format the tool can read, using the tool to check something, and making sense of the tool's output.

1. **Simplify the model.** Your model may need to be simplified, where the simpler model will have fewer elements and relationships than the original. The analyses performed by the tools generally work very quickly on small models, perhaps taking just a few seconds or minutes to run. But because of their computational complexity, larger models may take hours or even fail to complete in any reasonable amount of time. The relationship between this simpler model and your original model must be a refinement relationship, so that what you learn about the simple model will still be true about the more detailed model.

2. **Map to the tool vocabulary**. Your model must be adapted so that it is expressed in the primitive elements that the tool understands. Some tools only understand directed graphs or arrays, while others understand data structures like sets. This is roughly analogous to transforming story problems in math class, where the velocities of two trains are converted into variables in an equation. This transformation strips domain-specific details from your model, in the way that you do not care what color the train is, or what time of day it is traveling, or even that it is a train.

3. **Express model in the tool's language**. Your model must be expressed in the input language of the tool. This is similar to converting between pseudocode and the concrete syntax of a particular language, and could even be automated.

4. **Devise an assertion to check**. You must devise and express an assertion (a predicate) to check in the formalism. Sometimes the assertion is implicit, as with rate monotonic analysis: "These processes can be safely scheduled." Other assertions will be domain specific, like, "A call to Open is always followed by a single call to Close." The assertion must be converted from natural language into a form that the tool understands, which can be harder than it seems. Linear temporal logic, for example, has operators like *next*, *always*, and *eventually* that are used to express the assertion.

5. **Use the tool to check the assertion**. The tool analyzes your model and the assertion. Tools provide various results, but often they provide either an assurance that the assertion holds or they provide a counterexample of how the model could violate it.

6. **Reverse-map the tool output to a meaningful answer**. You must convert the results of the analysis back into the domain of your model. When the results are positive, as in "this model will not deadlock," this interpretation is rather easy. Sometimes a problem may be reported by the tool, yet impossible in the real system because of some constraints that you simplified out of the model. In that case you can revise the model to add these constraints back in, or otherwise reformulate the model.

Doing each of these steps yourself can be a lot of work, but analyses can be built into modeling tools to save effort. The following sections describe analyses grouped into categories based on quality attributes.

Security analysis. Security is a difficult quality attribute to achieve because small coding slips can result in gaping security holes. When securing a system, developers usually follow checklists, looking for known types of attack vectors and examining their code to ensure it is not vulnerable.

It is possible to formalize and automate such an approach by modeling the system as a data flow diagram (DFD) and building a program analyzer that would extract the same from source code (Abi-Antoun, Wang and Torr, 2007). They were able to look for attack vectors by analyzing the DFD and ensure that the source code had no deviations that could cause problems.

Security also provides design challenges because you can always apply more security measures. Each additional measure comes at a cost, yet it is hard for stakeholders to know which basket of measures will be optimal for them. Shawn Butler's security process guides stakeholders to understand their needs so that they can choose efficiently (Butler, 2002).

Reliability analysis. Reliability in software is usually achieved through both code quality and architecture. Code-level reviews reduce bugs to a minimum and processes are used to ensure high code quality from the start. Architecture comes into play because even the best code can fail, so architectures for high reliability can operate in different modes, such as steady state mode and degraded mode. Spacecraft that encounter problems may revert to a safe mode where they point their antenna towards Earth and wait for more instructions. Software architectures with single points of failure are dangerous for reliability and you can scour your runtime and allocation viewtype models to find them.

Because dynamism is hard to reason about, architectures for high reliability may be mostly static. For example, designers of a high reliability system might use *rate monotonic analysis* to ensure that the system cannot become overloaded by its jobs.

Performance analysis. Most often, performance is modeled coarsely based on back-of-the envelope estimates. For example, to analyze latency, you might annotate a runtime view of your system with numbers corresponding to how long processing should take in each element. The estimated latency is the sum of the latencies along a path, perhaps from user interface through the business logic and database.

Estimates can be made more accurate by using distributions instead of individual latency numbers and by taking measurements on a running system. At some point, you step up to *queueing theory*, which is a mathematical formalism you can use to estimate latencies and other properties, or *Monte Carlo analysis*, a numerical analysis suitable when there are many degrees of freedom in the system.

Accuracy, completeness, and other analysis. *Model checkers* are tools that evaluate a model with respect to a predicate. Some popular ones are Spin (Holzmann, 2003) and Alloy (Jackson, 2002). They are general purpose checkers, so you will need to transform your model for analysis as described above. Labeled Transition System Analyzer (LTSA) for Finite State Processes (FSP) (Magee and Kramer, 2006) models systems as finite state machines and can check that they meet properties, also mod-

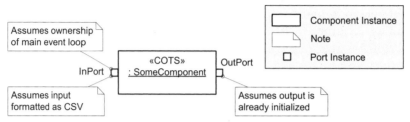

Figure 15.2: Architectural mismatch occurs when elements in an system have conflicting assumptions about the architecture. You can document these assumptions using UML notes so that others will watch out for them.

eled as state machines. It can be helpful in modeling concurrency and finding places where protocols can deadlock.

Models can have gaps with respect to the real world. They require experience to detect and expert modelers develop a spider sense in rooting them out. These gaps can only be identified by humans since the model itself may be internally consistent. Internal model inconsistencies, also called referential integrity violations, can be automatically checked. An example of an internal inconsistency is that a scenario refers to a component that is not defined in the model.

This concludes our brief tour of analysis techniques. The following sections discuss architectural mismatch, planning for your user interface, prescriptive and descriptive models, and how to model existing systems.

15.7   Architectural mismatch

The term *architectural mismatch* was coined when a team led by David Garlan built a system by assembling existing parts. They were burdened by difficulties that will be familiar to anyone who has done similar COTS integration, including code bloat, slow execution, re-implemented functions, concurrency difficulties, and error-prone composition. Their paper on the experience went beyond noting that integration is hard, and categorized the architectural properties that can make two pieces of software incompatible (Garlan, Allen and Ockerbloom, 1995). Their categories of potential architectural mismatch are:

1. Assumptions about components: infrastructure, who has control, data use
2. Assumptions about connectors: protocols, structure of transmitted data
3. Assumptions about system: system topology, component presence or absence
4. Assumptions about construction process: initialization sequence

The authors suggest a number of solutions that require a change in the landscape of COTS software. However, only one of their suggestions is helpful as you attempt to integrate some existing software: build models that highlight the architectural assumptions.

When your models point out potentially troublesome assumptions, you will be able to detect mismatches earlier, and can either choose different COTS software that is compatible, or change your system design to accommodate the assumptions embedded in the COTS software.

Conceptually, it does not matter where you document these assumptions, but in practice it is best to put them directly on the architecture diagrams as notes, since otherwise they can easily be overlooked. Figure 15.2 shows an example of a component and some assumptions it makes.

15.8 Choose your abstraction level

Models are abstractions and so, by definition, they omit details. When you build a model of a system you must choose which details to include and which to leave out. It is a particularly difficult choice for models of your system interfaces since you must decide: should the model represent the actual API operations, or be more abstract?

Your first instinct might be to model the actual API operations of the system. Such a model has the benefit that it is concrete and testable, since you can compare it with the source code. It can be used to detect problems in the actual API, which more abstract models cannot. For example, are the data interchange structures sufficient for your purposes? And you could use that model as API-level documentation.

But there are drawbacks related to size, since API-level models are usually quite large. Assuming that there are 1000 lines of implementation for every API operation, a 1MLOC program would have a thousand API operations to model. Though your ratio may be different, it is evident that building an API-level model for a large system is a considerable effort. Keeping it updated is perhaps even harder than the initial construction. An API-level model may also obscure your sight of the architecture, as it can be hard to see the forest for the trees. At the API-level, interfaces and modules are easy to see, but architecture abstractions like styles, ports, or connectors are not.

Perhaps most serious is that API-level models can be hard to reason about. Most obviously, size works against comprehension. Recall the story problems you worked on in math class, like the one where you must determine when two trains will meet. The model you built abstracted away every detail except for those relevant to answer the question at hand. If your architecture question concerns the system throughput, answering that question will be easier with a more abstract model, not the API-level model. In moderation, API-level models are valuable, but you should pause before building one for your entire system.

You must be aware that anytime you build a model, you are explicitly or implicitly choosing its level of abstraction. To choose effectively, know what questions the model must answer (e.g., security questions, performance questions, usability questions) and build the least expensive model that can answer them.

15.9   Planning for the user interface

The old wisdom concerning software design was that the backend and user interface (UI) could be built independently. The new wisdom is that the backend design will enable or inhibit usability of the user interface, perhaps to the point of making some user interface choices impractical (Bass and John, 2003). For example, a backend that simply supports individual CRUD (Create, Read, Update, and Delete) operations will likely have difficulty with undo and multi-element operations. Consider also what kind of backend support is necessary to support the increasingly common feature of text completion as you type.

Consequently, the user interface cannot be bolted on after-the-fact. Architecture models often include mockups of the UI and express the anticipated interactions between the UI and backend. An additional benefit of designing the user interface concurrently with other parts of the system is that user interface mockups can reveal errors or omissions in the low-level APIs (D'Souza and Wills, 1998).

15.10   Prescriptive vs. descriptive models

When you use an architecture model, you need to be aware of the distinction between prescriptive and descriptive models. *Prescriptive models* say how things should be while *descriptive models* say how things are. The standard set of architecture abstractions (modules, components, connectors, ports, roles, etc.) seeks to point future software development in the right direction, and so it is prescriptive in that it encourages encapsulation and clear channels of communication.

Architecture languages and the abstractions embedded in them overwhelmingly tend to be prescriptive in that their abstractions are cleaner than code you typically find in practice. When you model an existing system, you are creating a descriptive model, which will reveal some challenges, as discussed in the next section.

15.11   Modeling existing systems

You may already have an existing system and wonder if you can build an architecture model that explains it. Perhaps the system has a million lines of code and you do not have time to read every one. This book argues that building models is a good way to attack complexity and scale because you can apply knowledge, partitioning, and abstractions. But first you need to ask yourself why you want a model and what that model should do.

Reason for modeling	Candidate models
Understand current system better	Low detail: Domain model, boundary model High detail: None
Evaluate alternative architecture	Low detail: Boundary and internals models High detail: On selected tricky details
Re-architecting, new platform	Low detail: Boundary model High detail: Internals model, styles and invariants
Document for external developers	Low detail: Domain model, boundary model High detail: Styles and invariants
Investigate integration & compatibility	Low detail: Domain model, boundary model, internals model High detail: Selected domain modeling, connectors
Pre-purchase investigation	Low detail: Boundary model High detail: Domain modeling, connectors

Figure 15.3: There are many reasons to build models of existing systems, but the kind of model you build should depend on the reason. Here are some examples of reasons and corresponding candidate models that you could use to investigate designs and reduce risks.

Limit modeling based on needs. There are many common reasons to build an architecture model. You may want to understand the current system better, or evaluate how an alternative architecture could affect the system's quality attributes. The model could be a precursor to re-architecting or transitioning to a new platform. You may need to document the system for external developers, partners, or for outsourcing. You may be investigating the system's compatibility with a reference architecture or for integration with another system. Or perhaps the system is not yours but you are investigating purchasing it.

You should limit your models to those aspects of the system that will help you answer your questions. To give you an idea about choosing a reasonable subset, Figure 15.3 lists some possible reasons to build an architecture model and some corresponding candidate models (adapted from Fairbanks, Bierhoff and D'Souza, 2006). The candidate models and their level of detail are just ballpark estimates to illustrate that you can get value from just a subset of the possible models, and you should make adjustments on your projects. If you are investigating compatibility, watch out that you do not merely validate technical compatibility (e.g., the data files are XML) when the domain models are incompatible.

Prepare to find mud. If you are building an architecture model in order to understand the system better, be prepared for some level of disappointment. Clarity and a story at many levels (see Section 11.1) can be revealed by architecture models only if it is there to be found. Clean, well-thought-out designs are a result of careful design by the system's developers. If the system is built as a big ball of mud (see Section 14.7) then no amount of modeling will reveal anything but mud. If the system was built expediently and not refactored then expect to see a jumble of dependencies and communication paths. On the other hand, if the design is clean then models can make that evident.

Another thing you should expect is exceptions to general rules such as styles and invariants. It is common for a system to be "in style X, except ..." The architectural styles from books like this one are the purest expression of the style, so-called Platonic styles (see Section 14.2), but embodied styles are much more common in practice.

Building an architecture model of an existing system can be effective if you set your expectations appropriately, decide in advance what questions you want to answer with the models, and build appropriate models at the right level of detail. Section 16.1.1 describes some specific challenges you will face in modeling existing systems.

15.12   Conclusion

The ideas in this chapter should enable you to avoid some modeling pitfalls, such as sloppy or overly precise models. You should also know what to strive for when modeling: models that are accurate, predictive, and inexpensive; models that promote comprehension and have a consistent level of detail; and views that are monothematic. By building architecture models, you are striving not only to write models that are syntactically correct, but use those models to amplify your reasoning.

To be useful, models should be consistent with the real world, self-consistent, and falsifiable. Some models aim to predict, but all models should strive to be comprehensible by humans. One way to do this is to structure them as a story at many levels.

Decide in advance what questions your model should answer, then build a sufficiently precise model. Failing to do this means not knowing when you should stop modeling. You must embrace the fact that your models will be incomplete, yet still useful. Complexity and scale force you to use the long way around Shaw's commuting diagram (see Figure 6.1). You should do just enough modeling, since the goal is building a system, not building a model.

The general idea of working with views follows the divide and conquer strategy, where you break up a big master model into smaller views, each of which is more tractable and focused on a single concern. This strategy, however, introduces the problem of view consistency and being able to stitch together views to understand the whole system.

Fortunately, functionality scenarios are great for stitching together what would otherwise be disconnected views of your architecture. When you write them correctly, they engage you with the details of the architecture and help you to find problems and inconsistencies. You can animate them in your mind, just as you animate programs to debug them, and therefore gain an understanding of your system's behavior. Precise action specifications are another way to achieve this and are a great mental discipline to use, but they are usually too expensive to use all the time.

Techniques exist to improve the quality of your models. Some models can be tested; others must be proved correct. Proving usually entails transforming your model to be analyzed by a tool, then interpreting the results. It may have come as a surprise, but the most effective analysis tool is your own brain when it is looking at a clear model.

Quality attribute workshops, architectural checklists, design reviews, and the Architectural Tradeoff Analysis Method are all informal techniques you can use to analyze your architecture and improve its quality. There are formal analysis techniques and tools. They generally require you to transform your model and interpret the results that come out of the tool, but they let the computer grind through the calculations to find problems, rather than you.

When analyzing your architecture, you should be on the lookout for architectural mismatch. Seemingly compatible components can fail to integrate because of hidden assumptions about the components, connectors, the system, and its initialization process.

Oftentimes a system already exists and you want to build a model of its architecture. This can be effective if you set your expectations appropriately, decide in advance what questions the models should answer, and build appropriate models at the right level of detail.

15.13 Further reading

This chapter describes a list of desirable traits of models that is derived in part from other lists, including David Garlan's software graduate architecture course (Garlan, 2003), Grady Booch's software architecture presentation (Booch, 2004), and Bran Selic's presentation on UML2's desirable traits (Selic, 2003a).

Various authors have discussed techniques for achieving model quality. Philippe Kruchten (Kruchten, 1995) discusses how to use scenarios to tie together architectural views. Desmond D'Souza and Alan Wills (D'Souza and Wills, 1998) continue that idea and additionally discuss how precise action specifications can do the same. Many books advocate modeling using precise specifications, including Cook and Daniels (1994), Coleman (1993) D'Souza and Wills (1998), and Cheesman and Daniels (2000).

Chapter 16

Conclusion

The first part of this book described software architecture and gave an answer to the hard question, "How much architecture work should you do?" It suggested that your architecture and design efforts should address the failure risks you perceive, which lets you calibrate your effort based on how bad it would be to get that part wrong. It also showed that it is more effective to solve tricky problems using models, because models simplify the problems.

The second part of the book answered the logical next question, "What do architecture models look like?" It encouraged you to use the standard architecture models and abstractions to build up a conceptual model of architecture, which helps you see software the way that a coach sees a sports game.

Taken together, the first and second parts of the book exist to help you design software better. The next time you look at a computer system, you will not just see code written in a particular language, you will see a system that promotes or inhibits various quality attributes, one that exploits architecture hoisting, or one that is indifferent to its architecture.

In this concluding chapter, you will learn about challenges you will face when applying the knowledge from this book. The chapter also reprises and reinforces themes that run through the book, including using standard architecture abstractions, focusing on quality attributes, judicious application of constraints as guide rails, and the use of models.

16.1   Challenges

In Section 5.7, we looked at some challenges that you will face in applying software architecture and the risk-driven model. Now that you have seen the details of how to build architecture models, it is helpful to revisit that topic again and see some additional challenges. As before, the point of identifying these challenges is not to discourage you, but to forewarn you in the hope that you will recognize them and be more ready to overcome them.

The challenges are organized into three broad themes: the suitability of the architecture abstractions, the mechanics of architecture modeling, and the effectiveness of models.

16.1.1   Suitability of architecture abstractions

The architecture abstractions described in this book are the best that have been invented, but that does not mean that they are perfect. It can be difficult to align them with existing programs, abstractions in programming languages, frameworks, and non-object languages.

Misaligned architecture and programming abstractions. Chapter 10 discussed how architecture abstractions relate to those in programming languages, and described a set of patterns to make the alignment more visible. It would have been unnecessary if the architecture abstractions discussed in this book were the same as the abstractions available in your programming language, but that is not the case today. Consequently, there will be some friction when you try to implement your models in code, or try to interpret your code's architecture.

This friction is nothing new. The transition to structured programming saw some developers saying that they could not express their existing programs in the new, more constrained, programming languages. Some argued that their old programs were more efficient and perfectly understandable, so the new abstractions were undesirable.

When you discover code that does not line up neatly with software architecture abstractions, you could refactor the existing code into more explicit modules and components, but would likely be prohibitively expensive. It is more practical to think of your existing system as a collection of large modules or components, and not attempt to model its internal subcomponents.

By preparing for this misalignment of abstractions, you will be less tempted to reject architecture abstractions, and more likely to view it instead as the natural state of software engineering, where abstractions evolve and our programming languages catch up over time. You will experience difficulty with existing programs, but you should find it easier to line up your code and architecture models when you are writing new programs.

Frameworks. Frameworks present a particular example of misaligned abstractions because the interaction between client code and a framework does not neatly align with the standard architectural abstractions. Frameworks provide deep, wide interfaces to the clients that use them, often exposing the implementation details of the framework (i.e., its internals model). Ports, in contrast, provide shallow, narrow interfaces and encourage encapsulation (i.e., exposing only a boundary model). Some frameworks exist at runtime, so they can be represented as components, since components also have runtime presence. Other frameworks, especially older ones, are collections of code that cannot be instantiated until augmented with client code, so they can only be represented as modules, which lack runtime existence. The precise modeling of frameworks is an open research topic for academics, so perhaps this challenge will be addressed soon.

Object-oriented and other languages. As you have seen, every system will have at least one component instance at runtime, which is the entire system itself. When programming in object-oriented languages, it is comfortable to think about this component as having internal runtime structures that are objects, and not a big stretch to think about grouping those objects into subcomponents.

In non-object-oriented languages, such as functional, rule-based, or procedural languages, it is harder to envision what the runtime instances are. The entire running system is still clearly a component instance, but what subcomponents does it have? When you are building new code, you can ensure those subcomponent divisions are evident. You can deliberately create subcomponents, allocating responsibilities to them, and building them in whatever style of language is most appropriate, including non-object languages.

Even when using object-oriented languages, there are problems moving between the architecture abstractions and the object abstractions, because each has a different vocabulary and communication idioms. Objects, functions, procedures, etc., are concretely represented in programming languages and substantial design guidance exists for them. Architecture abstractions are not yet concretely available in mainstream programming languages, which raises the question of when to switch from one abstraction to another.

For example, a standard object-oriented pattern is to use an Adapter to convert from one interface to another. However, the Home Media Player in Section 4.2 represented an adapter as a component, not an object. There was a choice between putting this adapter into the existing components and revealing its existence as a new port, or making the adapter into its own component. Components range in size, but this example is unusual in that it has a single object as a component.

Within a single language, you can develop a coding style that makes the components and connectors evident (see Section 10.3). In practice, scripting languages are often used expediently and without the same attention to coding discipline as the rest of the code. Keeping up the discipline of an architecturally-evident coding style can be difficult with multiple languages, especially when they are substantially different and the conventions you are following in one do not translate well into the other.

16.1.2 Modeling mechanics

As you have seen, many architecture abstractions have been built up and guidance exists to help you build good models. Yet building models still presents challenges.

When to stop modeling functionality. The techniques in this book cover the modeling of both quality attributes and functionality. Architecture models that only describe quality attributes tend to reach a natural level of detail in modeling (i.e., you can tell when to stop), but models that include functionality can easily be elaborated until they describe details like individual operations on classes.

You rarely want to dig in deep, so when should you stop? Architecture modeling has the ability transition into design, then detailed design, then a paper-based version of coding. This ability to go deep is a benefit because you can dig into details when needed, but a challenge because you must decide when to dig in and when to resist. Time spent modeling has an opportunity cost: time spent building the system.

It is difficult to decide how much of the system's functionality you should model. As discussed in the Home Media Player example in Chapter 4, you can look at the risks you face and only model functionality if it addresses an identified risk. So, for example, you might build a use case model of the system only when you are asked to deliver a presentation that explains your architecture. Generally, you will need to be on guard that you do not dig down too far into modeling your system's functionality.

Non-static component configurations (Dynamic architectures). Most systems settle down into a stable set of runtime component instances, even though during initialization there are changes (see Section 9.7). When you draw diagrams showing the runtime configuration of component instances, you usually simplify the problem by not drawing diagrams of the intermediate configurations during startup and shutdown. You do this because reasoning about dynamic configurations is hard, and there are few tools or notations to make it easier.

However, some systems must change at runtime. For example, peer-to-peer systems evolve at runtime into different configurations of components, as do frameworks that can dynamically load new components. It is difficult to convince yourself that runtime re-configuration like this is free from problems, so developers tend to avoid it, but some problem domains demand a dynamic architecture.

View consistency. The ubiquitous advice on software architecture is to build multiple views of your system. Multiple views help by focusing attention on one aspect. Some views cannot be easily reconciled (recall the definition of a viewtype from Section 9.6), and creating a single view would create a muddle of details that defeats the purpose of having a model.

The downside of multiple views is reconciling the views for consistency. Today, tools have a limited ability to catch inconsistencies, so you will be doing most of your checking manually. Some view inconsistencies are simply cruft because you update one view but have not yet updated older views. Other consistency problems stem from design errors and may lead to un-buildable designs.

Crosscutting concerns. Components, modules, and nodes allow you to encapsulate your thinking, but some ideas will crosscut these abstractions. As discussed in Section 11.2, your choice of decomposition will affect which problems are easy to solve, and which are difficult. A design, for example, that makes horizontal scalability easy may result in poor encapsulation of your domain types.

Another example is concurrency, which often crosscuts your abstractions. Concurrency has always been one of the most challenging problems in developing systems. Novice developers may relish the challenge and seek out opportunities for concurrency, but jaded developers view it warily as a source of difficult bugs and are happy to get it right then leave it alone. Concurrency is introduced into systems either through forces in the problem domain or by a desire to improve a quality attribute, such as performance or usability.

With a clean-slate design, you may be able to perfectly align the threads or processes in your system with the component boundaries. If so, you can annotate the components and connectors, as the media player example in Chapter 4, to indicate the concurrency. Anytime a concern cross-cuts your decomposition (see Section 15.2) there will be trouble expressing it, and concurrency is particularly difficult.

Refinement. Models will become unsynchronized with other models and with code. Maintaining consistency between them is more difficult when there is a refinement relationship between models. For example, it is easy to forget to revise the high-level model of your system when you revise the low-level model. Forgetfulness aside, as discussed in Section 10.2, you may deliberately allow your various models to become out-of-date because it is expensive to keep them updated.

It is possible to be sufficiently precise in the refinement map so that you can detect refinement problems, but it is also prohibitively expensive. In practice, few developers even sketch the correspondences between high- and a low-level models, though they may eyeball each to convince themselves that the refinement is OK.

16.1.3   Effective modeling

Section 6.5 discussed the idea that some people can read models, fewer people can write syntactically correct models, and fewer still can use models to more effectively solve problems. As a software developer, building models is a necessary distraction from building code — necessary because you will have difficulty reasoning about large and complex systems without models. Two challenges that arise in using models as a reasoning aid are the choice of details to promote and building predictive models.

Promoting details. Choosing which details to promote to the architectural level is difficult. The challenge is how to select relevant details for the model while at the same time keeping the model minimally sufficient. Different developers are likely to choose different details, which means that some models will be better than others, yet there is no guidance on how best to choose.

It is difficult to know when your model is precise enough, or detailed enough. In general, you should make your model precise enough to answer the questions you ask of it, or sufficient to reduce the risks you perceive. However, this is easier said than done, because you may not be able to perceive the risk until after you have built the detailed model.

Prediction. Using architecture models to discover problems in advance is harder, and requires more effort, than modeling simply to document a design, because small details can distort predictions. A friend of mine built a model to predict performance of his web service. However, his performance predictions were substantially wrong because the actual distribution of requests into his system was burstier than in his model. Improved architecture modeling technology holds the promise of better predictions about performance, but producing a sufficiently detailed model for accurate predictions can be expensive.

Reflection on challenges. All of these challenges can cause trouble on your projects, but all of them can be overcome too. Despite imperfections in the techniques and abstractions, you are far better prepared to develop software with an understanding of architecture than without it.

We now turn our attention to several themes that run through the book: focusing on quality attributes, solving problems, using constraints as guide rails, and using standard architecture abstractions.

16.2   Focus on quality attributes

Software architecture encourages a shift in attention toward quality attributes. Mainstream software developers give most of their attention to a system's functionality rather than its quality attributes or extra-functional requirements. But architecture has a big impact on which qualities will be easy or hard to achieve, so when choosing a system's architecture, you should focus on quality attributes, such as performance, security, and modifiability.

Usually, any reasonable architecture will support the desired functionality, but only a carefully chosen architecture will enable the desired qualities. Unfortunately, it is expensive to change the architecture of even a well-maintained system, so it is worthwhile to consider quality attribute requirements early to avoid costly architecture mistakes.

Some domains have presumptive architectures that have been shown historically to be suitable for the desired quality attribute requirements in the domain. By using a presumptive architecture, a developer may succeed with *architecture-indifferent design*, where little attention is paid to architecture. When risks are higher, developers may use *architecture-focused design* to ensure that the architecture enables the required qualities and features. They may even choose to *hoist* some qualities into the architecture, such as scalability, so that the development team can focus on building the functionality instead of the hoisted qualities.

16.3 Solve problems, not just model them

This book advocates attacking complexity and scale by building models. This is the long way around the commuting diagram (Figure 6.1), but it should help you solve problems that you cannot solve directly. You should always remember, however, that the goal is to build a system that solves a problem, not to build models. Models are not running systems and you cannot eat a picture of a sandwich.

It is possible that your temperament may incline you to believe the problem is solved when the software is designed, but ensure that you validate your model by building a prototype or demonstrating it in the real system. To help you remember, here is a joke that reinforces the importance of validation:

> A fireman wakes up in the night to find his kitchen on fire. He pours water on the fire until it goes out and then he goes back to bed. An engineer wakes up in the night to find his kitchen on fire. He does some calculations, pours 2.3 buckets of water on the fire, observes the fire is out, and then he goes back to bed. A mathematician (software architect?) wakes up in the night to find his kitchen on fire. He does some calculations, says "Eureka!" and then he goes back to bed.

This advice is related to other obvious, but often repeated, fallacies from software engineering, like "the code must be correct because it compiles." Once you have a design, building a working system is almost always more difficult than just "turning the crank."

16.4   Use constraints as guide rails

An idea that runs through this book is that you can achieve a desired outcome by imposing constraints on your architecture. This idea is called *architecture-focused design* and you learned how it contrasts with architecture-indifferent design (Section 2.7). You have seen several examples of architecture-focused design:

- In the introduction, you saw how the Rackspace company switched from a client-server style to a map-reduce style in order to achieve scalability. You can think of architecture styles as a collection of pre-fabricated constraints with known benefits and drawbacks (Chapter 14).

- You saw another example of it in the Home Media Player system (Section 4.2), where overall reliability was promoted by running the unreliable COTS NextGenVideo component in its own process, isolating the main system.

- The Yinzer job advertising and networking system (Section 9.5.10) needed to send emails but also have good response times to web requests. It used an asynchronous connector (such as a message bus) to queue email messages rather than waiting for confirmation that they had been sent.

Tradeoffs. Most of the time constraints will involve tradeoffs. The older Rackspace client-server system could enjoy fresher results and ad hoc querying compared to the map-reduce system. The Home Media Player system became more complex and possibly less efficient by introducing concurrent processes. And you can easily imagine developers grumbling that the event bus in the Yinzer system made their lives more difficult than a simple method call would.

Guide rails. Constraints are not (or should not be) arbitrary and capricious restrictions, but *guide rails* that ensure that the system goes where you point it. If you are an enterprise architect, you are neither the designer nor developer of any one system, so constraints are your only tool to influence the direction of the set of systems.

Analysis. In addition to giving you control over where your system is going, constraints can give you the ability to *analyze* your system. If you have a hundred lines of unconstrained code, what can it do? Essentially anything. How fast does it run? No idea. Is it a security risk? Maybe. If the answers to questions like these is important to you, you could impose constraints to help you answer them. For example, the Android operating system constrains code by restricting its access to system services, so if code wants to access the internet, it must declare that it does, and users can inspect these properties before running an application.

Process sketch. But make no mistake: constraints close off design options. By choosing to impose a constraint you are saying that the system will *not* be a certain way. And if you are not the only developer, you are restricting potentially wonderful solutions that others may invent. With that warning in mind, consider the following process sketch for how you might choose to introduce constraints.

1. Start with no constraints.

2. Decide what the system's goals are. For example, it may need to inter-operate with other systems, be highly secure, or run fast. These goals will likely overlap or be the same as your architecture drivers (see Section 9.5.8).

3. Then ask yourself hard questions about how you will accomplish those goals. How could your system fail to accomplish its goals? Are there constraints that could guide it to success? How onerous are those constraints? What are the tradeoffs?

4. Finally, you may decide to impose constraints that promote or guarantee a desired feature, quality, or risk.

You will notice that this process sketch errs on the side of liberty rather than guarantees. If you follow this process, most of the time you will end up choosing to follow an architectural style because their constraints are relatively mild yet put the project on an appropriate foundation to achieve its goals. On projects with demanding requirements you may introduce more stringent constraints.

16.5 Use standard architectural abstractions

Developers build large systems and need to communicate about them with other developers. The language used by mainstream developers covers the most tangible development artifacts quite well: objects, classes, methods, interfaces, etc. However, there is great diversity and ambiguity when developers talk about larger chunks. One developer might call something a module while another calls it a component. And while design patterns have mostly standardized the vocabulary for talking about object patterns, the names of architectural styles are not as consistently used. When two developers chat at a whiteboard, they may sketch classes and objects that are pretty close to standard UML, but more often than not they invent notations for communicating architectural ideas.

When developers do not share a common set of architectural abstractions and notations, the bigger danger is not that they will communicate inefficiently, but that they do not communicate at all. Their discussions will center on the language they share, such as objects, rather than the language suited to their architecture discussion.

Large systems are built using architectural styles and have constraints that span more than a few objects. Developers who have not embraced architectural abstractions are at a disadvantage because they will communicate these ideas inefficiently, if at all.

Even before communication starts, developers benefit from architectural abstractions. Like a coach who watches a game and integrates all the low-level happenings into a big picture of what is happening, a developer looks at a system and integrates all the low-level interactions between objects into a big picture of the system's design. When developers do not think in terms of architectural abstractions, the big picture will be revealed more slowly and problems will be less evident. A developer who lacks architecture abstractions (like styles, components, and connectors) will struggle, both in recognizing those ideas, and in articulating why a proposed change is, or is not, appropriate.

Architectural abstractions co-exist with older ones. Protocols can still be described using state machines, and classes can still be described with class diagrams. Architecture abstractions are like a new tool in the toolbox that developers should reach for when they need to battle scale and complexity. Looking back, you can see that each decade has introduced new abstractions to combat new difficulties. Sharpening old tools is always helpful, but is unlikely to overcome the difficulties of the next decade.

Glossary

Action specification A (sometimes formal) specification of a method, procedure, or more abstraction behavior. Often consists of a pre-condition (what must be true for the method to successfully run) and a post-condition (what the method guarantees will be true after it completes). See *design by contract*.

Agile process A style of software development process characterized by iterative development. See *waterfall* process, *Extreme Programming*, *iterative process*, *agile process*, and *spiral process*.

Allocation element (i.e., *UML node* or *environmental element*) Hardware (such as computers) and geographical locations (such as datacenters) that can host *modules* and *component* instances. UML (Booch, Rumbaugh and Jacobson, 2005) refers to places where software can be deployed as *nodes* and the SEI authors (Bass, Clements and Kazman, 2003) refer to it as an *environmental element*.

Allocation viewtype The viewtype that contains views of elements related to the deployment of the software onto hardware. It includes deployment diagrams, descriptions of environmental elements like servers, and descriptions of communication channels like ethernet links. It may also include geographical elements, so that you can describe two servers in different cities. See *runtime viewtype* and *module viewtype*.

Analogic model In an analogic model, each model element has an analogue in the domain of interest. A radar screen is an analogic model of some terrain, where blips on the screen correspond to airplanes — they are analogues. Analogic models support analysis only indirectly, and usually domain knowledge and human reasoning are required. See *analytic model*.

Analysis paralysis The situation where a developer spends inordinate time analyzing or building models, and not building a solution.

Analytic model An analytic model directly supports analysis of the domain of interest. Mathematical equations are examples of analytic models, as are state machines. You could imagine an analytic model of the airplanes where each is represented by a vector. Mathematics provides an analytic model to evaluate the vectors, so you could quantitatively answer questions about collision courses. See *analogic model*.

Anonymous instance An instance (such as an object or a component instance) that has not been given a name. Graphically, it is labeled "*: TypeName*". In contrast, a named instance would have a name preceding the colon.

Application architect Application architects are developers who are responsible for a single application. It is possible for them to understand and manage thousands of objects that comprise their application. Application architects are like movie directors whose daily actions create the shape of the product.

Application Programming Interface (API) A set of operations that can be performed on a module, component, or object. When we refer to API-level operations, we mean that they are not abstract, and those operations are exactly what would be seen in the programming language.

Architectural style (i.e., architectural pattern). An architectural style is "a specialization of element and relation types, together with a set of constraints on how they can be used." (Clements et al., 2010)

Architecturally-evident coding style A style of programming that encodes additional design intent by providing hints about the system's architecture. It encourages you to embed hints in the source code that make the architecture evident to a developer who reads the code. It follows the *model-in-code principle*.

Architecture see *software architecture*.

Architecture description language (ADL) A language used to describe architectures that defines elements (e.g., components, connectors, modules, ports) and relationships. Examples include UML, C2, AADL, and Acme.

Architecture drift Architecture drift is the tendency for a system, over time, to violate its initial design. (Perry and Wolf, 1992)

Architecture driver *Quality attribute scenarios* or *functionality scenarios* that are both important to stakeholders and difficult to achieve. As such, they are the scenarios that you should pay most attention to when designing the system (Bass, Clements and Kazman, 2003)

Architecture hoisting When following an *architecture hoisting* approach, developers design the architecture with the intent of guaranteeing a goal or property of the system. The idea is that once a goal or property has been hoisted into the architecture, developers should not need to write any additional code to achieve it. See *architecture-focused design* and *architecture-indifferent design*.

Architecture refactoring A *refactoring* of a system's architecture, possibly from one architectural style to another, or the introduction of consistency (see *constraints*) where none were present before.

Architecture-focused design In *architecture-focused design*, developers are aware of their system's software architecture and they deliberately choose it so that their system can achieve its goals. See *architecture-indifferent design* and *architecture hoisting*.

Architecture-indifferent design In *architecture-indifferent design*, developers are oblivious to their system's architecture and *do not* consciously choose an architecture to help them reduce risks, achieve features, or ensure qualities. The developers may simply ignore their architecture, copy the architecture from their previous project, use the presumptive architecture in their domain, or follow a corporate standard. See *architecture-focused design* and *architecture hoisting*.

Baked-in risks When a process is designed to always address a certain risk, that risk is said to be baked-in to the process. For example, agile processes address customer rejection risk by building and delivering the system incrementally.

Big Design Up Front (BDUF) In Big Design Up Front (BDUF), the early weeks or months of a project are primarily spent designing instead of prototyping or building. It is a pejorative term coined by people, like agile advocates, who are concerned about *analysis paralysis*, a situation where a project spends too much time designing and not enough time building. BDUF is associated more with waterfall processes than spiral processes.

Binary connector A connector that can be attached to just two components. See *N-way connector*.

Binding (1) Using bindings, ports on an external component are bound to compatible or identical ports on internal components. Invariants and quality attribute scenarios on the external component must be satisfied by the internal components. (2) The binding relationship is used to show correspondence between parts in pattern and elements in a model using that pattern.

Boundary model The boundary model is what outsiders can see of the system (or an element in the system), which includes its behavior, interchange data, and quality attributes. The boundary is a commitment to an interface but not to implementation details. The boundary model describes what a user needs to know to understand how a system works. It is an encapsulated view of the system that hides internal details. When developers change the internal design, users are undisturbed. See *internals model*.

Business model A business model describes what a business or organization does and why it does it. Business models rarely talk about software. Different businesses in the same domain will have different strategies, capabilities, organizations, processes, and objectives and therefore different business models. It describes not only facts (which would appear in a *domain model*) but also decisions and goals that organizations must make.

Canonical model structure A set of models, ranging from abstract to concrete, that use views to drill down into the details of each model. It consists of three primary models: the domain model, the design model, and the code model. The canonical model structure has the most abstract model (the domain) at the top and the most concrete (the code) at the bottom. The *designation* and *refinement* relationships ensure that the models correspond, yet enable them to differ in their level of abstraction.

Classification relationship A classification relationship is the same one that exists between classes and objects in object-oriented programming.

Closed semantics In refinement with closed semantics, the refinement restricts what kinds of new items can be introduced by listing the kinds of items that will not change. See *open semantics*.

Code model The code model describes the system source code. The code model is either the source code implementation of the system or a model that is equivalent. It could be the actual Java code or the result of running a code-to-UML tool, but its important feature is that has a full set of design commitments. Where the design model has an incomplete set of design commitments, the code model has a complete set, or at least a sufficiently complete set to execute on a machine. Compare with the *domain model* and *design model*. All three are part of the *canonical model structure*.

Commercial Off-The-Shelf (COTS) *Modules*, *components*, or other source code available from third parties. This term is often used even if they are open source or from a non-commercial group.

Communication channel (i.e., *connection* or *environmental element*) Hardware that allows *allocation elements* to communicate. UML (Booch, Rumbaugh and Jacobson, 2005) refers to the communication channels between *nodes* as *connections* and the SEI authors (Bass, Clements and Kazman, 2003) refer to them as *environmental elements*.

Component "Components [are] the principal computation elements and data stores that execute in a system." (Clements et al., 2010) Usually refers to a component instance, but could also refer to a component type. See *module*.

Component assembly (i.e., component and connector diagram) A component assembly shows a specific configuration of component, port, and connector instances or types. Their arrangement is the component design and different arrangements will yield different qualities. It may show *bindings* between external and internal *ports*.

Component-Based Development (CBD) Software development whose end-product is loosely-coupled components to be sold in a component marketplace.

Conceptual model A conceptual model identifies salient features and how they operate. Introductory physics classes teach Newtonian mechanics, a conceptual model of how physical objects behave, which includes features like mass and forces.

Connector A connector is a pathway of runtime interaction between two or more components. This is just slightly different than the definition from (Clements et al., 2010), which states that a "connector [is] a runtime pathway of interaction between two or more components."

Constraint See *invariant*.

System context diagram A component assembly that focuses on the system being designed and includes all external systems that the system connects to.

Design by contract Bertrand Meyer popularized the concept of design by contract where method pre- and post-conditions as well as object *invariants* are inserted into the source code and checked by automated tools (Meyer, 2000). By relying on a method's contract, clients can safely ignore any internal implementation and treat the method or the entire object as a black box.

Design decision Decisions made by developers during the course of designing the system that commit the project to a particular design choice or restrict the design space. See *invariant*.

Design intent The understanding and intentions of the system's developers. Design intent is imperfectly contained in the source code of a system, forcing developers to infer parts of it.

Design model The design model describes the system you will build, and is largely under your control. The system to be built appears in the design model. The design model is a partial set of design commitments. That is, you leave undecided some (usually low-level) details about how the design will work, deferring them until the code model. The design model is composed of recursively nested *boundary models* and *internals models*. Compare with the *domain model* and *code model*. All three are part of the *canonical model structure*.

Designation A designation relationship allows you to show correspondences between two domains, for example between the real world and a problem domain model. It identifies that something from one domain corresponds to something in a second domain.

Documentation package A complete, or mostly complete, written description of a software architecture.

Domain connector A connector that bridges the domains of the components it connects. When two components interact, there is often some logic that is dependent on the domain of both components. By putting this logic into a domain connector, you insulate each of the components from knowing unnecessary details about the other.

Domain driven design Domain driven design advocates a embedding the *domain model* in the source code (Evans, 2003). It is compatible with the *model-in-code principle* but goes further by encouraging an *agile* development process and discouraging expressing domain models on paper.

Domain model The domain model describes enduring truths about the domain that are relevant to your system. In general, the domain is not under your control, so you cannot decide that weeks have six days or that you have a birthday party every week. The system to be built does not appear in the domain model. Compare with the *design model* and *code model*. All three are part of the *canonical model structure*.

Dominant decomposition The organizational system of a system that promotes a single concern. Problems related to that dominant concern will be easier to solve, but problems related to other concerns will be harder. For example, if you organize books by their size, then it will be easy to find the tallest books but harder to find ones by a specific author. This problem of one concern dominating others is referred to as the *tyranny of the dominant decomposition* (Tarr et al., 1999).

Driver See *architecture driver*.

Dynamic architecture model A model that generalizes all the possible instantaneous configurations (e.g., topology of component instances) of an architecture. Most systems change during startup and shutdown, but have a long steady-state configuration in between that is modeled as a static architecture model.

Effective encapsulation Encapsulation where the boundary does not unnecessarily leak abstractions across its interface. Ultimately, what counts as effective is subjective and requires good judgment.

Encapsulation "[T]he process of compartmentalizing the elements of an abstraction that constitute its structure and behavior; encapsulation serves to separate the contractual interface of an abstraction and its implementation." (Booch et al., 2007)

Engineering risk A risk related to the analysis, design, and implementation of the product. See *project management risk*.

Enterprise architect Architects who are responsible for many applications, who do not control the functionality of any one application, and who instead design an ecosystem inside which individual applications contribute to the overall enterprise. Enterprise architects are like movie producers in that they influence the outcome only indirectly.

Enterprise architecture The software architecture of an organization that spans multiple applications (systems).

Environmental element (i.e., UML node) Hardware with the primary purpose of running software that communicates via *communication channels*.

Event bus An *N-way* publish-subscribe connector.

Evolutionary design Evolutionary design "means that the design of the system grows as the system is implemented" (Fowler, 2004). Often paired with *refactoring*. Compare with *planned design*.

Extensional element Extensional elements are enumerated, such as "The system is composed of a client, an order processor, and an order storage components." Examples include modules, components, connectors, ports, and component assemblies. See *intensional element*.

Extreme Programming_(XP) A specialization of an *iterative* and *agile* software development process, so it contains multiple iterations (Beck and Andres, 2004). It suggests avoiding up-front design work, though some projects add an *iteration zero* (Schuh, 2004), in which no customer-visible functionality is delivered. It guides developers to apply *evolutionary design* exclusively, though some projects modify it to incorporate a small amount of *planned design*. Each iteration is prioritized by the customer's valuation of features, not risks. Compare with *waterfall* process, *iterative process*, *agile process*, and *spiral process*.

Framework (i.e., software framework or object-oriented framework) A form of software reuse characterized by inversion of control. Frameworks, in contrast with libraries, are an effective means of sharing or reusing a software architecture.

Functionality scenario Functionality scenarios, also called simply *scenarios,* express a series of events that cause changes to a model. A scenario describes a single possible path rather than generalizing many paths. See *use case*.

Generalization The relationship between a more general type and a more specific type, such as furniture and chair.

Goal connector A goal connector has an assigned goal, or objective, that it is responsible for accomplishing. A developer who builds a goal connector must avoid failure by looking into the problem, discovering possible failure cases, and ensuring that the connector handles them. Goal connectors are usually complex as they have real domain work to do, and are responsible for seeing it completed. See *micromanaged connector*.

Information model A set of types and their definitions that describes the things that exist in the domain. It also describes the *relationships* between those types. It can be drawn textually, often as a table, or graphically, often using UML class diagram syntax.

Information Technology (IT) A specialty inside software design that focuses on "the study, design, development, implementation, support or management of computer-based information systems, particularly software applications and computer hardware." (Information Technology Association of America).

Intensional element Intensional elements are those that are universally quantified, such as "All filters can communicate via pipes." Examples include styles, invariants, responsibility allocations, design decisions, rationale, protocols, and quality attributes. See *extensional element*.

Internals model An internals model is a refinement of a *boundary model*. Both are views of the design model but they differ in the details they reveal. Anything that is true in the boundary model must be true in the internals model. Any commitments made in the boundary model (the number and type of ports, QA scenarios) must be upheld in the internals model. See *boundary model*.

Invariant Approximately the same as a *constraint*. Can be expressed as a predicate that is always true with respect to the system or design. Sometimes divided into static invariants (or representation invariants) that deal with static structures and dynamic invariants that deal with behaviors. The term *invariant* is more often used to apply to source code or data structures. When referring to systems, the term *constraint* is more often used.

Iteration A period of time in an iterative process where all software development activities can take place.

Iterative process An iterative development process builds the system in multiple work blocks, called *iterations* (Larman and Basili, 2003). With each iteration, developers are allowed to rework existing parts of the system, so it is not just built incrementally. Iterative development optionally has up-front design work but it does not impose a prioritization across the iterations, nor does it give guidance on the nature of design work. See *waterfall process*, *Extreme Programming*, *agile process*, and *spiral process*.

Layer A layered system organizes its modules such that lower layers act as virtual machines to higher layers. Dependencies are (almost) exclusively downward, where higher layers can use and depend on lower layers but not the reverse.

Link An edge between two objects in a snapshot (or instance diagram).

Master model A model that contains a complete set of details necessary to project out the views you build.

Method signature A specification of a method or procedure that usually includes the method name, its return type, and the types of its parameters. It can be augmented with preconditions and post-conditions to form an *action specification*.

Micromanaged connector An connector that simply does a job you assign to it. If it fails that is because you did not supervise it sufficiently. Its job is only to do what you told it to do. Micromanaged connectors are simple connectors. See *goal connector*.

Minimal planned design (i.e., Little Design Up Front) In between *evolutionary design* and *planned design* is minimal planned design (Martin, 2009). Advocates of minimal planned design worry that they might design themselves into a corner if they did all evolutionary design, but they also worry that all planned design is difficult and likely to get things wrong.

Model A symbolic representation of a system that contains only selected details.

Model-code gap The difference between how we express the solution in the design model and how we express it in the source code. See *intensional element* and *extensional element*.

Model-in-code principle Expressing a model in the system's code helps comprehension and evolution. A corollary of this principle is that expressing a model in code necessarily involves doing more work than is strictly necessary for the solution to work.

Module (i.e., package) A collection of implementation artifacts, such as source code (classes, functions, procedures, rules, etc.), configuration files, and database schema definitions. Modules can group together related code, revealing an interface but hiding the implementation.

Module viewtype The viewtype that contains views of the elements you can see at compile-time. It includes artifacts like source code and configuration files. Definitions of component types, connector types, and port types are also in the module viewtype, as are definitions of classes and interfaces. See *runtime viewtype* and *allocation viewtype*.

N-way connector A connector that can join one to many components, usually three or more, such as an *event bus*. See *binary connector*.

Navigation The idea that you can traverse from node to node in a model across edges. For example, you can navigate across a UML class diagram from class to class across the associations. See *Object Constraint Language*.

Object Constraint Language (OCL) A precise language for expressing invariants and constraints over UML models. See *navigation*.

Open semantics In refinement with open semantics, the refinement can introduce whatever new items it pleases. See *closed semantics*.

Parnas module A modularization technique where you ensure that the details likely to change are hidden inside the module, and that changes to those details will not influence the module's interface. A Parnas module hides a secret to minimize coupling, rather than just grouping together related code. See *encapsulation* and *effective encapsulation*.

Partition (1) As a noun, a relationship between parts and a whole such that the parts combine to form exactly the whole, no more and no less. (2) As a verb, a loose synonym with "divide" or "decompose." Or as in (1), the division of a system into disjoint pieces.

Pattern A pattern is a reusable solution to a recurring problem (Gamma et al., 1995).

Planned design (i.e., up-front design) A kind of software development process where design is done mostly or completely before implementation begins. See *evolutionary design* and *evolutionary design*.

Port All communication in or out of a component is done via ports on the component. All of the publicly available methods that a component supports, and all of the public events it responds to, will be specified in its ports. There is no necessary connection between ports on components and ports in an operating system.

Pre-condition & Post-condition See *action specification*.

Presumptive architecture A software architecture (or, more carefully, a family of architectures) that is dominant in a particular domain. Rather than justifying their choice to use it, developers in that domain may have to justify a choice that differs from the presumptive architecture. For example, a 3-Tier architecture is a presumptive architecture in many Information Technology (IT) groups. See *reference architecture*.

Projection See *view*.

Project management risk Risks related to schedules, sequencing of work, delivery, team size, geography, etc. See *engineering risk*.

Property Model elements can be annotated with properties that elaborate details about the element. For example, a connector can be annotated with a property describing its protocol or its throughput.

Prototype (i.e., architectural spike or proof of concept) An implementation intended to reduce risk by demonstrating feasibility, evaluating properties, or similar. Not used pejoratively (i.e., "throwaway code") in this book.

Prototypical risk Each domain has a set of prototypical risks that is different from other domains. For example, Systems projects usually worry more about performance than IT projects.

Quality attribute (i.e., QA's, extra-functional requirements, or the "-ities") A quality attribute is a kind of extra-functional requirement, such as performance, security, scalability, modifiability, or reliability.

Quality attribute scenario (i.e., QA scenario) A concise description of an extra-functional requirement, consisting of a source, stimulus, environment, artifact, response, and response measure.

Rational architecture choice Rational architecture choices are ones where your tradeoffs align with your quality attribute priorities. They often follow this template: Since <x> is a priority, we chose design <y>, and accepted downside <z>.

Rational Unified Process (RUP) A meta-process that can be tailored, for example into an *iterative*, *spiral*, or *waterfall* process.

Refactoring A code or design transformation that improves its structure, or other quality, while preserving its behavior. See *architecture refactoring*. (Fowler, 1999)

Reference architecture A specification that describes an prescribed architectural solution to a problem. Reference architectures are often proposed by vendors or experts as the canonical architectures for given problems. See *presumptive architecture*. (Bass, Clements and Kazman, 2003)

Refinement Refinement is a relationship between a low-detail and a high-detail model of the same thing.

Responsibility-driven design In contrast to thinking about data and algorithms, responsibility-driven design focuses on roles and responsibilities.

Risk In this book, risk is the perceived probability of failure times the perceived impact.

Risk-driven model The risk-driven model of software architecture guides developers to apply a minimal set of architecture techniques to reduce their most pressing risks. It suggests a relentless questioning process: "What are my risks? What are the best techniques to reduce them? Is the risk mitigated and can I start coding?" The key element of the risk-driven model is the promotion of risk to prominence.

Role (1) In a UML class diagram, the name on the end of an association. (2) The typed end of a connector, roughly equivalent to a port on a component. (3) In a pattern, a part that can be bound or substituted for a concrete part in the implementation.

Runtime viewtype (i.e., component & connector viewtype) The viewtype that contains views of elements that you can see at runtime. It includes artifacts like functionality scenarios, responsibility lists, and the component assemblies. Instances of components, connectors, and ports are in the runtime viewtype, as are objects (class instances). See *module viewtype* and *allocation viewtype*.

Scale When referring to software, scale usually refers to the absolute size of a system, often counted in lines of code. Scalability (a quality attribute) refers to the ability of a system to handle a greater load than it currently does, such as running on larger hardware (as in vertical scalability) or more copies of the hardware (horizontal scalability). Somewhat confusingly, the question, "Will it scale?" refers to a system's scalability, not its lines of code.

Scenario Usually refers to a *functionality scenario* but could also refer to a *quality attribute scenario*.

Snapshot (i.e., instance diagram) A diagram showing objects or component instances at an instant in time.

Software architecture This is the standard definition from the SEI: "The software architecture of a computing system is the set of structures needed to reason about the system, which comprise software elements, relations among them and externally visible properties of both." (Clements et al., 2010)

Software Engineering Institute (SEI) A federally funded research and development center whose mission is to "advance software engineering and related disciplines to ensure the development and operation of systems with predictable and improved cost, schedule, and quality."

Source code The programming language statements typed by developers that appear cryptic to the uninitiated.

Spanning viewtype The viewtype that contains views that cross over between two or more viewtypes. An example of a tradeoff that spans viewtypes is: you decide to denormalize a database schema (which would be described in the module viewtype) in order to achieve greater transaction throughput (which would be described in the runtime viewtype), so you describe that tradeoff in the spanning viewtype.

Spiral process The spiral process (Boehm, 1988) is a kind of iterative development, so it has many iterations, yet it is often described as having no up-front design work. Iterations are prioritized by risk, with the first iteration handling the riskiest parts of a project. The spiral model handles both management and engineering risks. For example, it may address "personnel shortfalls" as a risk. The spiral process gives no guidance on the nature of design work, or on which architecture and design techniques to use. See *waterfall process*, *Extreme Programming*, *iterative process*, and *agile process*.

Stakeholder A customer or other person who has an interest in the features or success of a system.

Static architecture model A model of a system that shows it at an instant in time or in its steady state configuration. See *dynamic architecture model*.

Story at many levels A way of structuring your software such that each level of nesting tells a story about how those parts interact. A developer who was unfamiliar with the system could be dropped in at any level and still make sense of it rather than being swamped. Its primary benefit is cognitive, not technical.

Subject Matter Expert (SME) A domain expert, sometimes a customer.

System context diagram A *component assembly* diagram in the *top-level boundary model* that includes the system (as a component) and its connections (as connectors) to external systems. See *use case diagram*.

Tactic In Attribute Driven Design, a tactic is a kind of pattern that is bigger than a design pattern and smaller than an architectural style. Examples of tactics include: Ping/Echo, Active Redundancy, Runtime Registration, Authenticate Users, and Intrusion Detection (Bass, Clements and Kazman, 2003).

Technical debt The accumulated misalignment of code with respect to the current understanding of the problem (Cunningham, 1992; Fowler, 2009)

Technique A software engineering activity performed by developers. Techniques exist on a spectrum from pure analyses, like calculating stresses, to pure solutions, like using a flying buttress on a cathedral. Other software architecture and design books have inventoried techniques on the solution-end of the spectrum, and call these techniques *tactics* (Bass, Clements and Kazman, 2003) or *patterns* (Schmidt et al., 2000; Gamma et al., 1995). This book focuses on techniques that are on the analysis-end of the spectrum, procedural, and independent of the problem domain.

Top-Down Design Top-down design is the process of refining a high-level specification of an element (component, module, etc.) into a detailed design by decomposing the element into smaller pieces and specifying those pieces by allocating responsibilities.

Top-level boundary model The top-level boundary model is the single, topmost encapsulated view of the *design model*. It can be refined into an *internals model* to show internal, non-encapsulated design details.

Tradeoff Sometimes getting more of one thing entails getting less of something else. Tradeoffs can exist between *quality attributes*, such as adding security can trade off against usability.

Two-level scenarios A *functionality scenario* that has been elaborated to show an additional level of internal messages, such as between the *components* in an *internals model*.

Ubiquitous language A common language shared by developers and domain experts, as opposed to the developers using one term and the domain experts using different one for the same concept. See *domain driven design*.

Unified Modeling Language (UML) A common modeling language suited to object-oriented design and software architecture.

Use case Use cases are largely equivalent to *functionality scenarios*, but there are some important differences. Use cases are activities that are high-level and visible to the users of the system. Use cases are often defined to be accomplishing a goal of an actor outside the system, so internal system activities would not count as use cases. Where functionality scenarios are a single trace of behavior, use cases can include variation steps that allow them to describe multiple traces.

Use case diagram A UML diagram showing actors, the system, and *use cases*.

View (i.e., projection) A view shows a defined subset of a *model*'s details, possibly with a transformation.

Viewpoint The view of a system from a single perspective, such as the view of a single stakeholder. Used in the IEEE definition of software architecture. Viewpoints are used in the views-as-requirements approach, rather than the *master model* approach to views.

Viewtype A set or category of views that can be easily reconciled with each other (Clements et al., 2010). See *module viewtype*, *runtime viewtype*, and *allocation viewtype*.

Waterfall process The waterfall process (Royce, 1970) proceeds from beginning to end as a single long block of work which delivers the entire project. It assumes planned design work that is done in its analysis and design phases. These precede the construction phase, which can be considered a single iteration. With just one iteration, work cannot be prioritized across iterations, but it may be built incrementally within the construction phase. See *Extreme Programming*, *iterative process*, *agile process*, and *spiral process*.

XP See *Extreme Programming*.

Yinzer A slang term for someone from Pittsburgh, home of Carnegie Mellon University, and is derived from *yinz*, which is Pittsburgh dialect equivalent to *y'all*, the plural form of *you*.

Bibliography

Abi-Antoun, Marwan, Wang, Daniel and Torr, Peter, Checking Threat Modeling Data Flow Diagrams for Implementation Conformance and Security. in: ASE '07: Proceedings of the Twenty-Second IEEE/ACM International Conference on Automated Software Engineering. ACM, 2007, pp. 393–396.

Aldrich, Jonathan, Chambers, Craig and Notkin, David, ArchJava: Connecting Software Architecture to Implementation. in: ICSE '02: Proceedings of the 24th International Conference on Software Engineering. New York, NY, USA: ACM Press, 2002, pp. 187–197.

Alexander, Christopher, A Pattern Language: Towns, Buildings, Construction (Center for Environmental Structure Series). Oxford University Press, USA, 1977.

Alexander, Christopher, The Timeless Way of Building. Oxford University Press, 1979.

Ambler, Scott, Agile Modeling: Effective Practices for Extreme Programming and the Unified Process. Wiley, 2002.

Ambler, Scott, Agile Adoption Rate Survey Results: February 2008. Dr. Dobb's Journal, May 2008 ⟨http://www.ambysoft.com/surveys/agileFebruary2008.html⟩.

Ambler, Scott, Agile Architecture: Strategies for Scaling Agile Development. 2009 ⟨http://www.agilemodeling.com/essays/agileArchitecture.htm⟩.

Amdahl, Gene, Validity of the Single Processor Approach to Achieving Large-Scale Computing Capabilities. AFIPS Conference Proceedings, 30 1967, pp. 483–485.

Apache Software Foundation, Hadoop Website. 2010 ⟨http://hadoop.apache.org⟩.

Babar, Muhammad Ali, An Exploratory Study of Architectural Practices and Challenges in Using Agile Software Development Approaches. Joint Working IEEE/IFIP Conference on Software Architecture 2009 & European Conference on Software Architecture 2009 September 2009.

Bach, James, Good Enough Quality: Beyond the Buzzword. IEEE Computer, 30 1997:8, pp. 96–98.

Barbacci, Mario et al., Quality Attributes. Software Engineering Institute, Carnegie Mellon University, 1995 (CMU/SEI-95-TR-021, ESC-TR-95-021). – Technical report.

Barbacci, Mario R. et al., Quality Attribute Workshops (QAWs), Third Edition. Software Engineering Institute, Carnegie Mellon University, 2003 (CMU/SEI-2003-TR-016). – Technical report.

Barrett, Anthony et al., Mission Planning and Execution Within the Mission Data System. in: Proceedings of the International Workshop on Planning and Scheduling for Space (IWPSS). 2004.

Bass, Len, Clements, Paul and Kazman, Rick, Software Architecture in Practice. 2nd edition. Addison-Wesley, 2003.

Bass, Len and John, Bonnie E., Linking Usability to Software Architecture Patterns through General Scenarios. Journal of Systems and Software, 66 2003:3, pp. 187–197.

Beck, Kent, Smalltalk Best Practice Patterns. Prentice Hall PTR, 1996.

Beck, Kent and Andres, Cynthia, Extreme Programming Explained: Embrace Change (2nd Edition). 2nd edition. Addison-Wesley Professional, 2004.

Beck, Kent et al., Manifesto for Agile Software Development. 2001 ⟨http://agilemanifesto.org⟩.

Beck, Kent and Cunningham, Ward, A Laboratory for Teaching Object Oriented Thinking. OOPSLA '89: Conference Proceedings on Object-Oriented Programming Systems, Languages and Applications, 1989, pp. 1–6.

Bloch, Joshua, Extra, Extra - Read All About It: Nearly All Binary Searches and Mergesorts are Broken. June 2006 ⟨http://googleresearch.blogspot.com/2006/06/extra-extra-read-all-about-it-nearly.html⟩.

Boehm, Barry, A Spiral Model of Software Development and Enhancement. IEEE Computer, 21(5) 1988, pp. 61–72.

Boehm, Barry and Turner, Richard, Balancing Agility and Discipline: A Guide for the Perplexed. Addison-Wesley Professional, 2003.

Booch, Grady, Software Architecture presentation. 2004 ⟨http://www.booch.com/architecture/blog/artifacts/Software%20Architecture.ppt⟩.

Booch, Grady et al., Object-Oriented Analysis and Design with Applications. 3rd edition. Addison-Wesley Professional, 2007.

Booch, Grady, Rumbaugh, James and Jacobson, Ivar, The Unified Modeling Language User Guide. 2nd edition. Addison-Wesley Professional, 2005.

Bosch, Jan, Design and Use of Software Architectures: Adopting and Evolving a Product-Line Approach (ACM Press). Addison-Wesley Professional, 2000.

Bowker, Geoffrey C. and Star, Susan Leigh, Sorting Things Out: Classification and its Consequences. MIT Press, 1999.

Box, George E. P. and Draper, Norman R., Empirical Model-Building and Response Surfaces (Wiley Series in Probability and Statistics). Wiley, 1987.

Bredemeyer, Dana and Malan, Ruth, Bredemeyer Consulting. 2010 ⟨http://bredemeyer.com⟩.

Brooks, Frederick P, The Mythical Man-Month: Essays on Software Engineering. 2nd edition. Addison-Wesley Professional, 1995.

Buschmann, Frank et al., Pattern-Oriented Software Architecture Volume 1: A System of Patterns. Wiley, 1996.

Butler, Shawn A., Security Attribute Evaluation Method: A Cost-Benefit Approach. Proceedings of ICSE 2002, 2002, pp. 232–240.

Carr, Marvin J. et al., Taxonomy-Based Risk Identification. Software Engineering Institute, Carnegie Mellon University, June 1993 (CMU/SEI-93-TR-6). – Technical report.

Cheesman, John and Daniels, John, UML Components: A Simple Process for Specifying Component-Based Software. Addison-Wesley, 2000.

Chomsky, Noam, Syntactic Structures. 2nd edition. Walter de Gruyter, 2002.

Clements, Paul et al., Documenting Software Architectures: Views and Beyond. 2nd edition. Addison-Wesley, 2010.

Clerc, Viktor, Lago, Patricia and Vliet, Hans van, The Architect's Mindset. Third International Conference on Quality of Software Architectures (QoSA), 2007, pp. 231–248.

Cockburn, Alistair, Writing Effective Use Cases (Agile Software Development Series). Addison-Wesley Professional, 2000.

Coleman, Derek, Object-Oriented Development: The Fusion Method. Prentice Hall, 1993.

Conway, Melvin, How do Committees Invent? Datamation, 14 (5) 1968, pp. 28–31.

Cook, Steve and Daniels, John, Designing Object Systems: Object-Oriented Modelling with Syntropy. Prentice Hall, 1994.

Cook, William, On Understanding Data Abstraction, Revisited. OOPSLA: Conference Proceedings on Object-Oriented Programming Systems, Languages and Applications 2009.

Coplien, James O. and Schmidt, Douglas C., Pattern Languages of Program Design. Addison-Wesley Professional, 1995.

Cunningham, Ward, The WyCash Portfolio Management System. OOPSLA '92: Addendum to the proceedings on Object-Oriented Programming Systems, Languages, and Applications, 1992, pp. 29–30.

Dean, Jeffrey and Ghemawat, Sanjay, MapReduce: Simplified Data Processing on Large Clusters. OSDI'04: Sixth Symposium on Operating System Design and Implementation December 2004.

Denne, Mark and Cleland-Huang, Jane, Software by Numbers: Low-Risk, High-Return Development. Prentice Hall, 2003.

Dijkstra, Edsger, Go-to Statement Considered Harmful. Communications of the ACM, 11 1968:3, pp. 147–148.

D'Souza, Desmond F., MAp: Model-driven Approach for Business-Aligned Architecture RoadMAps. 2006 ⟨http://www.kinetium.com/map/demo/demo_index.html⟩.

D'Souza, Desmond F. and Wills, Alan Cameron, Objects, Components and Frameworks with UML: The Catalysis Approach. Addison-Wesley, 1998.

Dvorak, Daniel, Challenging Encapsulation in the Design of High-Risk Control Systems. Proceedings of 2002 Conference on Object-Oriented Programming, Systems, Languages, and Applications (OOPSLA) 2002.

Eden, Amnon H. and Kazman, Rick, Architecture, Design, Implementation. International Conference on Software Engineering (ICSE), 2003, pp. 149–159.

Eeles, Peter and Cripps, Peter, The Process of Software Architecting. Addison-Wesley Professional, 2009.

Evans, Eric, Domain-Driven Design: Tackling Complexity in the Heart of Software. Addison-Wesley Professional, 2003.

Fairbanks, George, Why Can't They Create Architecture Models Like "Developer X"?: An Experience Report. in: ICSE '03: Proceedings of the 25th International Conference on Software Engineering. 2003, pp. 548–552.

Fairbanks, George, Bierhoff, Kevin and D'Souza, Desmond, Software Architecture at a Large Financial Firm. Proceedings of ACM SIGPLAN Conference on Object Oriented Programs, Systems, Languages, and Applications (OOPSLA) 2006.

Fay, Dan, An Architecture for Distributed Applications on the Internet: Overview of Microsoft's .NET Platform. IEEE International Parallel and Distributed Processing Symposium April 2003.

Feather, Steven Cornford Martin and Hicks, Kenneth, DDP: A Tool for Life-Cycle Risk Management. IEEE Aerospace and Electronics Systems Magazine, 21 2006:6, pp. 13–22.

Firesmith, Donald G., Common Concepts Underlying Safety, Security, and Survivability Engineering. Software Engineering Institute, Carnegie Mellon University, December 2003 (CMU/SEI-2003-TN-033). – Technical Note.

Foote, Brian and Yoder, Joseph, Chap. 29, Big Ball of Mud. In Pattern Languages of Program Design 4. Addison-Wesley, 2000.

Fowler, Martin, Analysis Patterns: Reusable Object Models. Addison-Wesley Professional, 1996.

Fowler, Martin, Refactoring: Improving the Design of Existing Code. Addison-Wesley Professional, 1999.

Fowler, Martin, Patterns of Enterprise Application Architecture. Addison-Wesley Professional, 2002.

Fowler, Martin, UML Distilled: A Brief Guide to the Standard Object Modeling Language. 3rd edition. Addison-Wesley Professional, 2003a.

Fowler, Martin, Who Needs an Architect? IEEE Software, 20 (5) 2003b, pp. 11–13.

Fowler, Martin, Is Design Dead? 2004 ⟨http://martinfowler.com/articles/designDead.html⟩.

Fowler, Martin, Technical Debt. February 2009 ⟨http://martinfowler.com/bliki/TechnicalDebt.html⟩.

Gabriel, Richard P., Lisp: Good News Bad News How to Win Big. AI Expert, 6 1994, pp. 31–39 ⟨http://www.laputan.org/gabriel/worse-is-better.html⟩.

Gamma, Erich et al., Design Patterns: Elements of Reusable Object-Oriented Software (Addison-WesleyProfessional Computing Series). Addison-Wesley Professional, 1995.

Garlan, David, Software Architecture Course. 2003 ⟨http://www.cs.cmu.edu/~garlan/courses/Architectures-S03.html⟩.

Garlan, David, Allen, Robert and Ockerbloom, John, Architectural Mismatch, or, Why It's Hard to Build Systems Out of Existing Parts. in: Proceedings of the 17th International Conference on Software Engineering (ICSE). Seattle, Washington, April 1995, pp. 179–185.

Garlan, David, Monroe, Robert T. and Wile, David, Acme: Architectural Description of Component-Based Systems. in: **Leavens, Gary T. and Sitaraman, Murali, editors:** Foundations of Component-Based Systems. Cambridge University Press, 2000. – chapter 3, pp. 47–67.

Garlan, David and Schmerl, Bradley, AcmeStudo web page. 2009 ⟨http://www.cs.cmu.edu/~acme/AcmeStudio/index.html⟩.

Gluch, David P., A Construct for Describing Software Development Risks. Software Engineering Institute, Carnegie Mellon University, July 1994 (CMU/SEI-94-TR-14). – Technical report.

Gorton, Ian, Essential Software Architecture. Springer, 2006.

Harrison, William H. and Ossher, Harold, Subject-Oriented Programming (A Critique of Pure Objects). Proceedings of 1993 Conference on Object-Oriented Programming, Systems, Languages, and Applications (OOPSLA), 1993, pp. 411–428.

Heineman, George T. and Councill, William T., Component-Based Software Engineering: Putting the Pieces Together. Addison-Wesley Professional, 2001.

Hoff, Todd, Amazon Architecture. 2008a ⟨http://highscalability.com/amazon-architecture⟩.

Hoff, Todd, How Rackspace Now Uses MapReduce and Hadoop to Query Terabytes of Data. HighScalability.com, January 30 2008b ⟨http://highscalability.com/how-rackspace-now-uses-mapreduce-and-hadoop-query-terabytes-data⟩.

Hofmeister, Christine, Nord, Robert and Soni, Dilip, Applied Software Architecture. Addison-Wesley, 2000.

Holmes, James, Struts: The Complete Reference, 2nd Edition. McGraw-Hill Osborne Media, 2006.

Holmevik, Jan R., Compiling SIMULA: A Historical Study of Technological Genesis. IEEE Annals of the History of Computing, 16 1994:4, pp. 25–37.

Holzmann, Gerard J., The SPIN Model Checker: Primer and Reference Manual. Addison-Wesley Professional, 2003.

Hood, Stu, MapReduce at Rackspace. January 2008 ⟨http://blog.racklabs.com/?p=66⟩.

Ingham, Michel D. et al., Engineering Complex Embedded Systems with State Analysis and the Mission Data System. AIAA Journal of Aerospace Computing, Information and Communication, 2 December 2005:12, pp. 507–536.

Jackson, Daniel, Alloy: A Lightweight Object Modelling Notation. ACM Transactions on Software Engineering and Methodology (TOSEM'02), 11 April 2002:2, pp. 256–290.

Jackson, Michael, Software Requirements and Specifications. Addison-Wesley, 1995.

Jackson, Michael, Problem Frames: Analyzing and Structuring Software Development Problems. Addison-Wesley, 2000.

Jacobson, Ivar, Booch, Grady and Rumbaugh, James, The Unified Software Development Process. Addison-Wesley Professional, 1999.

Kay, Alan, Predicting the Future. Stanford Engineering, 1 Autumn 1989:1, pp. 1–6.

Kruchten, Philippe, The 4+1 View Model of Architecture. IEEE Software, 12 November 1995:6, pp. 42–50.

Kruchten, Philippe, The Rational Unified Process: An Introduction. 3rd edition. Addison-Wesley Professional, 2003.

Larman, Craig and Basili, Victor R., Iterative and Incremental Development: A Brief History. IEEE Computer, 36 2003:6, pp. 47–56.

Lattanze, Anthony J., Architecting Software Intensive Systems: A Practitioners Guide. Auerbach Publications, 2008.

Liskov, Barbara, Keynote address - Data Abstraction and Hierarchy. Conference on Object Oriented Programming Systems Languages and Applications, 1987, pp. 17 – 34.

Luhmann, Niklas, Modern Society Shocked by its Risks. Social Sciences Research Centre: Occasional Papers, 1996 ⟨http://hub.hku.hk/handle/123456789/38822⟩.

Magee, Jeff and Kramer, Jeff, Concurrency: State Models and Java Programs. 2nd edition. Wiley, 2006.

Maranzano, Joseph, Architecture Reviews: Practice and Experience. IEEE Computer, 2005, pp. 34–43.

Martin, Robert, The Scatology of Agile Architecture. April 2009 ⟨http://blog.objectmentor.com/articles/2009/04/25/the-scatology-of-agile-architecture⟩.

Meier, J.D. et al., Checklists for Application Architecture. 2003 ⟨http://www.codeplex.com/wikipage?ProjectName=AppArch&title=Checklists⟩.

Meyer, Bertrand, Object-Oriented Software Construction. 2nd edition. Prentice Hall PTR, 2000.

Meyer, Kenny, Mission Data System Website. 2009 ⟨http://mds.jpl.nasa.gov⟩.

Miller, Granville, Second Generation Agile Software Development. March 2006 ⟨http://blogs.msdn.com/randymiller/archive/2006/03/23/559229.aspx⟩.

Monson-Haefel, Richard, Enterprise JavaBeans. 3rd edition. O'Reilly, 2001.

Moriconi, Mark, Qian, Xiaolei and Riemenschneider, R. A., Correct Architecture Refinement. IEEE Transactions on Software Engineering, 21 1995:4, pp. 356–372.

Nyfjord, Jaana, Towards Integrating Agile Development and Risk Management. Ph. D thesis, Stockholm University, 2008.

Oreizy, Peyman, Medvidović, Nenad and Taylor, Richard N., Runtime Software Adaptation: Framework, Approaches, and Styles. in: ICSE Companion '08: Companion of the 30th International Conference on Software Engineering. ACM, 2008, pp. 899–910.

OSGi Alliance, OSGi website. 2009 ⟨http://www.osgi.org⟩.

Ould, Martin, Business Processes - Modeling and Analysis for Re-engineering and Improvement. John Wiley and Sons, 1995.

Parnas, David, Software Fundamentals: Collected Papers by David L. Parnas. Addison-Wesley Professional, 2001, Editors: Daniel M. Hoffman and David M. Weiss.

Perry, Dewayne E. and Wolf, Alex L., Foundation for the Study of Software Architecture. ACM SIGSOFT Software Engineering Notes, 17 1992:4, pp. 40–52.

Petroski, Henry, Design Paradigms: Case Histories of Error and Judgment in Engineering. Cambridge University Press, 1994.

Polya, George, How to Solve It: A New Aspect of Mathematical Method (Princeton Science Library). Princeton University Press, 2004.

Rosch, Elanor and Lloyd, Barbara; Rosch, Elanor and Lloyd, Barbara, editors, Cognition and Categorization. Lawrence Erlbaum, 1978.

Ross, Jeanne W., Weill, Peter and Robertson, David, Enterprise Architecture as Strategy: Creating a Foundation for Business Execution. Harvard Business School Press, 2006.

Royce, Winston W., Managing the Development of Large Software Systems: Concepts and Techniques. in: Technical Papers of Western Electronic Show and Convention (WesCon). 1970.

Rozanski, Nick and Woods, Eóin, Software Systems Architecture: Working With Stakeholders Using Viewpoints and Perspectives. Addison-Wesley Professional, 2005.

Schmidt, Douglas et al., Pattern-Oriented Software Architecture Volume 2: Patterns for Concurrent and Networked Objects. Wiley, 2000.

Schmidt, Douglas C. and Buschmann, Frank, Patterns, Frameworks, and Middleware: Their Synergistic Relationships. in: ICSE '03: Proceedings of the 25th International Conference on Software Engineering. Washington, DC, USA: IEEE Computer Society, 2003, pp. 694–704.

Schuh, Peter, Integrating Agile Development in the Real World. Charles River Media, 2004.

SEI Library, Software Engineering Institute Library. 2009 ⟨http://www.sei.cmu.edu/library⟩.

Selic, Bran, Brass Bubbles: An Overview of UML 2.0 (and MDA). 2003a ⟨http://www.omg.org/news/meetings/workshops/UML%202003%20Manual/Tutorial7-Hogg.pdf⟩.

Selic, Bran, The Pragmatics of Model-Driven Development. IEEE Software, 20 2003b:5, pp. 19–25.

Shaw, Mary, Abstraction, Data Types, and Models for Software. ACM SIGPLAN Notices, 16 January 1981:1, pp. 189–91.

Shaw, Mary and Clements, Paul, A Field Guide to Boxology: Preliminary Classification of Architectural Styles for Software Systems. Proc. COMPSAC97 21st Int'l Computer Software and Applications Conference, 1997, pp. 6–13.

Shaw, Mary and Garlan, David, Software Architecture: Perspectives on an Emerging Discipline. Prentice-Hall, 1996.

Simon, Herb, The Sciences of the Artificial. 2nd edition. MIT Press, 1981.

Society, IEEE Computer, IEEE 1471-2000 IEEE Recommended Practice for Architectural Description of Software-Intensive Systems. IEEE Std 1471-2000 edition. Software Engineering Standards Committee of the IEEE Computer Society, 2000.

Sutherland, Dean, The Code of Many Colors: Semi-automated Reasoning about Multi-Thread Policy for Java. Ph. D thesis, Carnegie Mellon University Institute for Software Research, 2008, ⟨http://reports-archive.adm.cs.cmu.edu/anon/isr2008/CMU-ISR-08-112.pdf⟩.

Szyperski, Clemens, Component Software: Beyond Object-Oriented Programming. 2nd edition. Addison-Wesley Professional, 2002.

Tarr, Peri L. et al., N Degrees of Separation: Multi-Dimensional Separation of Concerns. in: International Conference on Software Engineering. 1999, pp. 107–119.

Taylor, Richard, Medvidović, Nenad and Dashofy, Eric, Software Architecture: Foundations, Theory, and Practice. Wiley, 2009.

The Open Group, TOGAF Version 9 - A Manual. 9th edition. Van Haren Publishing, 2008.

Venners, Bill, A Conversation with Martin Fowler, Part III. Artima Developer, 2002 ⟨http://www.artima.com/intv/evolutionP.html⟩.

Warmer, Jos and Kleppe, Anneke, The Object Constraint Language: Getting Your Models Ready for MDA. 2nd edition. Addison-Wesley Professional, 2003.

Whitehead, Alfred North, An Introduction to Mathematics. Forgotten Books Reprint 2009, 1911.

Wing, Jeannette M., A Study of 12 Specifications of the Library Problem. IEEE Software, 5 1988:4, pp. 66–76.

Wirfs-Brock, Rebecca, Wilkerson, Brian and Wiener, Lauren, Designing Object-Oriented Software. PTR Prentice Hall, 1990.

Wisnosky, Dennis E., DoDAF Wizdom: A Practical Guide. Wizdom Press, 2004.

Zachman, John, A Framework for Information Systems Architecture. IBM Systems Journal, 26 (3) 1987, pp. 276–292.

Index